Pastors and the Care of Souls
in Medieval England

Notre Dame Texts in Medieval Culture, vol. 4

THE MEDIEVAL INSTITUTE

University of Notre Dame

John Van Engen *and* Edward D. English, Editors

Pastors and the Care of Souls

in Medieval England

EDITED BY

John Shinners *and* William J. Dohar

UNIVERSITY OF NOTRE DAME PRESS

Notre Dame, Indiana

Copyright © 1998 by
University of Notre Dame Press
Notre Dame, Indiana 46556

Colophon: Designed by Gary Gore
Set in Minion types by J. Jarrett Engineering
Printed in the United States of America by

Library of Congress Cataloging-in-Publication Data

Pastors and the care of souls in medieval England / edited by John
Shinners and William J. Dohar.
p.   cm. — (Notre Dame texts in medieval culture)
Includes bibliographical references.
ISBN 0-268-03821-X (cloth : alk. paper)
ISBN 0-268-03850-3 (paper: alk. paper)
1. Pastoral theology—Catholic Church—History of doctrines—
Middle Ages, 600–1500—Sources.   2. Catholic Church—England—
Clergy—History—Sources.   3. Clergy—England—Office—History—
Sources.   I. Shinners, John Raymond, 1954-   . II. Dohar, William
J. III. Series.
BX1913.P346   1998
253'.0942'0902—DC21   97-21480
                                                                CIP

The paper used in this publication meets the minimum requirements of the
American National Standard for Information Sciences—Permanence of Paper
for Printed Library Materials, ANSI Z39.48-1984.

For Leonard E. Boyle, O.P.

Contents
꿍

Chapter 6. Management of the Cure   213

Preface

A wealth of books now easily accessible to students and general readers harvests the fruits of recent research by medievalists exploring the history of women and the family, the lives of the lower classes, and the fortunes of people on the margins of medieval society—groups ignored for too long by too many scholars. Yet one social group still suffers from popular neglect and cliché: the medieval parish clergy, whose work daily and deeply affected most medieval people. Several decades of splendid research into these men's lives and how they performed their pastoral duties have made little headway in altering commonplace perceptions about them. Consequently, the typical portrait of the medieval pastor offered to the general reader is still gleaned from popular studies written almost a century ago. Even today the ideas of Edwardian scholars such as George Coulton, Cardinal Gasquet, and Lord Manning color the typical textbook snapshot of the parish clergy and their role in medieval religious life.

This older scholarship, though helpful in painting the broader outlines of the subject (and loaded with a trove of arresting detail so characteristic of the industrious gentlemen-scholars of the turn of the century), is generally out-dated, not only because it so often labors under the weight of sectarian special pleading, but also because it lacks the range of sources unearthed by recent scholars and the newer methods, insights, perspectives, and reestimations they offer.

Over the last forty years, historians like W. A. Pantin, Leonard Boyle, Peter Heath, and Roy Haines—to name just a few of a corps of modern scholars—have redefined our understanding of the English parish clergy and their work. What emerges from these recent studies of priests, their professional training, and their daily pastoral work is a better-rounded, more complex, and realistic picture of the medieval clergy. Yet despite these new historical labors, the old popular image of the village parson persists: a barely literate, barely celibate, barely sober bumpkin, more at home in a tavern or *in flagrante delicto* than at an altar or a *prie-dieu*.

Our own impatience with this durable stereotype and our regard for decades of still undervalued historical research inspired this sourcebook. It struck us that we might build a small bridge across the gap between current scholarly studies of medieval pastors and popular perceptions of them by assembling an assortment of documents that illuminate the richly varied lives of those members of England's medieval clergy engaged in the *cura animarum*, or pastoral care of souls.

The structures, agents, and institutions that developed in the medieval church cast a wide net over many aspects of religion and society, many of them only vaguely pastoral. Still, the church's mission then—as today—was the salvation of souls, and every effort brought to bear by men who exercised the pastoral office was, at least in theory, directed to that end. Principal among these pastoral duties were the celebrations of the sacraments and preaching; but the *cura animarum* also involved works of charity, education, correction, and the blessing of the many objects and events that filled the daily lives of parishioners.

Ideally the study of medieval pastoral care should simultaneously focus on the men who held the office of pastor—their backgrounds, their recruitment and training, the routines of their lives, their relations with their spiritual charges and the larger clerical community—and the elaborate systems of support created to aid them in their work—the administrative divisions of the institutional church; the methods for formulating and disseminating theological, canonical, and liturgical instruction; the legal apparatus formed to direct the cure of souls. It should also embrace parishioners—those individuals and communities that were the *raison d'être* of the church's pastoral mission.

In offering just such a broadly-focused introduction to medieval pastoral care, this sourcebook serves several purposes. First, it puts into print a large and varied selection of important material on pastoral care long overdue for translation. There is, of course, no pressing shortage of excellent sourcebooks for the history of medieval Christianity in general and of Christian England in particular. But the virtue of this collection, we believe, is that it focuses squarely on the parish clergy in its choice of documents, including the many never before translated. Thus, if chapter 5 seems top-heavy with pastoral manuals, this is because translations of these manuals, which offer such vivid glimpses into the routine concerns of curates, have very rarely been available before. Second, we hope this book will sharpen the historical awareness of its readers by highlighting the wider social and religious milieus in which the medieval pastor worked, thereby leading to a richer appreciation of the Christian religion's inextricable bond to nearly every facet of medieval society. This broader view necessarily includes selections pulled from a range of medieval sources: administrative, theological, legal, historical, and literary. We hope the range of documents we offer here will make this book suitable for an array of classroom applications and academic disciplines.

This book is definitely not a comprehensive history of medieval priests or of pastoral care. The general introduction to each chapter is meant purely to set the context and provide basic background. In medieval parlance, this a *florilegium*, not a *summa*. True, we hope a reader plowing straight through the book from cover to cover will come away with a solid sense of the multifaceted work of the *cura animarum* and the men who practiced it. But, as with any anthology, it is also fruitful to dip here and there as interest demands.

Finally, there are two overarching values implicit in this book. First, we hope that it will enhance our readers' historical image of the parochial clergy both as individuals and as members of a professional community. Considering the singular role they played in medieval life, the parish clergy have enjoyed relatively little attention from scholars. Consequently, historians, creating their portraits largely from anecdotal evidence, are too often prone to depict the clergy as a fairly anonymous and homogenous mass entity. This is the stereotyped image that still worms its way into many textbooks and general studies of the middle ages. In fact, no group of people occupied a more fluid status on the rigid ladder of social hierarchy that characterized medieval society. Priests could be noble or baseborn, rich or poor, brilliant academics or barely lettered, deeply pious or grossly opportunistic, utterly committed to their duties or derelict, and everything in between. By illustrating the clergy's assorted activities as communicators and implementers of the pastoral mission of the church; by offering concrete examples of their professional recruitment, training, and livelihood; by showing them at work side by side with their parishioners and other clergymen; by collecting portraits of the many kinds of men of many kinds of temperament who took up the *cura animarum,* our aim here is to provide a much richer and more nuanced view of medieval pastors, both as distinct personalities and as people interacting with other members of the Christian community.

Secondly, by shedding documentary light on the interplay between the clergy, the laity, and their daily practice of religion, this book further underscores the fundamental role that Christianity played in molding medieval culture. All Christians, priests and people alike, were ultimately preoccupied by one pressing question, the question posed by William Langland in his allegorical poem *Piers Plowman:* "How may I save my soul?" At least

ideally, this common pursuit of salvation lay at the heart of their relation-
ships. In the most fundamental sense, the parish clergy were the vital link
in the chain that stretched—sometimes quite slenderly—between the evangelical mission of the hierarchical church and ordinary peoples' grasp and
practice of their religion. The way that these pastors received the doctrinal
and disciplinary teachings of the church, and the methods they used to pass
those teachings on to lay people, yield a crucial perspective on the way that
Christianity shaped, suffused, and sustained medieval culture.

A few words about our decision to focus this collection on pastoral care
in late medieval England: In the last twenty years or so, a limited number
of documents from the medieval diocesan archives of, for example, France,
Spain, Italy, and the territories of the Holy Roman Empire have at last made
it to print. They confirm in very broad measure the basic patterns we have
long learned from the English model of pastoral care. It was tempting to
include some of this continental material here, since illustrations drawn
from throughout Europe would paint a rich canvas of the different regional
approaches to pastoral care and highlight the essential issues that faced any
parish priest, no matter what his country. But the *embarras de richesses* of
English archives remains unmatched in its ability to offer a detailed and
intricately cross-connected picture of the routine workings of pastoral care
from the loftiest levels of church administration to the smallest village parishes. English documents are readily at hand to illustrate almost any facet
of the medieval *cura animarum;* comparable sources from other countries
simply don't exist or have yet to be unearthed. Still, we include here many
excerpts from the law and theology of the international church to help suggest the ways that universal guidelines could find local expression.

We picked Pope Innocent III's great Fourth Lateran Council of 1215
(that most pastoral of medieval councils) as a benchmark in the history of
pastoral care and therefore the starting point, more or less, for our selections. Obviously there were pastoral efforts afoot before 1215, especially those
issuing from the budding schools of theology and canon law in the twelfth
century. Even earlier pastoral traditions reach back to Gregory the Great,
Augustine of Canterbury, and Boniface and the other Anglo-Saxon mission-
aries, not to mention the Celtic and continental penitentials, and the reform
programs of the Carolingians. But a fully viable system for delivering pastoral care to the parish really became feasible only when political, social, and
economic conditions in Europe were relatively stable; when the papacy was
organized enough and conscientious enough to spearhead pastoral reform;
when theologians had begun to fix their understanding of such crucial con-
cepts as "church," "sacrament," and "clergy"; when canon law had systema-

tized and disseminated these theological notions; and when administrative structures—from the papal curia, to the bishops, to the parish priests—were firmly in place. All these conditions coalesced around the time of the Fourth Lateran Council, when the church at large began to hone its techniques of pastoral care.

*   *   *

We owe many thanks to the people who helped this book along its way, none of whom bear fault for its faults. The valuable advice of Joseph Goering, Keith Egan, Jocelyn Hillgarth, and Joseph H. Lynch helped us orient the early stages of our work. John Van Engen and Edward English of the University of Notre Dame's Medieval Institute encouraged us along the way. And the keen eye of our editor Rebecca DeBoer helped us polish the final product. We also thank the Dean and Chapter of Norwich Cathedral and the Norfolk Record Office for their kind permission to translate documents in their archives. Throughout our work, our families, friends, and colleagues always encouraged us (even when we must have bored them) and propped up our sometimes flagging spirits.

A Note about the Translations

Our translations aim at clarity and fidelity, the first taking slight precedence over the second. Writings on pastoral care, like so much else in the legal-minded middle ages, were often crafted in exquisitely tortuous legalese. Long-winded verbal meanderings in themselves, of course, reveal something about a culture's worldview; but insofar as we have not consistently freed our translations from the encumbrances of confusing jargon and syntax, we offer our apologies. *Nostra culpa.* To keep the text as uncluttered as possible, we have not always noted words and phrases added to clarify Latin meanings implicit but unwritten.

Whenever possible we have tried to cast our translations in gender-neutral language. But, just like the traditional English use of the word "man," the Latin meaning of "homo" assumed either the human race in general or a specific *masculine* individual. Bearing this in mind, where we could use inclusive language without unduly marring the sense of the Latin, we have. But when the Latin uses gender-exclusive language that is not easily avoided without falling into awkward English, we have rendered it faithfully rather than insistently impose our very different values on past writers.

The Latin honorific *dominus,* or "lord," carried a range of connotations in the middle ages, meaning everything from Christ the Lord, to a feudal lord, to the head of a household, or any exalted person. It was widely applied as a title of respect for popes, bishops, abbots, monks, and priests. When *dominus* is prefixed to a priest's name, we have translated it as "Sir," with no implication of secular nobility.

Biblical translations and citations follow the Douay-Rheims version, which most closely corresponds to the medieval Latin Vulgate.

Many of the technical words and phrases that populate the medieval church's pastoral theology, liturgy, and law may be found defined in the concluding glossary.

A Note on Medieval English Currency

In medieval England, moneys of account (i.e., an abstract monetary denomination that does not circulate) were the shilling (= s. for *solidus*), equal to 12 pennies; the pound (= £ for *libra*), equal to 20 shillings or 240 pennies; and the mark, equal to two-thirds of a pound (13s. 4d.). (These values were abandoned when Great Britain decimalized its currency in 1971.)

From the late eighth century until the mid-fourteenth, the various mintings of the silver penny (= d. for *denarius;* plural = pence) and its fractions, the halfpenny and the farthing (worth one-quarter pence), were the only coins commonly circulating in England as legal tender. Both Henry III in the thirteenth century and Edward III in the fourteenth introduced gold coinage, but only Edward's gold noble (worth 6s. 8d.), half-noble, and quarter-noble—all first minted in 1344—caught on. In 1351 Edward also introduced the silver groat (worth four pence) and the half-groat. Henry VII minted both the first pound coin (the sovereign, worth 240 pennies) in 1489 and the shilling coin (worth 12 pence) in 1504. To put these amounts in perspective, in the thirteenth century the average daily wage of a carpenter was about 3d.; the statutory minimum annual wage for a vicar was five marks (£3 6s. 8d.).

Abbreviations

Bishop's Register	*The Bishop's Register,* ed. Clifford J. Offer (London: SPCK; New York: Macmillan, 1929).
Concilia, Wilkins	*Concilia Magnae Brittaniae et Hiberniae,* 4 vols., ed. D. Wilkins (London, 1737).
Councils and Synods	*Councils and Synods With Other Documents Relating to the English Church,* vol. 2, ed. F. M. Powicke and C. R. Cheney (Oxford: Oxford University Press, 1964).
Decrees, Tanner	*Decrees of the Ecumenical Councils,* vol. 1, ed. Norman P. Tanner (London: Sheed and Ward; Washington, D.C.: Georgetown University Press, 1990).
EETS	*Early English Text Society.*
EHD III	*English Historical Documents,* vol. 3, 1189–1327, ed. Harry Rothwell (New York: Oxford University Press, 1975).
EHD IV	*English Historical Documents,* vol. 4, 1327–1485, ed. A. R. Myers (New York: Oxford University Press, 1969).
Life, Coulton	*Life in the Middle Ages,* G. G. Coulton, 2 vols. (Cambridge: Cambridge University Press, 1935; reprint, 1967).
Reg. Boothe	*Registrum Caroli Bothe, episcopi Herefordensis, 1516–35,* ed. A. T. Bannister (Canterbury and York Society, 1921).
Reg. T. Charlton	*Registrum Thome de Charlton, episcopi Herefordensis, 1327–44,* ed. W. W. Capes (Canterbury and York Society, 1913).
Reg. Chichele	*The Episcopal Registers of the Diocese of St. David's 1397 to 1518,* vol. 1, transcribed and translated by R. F. Isaacson, Cymmrodorion Record Series 6 (London, 1917).
Reg. Corbridge	*The Register of Thomas Corbridge, Lord Archbishop of York, 1300–1304,* pt. 1, ed. William Brown, Surtees Society 138 (1925).

Reg. Grandisson	*The Register of John de Grandisson, Bishop of Exeter (1327–1369),* ed. F. C. Hingeston-Randolph, 3 vols. (London and Exeter, 1894–99).
Reg. Gravesend	*Registrum Radulphi Baldock . . . et Stephani Gravesend episcoporum Londoniensium, [1319–1338],* ed. R. C. Fowler (Canterbury and York Society, 1911).
Reg. Halton	*The Register of John de Halton, Bishop of Carlisle 1292–1324,* ed. W. N. Thompson, 2 vols. (Canterbury and York Society, 1913).
Reg. Mascall	*Registrum Roberti Mascall, episcopi Herefordensis, 1404–16,* ed. J. H. Parry, 2 vols. (Cantilupe and Canterbury and York Society, 1916–17).
Reg. Pontissara	*Registrum Johannis de Pontissara, episcopi Wintoniensis, 1282–1304,* ed. C. Deedes, 2 vols. (Canterbury and York Society, 1915–24).
Reg. Spofford	*Registrum Thome Spofford, episcopi Herefordensis, 1422–48,* ed. A. T. Bannister (Canterbury and York Society, 1919).
Reg. Stanbury	*Registrum Johannis Stanbury, episcopi Herefordensis, 1453–74,* ed. J. H. Parry and A. T. Bannister (Cantilupe and Canterbury and York Society, 1919).
Reg. Stapledon	*Register of Walter de Stapledon, Bishop of Exeter (1307–26)* ed. F. C. Hingeston-Randolph (London and Exeter, 1892).
Reg. Sutton	*The Rolls and Registers of Bishop Oliver Sutton, 1280–1299,* ed. Rosalind M. T. Hill, 8 vols., Lincoln Record Society (Hereford, 1948–86).
Reg. Swinfield	*Registrum Ricardi de Swinfield, episcopi Herefordensis, 1283–1317,* ed. W. W. Capes (Canterbury and York Society, 1909).
Reg. Trillek	*Registrum Johannis de Trillek, episcopi Herefordensis, 1344–1360,* ed. J. H. Parry (Cantilupe and Canterbury and York Society, 1910, 1912).

Excerpts from canon law are from the *Corpus Juris Canonici,* ed. E. Friedberg, 2 vols. (Leipzig, 1879, 1881). Citations follow modern practice but with expanded titles.

1

∽

Portraits of the Pastor

*M*edieval pastors were the heirs of a venerable and rich legacy from the ancient church on what should comprise the cure of souls. They knew, through the scriptures, liturgical language, and church doctrine, that they were to model their lives in a special way on the life of Jesus, to teach, heal, and guide as he did. Perhaps the most enduring image of the pastor (and appropriately so) is Christ the Good Shepherd leaving the otherwise well-tended flock to go out in search of the stray lest it be lost forever.[1] A point not to be lost on readers of the scriptures was that the goodness of this Shepherd applied equally to the errant one as to the ninety-nine. So, medieval pastors had much to reflect on when considering the scope of their vocations as shepherds of souls. While there was an abundance of material to inform them on this high matter—exegetical treatises, commentaries, prayers, hymns, religious art—they really had to look no further than the shepherds among their own parishioners who worked as if their lives, and the lives of their sheep, depended on the common-sense skills of vigilance, solicitude, and proper discipline.

Still, souls are not sheep, and the metaphor of the ecclesiastical shepherd in the middle ages was a multifarious reality. Like Jesus, medieval pastors were to know their respective flocks intimately, love them, and bring any straying soul back to the community of grace. Their path was to be lit by the scriptures and the laws of the church; the journey's end was nothing

[1] Luke 15:4–7.

1

less than eternal salvation itself. Souls lost along the way were prey to the wiles of Satan and, saving the intervention of the church, in dread peril. Even by the twelfth century, parish priests were the beneficiaries of an extensive documentary and literary tradition that reflected the image of the ordained minister as shepherd. But early on in the church's history it was realized that the expanding community of Christ and the developing understanding of ministry needed an institutional model to enhance and articulate the compelling but simpler image of the Good Shepherd. Thus, in the first generations of Christianity, a more definite model was offered in the words of St. Paul to Timothy in what are justly called the "pastoral epistles." [2] In 1 Timothy 3:1-7, Paul, by then a seasoned pastor and preacher, set out in brief the more salient qualities and virtues of an elder in the Christian community. The leader of the congregation, he wrote, should be a man of unimpeachable character, temperate in food and drink, discreet and courteous. He should be the husband of one wife, devoted to his family, preside over a household of obedient children, and be known far and wide as a man of virtue and reliance. (Medieval readers found allegorical meanings for these domestic images: if a priest was to remain faithful to one wife, let it be his church, and the children who owed him obedience were none other than his parishioners, his spiritual family.) Finally, but certainly not least importantly, the pastor needed to teach the faith he himself espoused. Certainly, he should be learned in the scriptures, but he also had to possess a full knowledge of the Christian life. His most eloquent preaching would occur in what he did, more than in what he said.

These words from 1 Timothy had a common currency in the writings of medieval exegetes, theologians, and church leaders on the subject of pastoral identity and ministry. But it was—and always has been—a developing identity, most effective when linked with the apostolic tradition on the one hand and responsive to the pastoral needs of the church within history on the other. The images and words of pastors offered in this chapter reveal some of the more significant lines of this composite portrait, with details that are both common to the long tradition of pastoral care and peculiar to various times and settings. They are as diverse as the sublime references in the writings of St. Thomas Aquinas (No. 3) and the barnyard imagery of a rustic song about the priesthood, "Many are the Presbyters" (No. 15).

These images had many derivations, but two individuals were especially influential regarding the ways in which medieval pastors understood (or

---

[2]There are three of these: two to Timothy and one to Titus, respectively.

were intended to understand) themselves. Pope Gregory the Great (590–604) summarized the early western church's tradition of the pastorate and set his own seal on the further development of the pastoral role in his *Rule of Pastoral Care* (No. 1). The book, written in the first months of Gregory's pontificate, had the pastoral work of bishops in mind, but it would be amplified in countless ways to include pastoral care broadly considered. One of the most significant contributions of Gregory's work was the solidification of an image already within the tradition and destined to influence pastoral theology for the remainder of the medieval period. For Gregory, the work of the pastor was the "art of arts" and its practice likened to the care of the physician, whose knowledge and actions contributed to the healing of the body. The *medicus animarum* needed to be adept at diagnosing spiritual ills, more deadly than any bodily affliction, and treating them with the ointments of preaching and penance. This imagery was echoed by another pope, Innocent III (1198–1216), who urged priests and confessors to be "discreet and cautious . . . in the manner of a skillful physician" when they listened to the sins of penitents and offered the saving grace of absolution. For Innocent and his contemporaries, the absolution of sins was the most potent medicine a spiritual physician possessed. Thus, this healer of souls had to be well-trained and spiritually fit to provide what his people needed.

The older image of the pastor as a shepherd was never lost in the tradition; it was augmented. The one who went out to find the stray could also apply the proper ointments of the church's healing sacraments to the wounded soul. But pastoral care, responding as it must to a variety of circumstances, entails more than absolution, and this too was represented in the developing tradition. Robert Grosseteste, the reforming bishop of Lincoln (1235–53), held that preaching and religious instruction were the most pressing pastoral skills for the church in his own time. These, he maintained, outweighed in importance the various other ministries and works available to priests (No. 4). He also urged pastors in his diocese to do everything that was required of spiritual shepherds: to feed the hungry, clothe the naked, visit the sick and those in prison. The fourteenth-century writer and theologian John Wyclif (c. 1330–84) would have found much to agree with in the bishop of Lincoln's estimation of pastoral virtues. But unlike Grosseteste, he was no friend of the friars who influenced greatly the course of pastoral care in the thirteenth century, nor did he agree that confession or most of the other sacraments and rituals of the church were necessary for salvation. Therefore, they should be of little concern to the zealous pastor. Rather, thought Wyclif, the true role of the pastor was as preacher, clarifying for the faithful the saving virtues of the word of God. Furthermore, this was a ministry not exclusive to priests but shared by all the baptized in the priesthood of the faithful (No. 6).

Thus, pastoral care was broad enough in its range of values and activities to allow for a similar variety of emphases. Still, there were some common features to the care of souls and the extensive writing on the subject. The clergy, because of their profession to follow Christ and to serve the church in special ways, were set apart from the laity. The curate was the cultic leader of the community and, as intermediary between God and his parishioners, he was elevated in ways that were spiritual but also social. It need hardly be said that the reality of clerical behavior was not always in keeping with the sort of rhetoric attached to the priestly office. Concern about moral lapses among the clergy was a constant in the writings of reformers, especially in matters touching upon chastity and public behavior (Nos. 7, 8). Another perennial concern among church leaders was the blurring of lines, spiritually and socially, between ordained clergy and the laity. Priests should wear a simple habit and bear the tonsure that distinguished them from secular society (Nos. 9, 11). There should be nothing in their outward bearing that would confuse them with the mammon of iniquity, which meant, among other things, they shouldn't carry weapons, play at dice, or engage in common trade (Nos. 8, 10). Avoiding such things would help the pastor preach convincingly to his flock about conversion of heart and moral reform; but these rules for good behavior also helped defend the special status given to clerics in medieval Christian society. As such, they enjoyed unusual protection and immunity from certain aspects of secular law and judicial processes, though there were many times when this legal point was at the center of raging disputes between civil and ecclesiastical governments (No. 12).

A portrait of the medieval pastor, even a composite one made up of many different types of sources, is at best impressionistic. The writings of theologians and lawyers are especially revelatory in their attempts to portray certain dimensions of the pastoral life, in the ideals that inspired and the laws that guided the behavior of medieval clergy. It must be conceded that such sources cannot tell the full story, moving as they do between moral hopes and pragmatic realizations. One has to look to a broader range of sources to find the variations in character, faith, and manner that collectively describe (in ways that no single source can) a group as disparate as medieval parish clergy. To humanize the face of the medieval pastor, we have chosen a few passages from literature which help flesh out the more formal features of theology and law. Chaucer's good parson (No. 13) and Langland's nearly worthless one (No. 14) help achieve this in obvious ways. There is an undeniable vitality to the parts they play on their respective literary stages: the good parson full of dedication, vigilant, and caring of his flock, but somewhat inaccessible in his personal holiness; in the opposite direction, the parish priest Sloth, patently self-indicting and comically embarrassing but just short of complete hopelessness. Like any stereotype, these images were derived from some truth. But, in fact, most flesh-and-blood medieval clerics took their place in pastoral estimation somewhere between these two extremes. There were good and dutiful men, hard workers more than saints, who tried to pull in their flocks like the pastors in "Many are the Presbyters" (No. 15). There were also priests who missed the mark often enough, and those who, whether they deserved it or not, won Everyman's faith in the grace of office (No. 16): "let us priesthood honor, And follow their doctrine for our souls' succor."

A. Theological

ℭ **No. 1. Pope Gregory the Great on the pastor's art (590).**

Gregory the Great, *The Book of Pastoral Rule*, trans. James Barmby, *A Select Library of Nicene and Post-Nicene Fathers of the Christian Church*, Second Series, vol. 12 (New York: The Christian Literature Company, 1895), pp. 1–2, 9, 24.

[Part 1, chap. 1] No one presumes to teach an art till he has first, with intent meditation, learnt it. What rashness is it, then, for the unskilful to assume pastoral authority, since the government of souls is the art of arts! For who can be ignorant that the sores of the thoughts of men are more occult than the sores of the bowels? And yet how often do men who have no knowledge whatever of spiritual precepts fearlessly profess themselves to be physicians of the heart, though those who are ignorant of the effects of drugs blush to appear as physicians of the flesh! But because, through the ordering of God, all the highest in rank of this present age are inclined to reverence religion, there are some who, through the outward show of rule within the holy Church, affect the glory of distinction. They desire to appear as teachers, they covet superiority to others, and, as the Truth attests, "they seek the first salutations in the marketplace, the first rooms at feasts, the first seats in assemblies" (Matt. 23:6), being all the less able to administer worthily the office they have undertaken of pastoral care, as they have reached the [teacher's] position of humility out of [vanity] only. For indeed, in [teaching], language itself is confounded when one thing is learnt and another taught. . . .

[Part II, chap. 1] The conduct of a prelate ought to so far transcend the conduct of the people as the life of a shepherd is wont to exalt him above the flock. For one whose ambition is such that the people are called his flock is bound anxiously to consider what great necessity is laid upon him to maintain [a life of] rectitude. It is necessary, then, that in thought he should be pure, in action [exemplary]; discreet in keeping silence, profitable in speech; a near neighbour to everyone in sympathy, exalted above all in contemplation; a familiar friend of good livers in humility, unbending against the vices of evil-doers through zeal for righteousness; not relaxing in his care for [the interior life] from being occupied in outward things. . . .

[Part III, prologue] Since, then, we have shown what manner of man the pastor ought to be, let us now set forth after what manner he should teach. For, as long before us Gregory Naziazen of reverend memory has taught, one and the same exhortation does not suit all, inasmuch as neither are all bound together by similarity of character. For the things that profit some often hurt others; seeing that also for the most part herbs which nourish some animals are fatal to others; and the gentle hissing that quiets horses incites whelps; and the medicine that abates one disease aggravates another; and the bread which invigorates the life of the strong kills little children. Therefore according to the quality of the hearers ought the discourse of teachers to be fashioned, so as to suit all and each for their several needs, and yet never deviate from the art of common edification. For what are the intent minds of hearers but, so to speak, a kind of [tautness] of the strings of a harp, which the skilful player, that he may produce a tune not at variance with itself, strikes variously? And for this reason the strings render back a consonant modulation, that they are struck indeed with one quill, but not with one kind of stroke. Whence every teacher also, that he may edify all in the one virtue of charity, ought to touch the hearts of his hearers out of one doctrine, but not with one and the same exhortation.

℅ No. 2. Thomas of Chobham's rules for priests (c. 1216).

Summa confessorum, ed. F. Broomfield, *Analecta mediaevalia Namurcensia* 25 (Louvain, 1968), pp. 79–85. Trans. JS.

The apostolic rule given to priests

Just as a monk must know the rule according to which he should live, a priest, too, must know why he was ordained and how he ought to minister in his orders. The Apostle [Paul] set forth this rule in his letters to Timothy and Titus, which has thirteen points to it. This is the rule: "A bishop then must be blameless" or "without crime" (which is the same thing), "married but once, vigilant, not a drinker, of good behavior," pure, "hospitable, a teacher; . . . no striker, . . . not a brawler, not covetous; one who rules well his own house . . . not a new convert" [1 Tim. 3:2–6; Titus 1:6–8]. Nine things are recommended here, four prohibited.

This rule applies as much to priests as to bishops for, as Jerome says, in ancient times bishops and ordinary priests alike were all commonly called bishops—in other words, superintendents or overseers, since all of them had to watch over and carefully guard their flock.

Whether, however, a bishop at his consecration receives some other order that an ordinary priest does not have is a question for experts in canon law. For some say that he receives no order beyond what he already had, but he does acquire a kind of rank or authority—just as a king does not receive holy orders when he is consecrated and anointed but only rank; whatever a bishop by virtue of his orders has the power to do an ordinary priest can also do; yet he does not have the same rank, because a bishop by the nature of his rank can ordain priests and confirm people, which an ordinary priest cannot do.

But in ancient times, according to the canons, any priest could ordain someone to the order of psalmist[3] and confer the first tonsure on him in accord with the ancient canons, just as all abbots in making a monk out of a layman give him his first tonsure; in fact, there are some abbots with special apostolic privileges who can ordain their monks as acolytes, and yet abbots are only anointed into the priesthood. Bishops, on the other hand, say that abbots do not confer any holy orders when they give the first tonsure but only the sign of a future order. Thus, when such monks come to a bishop to be ordained as priests, he first ordains them to the order of psalmist and then acolyte.

[1] When the apostolic rule says "a bishop must be without fault," the word "fault" here means something deserving blame and condemnation; in other words, something that would cause scandal if it were made public either through someone producing evidence or at a trial. This is thoroughly explained below.

[2] When it says "married but once," this should be understood to mean that someone who is going to be ordained should neither have been married to a widow nor have been married twice. This impediment to holy orders is not produced by any kind of sin but rather, so to speak, through a defect in

[3] The order of psalmist—a chorister who sang the psalms—was sometimes recognized as the eighth and lowest clerical order.

the sacrament. For matrimony is a sacrament of the body, that is, a sign of the marriage between Christ and the Church. Thus, just as Christ married only one virgin church, a priest, who is Christ's vicar, should have been the husband of only one woman who was a virgin. The church regards a virgin as any woman who has not been previously married, even though she may have lost her virginity. Thus anyone who marries a widow is not able to be raised to the priesthood. If he married a woman who had already lost her virginity, he can be ordained.

Saints Jerome and Augustine disagreed over this point. Jerome argued that if someone married one woman before he was baptized and then another after his baptism, he should not be considered to be twice married since baptism removed the impediment that had arisen from the first marriage. But Augustine's position prevailed, which argued that baptism removed nothing but sin and its consequences. Marriage, however, was neither a sin nor were its consequences sinful. Thus, the first marriage and its consequences were not removed by baptism.

When some other canonical impediment has occurred due to vice—for instance if someone has been convicted of theft or adultery—that infamy can be removed by baptism. But if someone has committed murder and thus been disgraced, this disqualification is not removed even after baptism since it is such a horrible thing to shed blood.

[3] That a bishop or priest should be vigilant is obvious since according to canon law anyone who is a half-witted dullard should be deposed from office, because a priest must possess the power of the keys, one of which is the key of knowledge. . . .

[4] Priests are required to be sober because of the danger that a priest might be called to visit a sick person but would be too drunk to go, and so that person would die without absolution; or perhaps he could go but, since he was drunk, he would not know how to give good counsel to the sick person. Thus, if someone is a drunkard he should not be ordained, or if he is already ordained he should be suspended.

[5] Next, good behavior. Here good behavior is understood to apply not only to his manner of life but also to his style of dress, for a cleric should wear the habit of his order. Thus, he who would live according to the requirements of canon law should be mindful that a clergyman is not allowed to wear green or red cloth, long-sleeved cloaks or gloves, laced shoes, and things like this. And since a clergyman swears canonical obedience to his bishop, and the canons forbid such clothing, a clergyman may rightly fear that he has perjured himself if he wears such clothing. His attire also in-

cludes a regulation tonsure; in other words, he should have his head shaved in the customary manner.

[6] That a priest needs to be pure is so obvious that it hardly needs saying.

[7] That a priest should be a teacher will be clear when we come to speak of the knowledge required of priests.

[8] Hospitality is necessary for a priest and every cleric because these men are more stewards than masters of the goods of their churches, since our goods are also the goods of the poor. For the church has been given such an abundance of worldly things so that the clergy may have the wherewithal to welcome guests; thus a priest's house could better be called a hospice for the poor than a dwelling for a priest.

[9] Next, "one who rules well his own house." He who does not know how to govern his household should not be assigned to govern a church. Thus, those who place a church in the hands of minors violate this regulation.

[10] Next, "no striker." A bishop must strike no one with his own hand, unless perhaps he is administering discipline to someone doing penance. However an ordinary priest may strike students if he is their teacher. Likewise, he may strike his servants to correct them if they are at fault—but moderately, so that the strokes of his whip are no greater than the misdeed itself. For this passage calls a striker someone who strikes out of malice, not someone who strikes in the abovementioned cases.

[11] Next, "not a brawler." This means not only a brawler over quarrels and base insults but also over lawsuits that are prosecuted in the secular courts; for a cleric—unless he owns secular things, i.e., lay possessions—should not bring litigation over ecclesiastical affairs into the secular courts. On the contrary, according to canon law if he does this he should be punished and also lose what he has won there. In this regard secular law says that it is shameful for a cleric to know civil law. Nevertheless, the church allows a member of the clergy to bring suit both on his behalf and on behalf of others in both the ecclesiastical and the secular courts and to receive a fee for his efforts. But according to canon law a member of a religious order may only be an advocate in a lawsuit involving his own monastery.

[12] That a priest should not be covetous is clear from both Testaments, since the cupidity of priests is linked to practically every evil thing in both the Old and the New Law.

[13] Next, "not a new convert," that is, not someone recently converted, because no one ought to be admitted to holy orders immediately after his conversion (unless he has had previous experience) since, given as much care as it takes to ordain someone, it takes an equal amount of difficulty to depose

him once he is ordained. For it would be a scandal for the church if the man who yesterday stood in the law court today stood in the choir, or if he who yesterday was a patron of actors today was a promoter of the saints.

These are the thirteen points, the apostolic rule; whoever does not know these precepts does not know how to be a priest.

∾ No. 3. Pastors and theologians: Thomas Aquinas' *quodlibets* on pastoral care (1269–70).

Quodlibetal Questions 1 and 2, ed. and trans. Sandra Edwards, Medieval Sources in Translation 27 (Toronto: Pontifical Institute of Mediaeval Studies, 1983), pp. 57–60.

Question 7, article 2: Whether someone is bound to give up the study of theology, even if he is suited to teaching others, in order to devote himself to the salvation of souls?

On the second [article] we proceed as follows: it seems that someone who can devote attention to the salvation of souls sins if he occupies his time in study.

1. For it is said in Galatians 6:10, "Let us do good while we have time." Also, no loss is more serious than that of time. Therefore, no one ought to spend his whole time in study, delaying to devote attention to the salvation of souls.

2. Moreover, the perfect are bound to do that which is better. But the religious are perfect so they ought especially to give up study to devote themselves to the salvation of souls.

3. Further, it is worse to wander off the moral path than a footpath. But a prelate is bound to call his subject back if he sees him wander off the footpath, therefore all the more is he bound to call him back from wandering off the moral path. But it is an error for a man to neglect what is better. Therefore a prelate ought to force a subject to apply his mind to the salvation of souls and neglect study.

On the contrary side, custom was brought in instead of reasoning.

I answer: it must be said that any two things can be compared with each other both absolutely and according to some particular case. For nothing prohibits that which is absolutely better from being the less preferred in some case, e.g., philosophizing is absolutely better than increasing your wealth but in time of necessity the latter is to be preferred. And any precious pearl is dearer than one piece of bread, but in a case of hunger the bread is to be preferred to the pearl, according to Lamentations 1:11, "They gave all valuable things for food in order to revive their souls."

However, we must consider that in any art the one who arranges the art and is called the architect is absolutely better than any manual laborer who carries out what is arranged for him by another. So also in constructing buildings, the one who arranges the building although he does no work with his hands is contracted for greater pay than the manual workers who hew the wood and cut the stones. But in a spiritual building there are the manual workers, as it were, who particularly pursue the direction of souls, e.g., by administering the sacraments or by doing some such thing in particular. But the bishops are like the principal artificers who command and arrange in what way the aforesaid workers ought to follow their office, because of which they are called "*episcopi*," i.e., superintendents. And likewise teachers of theology are like principal artificers who inquire and teach how others ought to procure the salvation of souls.

Therefore, it is absolutely better to teach theology and more meritorious if it is done with good intention, than to devote particular care to the salvation of this one or that. Whence the Apostle says concerning himself in 1 Corinthians 1:17, "For Christ did not send me to baptize but to teach the Gospel," although baptizing is especially a work bearing on the salvation of souls. And in 2 Timothy 2:2, the same Apostle says, "Commit to faithful men who shall be qualified also to teach others." Reason itself also demonstrates that it is better to teach those matters pertaining to salvation to them who can be of profit both to themselves and to others than the simple people who can be of use to themselves only. However, in a particular case where necessity requires, both bishops and teachers, having interrupted their own duties, ought to devote themselves particularly to the salvation of souls.

Therefore, to the first it must be said that someone who does what is better suffers no loss of time by teaching theology, nor does someone who disposes himself to this through study.

To the second it must be said that a person is called perfect because he has perfection or because he has a state of perfection. Now human perfection consists in the charity which joins a man to God, hence Genesis 17:1 says concerning love of God, "Walk before me and be perfect." Indeed the Lord says afterwards concerning love of neighbor, "Love your enemies," and in Matthew 5:48 he concludes, "Be therefore perfect." They are said to have a state of perfection, however, who are solemnly obligated to something connected with perfection.

Now something is connected with the perfection of charity in two ways. Something is connected in one way as a preamble and something preparatory to perfection, like poverty, chastity and such by which a man is drawn back from the care of worldly things so that he has more free time for these things which are God's, whence such men are more completely instruments of perfection. Because of this Jerome, expounding the words of Peter who said in Matthew 19:27, "Behold we gave up all and followed you," says that it is not sufficient for Peter to say "Behold we gave up all," but he adds what was perfect "and followed you." Therefore, those who preserve either voluntary poverty or chastity have indeed something preparatory to perfection but they are not said to have a state of perfection unless they obligate themselves to such a position by a solemn profession. Something solemn and perpetual is said to have a state, as is clear in the states of liberty, matrimony, and the like.

Something is connected to the perfection of charity in the other way as an effect, as when someone undertakes the direction of souls, for it pertains to perfect charity that someone out of love of God neglect the delight of the contemplative life which he loves more than the active and accept the occupations of the active life to procure the salvation of his neighbors. Therefore, he who applies himself in this way for the salvation of his neighbors has indeed an effect of perfection but not the state of perfection, except a bishop who, with a kind of solemn consecration, undertakes the direction of souls. Archdeacons and parish priests rather have certain duties committed to them than that they have been placed through them in a state of perfection, hence religious are made bishops but they are not made archdeacons or parish priests.

So when it is said that perfect persons are obliged to do what is better, it is true if it be understood of those who are called perfect because of the perfection of charity, for such are obligated from an inner law which binds by inclining so that they are obligated to fulfilling it according to the measure of their perfection. However, if it be understood of those who are called perfect because of a state, such as bishops and religious, it is not true for bishops are only bound to those things to which the charge of the governance undertaken extends, and religious are only bound to that to which they are obligated from the vow of their profession. Otherwise obligation would go on to infinity, but nature, art, and every law must have certain boundaries. Even given that the perfect are always bound to do that which is better, it would not be to the purpose as appears from what was said above.

To the third it must be said that although a prelate may be bound to call his subject back from all evil, he is not bound to lead him to everything better. This reasoning too has no place in the argument as neither do the others, etc.

No. 4. Bishop Robert Grosseteste on career choices (1235).

Grosseteste's *Epistolae*, ed. Henry Luard, Rolls Series 25 (London, 1861), pp. 57–59. Trans. JS.

Robert, by the grace of God bishop-elect of Lincoln to his beloved in Christ Master William de Cerda, greetings, etc.

We have received your letter, dear friend, saying that, since you do not wish both to lecture at the University of Paris and bear the cure of souls, right now you would rather lecture than carry the burden of pastoral care. So for the moment you have put off accepting the cure of souls to which we summoned you so that souls could be saved. We applaud and approve your academic studies: God willing they will be fruitful to many people. We praise even more your zeal so fervent that it would not allow you to be separated [i.e. non-resident] from your flock in the body of Christ if it happens that you accept their caretaking.

Nevertheless, since your zeal for the church so fervently graces your mind, it is not completely admirable that for the sake of continuing your short-term academic duties you refuse the everlasting duty of nourishing souls, since the one is a good that is fleeting, while the other is longer lasting, and—according to the rules for making choices—by virtue of this, is the better and more desirable choice, especially insofar as the Lord said to the chief of his apostles, "If you love me, feed my sheep" [John 21:17], not "If you love me, lecture to the pastors of my sheep." The Blessed [Pope] Gregory in his *Pastoral Care* said about this love: "If, then, the sign of loving is diligence in pasturing, whoever is strong in virtue but refuses to feed God's flock is guilty of not loving the Chief Pastor." Therefore, so that refusing a cure will not separate you from love for the Chief Pastor, you should allow the burden of pastoral care to be placed on your shoulders.

We certainly believe that you do not throw off this weight like a mule bucking against its burden; but we also realize that no one taking on this task looks upon it as a prize, and that, dragging and kicking, you agree to undertake it unwillingly because it is onerous and full of dread. Yet when it has been undertaken it can be borne tirelessly and with strength. Thus, so that it will not be counted my sin if the Lord's flock is robbed of the gift of your indispensable care, and my failing if you are cut off from the love of the Chief Pastor, prostrate at your feet in humility and love, with zealous heart I beg you, beseech you, and implore you through Jesus Christ's outpoured blood, that you do not reject the cure of souls toward which not only I, but Christ himself, who offered each and every one the complete reward of his blood, pulls you. For Christ pulls both you and the whole heavenly city by the rope of charity; he pushes you; he prods and goads you with the horrors of the infernal punishments that loom terribly over those who stubbornly refuse to undertake the cure of souls toward which they are led. Therefore, since my devotion—imploring you with total effort—and Christ's love, and the zeal for souls compel you not indifferently but fiercely, according to the advice of the Blessed Gregory, even though you flee from the cure of souls in your heart, you ought to obey and, against your will, take it up.

The Lord Jesus Christ came down from the bosom of the Father into the womb of the Virgin, and he suffered death on the cross to save souls; but you demur over stepping down from the teacher's chair in order to nourish through word, deed, and prayer those for whom the Son of God did not hesitate to surrender himself into hostile hands and suffer the torments of the cross!

But if the need for avoiding the scandal [of non-residence] compels you for the present to accept the teaching job, as your letter suggests, this ought not to stand in the way of you taking up the cure to which you are led. For even if your academic duties detain you, you would not have to be personally resident in the parish before the coming feast of St. Michael [September 29]. Thus, you will be able to continue your studies up until then without any anxiety about the defect of your non-residence. But if you so like and if it would be useful for you to continue studying for another half year or a year, I promise in good faith that I will take care to supply suitable preachers to carry out the duty of preaching to your parishioners in the interim during your absence.

∾ **No. 5. The dignity of the priesthood: an excerpt from a sermon (late fourteenth or early fifteenth century).**
Middle English Sermons, ed. Woodburn O. Ross, EETS o.s. 209 (1940), pp. 280–83. Modernized by JS.

. . . Perhaps you will say to me, sir, "Why should this confession be made to a priest?" Because, sir, the priest has the power in his hands to forgive you, to bless you, and to curse you. Put briefly, he is ordained to be your judge and your helper in everything concerning your spiritual governance. Insofar as it seems necessary to me to describe the dignity and power of the priesthood to this audience, so that gentlemen will know more truly how they should behave toward priests, I will show you the excellence of the priesthood in three or four ways. God would that I had the time and leisure that I might match the noble skill in this matter of St. John Chrysostom [c.

347–407], who wrote to St. Basil [c. 329–79], the great doctor of the church and bishop, in a book called *Dialogue of Chrysostom to Bishop Basil.*

Here are his words put in our own language: "A priest's office," he says, "contains great dignity. It is performed on earth but its minister is heavenly. This office of priesthood can be performed by no ordinary man, nor even by an angel or an archangel; no other creature can do it unless by the infinite goodness of Almighty God himself. He made the office of priesthood so perfect that no angel ever attained such a high, perfect office.

"Now, Father Basil," St. John Chrysostom says, "when you see Almighty God offered on the altar, you see the priest administering that Blessed Sacrament at the altar by his prayers. Where is your mind at then? Attending to earthly things? Or has it been translated to heaven? Truly this miracle is heavenly and wonderful, that God—Lord, God, and man, who sits in heaven upon his Father's right side and governs all the world—at the time of the sacrifice is contained in the priest's hands and desires to be intimate with man."

Furthermore, this saint says, "Let us make a comparison between the power of the great prophet Elijah in the Old Testament and the power of the simplest priest of the New Testament. Recall," he says, "how Elijah once stood with King Ahab with all the people about him. Remember further how, at the prophet's bidding, there was a sacrifice put on the altar on God's side; at the bidding of the false king and of all the priests of Baal another sacrifice was put on the other side. The people all waited in silence to see what miracle God would work by his prophecy. The prophet Elijah prayed and suddenly God sent down fire from heaven by a miracle, which burned up the sacrifice even though it was soaked with water—in fact, the fire licked up the water and burned it. This is the story in Holy Scripture, 3 Kings 18.

"Truly," says Chrysostom, "this was a wonderful miracle. But now let us see about the miracle that our priest does daily at the altar. The priest at the altar performing the mystery of the Blessed Sacrament brings down by prayer, not fire, the body of Almighty God to the altar, which enlightens and illumines man's soul and makes it purer than any gold or silver. Now surely," says this saint, "except for the gracious mercy of God that sustains the priest in his gracious working, no earthly man could bear the majesty of so high a presence. And yet," he says, "not just this power is given to priests; beyond this they have the power to open and shut the gates of heaven, which no angel nor archangel will ever attain. God gave this power to priests saying 'Whatever you bind on earth, shall be bound also in heaven; and whatever you loose on earth, shall be loosed also in heaven'"(Matt. 18[:18]).

This saint says that there is no earthly power equal to the power of the priesthood. "The power," he says, "of a king or of a temporal prince acts upon the body and upon material things; it does not affect the soul. But the power that priests have pierces heaven; it stretches to man's soul and makes it either free or bound, alive or dead. To put it briefly," he says, "all the power that the Blessed Trinity has over a man is given to priests. Therefore, scripture witnesses that the Father of Heaven has given his judgment to the Son. Now Christ has made priests his beloved tenants of this world.

"Now then," he says, "I may conclude and say this about priests: Without their power or service there is no help for any Christian man. Without them no man receives the sacrament of baptism perfectly. Without them no man may receive his Savior in the Blessed Sacrament. Without priests who may be reconciled to God when he is in a state of mortal sin? Do you not believe, Father Basil," he asks, "that these are men of great power and dignity, who by their prayers and offering of sacrifice stand for all the world in the sight of God? These priests in giving or offering these sacraments are guarded by angels against all their spiritual enemies."

Sirs, I have told this to you who are placed in high estate and to all gentlemen, in order to urge you to respect the priesthood as you should, as people did in the days of our fathers before us. Men know well enough how badly and dishonestly the priesthood is treated in various countries, often against the law. I see that they are accused of rape where there is no rape; they are oppressed and robbed of their goods grievously and foully. Truly this great wrong and mischief cannot be amended without the help of temporal lords—would to Jesus that they would do their jobs to amend it! And if they would complain to the bishops when they do see priests who are remiss or who live unchastely, I know that it would be corrected. For I know that the prelates of the church would punish them according to the law if they were informed of these things. And if those who are remiss are indeed punished according to the laws of holy church, they will be severely punished. If it happens that any prelates are negligent and do not correct these faults, I think that our sovereign lord, of his goodness, should bid them to take heed of such faults; then I have no doubt that they would soon be corrected. Surely, if this is not done, I sorely fear that the vengeance of God will smite the people of this realm for the constant perjury found in indictments made against priests and for the dishonor shown to the priesthood. O good Lord Emperor Constantine, what has become of the pity and honor that you once had for Christ's church? You know this. I pray God send you a successor who will follow in your footsteps. . . .

∽ **No. 6. John Wyclif, "On the Pastoral Office" (c. 1378).**

Ford Lewis Battles, ed. and trans., in *Advocates of Reform: From Wyclif to Erasmus*, ed. Matthew Spinka, The Library of Christian Classics 14 (London and Philadelphia: SCM Press, 1953), pp. 44–46; 47–49; 56–57.

I.16 It remains [for us] to examine the roots of sin, which have grown up out of this [human] law and of the devil's subtlety. Now certain curates feed themselves out of the superabundance of temporalities too elegantly; they are unsuited to preaching the gospel, and to beseeching God for their subjects. Since it ought to be accepted almost as a matter of faith that such curates are obligated to the pastoral office more than other officials, they ought to recognize themselves to be poor and needy, and that they receive their income from the meager gifts of widows and poor subjects. In so far as they depend upon the collections of the needy, they should recognize that they are going to answer individually for each one of those in the day of judgment. Where, then, is there a more straitened condition of miserable poverty? The Luciferine sign of pride is that the prelate is proud of the fatness of his benefice, which nevertheless he is able to spend each year. . . . To repress this pride one should recognize carefully that God expressly grants to each his part. Since the prelate is the bailiff of such a great Lord, he ought more especially to ponder that it behooves him to give a faithful account of the part due to God, how he has faithfully managed that part. And this would be a checkrein for rectors, not to play the wanton in banquets or to misappropriate for their own personal use the meager alms of their subjects.

This same ought to be applied to the four sects, namely, the bishops, the monks, the canons, and the friars, because all these wantonly spend in banquets and ornaments (contrary to the life and rule of Christ) the alms of their poor subjects. In matters such as these the poor prelate would blush if he were not blinded by devilish pride.

The third reason which should move the conscience of pastors of this sort consists in this, that the bishop of souls appoints the curate himself, not as the guardian of excrements for thus playing the wanton in his body, but as the guardian of souls which were made in the image and likeness of God. For this reason ought he to fatten the souls spiritually in the pasture of virtues; and he will follow the highest Pastor in morals, who attends to the feeding of the spirit and not to the feeding of the body, unless there is grace in this. . . . And if in this state perchance he become needy, as for example blind or lame or stricken with some other bodily infirmity, the provider of the necessities of the soul for his subjects ought according to the rule of the apostle be sustained by their alms. . . .

I.17 . . . How ought the curate to exemplify to his subjects the struggle against the three enemies of the soul? As for lust, many so-called curates are not content with a parish church unless they have a chapel attached thereto, or a wife sojourning with them or living sumptuously apart, yet near enough to be supported by parish funds. Yet they live outside of matrimony in open adultery, and it is clear how this sin ought to be detested by subjects and by curates alike. For subjects ought not to hear the Mass of such priests, nor as a consequence in other pastoral offices to participate in his wickedness, since prayer and whatever else he does are notoriously sinful in the eyes of God; as a consequence they ought not to give to him offerings of tithes lest they seem to be consenting to such a notorious crime in curates. . . . He would then not be a protector, but a plunderer of Antichrist, who would not blush, were his many sheep to perish out of hunger, and withal he would sustain his darling that she might go about in sumptuous raiment and in silver or gold net. Where, I ask, could be the conscience of such a pastor but rather more truly a ravisher, not fearing to seize the tithes of his poor parishioners in order to wallow with such a prostitute in lust, and with this to set himself up as worthy to exercise any pastoral office for the salvation of his own soul or of the souls of his subjects? Surely such a one seems to be not only a rapacious wolf but even a strangler of his simple sheep for salvation both of body and of soul. And the same seems to be true concerning a curate lingering in the Roman *curia,* seeking after other benefices or privileges, who secures the alms of his poor subjects, or living in London or other places of wantonness outside his own parish on what he has taken from them, however such sojourning of the Antichrist might be cloaked. . . . Thus in every respect ought curates engaged in human studies, law (as for example, civil or papal), to be detested, also those concerned with medicine or the teaching of Aristotle, although from such studies some good might proceed. In all such cases it is permitted to the parishioners wisely to withdraw their alms, lest they seem to defend and foster the frowardness of such a so-called pastor. . . .

II.1 We have touched superficially on the first part of the priestly office, holiness of life. . . . Now the second part pertaining to the pastor, that is, wholesomeness of teaching, remains to be looked at. While Jesus Christ "began to do and to teach" [Acts 1:1], the curate, who ought to be his vicar, ought to shine with sanctity in his own person, and, secondly, ought to be resplendent with righteousness of doctrine before his sheep. Otherwise his preaching would be useless, since it is written: "But to the sinner God has said, 'Why do you declare my justices, and take my covenant in your mouth? You have hated discipline and have cast my words behind you!' " [Ps. 49:16

f. Vg.; 50:16 f., E.V.]. Therefore the first condition of the pastor is to cleanse his own spring, that it may not infect the Word of God. And as for the second condition, which is very manifold, the first and particular function of the pastor remains to be seen. The pastor has a threefold office: first, to feed his sheep spiritually on the Word of God, that through pastures ever green they may be initiated into the blessedness of heaven. The second pastoral office is to purge wisely the sheep of disease, that they may not infect themselves and others as well. And the third is for the pastor to defend his sheep from ravening wolves, both sensible and insensible. In all these the especial office of the pastor seems that of sowing the Word of God among his sheep. God ordains for a good reason that by the teaching of the pastor and his own manner of life his preaching to his sheep may be made efficacious, since this acts more effectively than mere preaching. . . . The life of a good pastor is of necessity a mirror to be imitated by his flock. The highest Pastor could not depart from righteousness in deed or word; for this reason his life and moral example are, as it were, a vital spirit to be attended by individual Christians and especially by pastors, who say that they are the vicars of Christ. As a sign of this, because life and work ought to precede word in the pastor, righteousness of life is necessary in anyone who would be saved, but eloquence in preaching is especially necessary in curates. For "no one," either an infant or a feeble person, "can be saved unless his life according to the righteousness of Christ be found just through his grace." . . .

II.2 "Among all the duties of the pastor after justice of life, holy preaching is most to be praised," for Christ, the Primal Truth, . . . said to the woman commending the one who bore him in the womb and nourished his body, "They are blessed who hear the word of God and keep it" [Luke 11:28]. There is no doubt but that preaching the Word of God is as great as hearing it. Moreover, in Christ there were these three things: the highest was the preaching of the Word, [then] the hearing of it, and [finally] the keeping of it in deed. Yet in others preaching is more commendable than hearing, just as action is superior to being acted upon. In like manner, Christ, in highest wisdom, commanded his apostles when he ascended into heaven to preach the gospel to every creature [Matt. 28:19]; indeed the wisest Master would not have done this unless such preaching were more to be praised in apostle or curate. Hence, among his duties such an activity is more worthy [than the rest]. It is evident that preaching the gospel is the special work of the curate, for Christ advances more in his apostles by preaching to the people than by doing any miracle which in his own person he did in Judea. . . . Preaching the gospel exceeds prayer and administration of the sacraments, to an infinite degree. . . . Spreading the gospel has far wider and more evident benefit; it is thus the most precious activity of the Church. Just as the judges of the kings handing down their judgment to the people are especially designated next to the kings in honor, thus those preaching the gospel truly are to be set apart by the authority of the Lord.

II.8 Let us examine the supplying of a vicar for the office of pastor. Although many so-called curates have vicars, they usually explain the appointment of the vicar as being intended for this purpose: to collect (either by himself or through another) money or income, vulgarly called "the fruits of the benefice." Granted that it is not an inherited office, yet it seems that it is contrary to the law of God and reason for any such curate thus to fulfill his function through a vicar, for any such curate is personally held not only responsible to God for the sheep entrusted to him, but to the Church Militant, according to his merit. Since it is necessary that he answer for the sheep entrusted to him, it is therefore also necessary that he personally feed them. And since all the merit of the curate ought to be directed to God, it would seem exceedingly difficult for an absent curate spiritually to aid his sheep more than one bodily present. Yet it is known that the necessary spiritual works of mercy require a local relationship between pastor and flock. But to preach such works of mercy these pastors care little. In like manner no curate can satisfy God through a vicar without in his own person incurring sin. Although he were to institute a thousand vicars, yet he cannot thus excuse the leprosy of sin in his own spirit. For this reason it seems that this human tradition savors of heresy against the apostle's "Each one will carry his own burden" [Gal. 6:5]. And in the creed of Athanasius it is said, "Every man will render an account for his own actions." . . . In like manner before the tradition of paying such a curate with tithes and offerings was invented, that curate was required to aid the subjects given into his care as much as he was able; nor ought he to be lax or tardy on account of that human tradition; therefore he is still bound to aid spiritually the people given into his care as much as he is able. . . .

B. Legal

℺ No. 7. The rule of celibacy. First Lateran Council, c. 7 (1123).
Decrees, Tanner, p. 191.

We absolutely forbid priests, deacons or subdeacons to live with concubines and wives, and to cohabit with other women, except those whom the council of Nicaea [325 A.D.] permitted to dwell with them solely on account of necessity, namely a mother, sister, paternal or maternal aunt, or other such persons, about whom no suspicion could justly arise.

❧ No. 8. Forbidden professions and hobbies.

Gratian's *Decretum*, Dist. 34, 2–3; Boniface VIII's *Sext.* 3.1,1. Trans. JS.

A bishop, priest, or deacon is not allowed to have dogs, or hawks, or other birds of prey for hunting. If any person of this sort is often involved in this type of pastime, if he is a bishop he should be suspended from celebrating the mass for three months; if a priest, for two months; if a deacon, he should be removed from office. We forbid every servant of God from hunting or chasing wild beasts with dogs, or to own hawks or falcons.

Clergy who are entertainers, minstrels, or jesters greatly debase the dignity of the clerical order. If they practice this ignominious art for a year, or if they do it for a shorter time and have been given three warnings, they automatically lose all clerical privileges.

❧ No. 9. Clerical deportment. Fourth Lateran Council, c. 16 (1215).

Decrees, Tanner, p. 243.

Clerics should not practice business or callings of a secular nature, especially those that are dishonourable. They should not watch mimes, entertainers and actors. Let them avoid taverns altogether, unless by chance they are obliged by necessity on a journey. They should not play at games of chance or of dice, nor be present at such games. They should have a suitable crown and tonsure, and let them diligently apply themselves to the divine services and other good pursuits. Their outer garments should be closed and neither too short nor too long. Let them not indulge in red or green cloths, long sleeves or shoes with embroidery or pointed toes, or in bridles, saddles, breast-plates and spurs that are gilded or have other superfluous ornamentation. Let them not wear cloaks with sleeves at divine services in a church, nor even elsewhere, if they are priests or parsons, unless a justifiable fear requires a change of dress. They are not to wear buckles or belts ornamented with gold or silver, or even rings except for those whose dignity it befits to have them. All bishops should wear outer garments of linen in public and in church, unless they have been monks, in which case they should wear the monastic habit; and let them not wear their cloaks loose in public but rather fastened together behind the neck or across the chest.

❧ No. 10. Clergy bearing arms: the Legatine Council at St. Paul's London (1268).

Councils and Synods, pp. 751–52. Trans. JS.

[4] Concerning clergy bearing arms: Since the defence of Christian innocence relies on the virtues as a shield, the Apostle [Paul] teaches that we

should "put on the armor of God" and take up "the sword of the spirit" [Eph. 6:11,17], because ours is "not a struggle against flesh and blood, but against the Prince of Darkness" [Eph. 6:12], whom we fight against not with weapons of iron but with prayers, tears, and good works. Therefore, the authority of both divine and human law absolutely forbids the clergy, who have accepted Christ's noble inheritance, to bear arms, even in the defence of justice or in revenge. Burning with zeal for the church's honor, we abhor the enormous excesses of those who, ignoring the Divine Name and their own dignity, dare to carry arms. Falling in with thieves, robbers, and other criminals, they join in their robberies, pillaging, and thefts, committing these crimes against the property of ordinary people and even against churches and the things that others sometimes keep there or in their cloisters or churchyards for safekeeping. Bearing their spiritual welfare in mind, we intend to take action against clergy roistering in such thoroughly horrible crimes. Therefore, we order that no one in clerical orders may carry weapons; if he does, he will automatically incur the penalty of excommunication. And after this warning, unless he makes satisfaction within a time span fixed by his superior, then he will lose control of every ecclesiastical benefice he holds and he should realize that he may be deposed from his rank. And if he has no benefice, so that he will not remain unpunished, he will be ineligible to obtain any benefice for five years. His diocesan may not absolve him from this sentence of excommunication unless he first satisfies the diocesan's will regarding these regulations.

∾ **No. 11. Clerical attire described in Archbishop John Stratford's constitutions (1342).**

E. Cutts, *Parish Priests and Their People in the Middle Ages* (London: SPCK, 1898), pp. 164–66.

The external costume often shows the internal character and condition of persons; and although the behaviour of clerks ought to be an example and pattern of lay people, yet the abuses of clerks, which have prevailed more than usual in these days, in tonsure, clothing, horse trappings, and other things, have created an abominable scandal among the people; because persons holding ecclesiastical dignities, rectories, honourable prebends, and benefices with cure of souls, even men in Holy Orders, scorn to wear the tonsure, which is the crown of the kingdom of heaven and of perfection, and distinguish themselves by hair spreading to their shoulders in an effeminate manner, and walk about clad in a military rather than a clerical dress, with an outer habit very short and tight-fitting, but excessively wide, with long sleeves which do not touch the elbow; their hair curled and perfumed, their hoods with lappets of wonderful length; with long beards, rings on their fingers, and girded belts studded with precious stones of wonderful size, their purses enamelled and gilt with various devices, and knives openly hanging at them like swords, their boots of red and green peaked and cut in many ways; with housings to their saddles, and horns hanging from their necks; their capes and cloaks so furred, in rash disregard of the canons, that there appears little or no distinction between clergymen and laymen; whereby they render themselves unworthy through their demerits of the privilege of their order and profession. Wherefore we decree that they who hold ecclesiastical benefices in our province, especially if ordained to Holy Orders, do wear the garments and tonsure proper to their condition, but if they offend by using any of the foresaid abuses, too wide sleeves or too short outer coats, or long hair, or untonsured head, or long beard, and do not when admonished desist within six months, they shall incur suspension from their office until absolved by the bishop—to whom their absolution is reserved—when they shall forfeit a sixth of one year's income from their ecclesiastical benefices to the poor of their benefices; and if while the suspension lasts, they perform any act of their office they shall be deprived. [On the other hand] unbeneficed clerks publicly and habitually carrying themselves like clerks, if they exceed in these things, and do not, when admonished, correct themselves within four months, shall not be capable of holding a benefice. If living in universities, and bearing themselves as clerks, they offend in these respects, they shall be incapable of ecclesiastical degrees or honours. Yet we intend not to abridge clerks of open wide surcoats called table-coats with fitting sleeves to be worn at seasonable times and places, nor of short and close garments while travelling in the country at their own discretion. Ordinaries are commanded to make inquiry by themselves or by others every year, and to see that this canon is observed.

◌ No. 12. William Lyndwood's summary of clerical privileges (c. 1417–32). *Provinciale*, I.14, p. 69 (Oxford, 1679). Trans. WJD.

Clerical privilege entails many things: namely, that clerics should not be judged by lay persons; however, they may bring lay persons before church courts on ecclesiastical matters. Also, that lay persons or other non-clerical judges are excommunicated when they detain clergy, even without violence, in any place, public or private. In brief, this privilege consists of two basic things: one, that clerics are not to be harmed in their person precisely as stated above. Two, that no harm should befall their person or property. To consider the matter more extensively, there are fourteen aspects of clerical privilege: first, that clerics should not be brought before secular judges; second, that striking a cleric comes under canon law; third, that clerics are not called to worldly preoccupations; fourth, that they are permitted to form religious communities [*collegia*] where the laity may not; fifth, that they can make legal claim to something granted a church before it has been handed over; sixth, that this privilege is enjoyed by both individuals and households; seventh, that those who issue statutes against the clergy are ipso facto excommunicated; eighth, that clergy alone may receive church benefices; ninth, that a lay person cannot summon a cleric to court with a general citation; tenth, that in a civil case covering gifts, clerics are bound to give no more than four farthings. (In canon law, there is no such requirement.) Eleventh, that clerics can testify when it comes to family property; twelfth, that they may be litigants in cases having to do with recovery of their own property even without paternal consent; thirteenth, that they are not allowed to make contracts; fourteenth, that a serf who becomes a cleric with his lord's permission is freed from the lord's power.

C. *Literary*

∾ No. 13. Chaucer's "Poure Persoun" (1386).

"General Prologue" [A477–528] of *The Canterbury Tales*. In Albert C. Baugh, *Chaucer's Major Poetry* (Englewood Cliffs, N.J.: Prentice-Hall, 1963), pp. 249–50. Modernized by JS.

A good man was there of religion,
Who was a poor parson from a town;
But rich he was of holy thought and work.
He was also a learned man, a clerk,
That Christ's gospel truly would preach;
His parishioners devoutly would he teach.
Gentle he was, and wonderfully diligent,
And in adversity fully patient,
And such he proved oftentimes.
Full loath he was to curse [with excommunication] for his tithes,
But rather would he give, out of duty,
To all his poor parishioners
From his gifts and income;
He could be satisfied with just a little.
Wide was his parish, the houses set asunder,
But he left no one lie, even in rain and thunder,
In sickness; nor in danger did he fail to visit
The furthest person in his parish, either great or small,
On foot, and in his hand a staff.
This noble example to his sheep he gave:

First he acted and then he taught.
He got those words out of the gospel,
And this phrase he added too:
"If gold rusts, what shall iron do?"
For if a priest be foul, in whom we trust,
It's no wonder that a simple man will rust;
And a shame it is, if a priest take heed,
A shittied shepherd and a clean sheep.
A priest ought to give a good example
By his purity, of how his sheep should live.
He did not put his benefice out to hire
And let his sheep be encumbered in the mire,
And run to London to St. Paul's
To seek a chantry for souls,
Or to be supported by a guild;
He dwelled at home and kept well his fold,
So that the wolf did not make it go astray:
He was a shepherd, not a mercenary.
And though he was holy and virtuous,
He was not to sinful men contemptuous,
Nor by his speech was he haughty or superior,
But in his teaching he was discreet and benign.
To draw folk to heaven by fairness, this was his business.
But if there was anyone obstinate,
Whether he was of high or low estate,
Him he would rebuke sharply on the occasion.
I swear that there is nowhere a better priest.
He sought no pomp and honor,
Nor was he over-scrupulous.
Christ's teaching and his apostles' twelve
He taught, but first he followed it himself.

❧ No. 14. Parson Sloth in William Langland's *Piers the Plowman* (c. 1377–79).

The Vision of William concerning Piers the Plowman in Three Parallel Texts, ed. Walter K. Skeat,
vol. 1 (Oxford, 1886), pp. 166–72 (B-text, passus V, ll.392–468). Modernized by JS.

Then came Sloth all slobbered with two sleep-crusted eyes.
"I must sit," he said, "or I'll have to nap.
I can't stand, or stoop, or kneel without a stool.
When I'm in bed, unless my rear end makes me,
No bell-ringing rouses me till I'm ready to dine."

Belching a "Bless me, father," he struck his breast,
Stretched, sighed, and finally snored.
"Wake up, man!" Repentance cried, "Hurry up with your confession."
"If I were about to die this very day, I'd rather not know.
I cannot say the *Pater noster* perfectly as the priest sings it.
I do know rhymes about Robin Hood and Randolf, Earl of Chester,[4]
Though I don't know the shortest verse written about our Lord or
    Our Lady.
I've made forty vows and forgotten them by morning.
I've never done the penance the priest gives me.
And I've never been truly sorry for my sins.
When I say my prayers, unless I'm angry,
What I say with my tongue is two miles from what I mean in my
    heart.
I occupy each day, holy day or otherwise,
With idle tales told over my ale or else in church.
I seldom think about God's pain and his passion.
    I never visit the sick or people chained up in jail.
I'd rather hear a racy tale, or about the summer sports of
    cobblers,
Or laugh at lies about my neighbor,
Than anything that Mark, Matthew, John, or Luke wrote.
I skip vigils and fast days,
And lie in bed during Lent with my lover in my arms,
Until matins and mass are over, and then I go to the friars'
    church.
If I make it in time for 'Go, the mass is ended,' that's fine by
    me.
Sometimes I don't go to confession—unless I get sick!—
Even twice in two years, and then I guess at what I've done.
    I've been a priest and parson for the past thirty years,
Yet I don't know scales or how to sing, and don't read saints'
    lives.
I can hunt a hare in a field or furrow
Better than I can construe one clause
of 'Blessed is the man' or 'Blessed are they,'
Or explain them to my parishioners.

---

[4]The powerful baron Ranulph de Blundeville (c. 1172–1232). None of the ballads about him
survive.

I can arbitrate a dispute or audit a reeve's accounts,
But I can't read a line in the canons or the *Decretals*.
    If I beg or borrow something, unless it's written down
I quickly forget it; and if the lender asks me about it
Six or seven times, I swear I know nothing about it.
Such have I treated honest men ten hundred times.
    Sometimes I'm behind in paying my servants' salary;
It's a sorry thing to hear the reckoning when we read out the
    accounts,
As I pay my workmen with bad will and anger.
    If anyone does me a favor or helps me in need,
I am ungrateful for his courtesy and cannot understand it;
For I have and have always had a bit of the hawk's habits:
I'm not lured by love—there has to be a morsel held under the
    thumb.
The kindness that my fellow Christians showed me in the past,
I, Sloth, have forgotten sixty times since
By what I've said or failed to say.
Many times I've wasted
Both flesh and fish and many other victuals,
Both bread and ale, butter, milk, and cheese—
Spoiled while I held them till they're no good to anyone.
    I ran about in my youth and learned nothing;
Ever since I've been a beggar because of my foul sloth:
Woe is me that I spent a barren youth!"
    "Do you repent?" asked Repentance, but suddenly Sloth was
        snoozing,
Until *Vigilate*, the Watcher, tossed water on his eyes,
And dashed it on his face and earnestly cried to him
"Beware of Despair who would betray you!
'I am sorry for my sins.'—say this to yourself,
And strike your breast and ask God for grace;
For there is no sin so great that his goodness isn't greater."
    Then Sloth sat up and quickly crossed himself,
And made a vow before God about his foul sloth:
"There shall be no Sunday for the next seven years,
That I shall not go before daybreak to the dear church
    (unless I'm sick),
And hear matins and the mass as if I were a monk;
Drinking ale after dinner won't keep me

From hearing evensong—I swear this on the holy cross.
And I will repay—if I can—
All that I've wickedly earned since I had the know-how.
And even though I go broke, I will not cease to see
That each man gets back what is his before the day I die.
And from what remains, by the Holy Rood of Chester,
I shall seek truth first, before I seek pilgrimage to Rome."

∾ **No. 15. A poem on the priesthood: "Multi sunt presbyteri," an anonymous poem of the fourteenth century.**
Excerpted from *Collected Hymns*, trans. J. N. Neale (London and New York: Hadder and Stroughton, 1869, 1914), pp. 69–72.

Many are the Presbyters
    Lacking information
Why the Cock on each church tow'r
    Meetly finds his station;
Therefore I will now hereof
    Tell the cause and reason,
If ye lend me patient ears
    For a little season.

Cock, he is a marvellous
    Bird of God's creating,
Faithfully the Priestly life
    In his ways relating;
Such a life as he must lead
    Who a parish tendeth,
And his flock from jeopardy
    Evermore defendeth.
From what point the wind his course
    On the tower directeth,
To that point the cock his head
    Manfully objecteth:
Thus the Priest, where'er he sees
    Satan warfare waging,
Thither doth he turn himself
    For his flock engaging. . . .

Cock, he rules a tribe of hens,
    Laws and customs giving,

And hath many cares of heart
 For their way of living:
Even thus parochial cure
 Whoso entertaineth,
Let him learn and let him do
 That which God ordaineth.

Cock, he findeth grains of wheat,
 And his hens he calleth,
Giving to the dearer ones
 What to each befalleth:
Midst his people thus the clerk
 Scripture nurture shareth,
And for sick, and poor, and maim'd
 Providently careth. . . .

When it draws to vesper-tide,
 Cock neglecteth never,
But he goeth straight to roost,
 With his subjects ever:
So that then, when midnight comes,
 He may well and truly
Call God's Priests to rise and sing
 Matin service duly.

Cock at midnight croweth loud,
 And in this delighteth;
But, before he crows, his sides
 With his wings he smiteth:
So the Priest at midnight, when
 Him from rest he raiseth,
Firstly doeth penitence,
 After that he praiseth. . . .

Thus the cock hath preached to you;
 Hear with duty fervent,
Priests and Levites of the Lord,
 Every faithful servant!
That at last it may be said,
 "Come to joys supernal:—"

Yea, bestow on all of us,
    Father, Life Eternal!

∾ **No. 16. The dignity of the priesthood, from the anonymous play** *Everyman* **(c. 1509–19).**

Everyman, A Morality Play, ed. Montrose J. Moses (New York: J. F. Taylor and Co., 1903), pp. 39–41.
Modernized by JS.

[*Everyman, at the moment of his death, is confronted by his Five Wits, Knowledge, and Good Deeds, who counsel him to seek the eucharist and last anointing from a priest.*]

    Five Wits. Everyman, that is the best you can do;
    God will you to salvation bring,
    For priesthood exceeds all other things.
    To us holy scripture they do teach,
    And convert man from sin, heaven to reach;
    God has to them more power given
    Than to any angel that is in heaven.
    With five words[5] he may consecrate
    God's Body in flesh and blood to make,
    And handle his maker between his hands.
    The priest binds and unbinds all bands
    Both on earth and in heaven.[6]
    You minister all the sacraments seven;
    Though we kissed your feet, you were worthy.
    You are the surgeon that cures sins deadly,
    No remedy we find under God
    But all only priesthood.
    Everyman, God gave priests that dignity
    And set them among us in his place to be:
    Thus they are above angels in degree.
    Knowledge. If priests are good it is so, surely;
    But when Jesus hung on the cross with great smart   [pain]
    There he gave out of his blessed heart
    The same sacrament in great torment.
    He did not sell them to us, that Lord Omnipotent;
    Therefore, Saint Peter the apostle does say
    That Jesu's curse have all they

[5] *Hoc est enim corpus meum,* or This is my Body.
[6] See Matt. 16:19.

Who God their Savior do buy or sell,
Or who for any money do take or tell.   [reckon]
Sinful priests give sinners examples bad:
Their children sit by other men's fires, I have heard,
And some haunt women's company,
With unclean life, such as lusts of lechery.
These with sin are made blind.
Five Wits. I trust to God none such we may find.
Therefore, let us priesthood honor,
And follow their doctrine for our souls' succor.
We are their sheep, and they shepherds be,
By whom we are all kept in surety.

2

Education

*T*he image of the ignorant pastor—a clerical oaf stumbling bewildered over his Latin while his ignorant congregation looked on equally clueless—is the most potent modern stereotype of the medieval parish priest. But this caricature was sharply etched long before modern historians devised it. *Ignorantia sacerdotum*, "the ignorance of priests," was the catch phrase of ecclesiastical reformers and critics throughout the later middle ages. To their eyes as much as to ours, nothing seemed of more dubious value than an unlettered priest: the essential doctrines of Christianity and all its daily rituals were preserved in Latin texts; to be a minister of Christianity a priest had to be able to read them. All thoughtful churchmen knew the dangers that poorly educated pastors posed, and they were swift to draw on scriptural support—"If a blind man guide a blind man, both fall into a pit [Matt. 15:14]," a citation woven endlessly through medieval writings about the clergy. But the task of conceiving, much less executing, a plan to provide a uniform and sufficient education for every parish priest in Christendom daunted even the best-intentioned among them. In fact, until the Council of Trent decreed in the mid-sixteenth century that all aspirants to the priesthood must be trained in seminaries, the Catholic Church had no universally available system of vocational training for its priests. In the meantime, English pastoral education banked on catch-as-catch-can methods ranging from college study for the fortunate few, to the basic instruction offered to most priests-to-be in elementary and grammar schools, to private tutoring, to on-the-job training.

The burgeoning schools of the later middle ages were the fertile beds where theology, philosophy, and canon and civil law flourished—disciplines most exquisitely grounded in literacy. The college men who matriculated from these schools staffed the chanceries of popes, bishops, and kings alike. They spent their lives with books. Little wonder, then, that by the fourteenth century literacy was the hallmark of the clerical orders. The skill of reading was now so closely associated with monks and priests that literacy began to displace the tonsured head as the tell-tale mark of a clergyman.[1] In fact, even by the twelfth century, the word *clericus* was attached to anyone, clergy or lay, who could read. King Henry I, for example, whom contemporaries esteemed as *literatus,* won the nickname "Beauclerk." By extension, anyone who was illiterate was apt to be styled *laicus*—even a clergyman.

But just what was literacy and how were church authorities to measure it before admitting a man to the altar? The question stood unresolved throughout the middle ages. Canon law outlined a literate ideal to which priests should aspire (No. 17); yet commentators on that law admitted a wide range of reading proficiency when they tried to define the practical standards of literacy required for pastors. "Sufficient literacy" was the generally approved norm, but this could mean just a bit more literacy than the typical parishioner—in other words, not much literacy at all (No. 23). The medieval understanding of the word *literatus* itself complicated the debate. In the early middle ages it carried the meaning it usually carries today: the basic ability to read. (Writing was something else again. In the middle ages you could be literate and still be unable to write, which was a more selective, professional skill.) But by the twelfth century, *literatus* began to acquire a different connotation in educated circles. Now it meant more than just functional literacy; it implied a grounding in and love of Latin literature, what we would mean by "well-educated" or "book-learned." Thus, it was possible for someone to have perfectly functional reading skills, but still be thought illiterate since he was not *well*-read.[2] When late medieval reformers heaped scorn on what they reckoned the poorly-educated parish clergy, these critics—usually the products of university education—were typically using a different measure of literacy to gauge the learning of their rank-and-file brothers. A candidate for ordination deemed suitably literate by his examiners (who essentially wanted to be sure that he could handle the daily demands of the Latin liturgy) was apt to be considered illiterate by the loftier

[1] Leona C. Gabel, *Benefit of the Clergy in England in the Later Middle Ages* (Smith College Studies in History 14, nos. 1-4 [1928-29]; repub. New York: Octagon Books, 1969), p. 73.
[2] See Thomas Clanchy, *From Memory to Written Record, England 1066-1307*, 2d ed. (Oxford: Blackwell, 1993), chap. 7.

standards of university-educated men. Still, however fluid the meaning of *literatus*, medieval commentators agreed on one crucial point: the upright character of a priest's life was just as important as his learning.

Of course there were always isolated cases of flagrant illiteracy among the clergy (No. 28). The most infamous instance—the examination of the egregiously dumb Sonning clergy in 1222—gets a compulsory nod almost any time medievalists broach the subject of clerical learning (No. 34). But it is important to bear in mind that these seven chaplains are one anecdote; we should resist the temptation to use it to jump to conclusions. Against them must be placed, for example, Bishop Hugh of Wells' records for the examination of 1,958 men instituted to benefices in his diocese of Lincoln between 1209 and 1235. Over these twenty-six years, his examiners found only 101 candidates (just 5 percent, and only four of those already priests) unqualified due to illiteracy. Following the general practice of the times, these unfit men were conditionally ordained, pending their further education.[3]

But where did clerical candidates looking for an education go? Early in the twelfth century the Third Lateran Council ordered every cathedral church to appoint a grammar master to hold school for young boys seeking clerical careers (No. 18). Almost a century later in 1215 the trailblazing Fourth Lateran Council widened the scope of these cathedral schools, calling on every church which had sufficient revenue to establish grammar schools, and emphasizing just how vital education was for priests (No. 19). But schools had been sprouting up in England even before these papal initiatives. Most future parish priests received their earliest, and often only, education attending them. Prelates grasped their importance; during the thirteenth century several English bishops decreed that the office of the *aquabajulus*, or holy water clerk, should always be given to a young boy in minor orders so that he could use its small income to further his studies (No. 22).

By the later middle ages a boy inclined toward a career as a priest typically had a choice—limited by his locale and his income—of several avenues of schooling, formal and informal, to prime him for his calling.[4] The most basic was the "song school," the rough equal of today's elementary school. Here, when he was around seven, he could learn the alphabet, how to read and write in Latin the Lord's Prayer, the Creed, the Hail Mary, a few other basic prayers, and a little catechism. He also learned "song"—all the chanted hymns and responses that a server would need to know in order to assist a

---

[3] Nicholas Orme, *English Schools in the Middle Ages* (London: Methuen, 1973), p. 17.
[4] For song and grammar schools, see Orme, chap. 2.

priest saying mass (No. 20). There were song schools in most cities and towns, set up by cathedrals, by some houses of canons and collegiate churches, and sometimes even by lay guilds. Where a chantry was established in a church, the chantry priest, whose daily work was finished once he had sung mass for his patrons, was sometimes tasked with keeping a school. There were song schools in rural areas too, though here they were organized more casually and might be short-lived. Some priests taught song schools in their parishes. It would be an especially attractive job for unbeneficed priests hoping to supplement their meager salary. Parish clerks (factotums in minor orders whose job included their parish's secretarial work) likewise occasionally taught some basic reading and writing. One-on-one tutoring must have happened whenever a bright boy caught the eye of a discerning and solicitous priest. In fact, parish priests probably played a large role in providing elementary schooling, formally or informally, to promising boys leaning toward clerical careers. One chantry priest recalled in the 1460s that he had himself been taught to "learn, read, and sing" by a Somerset chaplain.[5] The example set by his own pastor, both in education and in morals, must have been a model of behavior for many an aspiring priest.

Older boys bright enough to manage it and rich enough to afford it could continue their education at a grammar school, where students immersed themselves in the careful study of Latin and its literature (No. 21). (The distinction between song schools and grammar schools was not rigid; the two could blend together, younger students studying song while older ones took up the demands of Latin grammar.) Grammar schools offered the most advanced education outside of Oxford and Cambridge or the secular cathedrals' schools of theology and canon law. Generally urban schools, they had patrons—ranging from the local bishop, to his archdeacons, to the local abbot, or even the local secular lord—who exercised the right to appoint the schoolmaster, usually a man with at least some university education.

For many parish clergy the rudimentary lessons they learned as boys at song school were the limit of their formal education. Before they received final orders and took up a cure of souls, they could polish their learning a bit by private tutoring or by studying whatever few books were at hand in their community. Though scarcely educated by either modern academic standards or those of the medieval university, these men at least had enough Latin to pass muster before their bishops at their ordination examination and to tackle the Latin that Christian liturgy and ritual required.

But curates also received on-the-job training coordinated by their bishop

---

[5] Orme, pp. 66–67.

and his agents. Archdeacons, the *oculi episcopi,* were especially charged with overseeing the ongoing education of the parish clergy. As far back as 1237, the papal legate Otto instructed archdeacons to ensure that priests learned in convocation the words of the canon of the mass and of baptism. Bishops throughout the thirteenth century ordered their archdeacons to keep an eye on their diocesan priests' education. Whenever a bishop issued statutes for his diocese, every parish was expected to have a copy made and to keep it near at hand (No. 55). Archdeacons were usually charged with examining these copies during their parish visitations. To assist their clergy in bearing the *cura animarum,* bishops sometimes issued special pastoral tracts, especially on penance (No. 78). In 1240 Bishop Walter Cantilupe even demanded that the texts of his diocesan statutes and a treatise on penance be publicly recited by every priest attending the archdeacon's synod. The archdeacon was then to explain any difficult points in them. The synod's president was to pass the two texts randomly to each priest, who was obliged to pick up reading where the last priest left off. Anyone lacking a copy of the works or ignorant of their contents faced a fine.[6] By these methods of oral and written instruction, the archidiaconal chapter became a classroom. Since attendance at these convocations was mandatory, local priests were kept up to date on the latest decisions of the church hierarchy. More importantly, through meetings and joint instruction with their fellow pastors, they polished their pastoral skills. In fact, professional networking among priests was probably a common way for pastors to stay abreast. Bishop Robert Grosseteste recommended, for instance, that priests whose Latin was shaky should turn to their neighbor priests for tutoring.[7]

By the middle of the thirteenth century, a wide variety of pastoral handbooks, large and small, also began circulating through England (Nos. 70–72). Priests with the wherewithal could afford to buy the larger, more comprehensive volumes. Almost anyone with the interest could probably manage to have the shorter ones copied. But a priest didn't need to buy a manual to consult it. Often priests left their books to their parish church when they died, creating in effect a community library for their fellow-priests. One bishop even established a pastoral resource library for his clergy (No. 27).

From a modern perspective, mandatory university education would seem the *sine qua non* for a proficient pastor. Though medieval church au-

---

[6] *Councils and Synods,* p. 321.
[7] Leonard Boyle, "Robert Grosseteste and the Pastoral Care," *Medieval and Renaissance Studies* 8, ed. Dale Randall (Durham, N.C.: Duke University Press, 1979), pp. 9–10.

thorities realized the potential of the growing universities to prepare men for the cure of souls, a college education posed two problems: how to finance it, and how to encourage university study without contributing to the non-residence of pastors in their parishes. Paying for college took money, but a rector could draw on the income from his benefice only after he had been installed in his parish; and once he was installed, he was strictly bound by canon law to maintain permanent residence and attend to the spiritual needs of his parishioners. So even if a rector could scrabble up enough money to pay for some college, he could not legally leave his benefice to go off to school. Though English bishops strained to find loopholes to this dilemma, it took papal action to resolve it (No. 24). Pope Boniface VIII (1294–1303) may be most remembered for his titanic wrangle with France's Philip IV. But he also prudently engineered a partial solution to the problems raised when priests wanted university education. In 1298 he issued the constitution *Cum ex eo.* Aimed at men just entering the lower ranks of holy orders, it provided rectors the means both to finance their university education and to avoid penalties for non-residence (Nos. 25–26).

Despite the incentives offered by *Cum ex eo,* university study was rare for most parish priests. Even rectors seldom had a college education. In the diocese of Norwich in the early fourteenth century, for instance, only roughly one in twelve rectors had attended college, and few of them actually completed degrees. Only the luckiest or most resourceful men aspiring to holy orders managed to get some higher education. When they settled back in their parish after a few years of study, they must have been invaluable sources of counsel for their fellow-priests, who could turn to them for advice about difficult pastoral matters. Even so, one overriding point remains: whatever its advantages, in the middle ages a college education was no more indispensable for a successful pastor than it is now. Some basic literacy, more moral character, still more charity, and probably patience too, were the medieval pastor's essential tools.

☙ No. 17. Books necessary for priests to know.
Gratian's *Decretum,* Dist. 38,5. Trans. JS.

These are the books necessary for every priest to know: the sacramentary, the lectionary, the antiphonary, the baptismal service book, the calendar, the penitential canons, the psalter, and the sermons suitable for each Sunday and feast day of the year. If he lacks knowledge of any one of these, the title "priest" hardly suits him, because the preaching of the gospel is put into great danger. As it is said: "If a blind man guide a blind man, both fall into a pit [Matt. 15:14]."

∾ **No. 18. Teachers at cathedral schools: Third Lateran Council, c. 18 (1179).**
Decrees, Tanner, p. 220.

18. Since the church of God is bound to provide like a mother for those in want, with regard to both the things which concern the support of the body and those which lead to the progress of the soul, therefore, in order that the opportunity of learning to read and progress in study is not withdrawn from poor children who cannot be helped by the support of their parents, in every cathedral church a master is to be assigned some proper benefice so that he may teach the clerics of that church and the poor scholars. Thus the needs of the teacher are to be supplied and the way to knowledge opened for learners. In other churches and monasteries too, if anything in times past has been assigned in them for this purpose, it should be restored. Let no one demand any money for a license to teach, or under cover of some custom seek anything from teachers, or forbid anyone to teach who is suitable and has sought a license. Whoever presumes to act against this decree is to be deprived of ecclesiastical benefice. Indeed, it seems only right that in the church of God a person should not have the fruit of his labour if through self-seeking he strives to prevent the progress of the churches by selling the license to teach.

∾ **No. 19. Education and the *cura animarum*: Fourth Lateran Council, cc. 11 and 27 (1215).**
Decrees, Tanner, pp. 240, 248.

11. Zeal for learning and the opportunity to make progress is denied to some through lack of means. The [Third] Lateran council therefore dutifully decreed that "in each cathedral church there should be provided a suitable benefice for a master who shall instruct without charge the clerics of the cathedral church and other poor scholars, thus at once satisfying the teacher's needs and opening up the way of knowledge to learners." This decree, however, is very little observed in many churches. We therefore confirm it and add that not only in every cathedral church but also in other churches with sufficient resources, a suitable master, elected by the chapter or by the greater and sounder part of it, shall be appointed by the prelate to teach grammar and other branches of study, as far as is possible, to the clerics of those and other churches. The metropolitan church shall have a theologian to teach scripture to priests and others and especially to instruct them in matters which are recognized as pertaining to the cure of souls. The income of one prebend shall be assigned by the chapter to each master, and as much shall be assigned by the metropolitan to the theologian. The incumbent does not by this become a canon but he receives the income of one as long as he

continues to teach. If the metropolitan church finds providing for two masters a burden, let it provide for the theologian in the aforesaid way but get
adequate provision made for the grammarian in another church of the city
or diocese.

27. To guide souls is a supreme art. We therefore strictly order bishops
carefully to prepare those who are to be promoted to the priesthood and to
instruct them, either by themselves or through other suitable persons, in the
divine services and the sacraments of the church, so that they may be able
to celebrate them correctly. But if they presume henceforth to ordain the
ignorant and unformed, which can indeed be easily detected, we decree that
both the ordainers and those ordained are to be subject to severe punishment. For it is preferable, especially in the ordination of priests, to have a
few good ministers than many bad ones, for if "a blind man guide a blind
man, both fall into a pit" [Matt. 15:14].

℘ No. 20. Preparing boys for clerical careers: from the statutes of Bishop John Gervais for the diocese of Winchester (1262–65).

Councils and Synods, pp. 713–14. Trans. JS.

[59] Furthermore, rectors, vicars, and parish priests should see to it
that the children of the parish know the Lord's Prayer, the Creed, the Hail
Mary, and how to make the sign of the cross. And when adult lay people
come to confession the priest should carefully inquire whether they know
these prayers so that, in case they do not know them (which often happens),
they may be instructed about them by the priests. Moreover, the parents of
children should be urged to have their children learn chant after they have
learned to read the psalter, so that when they turn to learning perhaps
harder subjects they will not be forced to go back and learn it, and so that
they will not be so ignorant about it as to make them for the rest of their
lives less able to carry out their ministry.

℘ No. 21. A grammar school curriculum: Bishop John Grandisson's mandate concerning the teaching of boys (1356).

Reg. Grandisson, vol. 2, pp. 1192–93. Trans. JS.

John, etc. to his beloved sons in Christ, each archdeacon in our cathedral
church of Exeter and to their officials, greetings, etc. Not without frequent
surprise and mental distress we continue to learn how the masters or teachers of boys and the uneducated in our diocese employ a preposterous and
useless method and plan of teaching grammar. It is downright supersti-

tious, more pagan than Christian. For while these students have learned—less than perfectly—to read and recite the Lord's Prayer, the Hail Mary, the Creed, the Matins, and the Hours of the Blessed Virgin as well as other things pertaining to the faith and the salvation of their souls, they do not know how to construe or understand them, or to decline the words in them, or how to identify their parts of speech. But then their teachers prematurely make them move on to harder texts and poetry or meter. Consequently, when they reach adulthood they cannot understand what they daily have to read and recite. Worse still, they do not even know the Catholic faith because of their lack of education. Wishing, therefore, to root out in whatever way we can such a terrible and foolish abuse now all too prevalent in our diocese, we order each of you to warn every master or teacher of boys in the grammar schools within your archdeaneries that when they enroll students in their schools they must not teach them just to read and learn by rote memory, as has previously been the case. Instead, putting aside everything else, they should first teach them to construe and understand the Lord's Prayer, the Hail Mary, the Creed, Matins, and the Hours of the Blessed Virgin. They should know how to decline and identify the parts of speech in these prayers before they move on to other books. Tell them, furthermore, that in the future we do not intend to confer clerical orders on any boys who discernibly have not been educated according to this method. . . . Given at our manor of Chudley, February 13, 1356, the thirtieth year of our consecration.

~ No. 22. Apprenticeship and the cleric: the parish holy water bearer (*aquabajulus*) and education. From the Statutes of Exeter (1287).
Councils and Synods, pp. 1026–27. Trans. JS.

[Chapter 29.] The holy water benefice should be assigned only to students.

We have often heard it said by our superiors that the office of holy water bearer was first instituted as a charitable gesture so that poor clerks could use its profits to support themselves at schools and, while there, would so progress in their studies that they would be fitter and better suited for greater things. Therefore, lest a practice begun for such a beneficial purpose should slip into abuse, we order that in churches which are within ten miles from the cities and towns of our diocese, the office of holy water bearer should be assigned only to students. Since we understand that many lawsuits often arise between the rectors or vicars of churches and their parishioners over the rights of appointment to this office, which (just as it pleases us) we are obliged to curtail, we order with discretion that rectors and vicars, whose duty it is to know which clerks are better suited to this office, should strive to appoint those clerks to the office who in their hearts have the knowledge and ability to devote themselves wholly to the church's worship and who wish to obey its mandates. If parishioners wish maliciously to withhold their accustomed offerings from these students, they should be diligently admonished to be generous to them and, if it becomes necessary, compelled to do so.

∾ No. 23. Canon lawyers discuss contemporary standards of clerical literacy (mid-fourteenth and early fifteenth century).

William Lyndwood, *Provinciale* (Oxford, 1679). Trans. JS.

A. John Acton's (d. 1350) gloss of Cardinal Otto's Legatine Constitutions, London (1237). Gloss for chapter 6 on the word *illiteratos, Provinciale,* pt. 2, p. 16.

The ignorance of these priests, which is what is meant here, is not only the mother of all errors but also should be particularly avoided.[8] Such ignorance should be much more despised in a bishop or a major prelate. For such men ought not lack the learning of other people—they should be their teachers. And in this case an automatic presumption [of learning] does not suffice while examining an ordinand who has said that he spent some time at school. A careful examination is required, though perhaps not so stringent as is done when consecrating a bishop. For they should be examined using simple, uncomplicated, words. Take into account their condition. For if they are poor—either because their parents were poor, or because their homeland is barren or has been devastated—and so were unable to attend school but had to seek a livelihood by their own hands, it is then fitting that they ought to be kindly encouraged, provided that they know a little more than lay people, especially about the sacrament of the altar which they must daily celebrate. For according to the Apostle, "knowledge puffs up, but charity edifies" [1 Cor. 8:1], and so imperfect learning may be made good by perfect charity. As to what sufficient literacy is, note well [the gloss] where it is also clearly distinguished whether ignorance is a mortal sin. It says there and in Innocent's gloss that if someone is found insufficiently literate, he should then not fail to acquire what learning he lacks, and he may not refuse to do this. Nor should the limb of the Devil be thus extended instead of the limb of Christ; for otherwise he is a fool. Such a defect may hardly be tolerated, except out of great mercy, because of the scandal it causes.

---

[8] Practically every sentence in both of these glosses cites references to chapters from canon law and other glosses. These citations are omitted here.

B. William Lyndwood's (c. 1375–1446) gloss on chapter 9 ("Ignorantia sacerdotum") of Archbishop John Pecham's Lambeth Council (1281)[9] on the word
sciat, Provinciale, I.1, p. 1.

From what has been said above, this means that everyone must know
the articles of faith (as it says in the gloss above, at the word "ignorance").
Here one may ask whether in matters of knowledge there ought to be equal-
ity or parity among everyone. I answer no, because those who bear the cure
of souls and must teach others should know the articles of faith unequivo-
cally and clearly so that they know how to explain and defend them. So we
understand from this that ignorance does not excuse those who bear the
cure of souls from knowing the articles of faith. Bishops should be able to
explain these articles to anyone who asks, though they are not obliged to
respond without deliberation. For others, however, who have little learning
or are lay people, it suffices that they believe these articles unquestioningly,
that is, just as the Catholic Church believes and teaches. According to some
commentators, the same should be said for those who are clerics and do not
have the resources to pursue study. But if such clerics have an income and
teachers are available to them, they sin if they do not know more than lay
people. But what about educated lay people—are they bound to know and
believe the articles of faith more clearly than other uneducated ones? According to Bernard of Compostella it is reasonable to expect them to know
the articles more clearly, but they do not sin mortally if they do not know
them more perfectly, or if they are not more careful about learning the articles, since, according to him, this is not their profession. And I agree with
this if they do not refuse to learn when they are able to. But clerics—making
the distinction between those with a cure and those sinecured—are bound
to know and believe the articles, just as it says above. Otherwise they sin
mortally, unless they are dispensed by some legitimate cause for their lack
of knowledge when they take up the cure of souls.

❧ No. 24. English bishops complain of papal measures that discourage education (1279).

Councils and Synods, pp. 862–64. Trans. JS.

To his eminence the Pope, etc. greetings, etc. Our venerable father in
Christ, the Archbishop of Canterbury John [Pecham], recently explained to
us your decision that those holding plural benefices in our kingdom should
vacate them unless they immediately obtain dispensation from the apostolic
see. He also explained the decision of Pope Gregory X about institutions and

---

[9]See No. 70.

commendations to benefices issued at the Council of Lyons,[10] and how it should be inviolably obeyed to the letter in England. Although your orders were authoritatively interpreted for us by John, our venerable father in Christ, they seem most burdensome—almost unbearable. But preferring the good of obedience over anything else, convenient or inconvenient, we have humbly bent our necks in order to shoulder, henceforward, the burden of these rulings. We will likewise put our shoulders together with those clergy who were present when these rulings were explained so that all of us together may effectively bear the weight of these mandates in the future, even though we were less than enthusiastic about observing them in the past—in our judgment not without reasonable cause—and, with a wink of our eye, permitted those deviating from them to go unpunished both out of regard for the outstanding demeanor of the English clergy and the nature of English benefices, few of which are without cure of souls, not to mention the persistent objection of the nobles and magnates which cannot be resisted without causing serious scandal.

Since up until now we erred through allowing, or at least tolerating this kind of error, we freely permit ourselves to be corrected by our venerable father in Christ, the archbishop. But we believe that the judgment according to our consciences supersedes the cause of our tolerance and our reason for it. Thus, unless your mandate is urgent enough to pull us in another direction and compel us to embrace the opposite position, it would be to the benefit of the English church to exempt institutions as well as commendations to benefices from such a rigorous decree, since there are few benefices here without a cure, and many men, noblemen especially, are not even going to try to get benefices with a cure of souls because of the severity of these statutes. When they realize that their path to these benefices is blocked, they will abandon their education, fall into poverty, and swell the number of notorious bandits. Learning, in great measure, will perish—especially the knowledge of civil law, the liberal arts, natural philosophy, and medicine. Unquestionably, thereafter competent ministers will be scarce in God's church.

Bearing all these things in mind, most pious father—both the utter ruin of the clergy entrusted to us and the needs of their flock—not for ourselves but only for our clergy and our churches, we humbly and devoutly come before you seeking your clemency with urgent prayers, and asking that you consent to mollify the severity of these statutes and temper their harshness so that beneficed clergy are not bound to be ordained to the priesthood

---

[10]The decree *Licet canon;* see No. 39.

within a year; also that at a bishop's discretion, the cure of souls may be given to a man less than twenty-five years old whom the bishop sees to be proficient and a suitable candidate for academic studies, just so long as he is ordained or about to be ordained to sacred orders. Also that either an educated man or someone otherwise deserving may hold a church in commendation[11] though he is neither priest nor [deacon] as long as he is in sacred orders; and that a predetermined time-limit is not fixed on a commendation, and a benefice can be put to the long-term use of the person to whom it is commended, especially for the sake of our regard for hospitality, which particularly thrives here, cherished in a way practically unmatched by any other nation.

We devoutly accept your decree, most holy father, though in this regard it is scarcely tolerable; but if only you would pitiably admit our prayers delivered up to your mercy for a favorable hearing, and by the merits of our obedience we could obtain this reward, and with humility we could gain the longed-for outcome, so that through our many intercessions the entire clergy of England could rejoice to receive a blessing of such compromise from your clemency. Farewell, etc. Given at London, etc.[12]

❧ No. 25. The constitution *Cum ex eo* of Boniface VIII (1298).
Sext. 1.6,34. Trans. JS.

Our predecessor of happy memory, Pope Gregory X, decreed in the constitutions of the Council of Lyons that those men taking up the direction of parochial churches should be ordained to the priesthood within a year from when they were instituted to their parishes and should personally reside in them; otherwise, if they were not ordained within that time, they were to be deprived of their churches without warning. Since that time, many men have refused to accept parochial churches and have thereby lost the opportunity for studying and improving themselves (since they neither have the means to support themselves nor do most of the church's prelates provide them with it from other benefices). This situation has caused great cost and loss to the Church Universal, which is known to depend particularly on learned men for its governance. Since many people have frequently and insistently encouraged us to address this issue, we wish to make suitable provision for those eager to advance in learning so that they can offer the fruits of their study to God's church in the future.

By the present constitution we decree that henceforward bishops and

---

[11] See glossary.
[12] This letter was never sent.

other superiors may legally dispense men who obtain such churches to delay being ordained beyond the order of subdeacon for a term of up to seven years while they are engaged in academic study. But we strictly require them to be ordained to the subdiaconate within a year of their institution so that they will not abandon their clerical status, which we know that many men supported by Christ's patrimony have done in the past. If they fail to be ordained to the subdiaconate, they will thereby incur the penalty decreed by the aforesaid council. In addition, during the course of those seven years, their bishops or superiors should make careful provision that the cure of souls is diligently exercised and divine services undertaken with laudable devotion by good, competent vicars appointed to their churches by the absent rectors. Their necessities shall be appropriately supplied from the revenues of these churches. When the seven years have elapsed, those so dispensed, as described above, are to be ordained to the orders of deacon and priest within one year, otherwise they should be aware that they will thereby legally incur the penalty stated above unless they have just cause.

ᗕ No. 26. A typical *Cum ex eo* study license and letter dimissory (1325).
From the Register of Bishop William Ayermine, Norwich, Norfolk Record Office Reg. 1, Bk. 2 (Ayermine), fols. 87r, 88r, 99r. Trans. JS.

November 28, A.D. 1325. . . . At London. Matthew, called le Palmere, acolyte, rector of the church of Brockdish, has been given dispensation and license to be absent for purpose of study for two years wherever there is a thriving university, according to this form: William by divine permission bishop of Norwich sends greetings, grace, and blessing to his beloved son in Christ, Matthew, called le Palmere, acolyte, rector of the church of Brockdish in our diocese. Recognizing your aptitude, by which academic studies would profit you, God willing, if you were free to pursue them, by the tenor of the present letter we grant you in the Lord the unrestricted opportunity and we mercifully dispense you by the authority of the constitution of Pope Boniface VIII issued in this regard, so that you will be legally free to pursue academic studies wherever there is a thriving university for two continuous years counted from the date of this present letter. Nevertheless, you must take care to be promoted to the order of subdeacon within a year from the date of your institution to your church. But for the duration of the said term of two years you will not be obliged to reside personally in your church or to receive final priestly orders. We reserve to ourselves the power of appointing in the meantime a suitable vicar to your church to exercise the cure of souls there and to undertake divine services with laudable devotion, and of providing appropriately for his needs from that church's fruits and revenues. But with this proviso: that at the end of each year of the two-year term, you should arrange to have exhibited to us testimonial letters about your course of studies where you are and about your conduct there. Given at London, November 28, A.D. 1325, the first year of our consecration.

[Letter dimissory] On November 28 in the abovesaid year [1325], Matthew, called le Palmere, an acolyte, rector of the church of Brockdish, received letters dimissory to proceed to all sacred orders.

Memorandum that on the Ember Saturday of Pentecost, namely, May 27, 1326, Matthew, called le Palmere, rector of the church of Brockdish (instituted into that church, just as he claimed at the time of its vacancy, by the Bishop of Norwich on behalf of the Lord Archbishop), a subdeacon, was ordained a deacon and has received letters dispensing him to be absent for two years for the purpose of study wheresoever according to the form of the constitution of Pope Boniface; he is not obliged to be ordained to priestly orders. He should report on his conduct at the end of each year.

[*He renewed his license for another two years of study in May of 1326, by which time he had been promoted to deacon. In 1333 he exchanged his benefice of Brockdish for Little Canefield in the diocese of Lincoln.*]

ᴄᴠ No. 27. Bishop Hamo Hethe's pastoral reference library (1346).
Life, Coulton, vol. 2, pp. 111–12.

To all sons of Holy Church to whose notice these letters present may come, Brother Hamo, by God's permission Bishop of Rochester, wishes eternal salvation in the Lord. Know ye all how we have learned by frequent experience (as we sadly remember) that some churchmen of our diocese, bearing not only the cure of souls but even the office of penitentiaries, although commendable both for their life and for their learning, yet have committed grievous and absurd errors for lack of books profitable to such cure or such office, especially in the matter of consultations and salutary advice to their flocks, of enjoining penances, and of granting absolution to penitents. We therefore, desiring greatly to bring such remedy as we can to the aforesaid evils, have thought fit to assign the following books, under the manners and conditions hereafter to be set down, for ministering some manner of information in future times to the aforesaid priests with cures of souls or who hold the office of Penitentiary, and for advancing the salvation of souls. We give therefore hereby as a gift between living persons, and with all prerogatives and favour of our last will we bequeath and assign to the Prior and Chapter and Cathedral of Rochester, our glossed books of Decrees and Decretals, the sixth book of the Decretals with two glosses in one volume, the seventh book (or Clementine Constitutions) unglossed, bound up with divers Provincial Constitutions, the book of Pope Innocent on the Decretals, a volume of Matthew and Mark with glosses, the Historia Scholastica of the Bible; also a volume of the Summa of Raymond [de Pennaforte] and one of Avicenna on the counsel of medicine, and one little book of the Vices and Virtues, and two stitched books whereof one begins *Qui bene presunt*[13] and the other treats of the articles of faith, the beatitudes, and the petitions; and lastly the book of Papas the Elder on Grammar; willing, commanding and ordaining that all these books be laid up and kept within our Cathedral, in a chest under two locks, there to be preserved under safe custody for ever, or as long as they may last. . . . Provided that none of the aforesaid books be carried out of the said Cathedral, and that each, when it has been inspected [by the reader] for a reasonable time, be forthwith returned to the custodians; Excepting only, during our own lifetime, the use of the said books be at our good pleasure, whether within or without the aforesaid Cathedral.

∾ No. 28. The illiterate Bishop of Durham (1316).

Robert Graystanes (Geoffrey Coldingham, William Chambre), *Historiae Dunelmensis Scriptores Tres* (London: J. B. Nichols, 1839), pp. 118–19. Trans. JS.

This Lewis [de Beaumont, Bishop of Durham, 1316–33] was a nobleman, related by blood to the Kings of France and Sicily. He was handsome, but he had bad feet, being lame in both of them. He was quite extravagant—many said he was prodigal. He was greedy, caring little for how he got what he wanted. His costly household and his lavish excesses, from which no counsel could restrain him, so afflicted his spirit with greed that he would forsake nothing that he could plausibly own. In fact, one wit said that he had never seen a person so greedy to get things and so rash about managing his estate. . . . He was chaste but illiterate [*laicus*]. He did not understand Latin and had trouble pronouncing it. Thus, during his episcopal consecration when he was obliged to make his profession, he was unable to read it aloud even though he had previously been coached for many days. With difficulty and whispered promptings he finally got to the word *Metropoliticae* [Metropolitan]. After stuttering over it a bit, he still could not pronounce it; so he said in French "let it stand as I've read it." Everyone around him was thunderstruck, mortified that this sort of fellow was being consecrated a bishop. Once when he was administering holy orders, he couldn't pronounce the phrase *in aenigmate* [from Paul's first epistle to the Corinthians, 13:12]. He said to those standing near him, "By Saint Louis, he was no gentleman who wrote this word here."

[13] See the introduction to chapter 5.

3

༄

Ordination and Admission to a Cure

*A*s men who held a certain prominence in local communities, medieval pastors were bound to be drawn into a wide array of activities and functions. Some of these had direct and immediate bearing on their pastoral cure—their celebration of the sacraments, leadership in prayer, and employment of assistant and junior clergy for the larger care of the parish—but others were not so obviously pastoral. Still, many of these activities, all brought into the wide embrace of administration, had an indirect bearing on the life of the parish. It was impossible for a local curate to remain aloof from the requirements of his superiors, ecclesiastical and lay, and a good deal of his time might be spent chasing down some commission given him by the bishop or in attendance on the local parish patron.

However he spent his time and whatever his status in the local community, either as curate, hired chaplain, or parish clerk, every practitioner of what Gregory the Great had called the "art of arts" was to be duly recognized, ordained, and canonically established in a local community. A cleric's place in the leadership of a church was not automatically guaranteed; there were winnowing processes along the way that helped assure that only abler men were advanced through the sacrament of holy orders and into service of the church. And when the sacrament was conferred or, after that, when a cleric was given a church to preside over, the bishop continued to hold considerable authority over who exercised the cure of souls and how.

The clergy were not all of one sort: there were various ranks within the body of clergy, each with its own appropriate function in the spiritual leadership of a community. There were seven ranks of holy orders excluding that of the bishop, who subsumed all lesser ministries into his own as the first pastor of the diocese, which was from ancient days the first *parochia*. Aspirants to holy orders began as apprentice clerics. These usually were parish youth who had demonstrated some talent and desire to serve the church. After tonsure, which was the portal to clerical life and open to boys as young as seven years old, the next step was the order of porter. This might entail any modest work needed around the church, but a porter's basic function was to open and lock up the church doors and otherwise keep some semblance of order in the holy place. After this came the order of lector, entitling the youth to read from scripture in the everyday settings of mass and prayer. As an exorcist he assisted at the blessings of people and things, and as an acolyte, the fourth minor order, he began to assist at the altar. A candidate for orders could pass through these lower offices quickly, often in a single day, but then came the more critical step of going on to the three higher orders of subdeacon, deacon, and priest. The graduation was not a minor matter: to become a subdeacon, the candidate had to profess a vow of celibacy and be willing to assist in the more prominent ministry of the altar. As a deacon, he was entitled to officiate at certain sacraments such as baptism and marriage; he was also allowed to preside at the graveside of a deceased parishioner. More often, he led the congregation in song and prayer and read the gospel passage for the day. A deacon's ability to sing was not a formality. Bishop Thomas Charlton of Hereford once delayed the ordination of a handful of subdeacons to the diaconate on the grounds that they were insufficiently trained in chant. He gave them another six months to improve on their musical skills before he would promote them to the next order.[1] After a deacon spent some time in the service of his order, he was advanced to the priesthood and to full pastoral ministry. His basic responsibilities included the celebration of daily mass, leadership in prayer, the absolution of repentant parishioners, and the run of blessings, baptisms, weddings, and funerals that told the life of a parish community. There were only two sacraments at which he could not preside: confirmation and ordination, which belonged to the bishop's ministry. In a sense, all ministry was derived from the bishop and ritualized in the liturgy of ordination when he invested the candidate with the symbols of his office and ministry (No. 38).

The sacrament of holy orders was celebrated seasonally, not only to mark the passing of major feasts in the liturgical year, but to sustain in a regular and predictable flow new clerics into the parishes and religious houses of the

---

[1] *Reg. T. Charlton*, p. 127.

diocese. Custom had long dictated that the bishop would usually hold ordinations on the four Ember Saturdays of the year (see glossary). But it was
necessary that the bishop confirm the day and, just as importantly, the place
where the ordination would occur. A letter was written and published
throughout the diocese (No. 33). In addition to these four seasonal days, a
bishop could ordain on the vigils of Passion Sunday and Easter (No. 29).
Which church he chose often depended on his itinerary. The cathedral was
a favorite place, a large enough space to accommodate the sometimes vast
crowds of candidates and their families. It was also bound to lend an aspect
of grandeur to the occasion. But travel to the cathedral was not always easy
and the bishop could choose a regional church or one of his own manor
chapels provided it was adequate in size and fairly accessible. Other circumstances influenced the choice of a site: Bishop Trillek of Hereford was asked
on one occasion to help out with ordinations in neighboring Worcester diocese during a vacancy there. In order to accommodate his own men as well
as Worcester candidates, Trillek chose the large parish church of Ledbury in
his own diocese but close to the Worcester border and situated on a road
that linked the two cathedral towns.[2]

Once the word had gone out that the bishop was intending to celebrate
the sacrament of holy orders, candidates readied themselves for the journey.
Every candidate was required to show his worthiness and ability to carry
out the function of the order he sought. There were preordination scrutinies
for every rank in holy orders, though these were generally uncomplicated,
especially among the humbler minor orders. As a candidate advanced in the
ranks and as the consequences of his ministerial activities grew more significant, so did the importance of the examination. Also, on account of the
occasionally large groups of men promoted to orders, there had to be time
enough to process each candidate. Long before the thirteenth century, the
custom had been established that candidates would appear four days before
ordination, usually the Wednesday preceding the celebration, and during
the course of those days undergo the necessary scrutinies (No. 30). The
bishop could examine candidates himself, and on occasion he did, but more
often than not this task went to episcopal assistants, men learned in doctrine and church law, who tested the candidates on basic aspects of their life,
learning, and the faith. The examination was a critical procedure, allowing
the bishop to separate the patently unworthy from the promising. Short of
the difficult and messy business of deposing a cleric from office, this scrutiny was the only real means a bishop had to assure that the right kind of

[2] *Reg. Trillek,* p. 480.

men were ordained and admitted to service in the church. At the same time, it is important not to overstate the intensity of the examination process: pastoral theologians and canonists were consistent in their appraisal of the scrutinies. They should be modest affairs, looking for some accomplishment in learning and holiness of life, but also for promising beginnings and a certain pliancy on the part of the candidate to learn well what only the exercise of his ministry could teach him. Pastoral care in the middle ages was, in many ways, on-the-job training.

More than learning and sufficiency of age was required for those men who aspired to the major orders. A potential subdeacon, deacon, or priest had also to show a title to orders, that is, some statement of affiliation with a parish or community. Part of this requirement had to do with the ancient tradition of the church that all clergy had to have a home within the community, a place to exercise their ministry. It also had a very practical purpose: the title was a guarantee that the candidate was economically self-sufficient and, against the possibility of unemployment, would not be a drain on the limited resources of any local community or, for that matter, on the bishop (No. 36). But, again, none of this was uniform. In the thirteenth century, a sufficient title was often the good word of a recognized leader from the candidate's parish community; or it might be a parcel of land, or the assurance of a benefice, or the patronage of a religious house. One ordinand appeared with a box of testimonial letters in hand as his title for ordination.

In spite of the church's efforts to screen candidates fairly, the system was far from perfect. By the late thirteenth century, ordination groups could be as large as several hundred candidates representing all ranks. It was no easy matter, even for a small army of examiners, to process these candidates in entirely satisfactory ways. Furthermore, candidates could show themselves far more able in getting around established requirements than in demonstrating modest learning and moral worth. Letters of testimony could be forged, candidates could hire imposters to take their examinations for them, and bribing officials was never out of the question. Sometimes, too, the examiners were slack in their duties and passed on men for orders who would not make it past more vigilant guards.

Though some physical or moral flaw might be detected in the course of the preordination scrutiny, this did not always signal an end to the candidate's aspirations. There were frequent applications for dispensation from some of the more typical impediments to holy orders, including illegitimate birth and insufficient age. Candidates were to be of sound body as well, but minor disabilities could be overlooked as was the case with a man who had lost a finger in a battle (No. 35). Such dispensations for physical disabilities were secured fairly easily, so long as the flaw did not interfere with the proper exercise of ministry.

Much depended on careful preordination scrutinies, but this was not the end either of examination or education for the cure of souls. Every subsequent promotion meant further clearance based on ability, intelligence, and work. At least this was the theory. There were bound to be exceptions, such as when nepotism or politics overshadowed the whole process. Parish clergy were also given opportunities for further pastoral education, sometimes through diocesan synods (larger and rarer events) or through more frequent meetings of local clergy in a deanery presided over by one of their own, the rural dean (No. 54). In fact, ordained clergy might undergo an examination at any time, for example, when a bishop or some other diocesan official was visiting a parish. If there were some doubt as to the good performance of the local clergy, officials could inquire into aspects of liturgical celebration or the more precise details surrounding a particular cleric's ordination—when and where he was ordained, by whom, and what sort of scrutiny had he then undergone. These seem to have been the embarrassing circumstances of a visitation by the Dean and Chapter of Salisbury to parishes in their care (No. 34).

Before we pass on from examination, one final point must be made. The whole procedure of scrutinies at ordination and afterwards could be expedited with letters, properly signed and sealed, that indicated the substance of what was looked for in an inquiry. A candidate for orders would be exempt from further scrutiny so long as he bore letters, usually from his archdeacon, rural dean, or religious superior, that indicated he had already been found worthy of the order sought (No. 37). The same message was typically conveyed in letters dimissory which indicated that the bearer had already been examined by his bishop and given leave, as circumstances required, to be ordained by any bishop who was willing to promote him. Letters were available to clerics even after ordination. A new cleric would often apply for (and pay for) letters testimonial, a statement that the bearer had been canonically ordained to a particular rank at a time and place by a particular bishop. These letters were to be on hand during a visitation when some verification of the cleric's status was wanted. Clerics also found such letters useful in the event that they were brought before a secular court and had to demonstrate their canonical status.

Ordination prepared a man for the exercise of pastoral authority in a local church, but not all clerics were destined for parochial work. Certainly most were, and the vast majority of secular clerics (to distinguish them from their regular brothers, such as monks and friars, who lived according to a rule or *regula*) had positions of one sort or another in the parish church (see chapter 4). Though it was, of course, ideal that the man who had charge of the church was also a priest who exercised the cure of souls, such was not always the case. Men of lesser rank such as deacons, subdeacons, and even acolytes could be made rectors of parish churches. In effect, they were administrators of the church and, limited in orders, they could not carry out all the pastoral requirements of the parish. They were, however, expected to manage the parish income in such a way that they could hire a priest who would serve as vicar of the parish, presiding at mass and celebrating the sacraments. As for the non-priestly rector, he had to agree to be ordained to the priesthood within a specified period of time or risk losing his benefice entirely (No. 39).

This arrangement was not uncommon in the medieval church and lasted for as long as it did because the parish was regarded as more than a center of spiritual life. It was a piece of property, possessing a guaranteed income with rights and obligations which had to be secured against all sorts of depredations, ecclesiastical and lay. Since parishes were also sources of wealth, it was inevitable that their guardians regarded them in this light. Thus, reform-minded churchmen were constantly concerned about the quality and vigilance of parish rectors. Two of the more prominent abuses were pluralism—holding more than one benefice with cure of souls—and absenteeism—failure to reside in one's benefice (Nos. 41, 42, 43). In order to avoid these and related abuses, the church had established a normative procedure for admission to an ecclesiastical benefice. This entailed presentation to the church, institution by the bishop, and induction to the benefice, usually by a local church official.

No vacant church benefice could be filled unless a cleric nominated by the parish patron had first been presented to the bishop. The patron of the parish owned the advowson of the church, a set of rights linked to the property of the church which included presentation. Patrons could be individual men or women, usually the sons and daughters of some local aristocratic family who had given land for the church in the first place. Another patron was the bishop himself, whose appointment of a candidate was a conflation of the two steps, presentation and institution, in a single act called a collation (No. 40). Other powerful patrons included the king and the pope, whose sights were set on the wealthier livings of cathedral dignities and royal chapels. Corporations could also act as patrons, such as a cathedral chapter, convents and monasteries, colleges, lay guilds, and religious confraternities.

Once a candidate had been presented to a benefice, he had to appear before the bishop or his delegate for institution. This process required establishing certain important details, such as whether the benefice sought was in fact vacant, the identity of the last inductee, the circumstances surrounding the vacancy, and whether the person(s) presenting was the true patron of the benefice. These conditions having been satisfied, the bishop needed to know that the candidate was worthy, and this entailed another examination.

The only step that remained in the process was the actual induction of the new rector to the church. For this task, the bishop usually appointed the rural dean of the neighborhood where the church was situated, and it was he who led the new curate into his parish church and the rectorial manse (No. 41). The newly inducted cleric now had the benefice for life and could only be removed from it for the gravest reasons. From the moment of his induction he was the pastor of the parish, duty-bound to see personally to the spiritual administration of his church or to secure and employ adequate clergy who would assist him in his duties.

ᴓ No. 29. The seasons for ordination in a letter from Pope Alexander III to Robert de Bethune (1131–48), Bishop of Hereford.
Gregory IX's *Extra* 1.11,3. Trans. WJD.

Now, regarding your inquiry, whether it is permissible to ordain anyone outside the four times of fast [the four ember days] to the orders of porter, lector, exorcist, acolyte, or subdeacon, we respond to your grace in this manner: bishops are permitted to ordain one or two men to minor orders on Sundays and other feast days; but no bishop, save the Roman pontiff, may ordain to the subdiaconate [and above] except on the four ember days, Holy Saturday, or the Saturday before Passion Sunday.

ᴓ No. 30. Canon law on clerical examinations.
Gratian's *Decretum*, Dist. 24,5–7. Trans. WJD.

Ch. 5. Ordinands should convene on the Wednesday [before the ordination] in order to be examined.

When a bishop decides to hold ordinations, all those who wish to come to the sacred ministry should be summoned to the city on the fourth day before the ordination along with their priests and those who are presenting them. Then the bishop should choose from his household priests and other good men learned in divine law and experienced in church law to examine diligently those who are to be ordained, especially in matters relating to their birth, upbringing, origins, age, education, and the place where they were schooled, whether they are well-educated or instructed in God's law, and if they are firm in their Catholic faith, and to answer these inquiries in simple words. They ought especially to be careful about men to whom the cure of souls has been committed, who for the sake of advancement or the lure of high office are wandering from the truth and, unworthy and ill-suited, approach the bishop for the laying on of hands and promotion to orders. But if this does happen and someone who is unworthy approaches, he shall be taken from the altar; also, let those who dared to sell the gift of the Holy Spirit be damned before God and stripped of their ecclesiastical dignities. Thus, for three days continuously let the examinations take place and, on the Saturday, those who have been found worthy are to be presented to the bishop.

Ch. 6. The bishop should not ordain clerics without the counsel of his own clergy.

A bishop should not ordain clerics without the counsel of his own clergy, so let him seek the advice and testimony of the community.

Ch. 7. Concerning those who are ordained without being examined and afterwards confess their sin.

Should any priest or deacon be ordained without an examination and the fact be discovered, either because the person confessed his sin or others detected it after ordination, let him be deposed from the clergy. Indeed, the same applies to any of the clerical orders and the church defends this [action] because the sin is so reprehensible.

℀ No. 31. Archbishop Walter Reynolds' rules governing ordination: Canterbury Provincial Constitutions, c. 1 (1322).
Wilkins, *Concilia*, vol. 2, p. 512. Trans. WJD.

That men should approach the sacrament of order reverently, contritely, and with devotion is shown in this: that it is conferred by none other than the high priest, that is, the bishop, and at certain times and places with fasting, not only by those being ordained, but by all the people. Therefore, with regard for the canons, we forbid any to come or be admitted to orders without canonical examination. Let no lesser clerics be admitted to the inferior degrees unless they have proper presenters, and upon their testimony let them be admitted. Let no simoniac, murderer, excommunicate, usurer, sacrilegious person, incendiary, liar, or any one under canonical impediment presume to go into any orders whatsoever; nor let him in any way be presented or admitted to them. Let no one who has been ordained in Ireland, Wales, Scotland, or elsewhere and who lacks the proper letters testimonial or dimissory be admitted for pastoral work in our province unless in case of great necessity. Even then, such men must obtain proper dispensations from appropriate authorities and the orders they have been admitted to must be confirmed by the bishops who receive them. Provided, notwithstanding, that they be in no way admitted without good evidence of their having been ordained and of their good life and learning. And we charge that priests we do not know, that have no evidence of their ordination, not be admitted to celebrate divine services in churches without the license of the diocesan bishop, after they have given sufficient assurance of their ordination by letters testimonial or by the testimony of good men. And we enjoin abbots and priors not to allow their monks and canons to be ordained by any other bishop except the diocesan, unless it be done with the letters dimissory of the bishop or his vicar general in the bishop's absence.

❧ No. 32. Procedures for clerical examinations (1384).
John de Burgh, *Pupilla Oculi*, VII.3,4. (London, 1516). Trans. WJD.

The Examination

1. On the times for the conferral of orders and the holding of a scrutiny. Holy Orders are generally celebrated on the four ember Saturdays and on the Saturdays before Passion Sunday and Easter; those ordained at any other time receive their orders but may not exercise them.

2. The bishop may legally confer minor orders on Sundays, solemnities, and some feast days but not so often and not in such a manner as they appear to be general ordinations. Also, one may receive all minor orders on the same day unless custom prohibits, the contrary of which might lead to scandal. But in no way can one be promoted to any major and minor orders or to two major orders at all on the same day. Anyone who secretly receives orders in this manner should be suspended.

3. There should be a twofold scrutiny before an ordination. The first is performed by the archdeacon, as is his right, or by other priests and wise men whom the bishop sends to the ordination site. These are to inquire diligently into the lives of those to be ordained: about the place where they live, their knowledge of the faith, and other things contained in the apostolic rule. This scrutiny ought to begin four days before the Saturday on which the ordination is held and continue up to that day. On Saturday, those who have been approved and accepted as worthy are to be presented to the bishop. This examination ought to be diligently made and, lest any of the unapproved pass furtively in among those who have been found worthy, let the names of the approved be written down at the examination, and at the or-

dination let the roster on which the names appear be read distinctly. The bishop is to keep this roster among his own records or it may be stored in the church.

4. The second scrutiny takes place at the ordination, when those to be ordained are presented to the bishop before the altar and the archdeacon says, "Holy Mother Church beseeches," etc. and the minister of ordination, namely the bishop, asks, "Do you know these men to be worthy?" The archdeacon answers, "In as much as human weakness can, I know and testify that these men are worthy of the burden of this office." Clearly, the presenter is not guilty of any sin when he responds in this way so long as he has not spoken against his conscience by finding unworthy men worthy. But if the archdeacon should know in advance that one of the candidates is unworthy or his conscience bothers him in the presentation of a particular candidate, let him make every effort to inform the bishop privately before the man approaches for ordination. If the bishop does not object, the archdeacon can see to the man's removal. If he is unable to do this without causing scandal, let him act as a true minister of the church, declining to judge what is hidden or in any way make public his brother's sins.

5. The one who is ordained without examination, if known to be worthy, has not sinned and should not be punished since such a person need not be examined. But, certainly if he is unknown, however worthy he might be in other respects, he should be deposed. And if both unknown and unworthy, he should be deposed all the more. If, however, he is known and found unworthy, he ought to be deposed because he did not admit his faults. In an examination, an ordinand is obliged to reveal his crimes or grave impediments, in law or deed, unless he has obtained a dispensation from them.

On the Age and Quality of Those to be Ordained
1. For an exorcist, lector, or porter to be ordained he must be older than an infant, that is, more than seven years of age. Similarly, the one who receives first tonsure in order to be ordained an acolyte should be more than fourteen years old. To be ordained to the subdiaconate, one must be more than eighteen years old, more than nineteen for the diaconate, more than twenty-three for the priesthood, and more than thirty for the episcopacy.

2. Anyone ordained under age sins gravely and should be suspended from executing the order received; not only is he automatically suspended, but so is the bishop who ordained him.

3. It should be noted that minority of age in no way impedes reception of holy orders as much as it does its execution, for even if this sacrament is conferred on a child in the proper manner, the [sacramental] character is de

facto received. Now, consent is not required in the one who receives this character, but the use of reason is required by the one to be ordained; this, because the dignity and reverence of the sacrament require it, but also because the vow of celibacy goes with it and such awesome power cannot be conferred unless it be received devoutly and with reverence. Thus, it is forbidden that anyone receive holy orders before the age set down by the church.

4. It is necessary that ordinands possess certain qualities fitting for the clerical state and be free from certain defects. First, the ordinand should be morally pure, modest in dress, temperate in eating and drinking, competent, not eminent, in learning, and calm and quiet, for according to St. Jerome, clerics need to live the common life. He needs to be a skilled preacher and one who corrects vices with the rod of discipline. He should not be pugnacious, litigious, or covetous, not a gambler, meaning a participant in vulgar games, especially dice; he should not be a merchant nor become preoccupied with secular business; he should not be unchaste or live with women. He should not be a novice, that is, a recent convert to the faith; such a person should not be admitted to minor orders, even tonsure. The reason for this is that such people are not sufficiently skilled in ecclesiastical and religious affairs and may grow haughty when promoted, thinking that the church could not do without them. In the same manner, public penitents should not be ordained even if they have already done penance for their sin. Though the sin is gone, the scar remains.

5. Court officials should not be ordained and by court officials we mean anyone who, by his condition, is bound to the court of any secular power, such as a knight, a judge, an advocate, an official, a court bard, or anyone else who has an office, worthy or no, attached to the court and because of it, can be summoned to the court. . . .

6. Others excluded from ordination for similar reasons include tutors, proctors, wardens, and the like. This means that anyone exercising administration on behalf of a secular person who is not poor should not be ordained during the period of employment. Those who work for ecclesiastical officials or for secular persons who are in dire need, such as the blind, the poor, orphans, and widows, if they are not impeded in the course of their administration, may be ordained. . . .

7. Those obliged to the public for the administration of some matter may not be ordained until the matter is resolved; except if they are public debtors.

8. One who is bound by oath or any other manner in service or debt to someone else may be ordained; but he remains bound just as before and may pay off the debt by doing secretarial work or other acceptable duties.

9. Anyone who in any way mutilates himself or another by his own hand

and without just cause, either out of anger, pride, or frustration, may not be ordained. Those who castrate themselves for the sake of continence and who think they are making themselves a gift to the Lord, should be barred from ordination and, if ordained, deposed. The same applies to one who loses an entire limb or a large enough part of one that he is unable to carry out the office of his order or gives rise to scandal. If one removes a part of his body for good reason, such as leprosy, or has some part of his body amputated to avoid infection in the rest, whether obvious or hidden, even if it be a finger (so long as it is not used in making the sign of the cross), he should not be rejected or deposed. . . .

10. Also, if a priest loses part of a finger in some conflict in defense of his own rights, as long as he can officiate with the missing part without causing scandal and provided that no one's murder or mutilation came about as a result of the fight, he may officiate with the dispensation of his bishop.

11. A cripple may be ordained so long as he does not need a crutch to get to the altar. There is no right or custom allowing a blind person to be ordained or any person with a visual defect that could develop into a deformity and a scandal.

12. Lepers, when they are expelled from common cohabitation, are absolutely prohibited from ordination. If, however, a priest should become leprous, he shall cease his ministry with those who are well; but he may celebrate the divine ministries among lepers or celebrate mass on his own in private.

13. A hump-backed person should not be rejected from orders unless his deformity is severe and causes disability. Those who have more or less toes than are usual for human beings are to be rejected.

14. But those who have six fingers or two fingers fused together, as long as there be no impediment in the use of the fingers, should not be rejected.

15. Madmen, lunatics, epileptics, and those who are possessed are not to be ordained even if they should be freed completely from their condition. But if they are ordained first and then suffer such diseases, they should abstain from celebrating the sacraments for a full year after their complete recovery.

16. Those who cannot drink wine should not be ordained to the priesthood since those who celebrate need to take communion.

❧ No. 33. A bishop announces an ordination (1286).

Reg. Pontissara (Winchester), p. 326. Trans. WJD.

A citation for the celebration of holy orders. John, etc., greetings to our beloved son in Christ, our Official, etc. Since we propose, God willing, to celebrate holy orders in our cathedral church at Winchester on the next Ember Saturday in September following the feast of the Exaltation of the Holy Cross [September 14], we strictly command you to cite or have cited all rectors and vicars of our diocese who have not yet been promoted to the presbyteral order, to appear at the stated time and place and receive orders as the cure of their benefice requires. And that you see to these things and make sure you certify for us at the said time and place the names of those who are to be ordained. Given at Brightwell, August 23 in the fifth year of our consecration [1286].

৩৯ No. 34. Examinations of the Sonning clergy (1222).
The Register of St. Osmund, in *Life*, Coulton, vol. 2, pp. 39–41.

Acts of the Chapter held by William, dean of Salisbury, at Sonning, in the year of our Lord 1222, on the Friday next before the Feast of St. Martin. . . . Vitalis, a priest, perpetual vicar of Sonning, presented the chaplain [i.e. curate] named Simon whom he has with him, and whom he lately engaged until Michaelmas. This Simon, examined as to his Orders, said that he was ordained subdeacon at Oxford by a certain Irish bishop named Albin, then suffragan to the Bishop of Lincoln, from whom also he received deacon's orders; and those of priest from Hugh [of Wells] now Bishop of Lincoln, four years past. He was examined in the Gospel of the first Sunday in Advent, and was found insufficient, and unable to understand what he read. Again he was tried in the Canon of the Mass, at the words *Te igitur, clementissime Pater*, etc.[3] He knew not the case of *Te*, nor by what word it was governed; and when we bade him look closely which could most fittingly govern it, he replied: "*Pater*, for He governeth all things." We asked him what "clementissime" was, and what case, and how declined; he knew not. We asked him what "clemens" was; he knew not. Moreover, the said Simon knew no difference between one antiphon and another, nor the chant of the hymns, not even of the hymn "nocte surgentes," nor did he know by heart aught of the service or psalter. Moreover, he said that it seemed indecent that he should be examined before the dean, since he was already in Holy Orders. We asked him where he was when he received his priest's Orders: he answered that he had forgotten. He is amply illiterate. ["Sufficienter illiteratus est."]

Wokingham is served by Philip, a chaplain, who hires that chapel on farm for ten marks, and the chapel of Sandhurst for a mark, but he takes

---

[3] These words which begin the canon of the mass or the Eucharistic Prayer are addressed to the Father: "Therefore, most heavenly Father . . ."

two marks from the priest who is there. He was not examined, since he is of approved life and good testimony. Where ordained . . . [hiatus in MS].

John of Hurst presented his chaplain, Richard by name, born at Ross. . . . He is a youth, and knoweth nothing. He saith that he received the sub-diaconate at London from Bishop William; the diaconate six years ago from Peter Bishop of Winchester; and the priesthood that same year from William Bishop of Chester. Examined on the Advent collect *Excita quaesumus Domine* ["Stir up, we beseech Thee, O Lord"] he said that he would answer naught of this matter; likewise also when we tried him in the Canon; (for, after his priest had left the church first after the examination, and had joined the rest, then all fell to one accord that they would not answer; yet some, at the earnest instance of the Dean, answered afterwards in detail). Having been questioned afterwards, he would not be examined at the end of the Chapter and remained suspended [from his office].

John of Arborfield presented his chaplain Reginald, born at Windsor. He was, as he saith, ordained to the subdiaconate at Salisbury, the diaconate and priesthood at Winchester, four years now past. Examined in the prayer, "*Excita,*" etc. and the passage of the Canon *Te igitur,* etc., he utterly refused to answer. Afterwards he came and offered himself for examination, and knew nothing, whether of reading or of singing.

The chaplain of Sandhurst, John of Sherborne, saith that he was or-dained subdeacon at Chichester, deacon at Winchester by the bishop God-frey in Ireland . . . [hiatus in MS], and hath now served the aforesaid chapel four years. Examined in the prayer *Excita* and in *Te igitur,* he knew nothing to answer. Examined in chant, in the Advent Sunday anthem *Ad te levavi,* he could not chant it.

Again Vitalis, priest, presented for the chapel of Ruscombe the priest Jordan, born at Shatton in Dorset, ordained subdeacon and deacon (as he saith) at Salisbury by Bishop Herbert, and priest by the Bishop of Rochester, Gilbert de Glanville, before the General Interdict [of 1208]. Examined, like the rest, in *Excita* and *Te igitur,* he knew nothing. A book was given him to chant from: he would not. We commanded Vitalis to find good chaplains for this place and for Sonning, or the Dean will take the benefices into his own hands.

At Arborfield also was an old man in the [priest's] house named Richard Bullock, a priest of Reading; and when the Dean examined him whether he could see and could pronounce the words completely, it was found that he could not completely pronounce a single word of the Gospel or the Canon. Wherefore the Dean bade John of Arborfield suffer him no longer to minister in that chapel.

∾ No. 35. Dispensations for ordination (1411, 1332).

A. For the loss of a finger (1411).
Reg. Mascall (Hereford), pp. 81–82. Trans. WJD.

At Hereford and with the authority of Anthony [the papal peniten-
tiary], the bishop dispensed John Dodley, also known as Phillips, from an
irregularity stemming from the loss of his ring finger cut off by a sword. He
is allowed to proceed to the orders of deacon and priest, this irregularity
notwithstanding.

B. For illegitimacy (1332).
Reg. T. Charlton (Hereford), p. 22. Trans. WJD.

At Prestbury, 18 September in the said year [1332], his lordship dispensed Henry of Rudmerley, clerk, from the defect of illegitimacy, having
been born of an unmarried man and an unmarried woman, that he may be
promoted to all orders and free to obtain an ecclesiastical benefice, even one
with a cure of souls. This was done according to the form of the letters
placed in Henry's keeping by lord Gaucelin, by God's grace, bishop of Al-
bano and penitentiary of the lord pope.

∾ No. 36. Ordination and material support (the ordination title). Third Lateran Council, c. 5 (1179).
Decrees, Tanner, p. 214.

If a bishop ordains someone as a deacon or priest without a definite title
from which he may draw the necessities of life, let the bishop provide him
with what he needs until he shall assign him the suitable wages of clerical
service in some church, unless it happens that the person ordained is in such
a position that he can find the support of life from his own or family inheritance.

∾ No. 37. A testimonial letter for a priest moving to another diocese (1297).
Reg. Halton (Carlisle), p. 98. Trans. WJD.

Greetings to anyone to whom the contents of this letter should pertain.
We wish to inform you by these letters that the bearer, one sir W. de S., priest,
has lived in the diocese of Carlisle for a very long time where he has celebrated the divine mysteries in a praiseworthy manner, has never been suspended, excommunicated nor charged with any crime. . . . And so we urge
and ask that you admit the said sir W. when he comes to you for the wor-
thiest execution of his office for whom we have written these letters testimonial. Given, etc.

◌ᴗ **No. 38. A bishop's instructions at ordination to First Tonsure and all other orders (thirteenth century).**

W. Maskell, ed., *Monumenta Ritualia Ecclesiae Anglicanae*, 2nd ed., vol. 2 (Oxford, 1882), pp. 237–49. Trans. WJD.

The first thing that identifies a cleric is his crown, since it is by this sign that the one chosen and given a share in the divine ministry is to reign. As Peter says: "you are a chosen race, a royal priesthood" [1 Pet. 2:9]. For this reason the hair is cut in the shape of a circlet and the top of the head shaved so that a cleric may realize that he has taken up a royal dignity in Christ. Also, nothing should come between him and God so that, as the Apostle teaches, he may contemplate the glory of God's face revealed [I Cor. 13:12]. For a cleric should not be ignorant of God as secular people are, since the cleric is God's ambassador to the people. Hence, his hair should be cut away from his eyes and ears so that worldly cares or earthly ambitions do not get in the way of his hearing or understanding God's Word. Indeed, it is for this that he should be supported by the church's contributions, instructed in sacred scripture, and instituted in an ecclesiastical office. And when there is good reason and a sufficiency in age, learning, and morals, he may assume holy orders under a particular title without which none may be ordained lest they become not clerics but men without heads. The rite of tonsure has its origins in the Old Testament from the Nazarites who, as it is written, for chastity's sake, burned their hair as pitch in the fire of sacrifice [Num. 6:18]. We also read in the Acts of the Apostles how Priscilla, Aquila, and St. Paul and certain others did the same thing, signifying in heart and deed the cutting away of vices as they grew [Acts 18:18].

Admonition to Porters, who have the first order

Porters were called doorkeepers in the Old Testament. Their office is to guard the keys of the church and to open and close [the doors] at the proper hours, but also to guard within, to receive the Christian faithful, and to shut out the excommunicate and the nonbeliever, just as the bishop teaches at ordination. Christ established and exercised this office himself when he ejected from the temple, whip in hand, the buyers and sellers who represent all heretics and nonbelievers.

Admonition to Lectors, who are the second order

Lectors have their origin in the prophets who, like Esdras and others, announced the word of God to the people. Hence they receive from the bishop the power to recite for the hearing of the people the prophets and other readings from the sacred writings. Therefore, they should be instructed in the holy scriptures and know what they read, speak well, and pronounce distinctly so that they may appear to their hearers intelligent as well as devout. They need to judge carefully in their reading what is indicative, what is interrogative, and where the middle and end of the sentence occurs. When these things are not done with care, listeners are prevented from understanding or it becomes a comedy. Furthermore, the lector's voice should not be heard as much in the ears as in the heart since, according to James, we ought to be doers of the word, not simply listeners. The lector should not look about or gesticulate affectedly, lest the people become spectators more than listeners: lectors should not have voices that are breaking or effeminate, oafish or rustic. In former times readers were called heralds or proclaimers. The Lord instituted and exercised this office when, at the age of twelve and seated in the midst of the learned and the elders, he opened the book of Isaiah and read there: "the Spirit of the Lord is upon me for he has anointed me and sent me to preach to the poor."[4] This means that readers who announce the word of God to the people ought to shine with a spiritual grace.

Admonition to Exorcists, the third order

Exorcists ought to lead a good life, in body and in spirit, because they receive power over evil and supernatural spirits and expel them from people who are possessed. They also perform the office of opening for the catechumens.[5] They constitute an order and office in the church since they first appear in Solomon's temple and, after Esdras' time, acquire a more distinct order. The Lord established and exercised this office when he touched the ears and tongue of the deaf and mute with his spittle and said, "*Ephphatha,*" which means, "be opened," teaching us to open the ears and mouth of our hearts in a spiritual way in order to know and profess Christ [Mark 7:31–37]. Jesus practiced this office frequently but no more so when he expelled seven demons from Mary Magdalene.

Admonition to Acolytes, the fourth order

The Greek word "acolyte" means *ceroferarius* or candle-bearer in Latin. These ministers carry lit candles when the Gospel is read or when the Host and Chalice are elevated or during the celebration of any other holy ministry, not for the illumination of this world but that, in a spiritual manner,

---

[4] The writer is conflating two stories: Jesus teaching the elders in the temple (Luke 2:41–50) and the beginning of Jesus' public ministry (Luke 4:16–19).
[5] A reference to the baptismal exorcism and Jesus' action in the passage from Mark 7:31–37.

they may show the works of light to those around them and offer a beacon of guidance to those who wander. They receive an empty ewer from the bishop since they are not yet ready to receive a full one. This signifies that though they touch holy vessels, they have not yet attained Holy Orders for the full exercise of ministry. The Lord referred to this very office when he said, "I am the light of the world. He who follows me does not walk in the darkness but will have the light of life" [John 8:12].

Admonition to Subdeacons, who hold the fifth place

The fifth order belongs to the subdeacons who among the Greeks are called *hypodiaconi* or underdeacons. It is they who are referred to in the Book of Esdras as "Nathanites," humble servants of the Lord. In the gospel, Nathaniel was of this order when the Lord praised him proclaiming, "Behold a true Israelite in whom there is no guile" [John 1:47]. They assist the deacons at the altar in taking up the paten and chalice for the Body and Blood of Christ and then returning them. For these reasons, the Fathers have maintained that those who participate thus in the sacred mysteries should observe the law of chastity, for, as it is written, "be clean, you who carry the vessels of the Lord." They accept the gifts from the people in God's church. It is also their duty to place on the altar the gifts [here, bread and wine] to be used for the people of God. In like manner, they are to wash the corporals, palls, and altar cloths and draw water for baptism. They also hold the ewer, the water for washing, and the bishop's finger towel and provide water for the priests and deacons for them to wash their hands at the altar. When they are ordained they do not receive the imposition of hands as do priests and deacons but the bishop gives them an empty chalice and paten and the archdeacon an ewer, water, and a finger towel in order to wash the hands of priests and deacons when celebrating the sacraments. The Lord exercised this office when, at table with his disciples, he girded himself with linen and poured water in a basin to wash his disciples' feet and dry them with linen.

Admonition to Deacons, who hold the sixth place

The order of deacons is called the sixth order with little surprise as the number six, as it is a perfect number, symbolizes the perfection of works. This order has its origins in the tribe of Levi in the Old Testament. This is what the Lord commanded Moses: that after the ordination of Aaron and his sons, the tribe of Levi should in turn be ordained for ministry of the divine cult and consecrated to the Lord. And they should serve Israel, before Aaron and his sons, in the tent of God. And they carried the ark and the tabernacle and all of its vessels and after transporting it, put it down in the encampment they had built. After the age of twenty or more they were commanded to serve in the tent. In the New Testament the Holy Fathers fixed this rule as Moses had instituted it for this order, since men at this age are strong and can carry burdens. It is from the New Testament that deacons are represented wearing a stole over their left shoulder and their dalmatic folded under the same shoulder on fast days, signifying that whatever labors or sustenance we carry in this life, we bear on the left and not the right until we have rest in eternity. The origins of this order are in the New Testament where, in the Acts of the Apostles, the disciples chose for the office of deacon seven men of good reputation, filled with the Holy Spirit [Acts 6:3–5]. And after they had prayed, they imposed their hands on them. From this, the apostles and their successors have decreed that in every mother church there should be seven deacons of the higher rank standing, as a seven-fold sign, about the cross of Christ, like columns around the altar. In this way, they represent the seven-fold gifts of the Holy Spirit, sanctifying body and spirit. They represent as well the seven angels of the Apocalypse sounding their trumpets or a burning candelabra with seven candles. They are the sound of thunder, a mighty voice like a preacher's urging those around him to pray or to bend the knee or sing or to read and to listen to God's word. It is they who preach and who administer the sacraments. Without them the priest has a title but no office, for consecration into priesthood is a consecration into diaconal ministry, which encompasses sacramental ministry. So as not to usurp the duties of the deacon, the priest at the altar is not supposed to take up the chalice unless it has been first handed to him by the deacon. The Levites place the sacrifice on the altar and they cover the Ark of the Covenant since not everyone should or can look upon these highest mysteries. They assist at the altar arrayed in white robes, the whiteness of their garb revealing the purity of their lives that they may approach the sacrifice, resplendent and without stain. For the Lord ought to have ministers who are untainted by ills of the flesh and who shine with spiritual perfection and chastity. The Apostle, in his letter to Timothy, describes what sort of men ought to be ordained as deacons [1 Tim. 3:1–13]. In describing the election of priests, he immediately adds that deacons, too, should be free of blame, that is, without fault just like bishops. They should be chaste, that is, always free from lust; not double-tongued so as to disturb the peace they enjoy; not heavy drinkers, for where there is drunkenness, lust and raging desire are strong; not pursuers of filthy profit or seeking after earthly gain while ignoring the heavenly host. After these things, he adds that they first ought to be tested and may minister if found without serious fault. And those who, like bishops, are examined before ordination and found worthy, are afterwards admitted to holy ministry. When they are ordained, it is only the bishop who imposes hands upon them since they are seeking ministry, not the priesthood.[6] The bishop places an *orarium* or a stole over their left shoulder representing their acceptance of the Lord's yoke which, in this life, means all things "sinister" and they bear their difficult trials bravely and submit themselves to God's love. They also receive from the bishop the Book of the Gospels by which they know they are heralds of the gospel of Christ. For as lectors read the Old Testament, deacons preach the New Testament, in particular the gospel, which they alone may proclaim in church. They are obliged to assist the priests in any sacramental ministry such as baptism, confirmation, offering and setting down the paten, chalice, and the gifts at the altar, arranging and dressing the Lord's table, carrying the cross and preaching on the gospel and the epistles. They also serve as announcers, calling out names. They are to urge people to attend to the Lord and to pray. They also proclaim and announce Christ's peace. The Lord exercised this office when, after the meal, he offered the sacrament which he had celebrated with his own mouth and hands; he exercised the office as well when he roused his sleeping apostles to prayer, saying, "be watchful and pray, that you may not enter into temptation" [Luke 22:40].

Admonition to Priests, who hold the seventh place

The order of presbyters follows in seventh place, those who in the Old Testament had their beginnings with the sons of Aaron. For those who were called priests are now called presbyters and those who were called the highest priests are now known as bishops. Priests are also called elders since this is what the Greeks call their priests. And so priests ought to be elders for the people of God, not merely in the matter of age, but in moral dignity and their mature behavior. As scripture says, "for venerable old age is not that of long time, nor counted by the number of years" [Wisd. of Sol. 4:8]. For gray hairs are human wisdom and old age a spotless life. Still, there is a difference between bishops and priests in our age because there are things only bishops can do: the ordination of clergy, the dedication of churches, the consecration of holy chrism, the imposition of hands, and the episcopal blessing. But both have common duties in the other sacraments, in catechizing, baptizing, celebrating mass and consecrating the Body and Blood of

---

[6] The inference here is that at an ordination to the priesthood, the bishop is joined by his priestly concelebrants in placing their hands on the heads of the newly ordained. Not so in diaconate ordinations, where the bishop alone imposes hands.

Christ and in preaching the Word in the churches. For that reason, some of these things just mentioned are reserved only for the highest priests, lest that same authority, if assumed by all and in every place, would make the lesser haughty before their ordained masters and, the chains of obedience thus broken, provoke scandal. Presbyters are the successors and vicars of the seventy disciples who preceded the Lord Jesus into every town and place where he was to go. So, the priests, to be sure, who are the bishop's helpers in catechizing, teach the common folk; in baptizing, they build up unity in the church, and minister every sacrament except for the laying on of hands.[7] Now the bishops are the successors of the apostles and, because they rule over such a multitude of people and need assistance and aid in their office, require the ministry of priests, just as Moses in the desert chose seventy good men with whose counsel and aid he more capably governed the multitude. Priests may be either in lower or higher orders, that is, either presbyters or bishops, bearing the charge of the highest pontiff in calling sinners to penance and healing with the ointment of their prayers, whence the Apostle says God reconciled the world to himself in Christ and placed the word of reconciliation within us. "We exhort you, for Christ's sake, be reconciled to God" [2 Cor. 5:20]. In this, priests are called to be mediators, for people pray to God for forgiveness of their sins and penitents are reconciled to God through absolution. And so it happens that there are good men, mediators between people and God, who through their preaching of the truth, teach the people God's commands and offer prayers on behalf of the people to God for the intercession of sinners. But a mediator, as the Apostle says, does not act on his own, for he who is not a member of the community, either through society or the bonds of friendship, cannot reconcile enemies. And so priests, when they are at peace with God through their holiness, need to build up peace along with compassion among their neighbors. Presbyters ought to be as the Apostle suggests in his letter to Titus: "It was for this reason that I left you in Crete to organize presbyters for the towns in the way that I told you."[8] This means anyone free from grave sin, who is the husband of one wife, whose children are believers, and who is beyond reproach or duplicity. Certainly, a bishop has to be beyond reproach, and by this statement Paul means to show how presbyters are included in the same category as bishops. When he writes his letter to Timothy concerning the ordination of bishops and deacons, he only touches on presbyters because he knows they are to be included among the bishops. Thus are presbyters

---

[7] This happens at confirmation and ordination.
[8] This sentence and the following are paraphrases of Titus 1:5-9.

included with bishops in the church, as the Apostle and the apostolic canons testify. When presbyters are ordained and the bishop, in blessing them, places his hands on their heads, all the priests who are present extend their hands along with the bishop over the heads of the ordinands and invoke the Holy Spirit to come upon them. The priests' hands are joined to the bishop's because they know they are co-consecrators in this sacrament and that all have a common mission in works of mercy. It is the bishop's duty alone to anoint the head of the ordinand, for he knows that he is the vicar of one about whom scripture has it "therefore God, thy God, hath anointed thee with the oil of gladness" [Ps. 44:8]. After the invocation of the Holy Spirit, the ordinands receive the stole over both shoulders which, as a kind of support, protects the sides right and left. Through this, presbyters know that they are guardians of the arms of justice, right and left, and that neither will hardships break them nor successes lift them up. They receive from the bishop the chalice with wine and the paten with bread with the understanding that they receive power to offer sacrifice to God through the use of these holy things. It is their duty to celebrate the sacrament of Christ's Body and Blood on the altar of God, to recite the prayers and bless the gifts of God. Our Lord Jesus Christ carried out this office when, after the meal, he instituted the sacrament by changing the bread and wine into his own body and blood and admonished his disciples to do the same in memory of his passion. He also showed how supremely he filled this office when, as priest and sacrifice, he offered himself to God the Father on the altar of the cross for the sins of the world and, by his own blood, brought peace to heaven and earth and entered eternity. How wonderful, then, is the priestly office by which the passion of Christ is celebrated every day on the altar and any sinner may be reconciled to God. All these things about the priestly office having been set forth, priests of Christ should realize that as they excel in rank of order, so too should they excel in holiness of life. In this way, the people entrusted to their care and instructed by their manner of living will obey them joyfully and grow in imitation of them until, in the passing of days, they attain their heavenly reward.

∾ No. 39. Admission to a cure: the constitution *Licet canon* (1274)
Gregory X, at the Second Council of Lyons, Sext. 1.6,14. Trans. JS.

The canon [Lateran III, c. 3] promulgated by our predecessor of happy memory Pope Alexander III ordered among other things that no one should be assigned the cure of a parochial church unless he has reached the age of twenty-five years and is of good learning and character; and that if a man assuming such a cure is warned that he should be ordained to the priesthood by the time limit set by canon law and he fails to do so, he should be removed from that office and it should be given to someone else. But now, since many men neglect to observe this canon, we, wishing to amend their dangerous negligence through the observance of the law, by this present decree order the following: No one may assume the cure of a parochial church unless he is of suitable learning, character, and age. From now on appointments to parochial churches of those who have not reached the age of twenty-five are completely invalid. Furthermore, anyone assuming the cure of a parish is bound to reside personally in the parish of which he is rector so that he may more diligently care for the flock entrusted to him. And he must be ordained to the priesthood within a year reckoned from the time when the parish was handed over to him. If he has not been promoted to the priesthood within that one-year period, by the authority of the present constitution he shall be deprived of his parish, even with no prior warning. Regarding the requirement, described above, that a rector reside in his parish, the local ordinary may grant him a dispensation to be absent from it temporarily for a reasonable cause.

∾ No. 40. Collation and presentation to a benefice (1286, 1290).
Reg. Pontissara (Winchester), pp. 27, 39. Trans. WJD.

A. A Collation (1290).

Collation of the church of Cheriton. John, by the grace of God, etc., greetings to his official, etc. Since we have been compelled by charity to confer the church of Cheriton in our diocese and vacant by the resignation of the last rector, Master William de [Monte Gangerii], with full right of collation to our beloved son in Christ John de Magnach, we command that you induct the same John or his proctor into full possession of the said church, etc. Given at Southwark, 3rd nones of June [June 3], in the year of our Lord 1290 and the eighth year of our consecration.

B. A presentation to a church (1286).

The lord bishop presented John de Hengham to the church of Portland. A memorandum that on the ides of September [September 13] in the year of our Lord 1286, the lord bishop presented John de Hengham to the church of Portland in the diocese of Salisbury vacant and under the bishop's patronage.

∾ No. 41. The presentation, institution, and induction of a cleric to a benefice (1335).

Reg. Gravesend (London), pp. 258–59. Trans. WJD.

A. Commission for institution after proof of age.

Stephen, by God's grace, bishop of London, to his beloved son in Christ, Adam of Murimuth, canon of our church in London, greetings, grace and blessing. Witnesses need to be admitted and received in order to confirm that John de Shobenhanger, cleric, presented to St. Mildred's church, is of legitimate age and these same witnesses should be compelled, if need be, by ecclesiastical censures. And, if in your presence, the proof of John's age should take place according to the terms of this inquest which we send to you by means of the official of the archdeacon of London included here and under our seal, he should be admitted to the same church of St. Mildred and canonically instituted to its rectory along with all other procedures that follow in such matters, either by law or custom. And we commit to you, our assistant, power of canonical sanction by these letters. Given at Horsted, the 17th kalends of May [April 15], in the year of our Lord 1335 and the seventeenth year of our consecration.

B. Institution to the church of St. Mildred in Broadstreet, London.

Adam Murimuth, canon of the church of St. Paul, London, special commissary of the reverend father in Christ, the lord Stephen, bishop of London by God's grace, to the beloved in Christ, John de Shobenhanger, cleric of the diocese of London, greetings in the Savior of all. I have received a mandate from the said father in these words: "Stephen, etc., to the beloved son in Christ, Master Adam Murimuth etc., greetings, etc. Let witnesses be admitted and received for the proof of legitimate age for John de Shobenhanger, cleric, etc. as above." Under the authority of this mandate, I admitted sworn witnesses as to the matter of your age, according to proper procedure, and took care to examine them with all diligence. By their testimony it was evident that you had completed your twenty-fourth year on the last feast of St. Andrew [November 30]. And since you adequately completed the inquest in this matter along with other articles, and since none of the canons disqualify you from being admitted to the said church, I admit you to the aforesaid church with the authority of the bishop and canonically institute you as rector of the church, saving all episcopal customs and the dignity of the church of London. In the testimony of which my seal has been affixed to these letters. And since there are some who do not know the seal, we add as well the seal of the officiality of the Court of Canterbury. Given at London, the 14th kalends of May [April 18], in the year of our Lord as above.

C. Certificate of Induction

To that reverend man of discretion, Master Adam of Murimuth, canon of the church of St. Paul, London, special commissary of the reverend father in Christ, the lord Stephen, by God's grace the bishop of London, the humble and devout official of the lord Archdeacon of London, offers his obedience with reverence and honor. I have received your mandate, the wording of which follows thus: "Adam Murimuth, canon of the church of St. Paul, London, special commissary of the reverend father in Christ, the lord Stephen, bishop of London by God's grace, to the beloved in Christ, the official of the Archdeacon of London, greetings in the Author of Salvation. Since, with the authority of a special commission of the said father which we sent you to examine and to return to us, we admitted John de Shobenhanger, cleric, to the church of St. Mildred, Broadstreet, London and instituted him canonically to the same, we [now] commit to you and command that you induct the said John into physical possession of the said church and defend the one you induct, withstanding all opponents and rebels through ecclesiastical sanctions, certifying to the said father or to ourselves that you did with these letters what you were required on behalf of the said John. Given at London under our seal and that of the officiality of the Court of Canterbury, 14th kalends of May, in the year of Our Lord 1335." By the authority of your mandate we inducted and defended the inductee, the said John, into physical possession of the aforesaid church of St. Mildred on the 13th kalends of May [April 19] with his rights and all other things that pertain. In the testimony of which, I have appended the seal of my office to these letters. Given at London . . . 11th kalends of May [April 21] in the above year of our Lord.

♋ No. 42. Decrees against pluralism from the Third (1179) and Fourth (1215) Lateran Councils.

Decrees, Tanner, pp. 218–19, 248–49.

A. Third Lateran

c. 13. Because some, seeing no limit to their avarice, strive to obtain several ecclesiastical dignities and several parish churches contrary to the decrees of the holy canons, so that though they are scarcely able to fulfil one office sufficiently they claim the revenues of very many, we strictly forbid this for the future. Therefore when it is necessary to entrust a church or ecclesiastical ministry to anyone, the person sought for this office should be of such a kind that he is able to reside in the place and exercise his care for it himself. If the contrary is done, both he who receives it is to be deprived of it, because he has received it contrary to the sacred canons, and he who gave it is to lose his power of bestowing it.

c. 14. Because the ambition of some has now gone to such lengths that they are said to hold not two or three but six or more churches, and since they cannot devote the proper care to two, we order, through our brethren and most dear fellow bishops, that this be corrected; and with regard to this pluralism, so contrary to the canons, and which gives rise to loose conduct and instability, and causes infinite danger to the souls of those who are able to serve the churches worthily, it is our wish to relieve their want by ecclesiastical benefices. Further, since some of the laity have become so bold that disregarding the authority of bishops they appoint clerics to churches and even remove them when they wish, and distribute the property and other goods of the church for the most part according to their own wishes, and even dare to burden the churches themselves and their people with taxes and impositions, we decree that those who from now on are guilty of such conduct are to be punished by anathema. Priests or clerics who receive the charge of a church from the hands of lay persons, without the authority of their own bishop, are to be deprived of communion; and if they persist, they are to be deposed from the ecclesiastical ministry and order. We firmly decree that because some of the laity force ecclesiastics and even bishops to come before their courts, those who presume to do so in the future are to be separated from the communion of the faithful. Further we forbid lay persons, who hold tithes to the danger of their souls, to transfer them in any way to other lay persons. If anyone receives them and does not hand them over to the church, let him be deprived of christian burial.

B. Fourth Lateran

c. 29. With much foresight it was forbidden in the Lateran council for anyone to receive several ecclesiastical dignities and several parish churches, contrary to the regulations of the sacred canons, on pain of both the recipient losing what he had received and the conferrer being deprived of the power to confer. On account of the presumption and covetousness of certain persons, however, none or little fruit is resulting from this statute. We therefore, desiring to remedy the situation more clearly and expressly, ordain by this present decree that whoever receives any benefice with the cure of souls attached, if he was already in possession of such a benefice, shall be deprived by the law itself of the benefice held first, and if perchance he tries to retain this he shall also be deprived of the second benefice. Moreover, the person who has the right to confer the first benefice may freely bestow it, after the recipient has obtained a second benefice, on someone who seems to deserve it. If he delays in conferring it beyond three months, however, then not only is the collation to devolve upon another person, according to the statute of the [Third] Lateran council, but also he shall be compelled to assign to the use of the church belonging to the benefice as much of his own income as is established as having been received from the benefice while it was vacant. We decree that the same is to be observed with regard to parsonages, adding that nobody shall presume to hold several dignities or parsonages in the same church even if they do not have the cure of souls. As for exalted and lettered persons, however, who should be honoured with greater benefices, it is possible for them to be dispensed by the apostolic see, when reason demands it.

ॐ No. 43. An infamous pluralist, Bogo de Clare (1291).

The Lanercost Chronicle, in *Life*, Coulton, vol. 1, pp. 54–55.

There died [1291 A.D.] in London Bogo de Clare [son of the Earl of Gloucester and Hertford], illustrious in name but not in life; whose end, as men report, was not very honourable yet accordant to his deserts; for he had held innumerable churches, and had ill governed such as Christ had bought with His trading. For he was a mere courtier, who cared not for Holy Orders but quenched the cure of souls and squandered the revenues of his churches; nor did he esteem Christ's spouse highly enough to provide the church out of her own revenues with necessary vestments untorn and undefiled; as might be proven by many profane instances, whereof I will tell one by way of example. In the honourable church of Simonburn, whereof he was rector, on the holy day of Easter, I saw, instead of a reredos[9] over the high altar, a wattle of twigs daubed with fresh cow-dung; yet that living was valued at seven hundred marks yearly. Moreover, he was so wanton and wasteful that he gave the old queen of France for a gift a lady's chariot of unheard-of workmanship; to wit, all of ivory, both body and wheels, and all that should have been of iron was of silver even to the smallest nail, and its awning was of silk and gold even to the least cord whereby it was drawn; the price whereof, as men say, was three pounds sterling;[10] but the scandal was of a thousand thousand.

[9] A carved wooden or stone screen or wall at the back of an altar.
[10] The correct price here is probably three *thousand* pounds, unless the figure refers to the cord only. By the time of his death, he held twenty-four churches or portions thereof, as well as several cathedral and collegiate prebends.

❧ No. 44. A pluralist defends himself (1366).

A. Hamilton Thompson, *The English Clergy and Their Organization in the Later Middle Ages* (Oxford: Oxford University Press, 1947), appendix 4, pp. 246–47. Trans. JS.

[*Master Roger Otery, a priest and bachelor of laws in service to the Bishop of Hereford, explained his pluralism in 1366:*]

By this document I say, adduce, and propose that I have been and still am of good life and honest demeanor, am snared in no crime or publicly defamed for any reason, am bound under no sentence of suspension, excommunication, or interdict, am most diligent regarding my secular and spiritual responsibilities, and am very strongly involved with the correction and reformation of the lives of the subjects of bishops according to the practice of the church of England and Wales just as experience teaches and has taught for many years.

The sacred canons stipulate that a good, industrious, and literate person has more ability and knowledge for administering two or even ten churches than another man has for administering one; and he knows how to minister at the altar whether he resides there or not provided that he lives well and spends what he receives from his labors fittingly. And I should add that it was and is the tradition of the English church—accustomed, practiced, and approved from time immemorial, and accepted by the Roman church—that bishops and other patrons of the English realm may provide any number of benefices, especially those without cures, to well-deserving clerics without any offense or contradiction to the apostolic see. Therefore, bearing in mind the aforesaid and other reasons, I show and make known to you by these letters the number of my church benefices and the taxes applying to them, clearly itemized and named one by one. . . .

[*He lists six benefices, five of which are sinecures, with a total value of £47 1s. 4d.*]

❧ No. 45. An unsuitable candidate: the underage Walter Paston (1479).

The Paston Letters, ed. James Gairdner, vol. 6 (London, 1904), pp. 6–7. Modernized by JS.

[February 2, 1479.]

To my Mistress Margaret Paston, at Norwich.

My worshipful mistress, I recommend me unto you, and thank you for your approved and ensured goodness evermore showed, and so I pray you to continue. I have received your letter and understand your desire, which is against the law for three causes. One is that your son Walter[11] is not tonsured,

[11]Margaret's son Walter was about twenty-three years old and studying at Oxford at the time of this letter. He died just months later in August, 1479.

in the mother tongue called *benett;*[12] another cause, he is not twenty-three years of age, which is required complete; the third, he ought of right to become a priest within twelve months after he has been made rector, without which he would need a dispensation from Rome by our Holy Father the Pope, which I am certain cannot be had. Therefore, I present not your desire unto my lord,[13] lest he would take displeasure at it, or else think your desire showed you to be greatly ignorant, which would cause him, in such matters as you shall take up with him another time, to show you the rigor of the law, which I would be loath; therefore, present another able man. Ask counsel of Mr. John Smyth, and cease your desire in this matter, for it is neither goodly nor Godly; and let not your desire be known, after my advice. Be not wroth, though I send unto you thus plainly in this matter. For I would you did as well as any woman in Norfolk, that is, with right, to your honor, prosperity, and to the pleasure of God, with you and yours, who has you in his blessed keeping.

From Hoxne on Candlemas Day.

William Pykenham.[14]

I send you again your present in the box.

---

[12] I.e., exorcist, the second highest of the four minor orders.

[13] The bishop of Norwich.

[14] A Paston family friend, he was then chancellor of the diocese of Norwich and Archdeacon of Suffolk.

4

~

The Clerical Community

T he diocese, the basic administrative unit of the church, was a region comprising parish churches, chapels, shrines, religious houses, hospitals, and schools where pastoral care could be provided in its many facets. At its center was the cathedral church where the bishop ceremonially presided over his diocese from his throne or *cathedra*. In the waning centuries of the Roman Empire, the Christian church had borrowed many of the official structures of imperial government, including the diocese, whose effective center was the *civitas*, the region's largest city or town. It was from there that the bishop, joined by his priests (the *presbyteri*) engaged in the work of preaching and sacramental ministry. In the course of this ministry, daughter churches were established to meet the pastoral needs of growing communities in the further reaches of the diocese.

These same structures endured through the medieval centuries, but as the church became increasingly involved in missionary efforts, the concept of the diocese changed in ways appropriate to new circumstances. For instance, in England, all the ancient dioceses were originally mission territories with a mother church or minster serving as a modest base for pastoral operations. With the growth of local communities of baptized Christians, churches were built, parish boundaries were gradually articulated, and clergy were assigned to their care. These parishes understandably took their shape according to the communities that comprised them: a village, a manor or local estate, a community of tenants who worked the lands of a monastery, a district or neighborhood in a town.

By the thirteenth century England's dioceses had been long established, though some parish boundaries within them were still being argued over, at times violently. Local demarcations might shift and settle differently from what they were in former times, but loyalties to a particular church or, more likely, to the saint whose dedication graced the church, remained unaltered. Also, the ownership of land whose value in tithes was a crucial fact for parish economies was, itself, not always easy to determine. But quandaries such as these have always been at the heart of litigation and dispute in the developments and changes associated with communities. Medieval parishes did not escape these frustrations.

The point here is that these communities so variable in shape, composition, and need, required ministers of the sacraments and leaders in prayer. The communities of clerics associated with parish churches varied from one place to another, based upon not only what was needed but also what was affordable. Certainly, every parish needed a curate, the one individual who was responsible for the spiritual leadership of the community (No. 56). There was a basic set of checks and balances to his authority, mostly provided by the bishop, who wielded certain real powers of intervention in the life of the parish community and curate; but the latter, for the most part, was the undisputed pastoral head of the local community.

As indicated in the last chapter, not all rectors were necessarily resident pastors. Some of them had been given their benefices because they were prominent servants of the bishop, the cathedral dean, or the king. After the late thirteenth and early fourteenth centuries brought papal reforms for clerical education, many rectors took advantage of new opportunities to leave their churches for a time and take up the life of a university student (No. 26). There were other reasons for the non-residence of rectors, but in every case they had to obtain the bishop's permission. Whatever reason they gave for leaving their churches, rectors had to provide for the pastoral care of the parish. In this case, a vicar was hired and paid out of the revenues the rector collected. The rector was responsible for finding a qualified vicar and for paying him a wage decent enough to support him in his work. This arrangement was generally workable but had to be supervised carefully by local church authorities. By the fourteenth century, most non-resident rectors were not individuals, however, but religious corporations, monasteries, and convents that had appropriated the revenues of parish churches with approval of the bishop (No. 57). These appropriations were not as unusual as they might sound. Since parishes were also economic units generating income in proportion to the vitality of the community and local markets, the revenues which flowed from them could be used to assist other religious en-

terprises in need. Poorer religious houses could make a good case for appropriating the revenues of a parish. But with this appropriation came certain
real responsibilities. The corporate rectors had to pour some of those revenues back into the local church, both in the form of hiring a vicar and in
shouldering the rector's time-honored responsibilities in the material upkeep of the church and the employment of assistant ministers. To be sure,
some of these rectors carried out their duties better than others, but this
was certain to be one of the bishop's major concerns when he visited a particular religious house or its appropriated parishes. Where corporate rectors
were deficient in carrying out their duties, a vicarage could be "ordained,"
that is, become a separate benefice. This was an administrative decision
made by the bishop and it did little to change the outward look of an appropriated parish. But the effects could be very significant in the administration and care of the parish. The vicar assigned to an ordained or perpetual vicarage was no mere hireling but a beneficed cleric in his own right,
possessing his freehold for life. He did not have to depend upon the charity
of the rectors for his income but, like any beneficed cleric, was assured a
certain portion of lands and tithes. Nevertheless, the rectors retained certain
obligations regarding the parish in the way of upkeep and, sometimes, the
employment of other clergy for service of the church.

It was unusual before the leveling effects of the late medieval plagues
for parishes to have but a single curate in residence. Depending on the size
of the parish community, its pastoral needs, and the available funds, the
curate of the place could hire as many assistant clerics or chaplains as he
needed to help shoulder the pastoral responsibilities. In fact, many of the
larger parishes had small communities of clergy of various ranks and duties
who lived in the parish manse or nearby. One of the more common clerical
assistants in parish churches was the chaplain, a priest hired by the rector
or vicar for a particular wage (No. 59). The chaplain's life could be busy,
carrying the larger pastoral burden of the parish, but his employment was
often tenuous, serving as he did at the rector's pleasure. Chaplains were
non-beneficed and potentially very mobile; they studied the market for
clerical assistance and went where the work was. They were far greater in
number than their beneficed counterparts and were, for the most part, the
pastoral workforce of the medieval church. Most chaplains were taken on
as assistant curates for a local parish, but there was another class of chaplains who became quite prominent in the later middle ages. These were
chantry chaplains who had been hired to serve an altar, founded usually by
wealthy individuals or parish collectives such as guilds, for the daily celebration of masses in memory of their souls and the souls of their departed

family members (No. 60). Chantries were extremely popular foundations, especially from the late fourteenth to the early sixteenth centuries, and were often lucrative posts for clerics. Chantry founders provided the chaplain with an annual stipend drawn from land revenues or a monetary fund. Strictly speaking, chantry chaplains had little else to do than sing their daily masses for departed souls, and this led to some resentment from their harder-working neighbors. But by the early fifteenth century, the chantry was increasingly connected with the provision of basic education for children of the parish and neighborhood. The chantrist would set up a modest school and spend a good part of his day teaching children how to read and write.

Every parish had, as well, junior clerics who offered what assistance they could in the exercise of their ministries. Parish youth who wanted to pursue a life of ministry in the church obtained holy orders as age and qualification would allow (see chapter 3). Usually, they worked in their own parishes as acolytes and lectors and took much of their ministerial and pastoral training as apprentices to the curate and chaplains in residence. After their ordination as deacons and priests, they might seek full-time employment in their home parish or join the many other priests in looking elsewhere for employment as chaplains or, for the fortunate few, promotion to a benefice.

The local curate needed the assistance of these other clerics as much as they needed the experience or the employment. When there were no other clerics around to help, one could be obtained from a neighboring parish. When curates grew old and feeble or fell sick, the local authorities might prevail upon the bishop to appoint part-time help for the parish in the form of an assistant or coadjutor (No. 62). This priest would assist the incumbent until such a time as his condition improved or a new curate was instituted to the parish.

Up to this point, our concern has been mainly with the parish community itself. While various priests and clerics were attached to the parish church, there were other ecclesiastical ministers whose work very much influenced the spiritual and religious life of local communities. The bishop of the diocese was an occasional but august presence in the parish, often brought there on visitation or to judge some dispute that had erupted into a controversy, or to ordain and confirm as his own pastoral ministry required. He would usually arrive in the company of an impressive retinue of clerics, diocesan officials, and men-at-arms to protect his travels through the wilder regions under his care. All pastoral authority resided in the person of the bishop (Nos. 47, 48) and, though local rectors and vicars possessed considerable autonomy when it came to running their parishes, the bishop had the authority to teach, judge, and correct as circumstances required (No. 50).

The bishop had extensive duties to perform in the diocese and, on occasion, beyond, when he was under some papal or metropolitan commission. His administration at home had, by our period, become increasingly demanding and complex. The need for qualified episcopal assistants was clear, and during the twelfth and thirteenth centuries a bishop's administrative household grew to match the augmentation of tasks and duties. These assistants were generally of two kinds: the first were those customary and long-established assistants who were attached to the bishop's cathedral, namely, the dean and certain chapter dignitaries and the archdeacons. Archdeacons were known as the *oculi episcopi,* or the bishop's eyes, and these local officials had special duties regarding pastoral care and the preparation, training, and examination of candidates for the clergy (No. 52). In turn, the archdeacons were served by local clerics who had been appointed their representatives in collections of parishes called deaneries. The rural dean was a modest but important person in this chain of command, linking the bishop's mandates to the clergy and parishioners of his own region (No. 54). He held local chapters of the clergy where he passed on any necessary information or instructions and was often the bishop's agent in formally inducting a new curate to his benefice.

These officials had a long tradition in local church leadership and were considered fixed in their spheres of responsibility. As episcopal administration grew more complex, the bishop needed other assistants who possessed a certain flexibility to match the nuances of administrative circumstance. Thus, by the thirteenth century, the bishop had gathered around himself an administrative *familia* or household to carry on the wide range of episcopal duties. These officers included the vicar general, the chief administrative authority after the bishop and the man who was in charge of the diocese during longer periods of his master's absence (No. 51). Other members of the household included the chief judicial officer or the *officialis,* who managed the bishop's courts, commissaries of various sorts, and the secretariat whose officers prepared and preserved important administrative records for the bishop.

All of these agents, permanent and ad hoc, assisted the bishop in his many duties regarding the government of the diocese. While few parishioners and even parish priests had much contact with these distant or itinerant officers, the pastoral order of the local church depended in large part on their vigilance and care.

Pastoral care was overwhelmingly the concern of the secular clergy, but their hegemony over the cure of souls did not go unchallenged. In the early decades of the thirteenth century, the mendicant orders began arriving in England. These friars, educated and expert in preaching and penitential matters beyond the wildest dreams of the typical parish curate, soon captured the hearts of Christians inspired by the evangelical piety of men who, by virtue of their voluntary poverty and their spiritual fervor, seemed to trod the very footsteps of the Apostles. In their early years they preached and heard confessions freely throughout the country. People sought tertiary membership in their orders, desiring to be buried, dressed in mendicant habit, in the friars' cemeteries; and they increasingly bequeathed money to them, imploring them to pray for their souls. Parish priests began complaining that the mendicants were illegally diverting income from them, depriving them of accustomed burial dues and legacies. Bad blood stained relations between the mendicant and secular clergy for the whole half century between 1250 and 1300 as the friars, still the darlings of the papacy, gained more and more papal privileges guaranteeing them the right to exercise pastoral offices that English bishops and parish priests regarded as gross encroachments on their local jurisdiction.

Finally, Boniface VIII's sensible decree *Super cathedram* (issued in 1300, briefly revoked, and then reissued in 1311) laid the legal groundwork for compromises that restored a great measure of civility between the friars and parish priests. The mendicants kept their right to preach, hear confessions, and bury the dead, but now the local bishop had to license their activities, and parish priests were not to be deprived totally of their customary burial dues (No. 64). Relations would still sometimes be rocky as one party or the other felt itself abused (Nos. 68, 69), but many parish priests must have welcomed the extra help that a band of friars passing through the village brought in preaching and hearing confessions (Nos. 65, 66, 67). Some priests still resented their presence; others surely admired—even envied—the unmatched mendicant talent for preaching the Word or soothing the guilty conscience of a sinner. While friars were never allowed to hold the cure of souls, they lent invaluable aid to the rank-and-file members of pastoral ministry.

ᴄᴠ No. 46. The life and character of a bishop: Third Lateran Council, c. 3 (1179).

Decrees, Tanner, pp. 212–13.

c. 3. Since in holy orders and ecclesiastical ministries both maturity of age, a serious character and knowledge of letters should be required, much more should these qualities be required in a bishop, who is appointed for the care of others and ought to show in himself how others should live in the house of the Lord. Therefore, lest what has been done with regard to certain persons through the needs of the time should be taken as a precedent for the future, we declare by the present decree that no one should be chosen bishop unless he has already reached the age of thirty, been born in lawful wedlock and also is shown to be worthy by his life and learning. When he has been elected and his election has been confirmed, and he has the administration of ecclesiastical property, after the time has passed for the consecration of bishops as laid down by the canons, let the person to whom the benefices which he held belong, have the free disposition of them. Further, with regard to the inferior ministries, for instance that of dean or archdeacon, and others which have the care of souls annexed, let no one at all receive them, or even the rule of parish churches, unless he has already reached his twenty-fifth year of age, and can be approved for his learning and character. When he has been nominated, if the archdeacon is not ordained deacon, and the deans (and the rest after due warning) are not ordained priests, within the time fixed by the canons, let them be removed from that office and let it be conferred on another who is both able and willing to fulfil it properly; and let them not be allowed the evasion of recourse to an appeal, should they wish by an appeal to protect themselves against a transgression of the constitution. We order that this should be observed with regard to both past and future appointments, unless it is contrary to the canons. Certainly if clerics appoint someone contrary to this rule, let them know that they are deprived of the power of election and are suspended from ecclesiastical benefices for three years. For it is right that at least the strictness of ecclesiastical discipline should restrain those who are not recalled from evil by the fear of God. But if any bishop has acted in anyone's interests contrary to this decree, or has consented to such actions, let him lose the power of conferring the foresaid offices, and let these appointments be made by the chapter, or by the metropolitan if the chapter cannot agree.

∾ No. 47. Episcopal authority in matters pertaining to the *cura animarum* and the bestowal of benefices: First Lateran Council, c. 8 (1123).
Decrees, Tanner, p. 191.

c. 8. We further resolve, in accordance with the statute of the most blessed pope Stephen, that lay persons, however religious they may be, have no power to dispose of any ecclesiastical business; but following the apostolic canons, let the bishop have the care of all ecclesiastical matters, and let him manage them as in the sight of God. Therefore, if any prince or other lay person should arrogate to himself the disposition or donation of ecclesiastical things or possessions, let him be regarded as sacrilegious.

❧ No. 48. The bishop's authority over benefices and their disposition: First Lateran Council, c. 4 (1123).

Decrees, Tanner, p. 190.

c. 4. Absolutely no archdeacon, archpriest, provost or dean may grant to anyone the care of souls or prebends in a church without the decision or consent of the bishop. Rather, as it is constituted by the holy canons, let the care of souls and the dispensing of ecclesiastical affairs remain in the decision and power of the bishop. Indeed, if anyone presumes to do something against this, or to claim for himself the power which pertains to the bishop, let him be banished from the bounds of the church.

❧ No. 49. The duties of suffragan bishops (1408).

EHD IV, No. 419, pp. 705-6.

[*A letter of appointment from Henry Bowet, Archbishop of York.*]

Henry etc., to our venerable brother the lord William by the same permission Bishop "Pharensis" [of Paros] greeting and fraternal charity in the Lord.

(1) To celebrate and confer minor orders on any of our subjects suitable for this, and for any others sufficiently recommended by their diocesans,

(2) To suspend churches, cemeteries, and altars whatsoever in our diocese which are unconsecrated or polluted by effusion of blood or semen, and to inquire about them in form of law and to inform us rightly and appropriately,

(3) To administer the sacrament of confirmation to any our subjects,

(4) To bless and consecrate portable altars . . . and chalices and patens and sacerdotal vestments,

(5) To bless, consecrate and veil abbots, monks, virgins and widows, with our previous canonical warning,

(6) To hear the confessions of any our subjects both men and women wishing to confess to you, and having enjoined on them the penance necessary for their salvation, to absolve them from their sins in all cases permitted by law and to perform and exercise the office of penitentiary,

Excepting however dispensations committed to us or to our vicar general by the Apostolic See, and apostolic mandates, and breaking into our parks or our liberties, and violations of our churches, and injuries, offences, and violences done to us or our church, incests, or perjuries in assizes which might cause disinheritance of grave poverty,

And to do, perform, exercise, expedite and rightly follow up all and singular in the foregoing items, or concerning them, or anything necessary or fitting in connection with them,

All these functions we commit to you, reverend father, in whose pure conscience and circumspect industry we confide entirely, and we give you power to act in all the above ways in our place as long as it shall please us, ratifying moreover so far as in us lies all and singular indulgences rightly conceded and afterwards to be conceded in any solemn masses.

In witness of which act our seal is appended to these presents.

Given at the castle of Cawood 29th December, in the year of our Lord 1408 and in the second year of our translation.

↬ No. 50. Episcopal statutes of Bishop Robert Grosseteste for the diocese of Lincoln (c. 1239).

Councils and Synods, pp. 265–76. Trans. JS.

Synodal Sermon

Since we, as bishop, are bound to render a good account about all of you (an account which, according to Augustine, is to speak, not to be silent; to weep when we speak and are not heard), we cannot leave unspoken those things which we believe it necessary for you to know and do.

1. Therefore, since there is no salvation for souls without obeying the Ten Commandments, we exhort you in the Lord, firmly enjoining you that every single pastor of souls and each parish priest should know the Ten Commandments—that is, the ten things commanded in the Mosaic Law—and should frequently preach and explain them to the people entrusted to him. He should also know the seven deadly sins and likewise preach to his people about how to avoid them. Furthermore, let him have at least a rudimentary understanding of the church's seven sacraments. And priests especially should know what things are required for a good confession and penance, and they should frequently teach lay people the formula for baptism in the vernacular. A priest should also have at least a simple understanding of the faith as it is contained in both the Greater and Lesser Creeds, and in the tract called *Quicunque vult* [i.e., "Whoever wishes to be saved"[1]] which is recited daily in church at Prime.

[1]See No. 73.

2. The eucharist, which is the sacrament of the Lord's Body, should be devoutly and faithfully stored and always maintained with honor in a special place which is clean and secure. And each priest should teach his people that when the saving host is elevated during the consecration of the mass they should reverently bow; they should do the same when they see the priest carrying the host to the sick. When a priest carries the host to the sick he should be dressed decently and a clean veil should be placed over the host which, with reverence and awe, he should display before him openly and with honor. The host should always be preceded by a lighted lamp since it is the splendor of eternal light. More is written in the general council about how these measures increase the faith and devotion of everyone. Along with the lamp, to venerate the Body of Christ a bell should also accompany the host so that its ringing will stir up the devotion of the faithful and they will duly adore this great sacrament. Also, priests should take great care to see to it that, due to cracks in the container where it is kept or because it has been stored too long, the holy eucharist does not become damp or moldy, which would make it either unpleasant to look at or disgusting to eat.

3. Day or night priests should be completely ready and extremely prompt to visit the sick when they require it lest due to their negligence (may it never happen!) a sick person dies without confession, communion, or the last anointing.

4. The altar cloths should be decently made and of correct size, and they should be firmly attached to the wood around the altar so that they do not move from it. Altar cloths should not be used for any other purpose except the celebration of divine services; thus, they should not be dyed nor should any other similar things be done to them.

5. Chrism-cloths should not be used for any profane purposes.

6. The divine office should be celebrated in church completely and devoutly. Specifically, readings, hymns, psalms, and those other things that are recited in church in praise of God should be said completely and thoughtfully word for word with devout attention paid to the meaning of the words so that (may it never happen!) a mutilated and dead sacrifice is not offered in place of a whole and living one.

7. And after all pastors of souls and parish priests have finished saying the divine office in church they should then diligently turn their attention to the prayers and readings of sacred scripture, so that through understanding scripture (which is their duty) they are always ready to give a satisfactory answer to every question asked them about hope and faith. Thus they should always apply their minds to prying open the teachings and inner meanings of scripture (just as a crowbar can pry open the lock on a chest)

so that through their assiduous reading—which should be their daily diet, so to speak—their prayers are nourished and grow fat.

8. Rectors of churches and parish priests should be careful to make sure that the children of their parishes are diligently taught and know the Lord's Prayer, the Creed, the Hail Mary, and how to make the sign of the cross. And because we have heard that even some adults do not know these prayers, we order that, when lay people come to confession, priests should carefully examine whether they know them and, as it is expedient, should teach them these prayers.

9. And since, as the prophet Isaiah says, those who bear the vessels of the Lord should be pure and should not touch polluted things [Isa. 52:11], earnestly cautioning you, we order that all beneficed clergy and those who are in sacred orders should shun the vice of lust and all willful impurities of the flesh, guarding the purity of their chastity.

10. No member of the clergy should take a wife. If anyone married before he entered sacred orders, he should not hold an ecclesiastical benefice, nor should he presume to perform the duties of those in sacred orders if he received them after he was married.

11. Since a priest should not only avoid evil but every appearance of evil, we strictly forbid members of the clergy to visit the convents of nuns without a clear and reasonable cause.

12. And we forbid any priest to keep a woman in his house, whether a relative or not, from which a reasonable suspicion could arise about his wrongful behavior.

13. In the book of Leviticus the Lord said to Aaron: "You shall not drink wine or anything that may make you drunk, thou nor thy sons, when you enter into the tabernacle of the testimony, lest you die" [Lev. 10:9]. Since in those times Aaron and his sons, the priests of the Old Law, represented the figure of the priest, and wine and other strong drink represented drunkenness, so also today priests ought to remain symbolically in the tabernacle day and night, keeping watch over the Lord lest they die, as it is written in Leviticus. Thus we strictly forbid beneficed clergy or anyone in sacred orders to be drunk or gluttonous or to spend time in taverns, lest they die the eternal death threatened by the law. Instead, through acts of abstinence and through their sobriety they should make themselves suitable, according to the Lord's teaching, to have the knowledge of discerning between the holy and the unholy, between the clean and unclean, and they should teach the people all the decrees of the Lord which he spoke to them through Moses [Lev. 10:10–11].

14. Also, because the priests of Levi were told that they would not have a

share of the inheritance among the sons of Israel [Num. 18:20; Deut. 10:9], so that the kindling wood of cupidity and filthy lucre could be pruned away from the church's ministers, earnestly cautioning you, we strictly order that those with benefices and those in sacred orders should not engage in secular business affairs, nor should they practice usury. Instead, they should lend money hoping for nothing in return, as the gospels teach [Luke 6:35].

15. Nor should they put churches and their belongings to farm or receive them at farm[2] except in the cases permitted by the councils.

16. In order to cut away every type of greed, we strictly forbid—not only by our ordinary powers but by special papal authority—anyone holding a benefice or in sacred orders to be appointed sheriffs or secular justices or to hold the office of bailiff through which they are required to render account to lay authorities concerning bailiwicks.

17. Also, we most strictly forbid any rector of a church to make the following sort of agreement with an assistant priest: to wit, that the priest receives the payment for celebrating annual and triennial masses instead of a fixed salary, since this sort of agreement is a clear indication that this priest is receiving a very meager payment; and it is also inevitable that either the priest fails to complete the cycle of annual or triennial masses which he has undertaken to say, or that the regular divine services in the parish church are not duly carried out.

18. Rectors of churches should pay such assistant priests a sufficient and decent salary so that the church will not lack divine services because of the inadequate maintenance of these priests, and they will not covet filthy lucre or have to beg for their living.

19. Also we strictly forbid any lay person to put to farm any land freely held by the Lord's churches—except perhaps those who serve as estate managers of these churches, and then this should be done with the license of the diocesan.

20. We forbid rectors or vicars to put church property in a lay fee outside of that church's endowment; and also we forbid them to put tithes into a lay fee instead of into that church's endowment.

21. Furthermore, we order that rents assigned to churches through the devotion of lay people for sustaining votive lights or for other pious uses in those churches should not be converted by those churches' rectors or vicars for their personal use or profit.

22. We strictly forbid priests to receive offerings from lay people after Eas-

[2]See glossary.

ter mass at which they take communion since this is a clear sign of greed and plainly harmful to the devotion of those receiving communion.

23. We also exhort them and order them not to attend the performances of mimes, jesters, or actors; nor should they play games of chance or dice, or watch others play, because, although some people consider these trivial things, according to the teachings of the church fathers, those who play such games are attending sacrifices made to demons.

24. Since a cleric ought to shine with nothing more than the splendor of Jesus Christ's humility and the perfection of the gospels (which counsel that if anyone strikes you on the left cheek, you should offer them the right one), we warn and order clerics not to carry arms. They should wear the tonsure suitable to their clerical status and their clothing should be appropriate both to their person and rank according to what the sacred councils have determined.

25. We also order, both by our authority and by special papal authority, that no one should hold multiple cures of souls for which they have not been dispensed by the Holy See.

26. Likewise, we order that the sons of those who have recently been ministers of churches who immediately succeed their fathers in that position should without question resign and the patrons should then present suitable candidates to those churches.

27. We have heard (and it grieves us terribly) that certain priests extort money from lay people for administering penance or other sacraments to them; and that others, driven by base greed, enjoin harsh penances: for instance, that a woman who has had sexual relations with a man after she has given birth but before she has been purified at church should carry an extra offering to the altar when the next woman from the same parish goes to the church to be purified. Or that someone who has committed a homicide or has arranged another's death should also make an offering for anyone else who has died in that parish. We absolutely forbid these things and others like them because they are filled with greed.

28. We forbid any priest from demanding, because of a similar kind of greed, that parishioners purchase annual or triennial masses for the dead. A priest who demands this is trying to make a profit from it.

29. We have also heard that there are certain priests who make their deacons hear the confessions of their parishioners. It is unnecessary to remind them how absurd this is since it is absolutely clear that the power of binding and loosing was not given to deacons. Priests who make their deacons do this are looking for leisure or for time to look after their secular business deal-

ings. For this reason we strictly forbid deacons to hear confessions or to enjoin penances or to administer any other sacrament which only priests are allowed to perform.

30. We wish and we order that all beneficed clergy be promoted to that sacred order which the pastoral office they were appointed to requires.

31. By special papal authority, we impress upon and order all rectors of churches and their vicars that they must be resident in their benefices, living in them in a praiseworthy and upright manner, unless there is some reasonable cause for which they have been given dispensation not to reside in their parishes.

32. In every church which has the wherewithal to support them, there should be one deacon and one subdeacon ministering to the needs of the church as is fitting. In other churches there should at least be a cleric in minor orders who is suitable and upright, and who can assist the priest in conducting divine services appropriately dressed.

33. Also we strictly order by the authority of the gospels and also with special papal indulgence that no markets should be held on sacred ground (since the Lord ejected the buyers and the sellers from the temple), so that a house of prayer will not become a den of thieves.

34. In addition to this, we order that graveyards should be satisfactorily enclosed, and that churches as well as any dwellings pertaining to them should be competently constructed according to the financial resources of the church. These churches should be decently furnished with both service books, altar plate, and vestments. The church's furnishings and its sacred vessels should be given secure and decent safekeeping at night. They should not be kept in the houses of lay people nor put under their custody unless a clear and reasonable circumstance makes this necessary.

35. Some churches have traditionally practiced the detestable custom of celebrating the Feast of Fools.[3] By the special authority of a papal rescript we absolutely forbid the house of prayer to be made into a house of mockery; the solemn nature of the feast of the circumcision of our Lord Jesus Christ should not be derided by jokes and wantonness.

36. We forbid priests to celebrate mass using wine that has soured.

37. Since whoever is a master of one art ought to attend to that art rather than to another, we order rectors of souls to attend vigilantly to the art of guiding souls, because the art of arts, as Pope Gregory the Great witnessed,

[3] A holiday of role-reversal where lower clerics usurped the positions of their superiors and parodied religious rites, usually celebrated on New Year's Day, the feast of the Circumcision. In England it was presided over by a "Lord of Misrule" or, more commonly, a "Boy-Bishop"—a minor clerk decked out in bishop's regalia.

is the guidance of souls. So that priests will not be distracted from this art, we strictly forbid any priest to study or teach civil law in schools.

38. We also order that in every church the canon of the mass should follow the rite of the local church.

39. We order that those who mount quintains[4] on wheels, or hold other contests where people fight for prizes, or anyone present at such contests should be solemnly denounced in every church. Similarly prohibited are drinking parties, called "scot-ales"[5] in the vernacular.

40. No games or secular courts should be held on sacred ground.

41. Through frequent preaching, mothers and nurses should be warned not to place their infants in bed next to them.

42. Clandestine marriages should be strictly prohibited.

43. Rectors of churches and priests should not permit their parishioners to compete with each other over whose banners should go first in the annual visitation of the mother church, because brawls and even deaths result from this.

44. Also we firmly order to be solemnly denounced in church anyone who knowingly and purposely gives lodging to the concubines of clerics unless they are simply passing through—in which case they should be cautious that a cleric known to be a fornicator is not also lodged there.

45. We add to this that lay people should not stand or sit with the clergy in the chancel of the church while divine services are being conducted. Patrons alone, however, may be allowed to do this if they do it out of reverence or for some other clear and reasonable cause.

46. Since we believe that copies of the constitutions of the Council of Oxford[6] are not available in many churches, we have directed that the beginning of that council dealing with the excommunications made in the same council in order to terrify the wicked and to restrain their evildoing be adjoined to this document. We order that these excommunications should be reviewed annually in every church, using the words which are contained in the same Council of Oxford. . . .

[*For an expanded version of these excommunications see* No. 83.]

Therefore, we wish and we order you to observe these things reverently

---

[4]A target mounted on a rotating post used for practicing tilting. Here it would seem that the target is set on a wheel that spins on its side, like a potter's wheel.

[5]A scot-ale (i.e., "ale payment") was a festival sponsored by a manorial lord, bailiff, or game warden. Villagers were forced to attend and to pay a fee for drinking the ale served there.

[6]The provincial council held in 1222 by archbishop Stephen Langton, which promulgated the decrees of the Fourth Lateran Council in England and issued other decrees repeated in subsequent English ecclesiastical legislation until the Reformation.

and strictly, just as they are ordered by canon law. Insofar as we are able and with the help of our Lord Jesus Christ we will canonically punish those who scorn or transgress these articles, if they are duly convicted of or confess to their contempt or transgression.

ᖇ No. 51. The pastoral duties of the bishop's vicar general (1408).
Reg. Chichele (St. David's), pp. 417–19. Revised WJD.

Henry [Chichele], by divine leave bishop of St. David's, to our beloved son in Christ, Master John Hiot, archdeacon of St. David's, greetings and benediction. The charge of pastoral care to which He has raised us, though unworthy, bids us while outside our city and diocese engaged in distant parts for the good of our subjects to commit safely those things which would not be easily accomplished by us and rest upon our shoulders to prudent and discreet men constituted in these parts. We therefore, fully confident in your vigilance and hard work, commit to you our functions with the power of every canonical coercion: to ask for and receive the oath of canonical obedience, and canonical obedience from every one of our subjects who is bound to this by right or custom; to celebrate a synod; to assemble the clergy and people of our city and diocese; to publish and punish the contumacious; to receive all presentations to ecclesiastical benefices, with or without cure of souls; to answer these and inquire in the usual form regarding them; to examine those presented as to their fitness, and to admit and institute them canonically in the said benefices and induct them or see to their induction into full possession of such benefices; to commit also anything regarding orders to any Catholic bishop who has the grace of the apostolic see and the exercise of his office, and to grant letters dimissory to clerics of our diocese; also, to make probations and records of the wills of all persons who die within our city and diocese and elsewhere of which the proving and recording pertain to us . . . ; also, to hear confessions of all our subjects willing to confess to you in the court of penitence and enjoin salutary penances for sins committed, and absolve them from the things which they have confessed even in cases reserved to us; to hear and determine in a due end all causes whatsoever either at the instance of a party, or *ex officio* . . . and to answer all appeals and end them canonically; to pass sentences interlocutory or definitive; and to visit the clergy and people of our city and diocese, to inquire in due form of crimes committed, to punish and reform all crimes, and to do and exercise each and every other thing necessary. . . . And we appoint you, by these letters, our vicar general in spiritualities for the period of our absence. In testimony whereof we have set the seal of our officiality to these letters. Given at London, 16 September, 1408, the first year of our consecration.

ᐁ No. 52. The archdeacon's duties: A letter from Pope Innocent III to the Bishop of Coventry and Lichfield.
Gregory IX's *Extra* 1.23,7. Trans. WJD.

Well it is that fraternal zeal has prompted you to inquire about the office of archdeacon, what things pertain to it, and how the office may assist the bishop in doing his pastoral work. And we, as far as we may, respond that the archdeacon, according to the statutes of St. Isidore, supervises subdeacons and Levites, oversees the parishes, their care and all that pertains to them, and hears the disputes of their members. Now, archpriests, who many refer to as deans, are under his jurisdiction. According to the Roman canons, the archdeacon is reckoned as first after the bishop and the bishop's vicar; he is concerned fully with the care of the clergy and their churches and delivers judgments on matters stemming from local inquests. Furthermore, Pope Clement, our predecessor, wrote in a letter that the archdeacon is the "bishop's eye," as it were, gazing over the diocese in the bishop's place, seeing what needs to be corrected and acting on it, except in matters too weighty. In such cases, he ought not resolve them in his master's absence.

We recall having stated in our own constitution on this subject that the archdeacon is also responsible for the induction of clergy to benefices and other dignities as well. He is also to examine clerical candidates for holy orders. In matters regarding institution to benefices, he is to examine nominees to ecclesiastical benefices first and then present them to the bishop.

Finally, in your letter, you asked whether rural deans, whose positions are temporary, should be appointed, dismissed, or transferred on your own authority, by the archdeacons or both of you. To this we respond briefly: since, under the authority of imperial decree, what affects all should be approved by all, and, since the dean's office is an aid [to both bishop and archdeacon], the two should appoint and remove.

ᐁ No. 53. To a negligent archdeacon from Bishop Simon de Gandavo (1301).
EHD III, No. 147, pp. 722-23.

To the archdeacon of Salisbury because of the manifest defects in the chancel of the church of Urchfont discovered by his lordship.— Coming in person lately to the church of Urchfont to proclaim the word of God we found the chancel of that place unroofed so much that if then rain, snow or hail had fallen even lightly there would have been no more convenient place in it to celebrate the solemnities of the mass than under the open sky; in which case it certainly behooves our solicitude to make clear the default of the rector of the place and we cannot commend your diligence. Furthermore, we have found that the aforesaid rector without our leave has not only left the aforesaid church, but, in addition, from the time when he obtained possession of it, as is set out above, he has always been absent and has not hitherto come near it, but without license sending to other places the revenues and offerings belonging to the rectory of that church, and by means of an illegal contract he has granted and still grants it to a layman to farm yet by some fraudulent subtlety of language inserted in the said contract by a change not of substance but of wording, as by the substitution of the word farmer for layman, to the peril of his own safety and the no mean prejudice of the parishioners of the said church and the scandal of very many. Since therefore we cannot with averted eyes let them go without correction, we, by the tenor of these presents, commit the aforementioned things to your zealous attention and order you in our place and by our authority for the aforesaid and certain other legitimate causes to sequestrate the aforesaid fruits, revenues and offerings and have them kept in safe sequestration by the vicars of that or neighboring places until you have orders from us touching on these things. Farewell. Given at Poterne, 11 December A.D. 1301, and in the fifth year of our consecration.

∾ No. 54. A rural dean is appointed (1523).

Reg. Boothe (Hereford), pp. 137–38. Trans. WJD.

On the twenty-fourth day of the month of January, in the aforesaid year and place [Prestbury, Worcestershire, 1523], the reverend, etc. [bishop], ordered and appointed, by these letters, Sir John Allen, vicar of Ditton, as rural dean of Stottesden, with authority to hold inventories of all goods and debts of any who die within the said deanery and to do any and all things that have pertained to the office of rural dean from ancient times and to put into effect whatever letters or mandates he receives.

∾ No. 55. Admonitions to rectors, vicars, and curates: Archbishop John Pecham's injunctions to the parish clergy of Canterbury (1287).

Councils and Synods, pp. 1079–80. Trans. JS.

Though nothing is more precious on earth than the cure of souls since Christ offered himself on the cross for this alone, nowadays nothing is reckoned more vile among many people. Indeed, there are countless people who, boldly seizing church property, reap the flesh where they have sown not the spirit but rather scandal. To serve up a remedy for this sacrilege, since nothing is more despised in God's sight than this, in virtue of strict obedience we order you to see to it that the articles enclosed in the letter we are sending you be written clearly and plainly in the missal or some other book of every church subject to your jurisdiction in our diocese of Canterbury. They should be solemnly and publicly recited so that they will frequently cross the minds of the ministers of these churches, and they should be shown to officials making visitations of these churches. Once written, no one should dare to erase any of these articles in whole or part under pain of excommunication, into which we wish anyone violating them to fall. Wherever we happen to be in our diocese or province, you must send us your letters patent describing what you have done regarding this matter by the feast of the Assumption of the Glorious Virgin [August 15]. Given at Otford, July 8, 1287, the ninth year of our episcopate. Similar letters have been sent to the commissary [general] of Canterbury and to each dean of exempt jurisdictions.

Articles to be observed by rectors and vicars of the diocese of Canterbury and its jurisdictions

We, Brother John, by divine permission humble minister of the Church of Canterbury and Primate of all England, order that the articles noted below be inviolably observed in virtue of obedience and duly under oath by all rectors, vicars, and anyone else bearing the cure of souls in our diocese or in other places subject to our immediate jurisdiction.

First, they should perform their church offices with all the reverence and decency with which worthy ministers can celebrate them at the appropriate times without interruption.

Second, they should faithfully provide the flock entrusted to them with spiritual offices: namely, preaching the word of God and dispensing the sacraments of the church, especially hearing confessions; and where they are unable to do this adequately, they should call in pious men specially appointed for this task to help them.

Third, they should take special care to provide the poor and indigent in their care with bodily necessities insofar as their church's resources allow, drawing at least on what is left after their own needs and those of their assistants are met; they should offer the hospitality that canon law calls for.

Fourth, they should not enter into any contract privately or publicly with any literate or illiterate person in any court whatsoever which could injure their successors' spiritualities or temporalities by hindering their ability to forward their church's rights.

Fifth, they should maintain the buildings of the rectory or vicarage in a decent state insofar as the church's resources allow.

Sixth, out of respect for God and justice they should try to recover any church property or liberties alienated in violation of common law.

Seventh, they should take pains to preserve the property and the rights of the church entrusted to them for the sake of the people, not alienating it or otherwise causing it any serious damage.

Eighth, they should not sell the fruits of their churches together all at once without our special license, because this kind of transaction, which resembles farming a church, sweeps away every pious office and puts those tithes up for sale which should be used to provide necessities for the poor dwelling in God's house.

We order every church to have these articles written plainly, distinctly, and clearly inside its missal or some other book so that they will frequently come to the notice of the church's ministers. They should be shown to officials during the visitations of the church; those doing otherwise will be seriously punished.

∞ No. 56. A parishioner remembers the curates of Braughing, Hertfordshire (1514).

Peter Heath, *The English Clergy on the Eve of the Reformation* (London: Routledge and Kegan Paul, 1969), appendix 2(b), pp. 207–9. Trans. JS.

[*This is the testimony of John Broke, a maltman from the parish of Braughing, regarding his vicar Robert Philippson, who was accused of withdrawing material support for the parish chaplain.*]

To the first article of the libel he says and deposes that from the time he reached the age of discretion, that is, since nearly fifty years ago, the vicar was obliged to reside there in the vicarage together with another chaplain supported at his expense to the purpose and end specified in this article.

To the second article he swears under oath that fifty years ago or more he knew a certain vicar of the said vicarage, whose name he now does not remember, so he says, who afterwards was the rector of the parish church of Fenchurch in London; he does not know how long he had been the vicar of Braughing. But he says that this same vicar personally resided there together with his chaplain, whom he supported at his expense, whose name he does not at the moment remember; he says that he first learned his letters from that priest. And after that a certain vicar named Master Sowthwell succeeded to the vicarage there, and he too likewise resided there with his chaplain similarly supported by him. He does not remember now how long he remained vicar there. Sir Thomas Miton succeeded Master Sowthwell as vicar of the said vicarage, who likewise resided there with his chaplain whom he supported at his expense. But how long he continued as vicar there he does not now remember, so he says. After him, a certain Sir Hugo Ysaac, who was born in the said village, became vicar and remained there for six or seven years, as he recalls, and he also resided there with his chaplain, who was named Sir John and was born up north, and with whom the witness also learned some grammar, making good progress under his instruction, so he says. After him came a certain Sir William Sawge, as he recalls, who was vicar there for twenty years. And in the same way he resided there along with whomever was his chaplain for the whole time he was the incumbent. But he stopped the maintenance of his chaplain and so the parishioners there brought a suit against him for non-support of his chaplain before the reverend father Lord [Thomas] Kempe, then the bishop of London [1448–89]. As a result of this suit, by the order of the said reverend father, this same Sir William Sawge once more began to hire and maintain a chaplain. And then a certain Sir John Kent succeeded him as vicar and was vicar there for seven or eight years, so he recalls; and while he was there he had with him one chaplain, his associate or coadjutor, whom he supported at his expense. And he says that this Sir John Kent went to Rome with Master David Williams who was then Master of the Rolls. While he was away he sent two chaplains hired and supported at his expense to carry out divine services there. His surrogate was a certain Sir Richard Taillour who was vicar there for around eight years, who likewise had a chaplain with him there, and he himself was personally resident there until he died. He further says that after Sir Richard Taillour, a relative of a certain Master Yarford of London was vicar there for half a year, but he does not remember his name, so he says. This man spent his time studying at Oxford and only a parish priest was resident and ministering the cure there. After him, Master Bulgen, the chaplain of the reverend father Lord Richard Fitzjames, the current bishop of London [1506–22], arrived, who was vicar there for a year and a half, as he recollects; and while he was there he resided together with his chaplain whom he hired and supported. But for the most part he spent his time at the household of the said reverend father, so he says. And then after he resigned the vicarage, Sir Thomas Percy, then prior of the monastery of Holy Trinity, London, obtained and occupied the vicarage and personally resided there together with the parish chaplain and also with an assistant chaplain whom he hired and supported at his expense. And when he was absent, there was a parish priest and one canon resident there. Afterwards a certain Master Oressell was vicar there for fourteen years, who after taking possession of the vicarage did not personally reside there, but only hired a parish priest, so he says. Finally the current vicar, Sir Robert Philippson, was instituted as vicar there who has personally resided there for a definite time since the beginning of his incumbency, and he too has a chaplain whom he supports at his expense. And the witness says that he has reported the above based on his own witness and hearing. Furthermore, he says and deposes that he has heard it said from older and more mature people there, in whom he puts trust, that once there was a certain vicar there, a good man whom the parishioners so loved because of his virtue and kindness that they did not require him to personally support a chaplain during the first year of his residency. But after a year had passed they told him that he was obliged to provide support for one chaplain who was also to be personally resident there, and that they had written evidence and documents bearing this out. When he heard this, he thanked them for their kindness and good will toward him, but if this obligation was his responsibility, he was not satisfied that they had not informed him about this from the outset. And so he made amends and hired and supported two chaplains there at his own expense, inasmuch as he had not done this during the time before he was personally resident there—so he says he heard them say. Furthermore he says that the current parishioners of Braughing have evidence or documents with a seal which make it clear that the incumbent vicar is bound to provide support for a chaplain as is specified in the first and second articles; he knows this from his own witness and knowledge, so he says.

ᗡ No. 57. Appropriation of a parish to a monastic house (1318).
Reg. Halton (Carlisle). *Bishop's Register*, p. 70. Revised by JS.

To all the sons of Holy Mother Church to whom these present letters may come, John by divine pity bishop of Carlisle sends eternal greetings in the Lord. Know all of you by the inspiration of charity and piety, that we have regard and consideration for the alms and the hospitable reception of paupers the support of which we know to be the daily duty of the religious men the prior and convent of St. James of Warter of the diocese of York, both in the place where they live as in their church of Askham of our diocese which they hold for their own uses (at which men both well known and strangers and the poor of many nations and places commonly come together). We also have consideration for the other works of piety which they perform, and we wish to compensate them for the destruction, laying waste, and devastation which they sustain and hitherto have sustained on account of the hostile invasion of the Scottish enemies of the kingdom of England and the depredations of others, by which they are greatly impoverished and even destitute. Directing, therefore, our thoughts and the gaze of charity towards them for the relief of the foregoing, so that they may be better able to sustain their said works of charity, we concede to the same religious men the prior and convent aforesaid and to their monastery, the patronage over the church of Bartor in our diocese upon the resignation or death of the current rector of the same church or when the church falls vacant in any other way whatsoever, to be held canonically for their own use for all time: namely, when the present rector of the church resigns or dies or the church itself falls vacant in any other way whatsoever, the said religious themselves or their proctor shall be permitted to seize lawfully the same church and to enter into possession of it and to retain it for their own uses as above said, without asking for license and consent of us and our successors or of any persons whatsoever. With this proviso: that a suitable portion (consisting of one-third part of the true worth of the said church according to our valuation, based on the land, meadow, property, and revenues of that church along with half of the manor of the said church) be assigned for a perpetual vicar to serve the same church and to support the ordinary expenses of that church. However, the vicars for the time being shall be content with this portion. We specially reserve forever the collation of that church, when it will be vacant, to us and to our successor bishops as a recompense for the injuries to the rights of our church of Carlisle from this time onward; and we will and ordain that both the said religious and the vicars for the time being shall recognise and support from their portions half the extraordinary burdens attaching to that church in proportion to their allowances. But the said vicars will support as of old all the ordinary burdens whatsoever arising out of or touching that church at whatever times they may arise. In testimony of which matter we have caused these our letters patent, strengthened by the fortification of our seal, to be written to the said prior and convent. Given at York, 23rd November, in the year of grace 1318.

ᴏⱳ No. 58. Ordination of a vicarage (1304).

The Worcester *Liber Albus*, ed. James M. Wilson (London: SPCK, 1920), pp. 79–83.

To all members of Holy Mother Church to whose knowledge this writing may come, brother William [Gainsborough], by divine permission bishop of Worcester, everlasting salvation in the Lord.

We make it known by these presents to all of you that recently we found that the church of Child's Wickham in our diocese, which under the title of appropriation had been applied to the personal needs of the men of religion, the abbot and convent of Bordesley of the Cistercian order, by the lord Godfrey of good memory our predecessor, was destitute of the solace of a vicar; and that no sufficient provision for the support of a vicar had been arranged by our predecessor or by anyone else, or was in any way existing. We being anxious to keep in view that the said parish should suffer no loss; and that the souls of the parishioners should be provided for; anxious also to obey canonical laws as we are bound to do; having first obtained the written and explicit submission of brother J. the abbot, and the convent of the said place, sealed by their seal and now in our custody, do make order henceforth that a vicar shall be appointed in that church with whom will rest the cure of souls, and who should reside there continually; and for his support in the aforesaid church of Wykewane[7] we make order as follows:

We . . . after inquiry made in accordance with our mandate by trustworthy men, rectors, vicars, chaplains, and laity in sufficient numbers, men who were likely to have the fullest knowledge of the true value of all sources of income, sworn and straitly charged to report the true value of all the income of the said church, and of every particular of its income, such as it produces in ordinary years, do hereby order, decree, appoint, and will that the support of suitable sustentation for the perpetual vicar whose duty it is to serve the said church shall consist of the payments written below.

To wit, of a certain area in the township of Wykewane, in which is situated a certain house called the priest's house, with all the area adjacent to it; and of a certain garden defined on the western side of the rectory manse by hedges and ditches, as are now included, lying between the manse on one side and the pool of the watermill on the other, to be satisfactorily built by the abbot and the convent before St. John the Baptist's day [24 June] next occurring; and of tithes, and other payments to the said church written below.

That is to say, of the tithe of wool, milk, calves, young pigs, geese, eggs, honey and bees, gardens, curtilages, land dug with spade, doves, mills of every kind, flax, hemp.

Also of all mortuary fees save only those which have to be paid in live animals.

Also of offerings of all kinds at the altar, annuals, trentals, oblations for the dead and in general all small tithes and contributions to the altar by whatever name either now or at a later time they may be described.

Also of the tenth of meadow land hitherto paid in money.

Also of one quarter of wheat, and of one quarter of barley, pure and clean grain, to be received from the grange of the abbot and convent in the town of Wykewane every year in future on St. Martin's day in the winter.

We also ordain and decree that the said abbot and convent and their successors for ever, shall pay to the vicar for the time being of the aforesaid church of Wykewane sixty shillings sterling, at the times named below, viz.,

[7]Child's Wickham.

on the feast of the Purification of the glorious Virgin, twenty shillings; on the feast of the Annunciation, twenty shillings; and on the feast of the Holy Trinity, twenty shillings.[8]

We further order and decree that the said abbot and convent shall repair, rebuild, or reroof the chancel, whenever it shall be necessary, and shall for the future provide sufficient books in the same.

We further order and decree that the vicar for the time being shall entertain in future the archdeacon of the place, and besides his procuration shall pay him annually half a mark sterling, on the feast of the Purification of the glorious Virgin; and that he shall be bound to find linen, vestments, and other ornaments necessary for divine service in the chancel, and also to provide a competent clerk.

We also ordain that both the said abbot and convent and the said vicar and their successors shall always acknowledge extraordinary claims from time to time, and bear their share, to be divided as in future may be decided.

To this ruling we hereby add that the archdeacons of the place and their officials for the time being shall, notwithstanding any privilege whatever obtained or to be obtained by the said abbot and convent and their successors, possess the free power to correct, punish, and otherwise exercise archdiaconal powers, as they have been accustomed to exercise them in their own time and that of their predecessors over the transgressions and sins of the parishioners of the said church, and also of the ministers and servants of the said abbot and convent, if committed in the parish itself, and those of all others of whatever state and condition, who have been guilty in the parish or in the rectory manse.

That this our ruling may have its due result in every detail, and not be exposed to blame in the future, we ordain that we, and the archdeacon of the place, and our successors, and our officials, shall possess the power, without troublesome judicial proceedings, or any form of law, or any warning given, of compelling, when occasion requires, the said abbot and convent and their successors to observe all the foregoing, if in any respect, which may God forbid, they wish to infringe our ruling; and to satisfy in the matter of losses or any interests those who may be interested in this matter, by sentences of suspension, excommunication, and interdict, or any other ecclesiastical censure, and by the sequestration of all their property, wherever found, whether in the parish itself or elsewhere in the diocese.

We reserve for ourselves and our successors four marks sterling as procuration, from the income of the said abbot and convent in the said church,

<hr/>

[8] I.e., on February 2, March 25, and (according to the year) a date in May or June.

to be paid every year in future, to those who are appointed by us or our successors to visit the church, under penalties notified above.

We reserve also for ourselves and our cathedral church of Worcester the dignity in all matters due to the bishop and the cathedral, and that of the archdeacon for the time being.

Given at Alvechurch, the 3rd of the Ides of January [January 11], A.D. 1304, in the year of our consecration.

ᴄᴡ No. 59. Parish chaplains and their duties: episcopal rules for the clergy of Lynn (1373).

Norfolk Record Office, Norwich, Dean and Chapter Norwich, Episcopal Charters (R235C) Box 2, No. 4385. Trans. JS.

Henry [Despenser], by divine permission bishop of Norwich [1370–1406], sends greetings, grace, and blessing to his beloved sons in Christ, the prior and subprior of the parish church of St. Margaret in our town of Lynn, to the parochial chaplains of the chapel of St. Michael and the chapel of St. James in the same town, and to all the chaplains and clerics associated with this church and these chapels in the said town of Lynn.

Among the concerns of our office we should especially take care that church personnel live upright lives, that they devoutly and vigilantly say the divine office at the proper times and places, and that they observe the rules just as we have lawfully decreed them.

[1] Therefore, we ordain and decree and, by decreeing, we direct that the priests and clergy, each and every one, appointed to celebrate divine services in our town of Lynn, for as long as they happen to remain in any sort of service, should bear themselves honorably in deed, behavior, and way of life, completely refraining from quarrels and disputes, from taverns, public entertainments, and other vanities and unlawful things from which scandal may arise. And particularly they should not be abusive or talkative while divine services are being celebrated in the aforesaid church and chapels, which sets a bad example for lay people whom they should instruct not by their bad habits, but rather by their devoted service to God.

[2] Also we order and decree that each chaplain and cleric should be present dressed in a surplice during the celebration of divine services every day and feast day at the church or chapels where they serve, according to the need of each church. We especially order that they be present at matins, vespers, processions, and the mass of the day on great solemnities. They should be present dressed in a surplice every Sunday during the mass and at processions and at vespers, unless there is some reasonable excuse—namely,

they should probably be excused if they are in the service of their lords or for other evident reasons.

[3] On the Sundays and feast days during which parishioners are legally obliged to attend divine services (namely, matins, the canonical hours, vespers, and the parishioners' public mass), we forbid each and every priest to leave the choir from the time of vespers until the saying of vespers in the chapels or side chapels before evening services are finished for that day unless they have the special permission of the curate.

[4] Also we decree and order each anniversary chaplain to show obedience at least once a year to the prior or subprior then in office; namely, before they celebrate divine services in the said church or chapels they should perform a physical act of obedience[9] and they should offer a physical guarantee that, to the best of their ability, they will completely preserve unharmed the parochial church of St. Margaret together with its annexed chapels, by not seizing or holding anything at all which ought to pertain to the churches or to the office of its guardians, whether by appropriating for their own or for another's use required offerings and candles, or by usurping other things that pertain to the curate or to these churches without the special license of the prior or at least of the curate.

[5] We also decree that the aforesaid priests and ministers of divine services should sing the daily lessons clearly and distinctly, and they should wear a surplice. They should read the lesson in order, and should say the whole divine office devoutly and humbly.

[6] We also decree that all priests celebrating services in the aforesaid church and chapels should be obedient and attentive to celebrate the mass with singing, to read the gospels and epistles, and to baptize children as often as it is necessary and they are so requested by the curate unless they are excused because they are in service to their lord or for some other reasonable cause.

[7] Furthermore, we forbid any priest to be allowed to celebrate services in the aforesaid church or chapels unless he has shown letters of ordination and recommendation to the prior, and he has been examined by the lord prior, acting on our behalf.

[8] We likewise forbid any priest to presume to celebrate mass in the church or the chapels while the word of God is being preached to the people there, or while community matters are being explained by the parish chaplains on Sundays, or while prayers are being said according to custom. But

[9]I.e., kissing the hand, etc.

these priests may celebrate at other appropriate times at the will of the curate.

[9] We also forbid any chaplain to presume to celebrate mass before the Preface of the high mass is completed during major feast days (especially Christmas Day, Easter, the Ascension, Pentecost, and the Assumption of the Blessed Mary) and other feast days on which parishioners, because of their devotion or out of obligation, are accustomed to make offerings to God in the aforesaid church or chapels during high mass.

[10] Also, no priest should presume to administer holy water or to consecrate and administer blessed bread to any parishioners of the said church and chapels, or to visit sick parishioners with the gospel book, or read these to them in the manner of a curate, or do anything which is recognized as belonging to the office of the curate unless he is so requested by the curate and he does this with the curate's special permission.

[11] We also forbid any stipendiary priests or anniversary priests to presume to hear the confessions of any of the parishioners of our town of Lynn, either lay people or clergy, or even of a priest, without seeking and obtaining the special license of the prior.

[12] We also forbid any priest or anyone else to hold schools or admit children [pueros] for instruction in the same church or chapels lest when the children are crying while being whipped, divine services are interrupted and the people's devotion is more easily distracted.

[13] We also forbid each and every anniversary chaplain celebrating divine services in the church or the chapels to celebrate masses for the purification of women after their childbirth. Nor should they lead into the church any women coming for purification unless the curate has specially requested them to do this.

[14] Under pain of major excommunication (which those violating the above rules will incur after they have been given canonical warning) we forbid each and every priest celebrating divine services in the said church and chapels to use these regulations, which we have made and collected here with the thought of increasing devotion to God, to sue or slander the prior or his curates in the presence of lay people or elsewhere; nor should they inflict injury on the prior or his chaplains because of these regulations or in any other way.

[15] And because it is empty and pointless to make and write these sorts of constitutions or statutes unless they will be obeyed by those for whom they are made, we direct and order you, the prior or subprior of the said church and annexed chapels, firmly enjoining you by virtue of your holy obedience, that three times every year and as many other times as you

deem suitable, accompanied by our official at Lynn, you assemble or cause to be assembled before you by the authority of the present document each and every chaplain who celebrates any kind of divine services in the said town, and also each and every minister of the said church and its annexed chapels. You should carefully inquire about their failings in regard to the points mentioned above. And if you find anyone guilty of these things, especially if they have perjured themselves, acting as our deputy and wielding our authority bind them with the chain of suspension from celebrating divine services, from which we do not wish them to be absolved until they have promised under oath henceforward to observe with complete and humble obedience everything mentioned above down to the last detail.

To carry out all of these things we entrust to you our assistants until we order them to return to us. In addition, we especially reserve to us the power to increase, decrease, renew, or cancel everything pertaining to what is written above down to the last detail.

In witness to all of the above we have attached our seal to this document. Given at Gaywood, June 17, 1373 A.D., the fourth year since our consecration as bishop.

No. 60. The founding of a chantry (1407).

The Medieval Records of a London City Church (St. Mary at Hill), A.D. 1420–1559, ed. Henry Littlehales, EETS o.s. 128 (1905). Modernized by JS.

[*Since founding a chantry required setting aside rents from parcels of land in perpetuity in order to provide a salary for each consecutive chaplain of the chantry, legal instruments of chantry foundation were often quite lengthy and detailed, describing not only each parcel of land and its income, but also the daily duties of the chantry priest. But the basic formula for founding a chantry could also be contained fairly briefly in a last will. In this excerpt from his testament (1407), the London merchant John Weston makes provision for a perpetual chantry established on his and his family's behalf.*]

. . . I also give and bequeath, after the decease of my said wife Joanna, all the aforesaid tenements and their appurtenances to God and to the church of St. Mary at Hill, and to Thomas Atherston, now parson of the same church, and to his successor parsons of the same church forevermore, and to the churchwardens and other parishioners of the said church forever, therewith to do and fulfill my will described below. That is to say, to pay from the income and profits of the said tenements and their appurtenances when they shall come into their hands after the decease of my wife Joanna, annually forever six marks sterling to help support a priest—an honest man—to sing divine services in the said church of St. Mary at Hill at the altar of St. John the Baptist there, for my soul and the soul of the said Joanna my wife, and the souls of our fathers and mothers, and of all the souls for whom we are obliged to pray, and for all Christian souls, so that always the parishioners of the said church of St. Mary at Hill will fulfill the full and complete support of such an honest priest to sing the divine service in the form aforesaid. . . . And I will and ordain that the said priest be chosen by the said churchwardens and by two other worthy men of the same parish for the time being. And I will that the said priest be an honest man of good reputation. And that the said priest be in the said church at matins, mass, evensong, and at the *Salve regina* with the collect and the *De profundis,* and at all other canonical hours as it is befitting. And if the same priest so chosen behaves dishonestly, then I will that he be removed from service by the said wardens and the parishioners and another honest priest chosen by them be put in his place, and to do so from time to time as the case arises. . . .

∾ No. 61. The settlement of a dispute between two chantry chaplains (1450).

EHD IV, No. 443, pp. 735–36.

This is the award given by the reverend father, Thomas, Prior of Christ Church [Canterbury], and Master Richard Cost and Sir John Chamberleyn, for all manner of matters pending between Master William Scarborgh and Sir William Dyolet, which award to be faithfully kept the said Master William and Sir William have solemnly promised in the hand of the said prior, on the word of a priest.

First, that Master William and Sir William Dyolet have a man in common, to serve them both equally, as it has been the custom of old time, in doing all the work that belongs to them in common, always remaining with the incumbent who is home. And each of them is to have a child to serve him at his meals, and to go with him, and hear from him what he orders.

Also that Master William and Sir William contribute equally to all that is needful to the repairing of household stuff, and that they pay equally for such stuff when need shall require at any time. Also that the due hours of their meals be kept; that is to say at ten o'clock on the flesh day and five at supper, and on fasting day at eleven; so that there be no preventing of the due hour without reasonable cause, which is to be notified in person, each to the other, as the cause requires. Also, that William and Sir William have assigned between them reasonable hours for saying their services, as their virtuous occupation requires, that is to say, at seven in the morning and at three in the afternoon, so that neither of them is to be delayed by the other

... and if one of them be prevented so that he may not come, then the other is to proceed and say his service as soon as the hour is passed.

Also that all debates, trespasses, injuries, and hurts and all demands by way of debt or plea or otherwise, be pardoned and remitted and relaxed, and forgiven; and true friendship be had between the said parties ... and if it should befall that one of them should be ill-advised in word or deed, that then the other fellow shall bear with him, and leave and depart from his presence at that time. Also, that the said parties restrain their tongues from all unclean language and shameful word and unkindly word, which is the root of all debates between man and man, on pain of 6s. 8d. the first time and 13s. 4d. the second time, and 20s. the third time, and so from time to time to multiply the penalty according to the quantity of the offence; so that the fines be kept in the hands of the said father prior, and expended by the decision of my lord of Canterbury; and also on pain of removing the one who shall offend from his livelihood, by exchange or otherwise, by the will of my said lord of Canterbury, according to the form of their foundation and ordinance.

∾ No. 62. A coadjutor is appointed for a blind rector (1298).
Reg. Halton (Carlisle), p. 113. Trans. WJD.

John, etc., to his beloved son in Christ, Master W. Bonkes, greetings. Having the deepest confidence in your honesty, hard work and excellent and praiseworthy judgment, and urged on for the sake of justice, we appoint you coadjutor by these letters and grant you wardship of our beloved son in Christ, the reverend W. de C., rector of the church of Morton in our diocese, who, most sadly, has lost his sight, to relieve him and provide care for the goods of his church. We firmly enjoin upon you that you hold William, who has always governed himself and his goods well, with care and discretion so that we may regard your person and your reputation with increased grace and favor. The terms of this letter shall stand for as long as William lives. Given at Graystoke, on the kalends of August [August 1], in the year of our Lord, 1298.

∾ No. 63. The parish clerk and the sexton (c. 1442–83 and 1540s).
Edwin Freshfield, "Some Remarks upon the Book of Records and History of St. Stephen, Coleman Street in the City of London," *Archaeologia* 50 (1887): 17–57. Modernized by JS.

STATUTES [c. 1442–83] of the office of clerks and how they should behave toward curates, priests, and all parishioners.

First, clerks in their office shall give sufficient guarantee to the curate

and churchwardens that they will guard all books, all vestments, all ornaments, and see to the altar cloths, including their washing and mending, as
if they were their own.

Next, they shall be obedient to the curate and to all the priests in the
church, giving them reverence and being ready day and night and at all
times to go gladly with the curate or his deputy to visit the sick and to help
in administering the Sacrament. Also they shall be diligent and ready daily
both holidays and workdays to attend all divine services that are held in the
church of St. Stephen, not quarreling or talking during the service, but being an exemplar of devotion.

Also they shall be ready to provide the books, vestments, chalice, and
all other necessary things to the curate, to the morrow-mass[10] priest, and to
all other priests of the said church; that is to say: to ring three peals with the
smallest bell for the morrow mass, and before the last peal to warn the morrow-mass priest and ask him if he should ring the final peal. He should do
the same for the curate or his deputy on Sundays and holidays, following
the good custom of London.

Also, during the summer they shall open the church doors at six o'clock
and provide fresh water, wine, and bread. They shall ring the call to morning
mass during summer at five o'clock, and in winter at half an hour before six
so that mass can be said at seven.

Also, wearing a surplice, they shall help the morrow-mass priest to say
mass, and also high mass daily. And since no other priest in the church may
say mass at the side altars at his own will except the curate, one of the parish
clerks shall help him say mass or see that he has a server. They shall be ready
to ring the call to all types of divine services at the due hour assigned by the
curate or his deputy following the usage and customs of the City of London;
they shall not ring the last peal until the curate or his deputy is present. They
shall sweep clean all the images and glass windows of the church twice a
year at Easter and at the feast of the Translation of St. Stephen [August 4];
and they shall maintain the footpaths in the churchyard, and allow no grave
or pit to be dug along the procession way without great need under fine of
twelve pence.

Also every Sunday after matins are said they shall be ready to get water
and salt and to cut the holy loaf (2s. ½p.) and a half loaf for the slices under
pain of fine of one penny to be paid to the church.

They shall oversee the profits accruing to the curate in offerings of wax,
wine, bread, offerings made for purifications after childbirth, and in all

---

[10]The first mass of the day.

other rights and payments that pertain to God's altar, increasing and multiplying at their power.

They shall encourage no discord nor arguments nor ill-feelings between the curate and parishioners or any other priest. And if they hear about any conspiracies or plots or slanders against the curate or any of the priests associated with the church, they shall reveal these and the names of the people so plotting to the curate with all haste in confidence.

Also they shall "be obedient in all lawful things" to all the parishioners, and they shall be courteous in their bearing and behavior. They shall answer to both high and low as servants and members of the church of God, asking them amiably for their quarterage and incidental payments, and other things that rightfully belong to them. If any man or woman will not pay his or her dues, they shall inform the curate and the churchwardens who shall fix a remedy with the grace of God.

And if any person breaks this good and godly ordinance, may the indignation of Almighty God fall on him. Amen.

Duties of the Sexton [1540s][11]

Also the sexton shall sweep the church and its aisles at least once every week and sprinkle water on the ground to remove the dust. Also he shall light the candles every Sunday and holy day in the year and put them out again when it is time. Also he shall ring curfew with one bell and the call for help when it is rung with more. Also he shall pump the organs every Sunday and holy day in the year. Also he shall carry the cross in processions and carry holy water every Sunday and ceremonial fire when it is required. Also he shall dig the graves for dead bodies deep enough to avoid corrupting the air, that is to say four feet deep for men and women and three feet deep for children. Also he shall sweep the church roof four times a year, the church supplying the brooms and poles. Also when any procession is scheduled.

[*The text ends abruptly, but there is no indication that it is incomplete.*]

Duties of the Two Clerks [1540s]

Also they shall clean the baptismal font and fill it again with clean water twice a year at Easter and Pentecost and at other times if it is required.

Also every week they shall certify to the curate and the churchwardens

---

[11]Though these next texts both date from the latter part of Henry VIII's reign, his reform of the English church had not progressed so far that these customs would be much different from pre-Reformation practices.

all the names and surnames of those who were married, christened, or buried in the parish that week, under the pain of a one penny fine to be paid to the church.

Also they shall keep the property of the church committed to their custody in the best condition, saving it from harm or loss to their utmost power.

Also the said clerks should never be unavailable, but one of them should always be ready to help the curate in ministering whatever sacraments and sacramentals are needed and to notify him when he is needed. None of the clerks shall go or ride out of town without special license from the vicar and the churchwardens.

And every Sunday and other holy days they shall help the sexton ring the second summons to matins in due time, and to the mass at evensong, and during Lent to compline; in the absence of the sexton they shall ring curfew.

Also they shall daily bring forth the books that belong in the choir and return them again for their safeguard since they are responsible for them. On principal days and other feast days they shall bring forth the copes, vestments, and apparel for the altars in the church, with the ornaments to be set on the side altars. They shall remove them when it is time and return the said ornaments to themselves for safekeeping.

Also they shall help the curate and priest with their copes and see that fire is made ready for the censers before it is needed. Also they shall seat the children who serve in the said choir. They must light the tapers that go with the censers and see that they are taken to the choir to be censed, and many more small things such as singing and reading and preparing the books and turning their pages to the divine service before it begins, in accordance with a laudable and ancient custom that has been done in the past.

Also they shall carry the holy water every Sunday in the year. Also the clerk shall determine, collect, and take to the church all such incidental payments that belong to the churchwardens. And if a payment falls due while the churchwarden is out of town, the clerks shall bring them to the acting churchwardens.

❧ No. 64. Papal regulations on the rights of the secular clergy and the friars (1311).

Super cathedram (as reissued at the Council of Vienne, c. 10). *Decrees,* Tanner, pp. 365–67.

The following decretal, published a little while ago by our predecessor pope Boniface VIII [in 1300], was revoked by our predecessor pope Benedict XI [in 1304]. Since, as results have proved, the revocation did not bring with it the peace hoped for by its author, but rather stimulated the discord which it was designed to allay, we annul it altogether and renew, with the insistence and approval of the sacred council, the said decretal published by Boniface which runs as follows.

"Boniface, bishop, servant of the servants of God, for the everlasting record. . . . For a long time past there has existed between prelates and rectors or priests and clerics of parish churches throughout the different provinces of the world on the one hand, and the friars Preacher and Minor on the other, grave and dangerous discord, produced by that enemy of peace, the sower of cockle, in the matters of preaching to the faithful, hearing their confessions, enjoining penances, and burying the dead who choose to be buried in the churches or lands of the friars.

"As an affectionate father rightly suffers with his children, we carefully considered and turned over in our mind the great danger and loss that such discord brings, and how detestable it is in the sight of the divine majesty. We therefore intend with all the energy of fatherly care to eradicate and remove it wholly, so that with the Lord's favour it may never revive in the future. . . . After careful deliberation with our brothers, we decree and ordain . . . that the friars of the said orders may freely preach and explain the word of God to the clergy and the people in their churches and other places as also in public places, except at that hour only when the local prelates wish to preach or have someone to give a special sermon in their presence; at this hour they shall not preach, except the prelates decide otherwise and give special permission. . . . In parish churches, however, the said friars may not preach or explain God's word, unless invited or called to do so by the priests of the parishes, and with their good will and assent, or having asked and obtained permission, unless the bishop or higher prelate should through them commission a friar to preach.

"By the same authority we also decree and ordain that in each city and diocese in which the friars have houses, or in neighbouring cities and dioceses where they have no houses, the masters and priors provincial of the Preachers or their vicars, and the ministers general and provincial and the guardians of the Minors, should gather in the presence of the prelates of those places either personally or through friars whom they judge will be suitable delegates, and humbly request that friars chosen for the purpose may freely hear the confessions of those of the prelates' subjects who wish to confess to them, may impose salutary penances as they shall think right in God's eyes, and may grant absolution to them, with the leave, favour and good will of the prelates. The masters, priors, provincials and ministers of the orders are then to choose diligently sufficient persons who are suitable, of approved life, discreet, modest and skilled for such a salutary ministry and office. These they are to present or have presented to the prelates that by their leave, favour and good will, they may hear the confessions of those wishing to confess to them in the prelates' cities and dioceses, impose salutary penances and grant absolution, as has been said above. They are by no means to hear confessions outside the cities and dioceses for which they were appointed. We want them to be appointed for cities and dioceses, not for provinces. The number of persons to be chosen for this ministry ought to be in proportion to that which the number of clergy and people demands.

"If the prelates grant the permission requested for hearing confessions, the said masters, ministers and others shall receive it with thanks, and the persons chosen should carry out the duties entrusted to them. If the prelates do not accept one of the friars presented to them, another may and should be presented in his place. But if the prelates issue a general refusal to the friars chosen, we graciously grant, from the fullness of our apostolic power, that they may freely and lawfully hear the confessions of those wishing to confess to them and impose salutary penances, and then impart absolution. By this permission, however, we by no means intend to give more ample power to such friars than is granted by law to the parish clergy, unless perhaps the prelates of the churches think that such power should be given to them.

"To this decree and regulation of ours we add that the friars of the said orders may provide free burial everywhere in their churches and cemeteries, that is, they may receive for burial all who have chosen these places for their burial. Yet, lest parish churches and their clergy, whose office it is to administer the sacraments and to whom it belongs by law to preach God's word and to hear the confessions of the faithful, should be denied their due and necessary benefits, since the labourer deserves his wages, we decree and ordain by the same apostolic authority, that the friars are obliged to give the parish clergy a fourth part of all the income from funerals and from everything left to them, expressly or not, for whatever definite purpose, even from such bequests of which a fourth or canonical part is not claimed by custom or by law, and also a fourth part of bequests made at the death or at the point of death of the giver, whether directly or through a third party. We set and also limit this amount to the fourth part by our apostolic authority. . . . The rectors of parishes, pastors and prelates may not, however, exact more than this portion, nor are the friars obliged to pay more, nor may they be compelled by anyone to do so.

"In order that everything may go forward evenly and peacefully with the Lord's favour, we revoke, void, annul and invalidate completely all the privileges, favours and indults granted orally or in writing, in any form or expression of words, by ourself or our predecessors as Roman pontiffs to any of the said orders. . . . Furthermore, by this present decree, we earnestly ask and exhort, indeed we strictly command, all prelates of churches, of whatever preeminence, status or dignity, and the parish priests, pastors and rectors, out of their reverence for God and the apostolic see, to show friendliness to these orders and their members, not being difficult, severe, hard or austere to the friars, but rather gracious, favourable and kind, showing them a spirit of holy generosity. They should accept the friars as suitable fellow-workers in the office of preaching and explaining God's word and in everything else mentioned above, admitting them with ready kindness and affection to a share in their labours, so as to increase their reward of eternal happiness and the fruitful harvest of souls. Nor let them be unaware that if perhaps they act otherwise, the kindness of the apostolic see, which honours these orders and their members with great favour and holds them in its heart, will with good reason be roused against them, nor can it tolerate with good will such behaviour without applying a suitable remedy. The indignation, moreover, of the heavenly king, the just rewarder, whom the friars serve with all earnestness, will not be lacking."

∾ No. 65. Bishop John Gynwell of Lincoln commissions an Austin friar to hear confessions (1347).

Arnold Williams, "Relations between the Mendicant Friars and the Secular Clergy in England in the Later Fourteenth Century," Duquesne Studies, *Annuale Mediaevale* 1 (1960): 45–46. Trans. JS.

John, by divine permission bishop of Lincoln, to his beloved son Brother William of Brinton of the Order of Friars Hermit from the convent of Northampton in our diocese, greetings, grace, and blessing. Trusting in your discretion and the seriousness of your zeal which are fit for securing the salvation of souls, by virtue of this present letter we grant you for one whole year the power to act as our penitentiary within the jurisdictional boundaries assigned to the said friars, and to hear the confessions of all parishioners subject to us within the said boundary who wish to confess their sins to you, and to enjoin a proper salutary penance upon them, and to absolve them by our authority in the following cases: adulterous incest, violation of vows, deflowering of virgins, sodomy, breach of faith, laying violent hands on clerics, blasphemy against God and his saints, and all cases of perjury excepting cases committed at assizes, inquisitions, procurations, and where intended to injure other witnesses. We remove all authority to grant absolution in other cases not further granted to you. Given at Nottingham, 14th kalends of April [March 19], the year of our Lord 1347, and the first year of our consecration.

ᖰ No. 66. Carmelite friars licensed to preach (1293).

Reg. Swinfield, p. 300. *Bishop's Register*, p. 151.

On behalf of the brethren of Mount Carmel, Richard [bishop of Hereford], etc., to the discreet men and beloved of him in Christ, the Provincial prior and brethren of the order of Mary of Mount Carmel established in England, greetings, etc. The worthy honesty of your religion excites and persuades us to treat you with grace and favour. We therefore concede a special license to your devotion that the brethren of your order to whom God has given the power and grace of preaching, obtaining a license for this in your provincial chapter, shall have in our diocese in every place to which it shall happen that they shall come power freely to preach lawfully in parish churches the word of God to the people, to hear confessions, and to enjoin salutary penances according to the tenor of your privileges unless they entrust to you in confession anything of such a kind that the Roman court should be consulted or the diocesan bishop. To those also who have listened to your preaching in our diocese and have been penitent for their sins and confessed, we concede by these present letters twenty days' indulgence, with the Lord's authority. In which, etc. Given at Ross, June 7th, A.D. 1293.

ᖰ No. 67. Bishop Hamo Hethe of Rochester presents a credentialed Franciscan friar to his clergy (1326).

Arnold Williams, "Relations between the Mendicant Friars and the Secular Clergy in England in the Later Fourteenth Century," Duquesne Studies, *Annuale Mediaevale* 1 (1960): 31. Trans. JS.

Brother Hamo, etc. to his beloved sons the rectors, vicars, and parish priests of our diocese within the jurisdictional boundary of the Friars Minor of Winchelsey, greetings, grace, and blessing.

Since Brother John de Witele of the said order and religious house has presented himself before us according to the terms of the recent constitution which begins "Super cathedram," we have granted that within the said diocese and boundary he has the authority to preach the word of God, and to hear the confessions of our subjects wishing to confess to him, and to impose salutary penances on those confessing to him as he shall think it right in God's eyes, and he may grant absolution to them according to the terms and the obligation of the said constitution; we grant no more power to him in this matter than that which has been conceded by law to parish priests. In the Lord we admonish and exhort all of you to be sure to receive the aforesaid John, whom we have inducted as explained above, with kind support as your coadjutor; and you should not presume to obstruct this same man in any way whatsoever from freely carrying out the aforesaid unless someone else shall be substituted in place of him, or you have received further instructions from us in this matter. Given at Hall, 9th Kalends of March [February 21], the year of our Lord 1326.

◌ No. 68. Dominican friars deprive a parish priest of his burial dues (1402).

EHD IV, No. 437, p. 730.

To the very noble, etc. supplicates humbly your poor clerk, may it please you, R. T., parson of the church of E. in the diocese of Lincoln, that, as his very noble lord the Duke of York, whom God pardon, passed to God in his said parish [in August, 1402], and during his life devised his body to be buried at the friary in Langley, and immediately after his death his body was carried to Langley without any divine service being said in his said church for his soul and R has visited the prior of the friars to require from him the fourth part of the duke's armour and horse which will be offered for the principal[12] and other oblations whatsoever to be made, as the common right of the Holy Church demands, and the prior denies him, saying that he shall have nothing of this,

May it please your very noble and very gracious lordship and reverend paternity in God, as you are the primate and chief of the clergy of England, to ordain that the said R may have what the law of the church demands in such a case. For God and as a work of charity.

◌ No. 69. A concord between a parish rector and Carmelite friars (1301).

Reg. Corbridge, pp. 60–64. Trans. JS.

Acceptance of a settlement between the rector of the church of St. Savior, York and the prior and brothers of the order of St. Mary of Mount Carmel, York: To all the sons of holy mother church to whose notice these present letters come, Thomas, by the grace of God bishop, etc., greetings in the Savior's embrace.

Sir Stephen de Burton Anneys, rector of the church of St. Savior [Peaseholme] in the Marsh, York, had acquired certain papal letters (whose contents are described below) against the prior and brothers of the order of

---

[12] The best possessions someone bequeaths.

St. Mary of Mount Carmel in York, and these two parties were litigants against each other by virtue of these letters; but after friends intervened between them, they unanimously consented to the following written agreement, signed by the seals of the rector and the prior and brothers, the tenor of which follows:

In the name of God. Amen. Sir Stephen de Burton Anneys, rector of the church of St. Savior in the Marsh, York, obtained two different papal letters whose contents are as follows:

"[Pope] Boniface [VIII], bishop, etc. to his venerable brother the archbishop and to his beloved sons the dean and Master Robert de Pickering, canon of York, greetings and apostolic blessings. The rector of the church of St. Savior, York, showed by his petition to us that the prior and brothers of the order of St. Mary of Mount Carmel, York, have abandoned the place where they formerly resided in the suburbs of York and have newly acquired another place within the parish of the said church against the rector's will; they have presumed by their own rashness to relocate themselves to the serious detriment of the rector and his church without license from the Holy See in violation of the tenor of our constitution[13] promulgated about this issue, long after it was published in these lands. Therefore, at your discretion we order you by this papal letter to call together the parties in the dispute, hear the case, and, barring an appeal, deliver an appropriate settlement, seeing to it that your decision is firmly obeyed under pain of ecclesiastical censure. If the witnesses named in the case refuse to appear out of favor, hate, or fear [of the litigants], you should compel them to adduce true testimony, barring any similar appeal as above. But if you are unable to be present to see all these things through to an end, you should have someone else see to their fulfillment. Given at the Lateran, April 1, 1300, the sixth year of our pontificate."

"Boniface, etc. as above. The rector of the church of St. Savior, York, has complained to us that the prior and brothers of the order of St. Mary of Mount Carmel, York, have attempted by their own rashness to construct a new church or oratory within the parish of the aforesaid church, without obtaining license for this from the Holy See or from the local ordinary, and completely against the objections and the will of the said rector, to the great harm and oppression of the rector and his church; and so, at your discretion,

[13]I.e., *Super cathedram.*

we order you by this papal letter, etc. . . . Given at the Lateran, February 5, the sixth year of our pontificate."

A matter of dispute arose between the said rector on one hand and the said prior and brothers on the other which prompted his petition to the pope. But when mutual friends intervened, urging them to restore peace between them, and after both parties weighed the intricate entanglements of the lawsuit and the injuries that come from litigation, striving in harmony for the sweetness of concord, by the unanimous consent of the two parties the said matter of dispute has been completely settled under the terms that follow: namely, that the aforesaid rector Sir Stephen, on behalf of himself, his church, and all his successors to the church, concedes that the said friars and their successors may erect a church or oratory within the boundaries of the said parish church of St. Savior, and they have the right to bury themselves or any others wishing or choosing to be buried in the place where they now dwell (as is made clear below), so long as all the parochial rights of the church are protected, and at the express consent of the monastery of the Blessed Mary, York (the patron of the said church), and according to each and every thing contained in the said letters. . . .

[*A description of the boundaries of the friars' property, omitted here.*]

The rector willingly has surrendered and released in perpetuity to the same prior and brothers all claims, actions, charges, pleas, and demands which now or in the future he and his successors might seek or exact by whatever right forevermore against the prior and the brothers for tithes, offerings, incomes, and proceeds whatsoever. An exception is granted to the rector Stephen and his successors for whatever they are due and accustomed to have and claim according to parochial rights in the way of tithes, offerings, and proceeds from the servants of the said prior and convent (as from the other parishioners of the said church). And for the concession, renunciation, remission, and also compensation of all the tithes, offerings, and proceeds whatsoever, mentioned above, the said prior and brothers on their behalf and on behalf of their successors have conceded and promised to give and to pay each year in perpetuity to the said rector of the church and all his successors thirty shillings of pure and legal sterling in equal portions; namely, half at the feast of Pentecost [7th Sunday after Easter] and the other half at the winter feast of St. Martin [November 11] without further delay. The prior and brothers oblige themselves in good faith by the tenor of the present letters to pay faithfully on the said days, promising that they will give or pay one-half a silver mark to the fabric fund of the cathedral church of St. Peter, York if they are in arrears in making payment for fifteen days after the feasts, with the exception nevertheless of paying the thirty shillings pension to the said Stephen and his successors every year as stated. So that this settlement may stand perpetually valid, the two parties expressly renounce on their behalf and on behalf of their successors all challenges and appeals, every opportunity to interfere with the abovementioned, all privileges, letters, and grants petitioned from the Holy See, from any lower ordinaries whatsoever, or from the royal courts, and each and every thing that could infringe on or impede directly or indirectly the present settlement. To observe this settlement inviolably and perpetually in each and every one of its clauses, the two parties have submitted themselves to the jurisdiction and coercion of the lord archbishop of York and his official, expressly conceding and consenting that they or someone else at their request have the power to call to account without judicial formality the party going against the present settlement or anything in it, and to restrain him through ecclesiastical censure as seems most suitable to them.

In witness of this at the request of the parties the common seal of the aforesaid prior and the brothers is appended to this chirograph together with the seal of the Dean of York, and it is put into the possession of the said rector. Given at York 16 kalends November [October 17], the year of grace 1301.

5

The Curate's Spiritual Duties

*I*n the framework of medieval Christian theology, the sacraments were those rituals instituted by Christ as conduits of divine grace to God's people. In his role as the spiritual overseer of a Christian community, the curate's chief duty was to be the minister of these vital, grace-giving sacraments. Medieval theologians, after prolonged debate, had decided by the twelfth century that they numbered seven: baptism, confirmation, the eucharist (celebrated within the mass), penance, marriage, extreme unction (the last anointing), and holy orders. A parish curate could administer all but two of these, confirmation and holy orders, which were reserved to bishops.

Twelfth-century advances in sacramental theology and the codification and analysis of canon law, both disciplines honed in the new schools sprouting throughout the West, compelled the development of practical aids for administering the cure of souls: theory had to pass into everyday practice. Nothing more clearly illuminates the links between pastoral theology, its institutionalization through law, and its routine application to Christian people than the sacrament of penance.

Innocent III's Fourth Lateran Council of 1215 was the bellwether in the history of medieval pastoral care. Of its seventy-one canons, over half were concerned directly or indirectly with the conduct of the clergy and matters touching the cure of souls. The most influential of its decrees was canon 21, *Omnis utriusque sexus,* which required all adult Christians (usually those fourteen and older) to confess their sins at least once annually and to receive communion at least at Easter (No. 77). The canon reflected the outcome of at least a century of rethinking confession, for by the twelfth century the theology of the sacrament of penance was in transition. Rapidly moving away from the old penitential practice that prescribed fixed or "tariffed" penances for specific sins, the new theory of penance pronounced that "penances are arbitrary"—in other words, it was at the confessor's discretion to tailor the penance imposed for a particular sin to the character of the sinner. In the earlier penitential tradition, a confessor simply matched the penance to the sin; on the face of it, it called for no real psychological discernment. The twelfth-century reestimation of the sacrament made far greater demands on a priest, obliging him to weigh the personality of each penitent carefully. Now he had to be a discerning reader of souls, someone who could judge intentions, consider temperament, listen for subtleties and extenuating circumstances, and impose penances that would reform sinners, calling them back to God's love rather than crushing their spirits with severe penances that might lead them to spiritual despair. Gregory the Great's ancient metaphor of the pastor as a "doctor of souls" became even more apt: now a priest had to do more than simply dispense patent remedies. Faced with this new theory of penance, he had to become an expert diagnostician as well.

By the end of the twelfth century, theologians, canonists, and pastoralists were churning out all kinds of treatises, brief or rambling, meant to help ordinary priests cope with the new demands placed on them in promoting the Christian life in general and administering penance in particular. The pastoral reforms enacted shortly thereafter by Innocent's Fourth Lateran Council gave even more inspiration to theorists and administrators already trying to prepare priests to carry out the cure of souls as effectively as possible. In England, a great flurry of pastoral manuals began circulating by the mid-thirteenth century.

The *locus classicus* for many of these pastoral aids was Archbishop John Pecham's tract named after its opening words, *Ignorantia sacerdotum,* or *The Ignorance of Priests*—an oft-repeated allusion to the scriptural warning about the blind leading the blind. Issued in 1281 as a chapter (titled "Information for Priests of Simple Learning") in the decrees he issued for the province of Canterbury, this small tract was in effect a pithy outline of the fundamental theology that every priest was expected to know (No. 70). In time-honored fashion it assembled all the various sevens so dear to medieval scholars: the seven sacraments, the seven deadly sins, the seven virtues, the seven works of mercy. It quickly rehearsed the Ten Commandments with examples of typical violations against them. And it briefly summarized the articles of faith. Copies of it, in its original Latin and in a later English translation, circulated throughout England for almost the next three centuries. Manuals large and small, obscure and popular, would hew, with minor variation, to Pecham's basic schema—a mix of theory and practice, theology and law—for the rest of the middle ages. If the ideas and even the phrases in the manuals translated here seem repetitious, this reflects less a failure of their authors' originality than a common grounding in and respect for a time-honored body of knowledge deemed essential for the successful pastor.

Pastoral manuals ran the gamut. Some were contemplative and theological, moral entreaties to inspire the sweetest Christian spirits; some, peppered with abundant citations to canon law, proffered terse practical advice for pastors guiding Christians all too apt to stray. Some, following the spirit of Pecham's short tract, were mere booklets of a few folios, portable enough to be called "fist-books." Sensible, theological, and humane, *Quinque verba* (*Five Words*) is just this sort of brief yet informative piece that would be relatively easy for a priest to get his hands on (No. 71). Where the anonymous *Quinque verba* filled just four or so easy- and cheap-to-copy pages, the Salisbury vicar William of Pagula's *Oculus sacerdotis* (*The Priest's Eye*) ran to over 250 pages, covering in meticulous canonical detail every possible question a priest might raise about the cure of souls. We include here just one chapter from it that demonstrates the sweep of its author's canonical and theological learning and the range of things a parish priest needed to know (No. 72). This little chapter, easily lifted from its much larger parent, could itself serve as a short pastoral handbook, and in fact did circulate independently. Dozens of other pastoral manuals emerged during the later middle ages. From the thirteenth century came works like Thomas of Chobham's *Summa confessorum; Qui bene presunt* by the Chancellor of Cambridge, Richard Wetheringset; Simon of Hinton's *Summa iuniorum;* and Robert Grosseteste's schematically-organized *Templum domini* (*The Lord's Temple*). Still more manuals appeared in the fourteenth century: the *Speculum curatorum* (*Mirror for Curates*), the *Memoriale presbiterorum* (*Memorabilia for Priests*), and Robert Mannyng's *Handlyng Synne*—an English rendering of the important thirteenth-century *Manuel des péchés*. The *Oculus sacerdotis* itself inspired a host of imitators that freely took material from it: the *Cilium oculi* (*The Priest's Eyelid*), the *Regimen animarum* (*Guidance of Souls*), and John de Burgh's *Pupilla oculi* (*The Pupil of the Priest's Eye*). The curate John Mirk wrote a Latin *Manuale sacerdotis* (*The Priest's Manual,* which should always be "at hand") and, in his *Instructions for Parish Priests,* translated parts of the *Oculus* into English verse. And the list is hardly begun. Even Chaucer penned one: the prose "Parson's Tale" that caps the *Canterbury Tales* is, most appropriately given what has gone before, a tract on the deadly sins and confession adapted from two other treatises. That literature meant to guide parish priests could filter into contemporary popular literature shows just how widespread these manuals were. Still, although many of them were brief (and therefore inexpensive to borrow and copy), and although many bishops either appended them to their diocesan statutes or circulated them independently to be possessed by curates on pain of fine, not every priest had access to such up-to-date material. Many priests had to be content with whatever ad hoc pastorally-oriented episcopal legislation was issued in their diocese. Lacking even this, every priest at least had access to a basic summary of Christian belief about God in the Athanasian creed (known by its incipit *Quicumque vult*), which was contained in the breviary (No. 73).

Ironically, despite all the pastoral *summae*, handbooks, treatises, and tracts, the new theory of discretionary penances never entirely dislodged the older practice of tariffed penances. Though fully in sympathy with the new thinking, William of Pagula himself (who had served as a penitentiary in his diocese) still found it inconceivable for a priest to be ignorant of the ancient penitential canons. These canons—many of which the canonist Gratian drew from penitential handbooks that flourished from the sixth century onwards, especially among the Anglo-Saxons and the Franks—represented the oldest strains of medieval penitential theory. The Italian canonist Henry of Susa (called Hostiensis) compiled a comprehensive list of the canons in 1253, long after the new theory of arbitrary penance was in place (No. 79). Set next to a confessional *summula* issued for the diocese of Exeter in the thirteenth-century (No. 78), they seem draconian and far behind the times. But if a late fourteenth-century inventory of the books in over 350 Norfolk churches is any indication, even at this late date the penitential canons were still firmly rooted in the average priest's pastoral arsenal. Far more of these churches (40 percent) owned copies of the penitential canons (which filled only a few folios of parchment at most) than they did more sophisticated and up-to-date manuals.[1] Perhaps the commonplace book of a fifteenth-century York pastor gives us the best—and almost unique— glimpse into the kinds of things a parish priest himself really thought worth knowing (No. 74).

Pastoral handbooks offered priests guidelines for the exercise of their office; they were particularly useful for aiding priests hearing confessions, the most difficult sacrament to which they had to attend. Liturgical service

---

[1] This percentage is compiled from *Archdeaconry of Norwich Inventory of Church Goods, temp. Edward III*, ed. Dom Aelred Watkin, Norfolk Record Society 19, pts. 1 and 2 (1947–48), passim.

books laid out the formulas to be followed with painstaking care in administering the church's other sacraments and performing its rituals and blessings. Baptism admitted an infant into the Christian community and was the doorway to the other sacraments. So vital was it to salvation that even lay people could bestow it in an emergency (No. 75). Holy communion, the sacrifice of the mass, gained increasing reverence during the middle ages—so much so, that by the twelfth century receiving communion was increasingly rare for ordinary people, since prelates feared that frequent reception would make its great mystery and power seem commonplace. Around this time, too, the chalice of consecrated wine was withheld from lay people. Most Christians received communion at least at Easter and perhaps a few more times a year at most (No. 76). Marriage theory, like penance, had evolved over the course of the twelfth century. The new understanding of marriage was that consent alone sufficed to make a valid marriage; sexual intercourse between the couple consummated the union but did not create it. Since the exchange of vows was all that was required to form a marriage, priests had to take care to urge their parishioners not to marry clandestinely without the church's blessing, and to wait for the announcement of banns. The ritual itself is remarkably familiar even today (No. 80). Since medieval medicine could do little to help the sick and dying, spiritual solace offered what physicians could not. In a society haunted by the consequences of a sudden death (which left the soul stained by sin and thereby damned), the desire for a "good death"—one accompanied by the presence of a priest and the church's rites—became an obsession for all Christians. Extreme unction, the last anointing, cleansed sin from those who were mortally ill and prepared them to finish their earthly pilgrimage and journey safely home (No. 81). Though the sacraments marked life's decisive moments, the church was present in people's lives every day. Blessings geared to an array of occasions helped to sanctify the community from moment to moment (No. 82).

Parish priests were obliged to conduct the church's rituals; they were also bound to preach Christian scripture and interpret it for parishioners who rarely were capable of reading it for themselves. How frequently pastors preached to their congregations is a question that still stirs controversy. The formal university sermon, written in Latin and composed according to elaborate rhetorical rules, was never delivered in parish churches; such productions were compositional exercises meant to edify an elitely-educated audience. If a Latin sermon was delivered before lay people, it had to be substantially edited and translated into English. All preaching to the laity was vernacular preaching—sometimes so vernacular that sermons were delivered in the local dialect of the people. For example, Bishop John Grandisson, passing through a parish in the Welsh hinterlands, delivered a sermon and then had an interpreter translate it into Cornish for those who could not understand him.

The talents of the mendicant preachers set a new standard for sermons. Abandoning the dry scriptural exegesis of the formal university sermon, the mendicants composed their sermons with an eye to the tastes and understanding of their lay audiences. Their task was to preach, as St. Francis put it, "vices and virtues, punishment and glory,"[2] which they did by creating a popular style of preaching laced with colorful stories underscoring a moral message. Critics of this new style so frankly aimed at popular taste complained that the faithful were as apt to hear stories about King Arthur's Round Table as about the Last Supper. There is some truth to the charge. Medieval sermon manuals, usually compiled by the educated mendicants, were crammed with anecdotes (called *exempla*) that preachers could draw on to lend concrete illustration to subtle theological doctrines. But the *exempla* were seldom subtle: they painted spellbinding verbal portraits of miraculous interventions, dreadful retributions, and sanguinary martyrdoms. Parish priests could hope to emulate, but could hardly compete with the friars' gift for pulpit oratory.

Some historians note that bishops themselves seemed to have expected little preaching from their parish clergy. For instance, Archbishop Pecham's *Ignorantia sacerdotum* required parish clergy to preach about doctrinal matters only four times during the year (though of course they were free to do more if they wished). Still, in their mandates to their priests, bishops consistently emphasized priests' duty to instruct lay people in matters of faith and morals. Some form of preaching, whatever its level of rhetorical sophistication, was essential for the medieval curate. The hundreds of medieval sermons and scores of preaching handbooks that survive in manuscripts still hardly tapped by scholars suggest that, if nothing else, many medieval priests had a keen interest in sermons and sermonizing. Whether a parish priest ventured much beyond Pecham's minimum requirement depended on his education and his initiative. If he was enterprising, lack of material was no barrier. By the middle of the fourteenth century, collections of potted sermons were circulating in clerical circles. Several popular manuals took the title *Sermones dormi secure,* or *Sermons for Sleeping Soundly,* since these pre-written homilies ensured unworried sleep for the unprepared pastor on a Saturday night. With a handbook of *exempla* at his side, a clever pastor could easily cobble together a coherent homily that, while not passing mus-

[2] St. Francis' *Rule,* chap. 9.

ter for men sensitive to the rhetorical niceties that guided formal sermon writing, would probably enthrall his mostly illiterate parishioners (No. 85). The wall paintings that decorated churches even in many humble rural parishes undoubtedly served as visual aids for preaching pastors. Simply and vividly drawn, their subjects ranged from the biblical, to the hagiographical, to the didactic. Among the more popular were depictions of Christ's Passion, the Last Judgment, incidents from the life (or better still, the martyrdom) of favorite saints, St. Christopher ferrying the Baby Jesus (an image thought to ward off evil during the day it was seen), and the allegorical tree of the seven deadly sins—all images guaranteed to lend color to even the dullest homilist's sermon.

Sermons aside, parish priests passed on much other important information from their pulpits: announcements of banns of marriage; cautions to parents to watch after the safety of their children; admonitions to tithe; exhortations for prayers for good weather or to ward off plague; entreaties to donate money or time to such pious causes as repairing churches, roads, and bridges; announcements of spiritual indulgences granted for pilgrimages to saints' shrines or other holy sites; bulletins about community and national affairs; even notices to be on the lookout for parishioners' stolen goods. And four times yearly priests were obliged to read to their congregations the Great Excommunication that threatened damnation for a harrowing litany of crimes both spiritual and secular (No. 83).

A. Manuals of Instruction

ᑲ No. 70. Archbishop Pecham's *Ignorantia sacerdotum* (1281).
"De informatione simplicium sacerdotum", c. 9 of the Council of Lambeth. *Councils and Synods,* pp. 900–905. Trans. JS.

[9] Information for priests of simple learning
The ignorance of priests casts the people down into the ditch of error, and the foolishness and lack of learning of clerics, whom the decrees of canon law order to teach the sons of the faithful, is all the worse when it leads to error instead of knowledge. For some blind preachers do not always see the places which stand in greatest need of the light of truth; the prophet testifies that "the little ones have asked for bread, and there was none to break unto them" [Lam. 4:4], and another cries that "the needy and the poor seek for waters, and there are none: their tongue hath been dry with thirst" [Isa. 41:17].

To remedy this dangerous situation we order that four times during the year, that is once in every quarter on one or several solemn days, each priest in charge of a parish should personally explain or have someone else explain to the people in their mother tongue, without any fancifully woven subtleties, the fourteen articles of faith, the Ten Commandments of the Decalogue, the two precepts of the Gospel (namely the twin laws of charity), the seven works of mercy, the seven capital sins and their fruits, the seven principal virtues, and the seven grace-giving sacraments. And lest anyone, claiming ignorance, should try to excuse himself from knowledge of these things, which all ministers of the church are required to know, we have outlined them here in a brief summary.

Thus, one should know that there are seven articles of faith that pertain to the mystery of the Trinity: four concern the interrelationship of the godhead, and three concern its effects. The first article is that there is one divine essence contained in a trinity of three indivisible persons. As the creed says: *I believe in one God.* The second article is to believe that the Father is the unbegotten God. The third article is to believe that the only-begotten Son is God. The fourth article is to believe that the Holy Spirit is God neither born nor unbegotten, but proceeds equally from the Father and the Son. The fifth article is the belief that heaven and earth, that is, all creatures visible and invisible, are the creation of a totally indivisible trinity. The sixth article is the sanctification of the church through the Holy Spirit, the grace-giving sacraments, and all the other things in which the Christian church communicates. By this is to be understood that the church with its sacraments and laws through the Holy Spirit suffices for the salvation of every man, sinner though he be, and that outside the church there is no salvation. The seventh article is the fulfillment of the church through everlasting glory in the truly-resurrected soul and body; the opposite of this means the eternal damnation of the reprobate.

The remaining seven articles of faith pertain to the manhood of Christ. The first is his incarnation, or real assuming of flesh from the glorious virgin through the Holy Spirit. The second is the birth of the truly incarnate God from the inviolate virgin. The third is the real passion and death of Christ God on the cross under the tyranny of Pontius Pilate. The fourth is the descent in the spirit of Christ God into hell to harrow it, while his body lay in the sepulcher. The fifth is the true resurrection of Christ. The sixth is his true ascension into heaven. The seventh is the most certain expectation of his coming in judgment.

Out of the Ten Commandments of the Old Testament, three (called the laws of the first tablet) are ordained for God; and seven (called the laws of the second tablet) are ordained for our neighbors. The first commandment forbids all idolatry when it says: "Thou shalt not have strange gods before me" [Exod. 20:3–17]. Implicitly it forbids all sorcery, incantations, and superstitious uses of written letters or other types of images. The second commandment, when it says "Thou shalt not take the name of the Lord thy God in vain," primarily forbids all heresy and secondarily forbids all blasphemy and irreverence for the name of God, especially in perjury. When the third commandment says "Remember that thou keep holy the sabbath day," it orders the promotion of the Christian religion to which clergy and laity alike are obliged. From this it should be understood that the legal obligation to fast on the sabbath along with other legally required rituals contained in the Old Testament completely ceased and was succeeded in the New Testament by the rule for keeping Sundays (and other holy days designated by the church's authority) free for divine worship. This new rule was not adduced from the superstition of the Jews but through the creation of the holy canons. The fourth commandment (the first commandment of the second tablet) explicitly is to "honor thy father and thy mother," both in temporal and spiritual affairs. An implicit and secondary meaning of this commandment is that anyone should be honored by virtue of his status. One should also understand this commandment to mean that we should honor not only our natural father and mother but also our spiritual parents. Thus, our father is also any prelate of the church, mediate or immediate; and our mother is the church itself whose children are every Catholic person. The fifth commandment is "Thou shalt not kill," which explicitly forbids the illegal destruction of a person by conspiracy, word, deed, or approval; but implicitly this commandment forbids every unjust injury to someone. They commit spiritual murder who do not relieve the needy; similarly, they kill who slander, or who oppress or harass the innocent. The sixth commandment is "Thou shalt not commit adultery," which explicitly forbids adultery, but also implicitly fornication (which Deuteronomy 23 explicitly forbids where it says: "There shall be no whore among the daughters of Israel, nor whoremonger among the sons of Israel" [Deut. 23:17]). This commandment also forbids all sexual relations between men and women which the blessings of marriage do not allow, and every willful act of sexual pollution achieved in any eager or voluntary fashion. The seventh commandment is "Thou shalt not steal." It explicitly forbids any clandestine withdrawal of another's things without the owner's consent. Implicitly, it also forbids any harmful seizure of another's things whether through fraud, usury, violence, or intimidation. The eighth commandment is "Thou shalt not bear false witness against thy neighbor," which explicitly forbids false testimony harmful to someone. However, it implicitly forbids false testimony that speaks on behalf of someone who, based on merits, is unworthy. This commandment also condemns all lies, especially pernicious ones. The ninth commandment is "Thou shalt not covet thy neighbor's house"; that is, by damaging it. This commandment implicitly forbids greed for another's real property, especially that of any Catholic. The tenth commandment is "Thou shalt not desire his wife, nor his servant, nor his handmaid, nor his ox, nor his ass, nor anything that is his," which condemns greed for another's possessions, including his chattel.

The gospels [Matt. 22:37–39, etc.] add two other commands to these ten commandments—namely, love of God and of neighbor. He loves God who keeps the aforesaid commandments chiefly out of love, not fear. In addition everyone ought to love his neighbor as himself. This conjunction "as" does not mean "equally," but "similarly." So you should love your neighbor for that which you love in yourself (that is, for the good in him, not the bad), and in the manner in which you love yourself (that is, spiritually, not carnally, insofar as carnality can be called a vice), and to the degree you love yourself (that is, in good times and bad, in health and in sickness), and in comparison to temporal goods (insofar as you should love every single person more than any temporal wealth), and as you love yourself (insofar as you should love the soul of your neighbor or the eternal salvation of the soul more than your own earthly life—just as you should put the life of your soul above the life of your body), so that you should go to the aid of every other person in an emergency, just as you would wish to be aided in similar circumstances. All these things should be understood by the phrase "Thou shalt love thy neighbor as thyself."

There are six works of mercy revealed in the Gospel of Matthew [Matt. 25:35–36]. They are to feed the hungry, to give drink to the thirsty, to give shelter to strangers, to clothe the naked, to visit the sick, and to comfort those in prison. The Book of Tobias [Tob. 1:21] adds a seventh: to bury the dead.

These are the seven deadly sins: pride, envy, wrath (or hate), sloth, avarice, gluttony, and lust. Pride is love of your own excellence, from which arises boasting, ostentation, hypocrisy, schism, and other such things. Envy is hatred for your neighbor's happiness, from which arises disparagement, querulousness, disagreement, wrongful judgments, and similar things. Wrath is a craving for vengeance against or for harming another; when it endures in the heart it becomes hatred from which arises persecutions in words and deeds, fighting, murder, and things like these. Sloth is lethargy toward spiritual goods, from which a man takes delight neither in God nor in divine praises for him. From it arises listlessness, faint-heartedness, despair, and similar things. Avarice is an immoderate love of movable and immovable wealth, either by unlawfully acquiring it or unlawfully detaining it. From it arise fraud, theft, sacrilege, simony, and all ill-gotten gains. Gluttony is the immoderate love of the pleasures of the sense of taste through eating and drinking. There are five varieties of the sin of gluttony: First one can sin according to interval, as when one eats too early in the morning or lingers too long when eating or is too hasty. Second, one can sin through quality when one craves sumptuous food, that is, food that is too rich. Third, one sins in quantity when one eats or drinks too much. This is the commonest type of gluttony; it is this surfeit of food and drink which aggravates the heart, impedes both the exterior and the interior senses, and injures the body's health. Fourth, once can sin in the overeager or voracious quality of one's eating; and finally one can sin in the over-meticulous and exquisite preparation of food meant to arouse the savory pleasures of taste. These five circumstances for gluttony are summarized in this verse: "Too hastily, too sumptuously, too much, too ardently, too meticulously." It is not fitting to say much about lust whose infamy infects every breath we take.

The seven principal virtues are faith, hope, and charity (which were ordained by God and so are called the theological virtues), and prudence, justice, temperance, and fortitude (which were ordained by man for himself and his neighbors). To act with prudence is to choose the good; to act with justice is to do the good; to act with temperance is to be unimpeded by pleasures; to act with fortitude is to do good despite whatever difficulties and troubles. These four are called the cardinal (or principal) virtues. There are many other matters concerning these four, but because we are writing here for those of only a little learning, right now we will not discuss them further.

There are seven sacraments of grace, whose ministers are the prelates of the church, five of which all Christians ought to receive: namely, baptism, confirmation, penance, the eucharist (at the proper time), and the last anointing. (The last anointing ought to be given only to those who seem be in danger of death from some grave illness; however, if possible it should be given to them while they are still of sound mind. But if it happens that they are delirious or out of their minds, and before this happened they showed concern for their salvation, we nevertheless advise that this sacrament be faithfully ministered to them. For we believe and have learned by experience that the reception of this sacrament, inasmuch as it increases grace, will be of profit no matter how mad someone may be—providing he is a predestined son of God—by giving him a lucid moment or at least some spiritual benefit.) There are two other sacraments—holy orders and matrimony—the first of which is appropriate for those seeking perfection, while the second is appropriate only for the imperfect, so long as the law of the New Testament endures; still, we believe it bestows grace through the power of the sacrament if is contracted with a sincere spirit.

∾ No. 71. A pastoral vade mecum: *Quinque verba* (fourteenth century?).
BL Harley MS 52, fols. 83r–84v. Trans. WJD.

In the name of our Lord Jesus Christ. In an effort to remedy the ignorance of simple priests, we have gathered a few things from the teachings of our fathers that tell priests how they can preach with confidence to the people and administer more carefully the church's sacraments. Thus, we have written these things in a simple and almost child-like manner lest anyone try to excuse himself from knowing this material. Furthermore, we have divided these things into five chapters: in the first, an explanation of those things which must be believed; the second, the things that should be loved; the third, what works should be done; the fourth, what should be watched out for or avoided; the fifth, those things that priests should do.

Chapter 1. Since faith is the foundation of every spiritual good, the first thing that should be known are matters of faith. It is necessary to believe that God is one and absolute in essence, three in persons, Father, Son, and Holy Spirit, as is clearly and manifestly stated in the hymn sung at Prime, "*Quicumque vult salvus esse,* etc."[3] Namely, that God created out of nothing and formed all things in heaven and on earth, things visible and invisible. Also, that God sustains, protects, and rules all creation. It must also be believed that the Son of God took on human form and was born of the Blessed Mary ever virgin. Also, that the same Son of God suffered bodily on the cross for our salvation, died and his body was buried, that his soul went down to the netherworld to harrow hell and free the elect and just who had been held there. And that on the third day he truly rose from the dead and after forty days ascended to heaven and sent the Holy Spirit upon the apostles and all who believe. He gave these same apostles and their successors the power to bind and loose souls of all sin through the ministries of the church he established; he also gave them power to sanctify souls through the church's sacraments, in particular, baptism, penance, and the others. And that the same Son of God will come again at the end of the world to judge the living and the dead and the good he shall lead into eternal life, but the wicked he shall send to the everlasting flames.

Chapter 2. The second thing one must know is what should be loved in

[3] See No. 73.

true charity without which neither faith nor good works can suffice for everlasting life. First, God should be loved above all things and, especially, more than you love yourself to the extent that you would rather lose everything including your own life than offend God through mortal sin. Second, you should love yourself, that is, out of charity you should love your soul which is true love. In this way you desire for yourself virtues and grace in order to merit eternal life. For, as the prophet says, whoever loves sin and iniquity hates his soul. Third, you shall love your neighbor, which means everyone, as yourself and this is that good for which you love yourself. As the saying goes, you should love the good in every person, the noble manners and the grace through which eternal life is won, just as you love the same in yourself. As the Lord says, "Love your neighbor as yourself"; he does not say how much you should love yourself, but you should love your own soul more than your neighbor, and you should love your neighbor's soul more than your own property or worldly goods. Fourth, out of charity, you should love your body to the extent that it serves your soul for glorification in the life to come. For there are seven principal virtues with which you ought to decorate your soul and which you should encourage among your neighbors: the first is faith by which you believe in God; the second is hope by which you confide and hope in God; the third is charity by which, above all things, you shall love God and neighbor. These are called the three theological virtues since they direct one to God. The four other virtues are called cardinal virtues and they are, first, prudence by which good is chosen and evil avoided; second, justice by which one gives to another his or her due; third, temperance by which one uses all things in reasonable measure; and fourth, fortitude or magnanimity which makes a person unafraid to suffer pain or persecution for justice's sake.

Chapter 3. The third thing one ought to know are those works which need to be done, since faith without works is dead and true charity is never idle. These works include the Ten Commandments of the Old Testament: the first commandment is: "you shall not have strange gods," in which holy church forbids every kind of sorcery, incantations, spells, and superstitions. The second commandment is: "do not take the name of your God in vain," wherein lies the prohibition of false and empty oaths and any blasphemy, that is, words and sayings which are against the honor of the Divine Majesty. The third commandment is: "You shall make holy the sabbath day," which means the devout observance of the church's ancient feasts, worshipping God through pious acts, listening attentively to the word of God and the Divine Office and doing other things that are similarly good; it also means avoiding those things which are not holy, such as all uncleanliness, going to the taverns, wrestling, and dancing. The fourth commandment is: "Honor your father and mother," which requires not only the respect due to one's natural parents, but also the honor and humble obedience due to spiritual fathers, the prelates and guardians of your soul, and the worthy veneration to the spiritual mother, that is, the church. The fifth commandment is: "You shall not kill," which forbids every sin of killing, in deed but also in forethought, counsel, consent or support; also, this same commandment forbids any violence done to one's neighbor, for scripture calls murderers all those who plunder the poor, oppress and subjugate the innocent. It is the same for those who hate their neighbor, who do not feed the poor or allow others to die through neglect. The sixth commandment is: "You shall not commit adultery," by which all fornication is forbidden along with every kind of lustful and unchaste act which is intentional and willingly engaged in. This sort of act is a mortal sin. The seventh commandment: "You shall not steal," which means not only the furtive theft of someone else's possessions, but any unjust acquisition or appropriation by means of plunder, fraudulence, usury, violence, threats, or fear. The eighth commandment is: "You shall not give false witness against your neighbor," which includes any lie, especially slander which harms you or your neighbor. The ninth commandment is: "You shall not unjustly covet your neighbor's property." This is a prohibition as well of the desire to possess another's immovable goods, such as land or fields. The tenth commandment is: "You should not desire your neighbor's wife," servant or maid, ass or any movable goods which your neighbor owns. Do not covet these things for God forbids willful sin or the sin of the heart.

Chapter 4. The fourth matter to be known are those things which ought to be avoided or shunned, as much in heart as well as in word and deed. These are the deadly sins and are so called because any one of them kills the soul, destroys charity and all virtue, and is deadening like poison. The first deadly sin is pride, which is the inordinate love of one's own greatness from which all other vices are born: boastfulness, discord, quarreling, hypocrisy, vainglory. The second deadly sin is envy, which is a yearning for another person's goods. Other sins arise from this, such as detraction, back-biting, slander, and delight in another's misfortunes. The third deadly sin is anger, a desire or craving for the punishment or harm of another. If this endures, it gives rise to hatred in the heart. Anger's progeny are quarrels, fights, blows, harsh words, murder, and the like. The fourth deadly sin is sloth, a lethargy about spiritual goods from which a person fails to delight in God or sing God's praises. From sloth comes laziness, evil-doing, despair, an indifference towards God's commands, and other like things. The fifth deadly sin is greed, the inordinate love of wealth. To be greedy is to seek after something more than is necessary. Thus, greed is equivalent to desiring and holding on to more than one needs. From greed come other sins: theft, pillage, false oaths, fraud, sacrilege, simony, and profit from base things. The sixth deadly sin is gluttony, an excessive love of delicacies in food and drink. There are five types of gluttony: hastiness, indulgence, excess, voraciousness, and over-fondness. One is hasty when one has too little time, or is too early or eats something too quickly or too often, especially on fast days. One is indulgent when eating too many delicacies or rich foods. Excess occurs when one does more than is good for one's health or when one becomes so ill because of drink that one is unable to eat. Voracity happens when there is an excess of desire and greed. To be overfond of something is manifest in excessive preparation in the creating of delicacies. Lust is the seventh deadly sin, and lust means the desire for illicit pleasures in many forms such as fornication, whoring, adultery, debauchery, incest, sacrilege, unnatural vices, and other horrendous sins. Still, it is not a good thing to dwell on these sins or speak of them at too great length, but, rather, to grieve over and fear them. The best antidote is to avoid at all costs the company of women and to resist any thoughts of this sort as soon as they arise. It is important to know that the above sins are grave, dangerous, and mortal when a person gives full consent to them and knows that they are against the laws of God. But when one resists them entirely when inclinations or thoughts of them first arise, then they are venial or less serious sins.

Chapter 5. The fifth subject that every priest ought to know for his pastoral work is the seven sacraments, which are the medicine of the soul. They are seven and were established by God for the remission of sins and the transmission of grace. A sacrament is the visible form of an invisible grace; a sacrament is also the sign of a sacred thing.

The first sacrament is baptism, which takes place only with water and these words: "I baptize you N., in the name of the Father and of the Son and of the Holy Spirit. Amen." This may be done by anyone who has the intention of baptizing according to ecclesiastical form. Without these aspects, it is not the sacrament of baptism. Anything else which takes place or is said before these words is not essential for baptism but belongs to its celebration and the devotion of the people. Baptism's effect is to wash the baptized clean of every sin, original and actual. Actual sin is what a person does, namely through doing, speaking, or thinking in an evil manner, either mortally or venially. Original sin is what a person takes on or receives as a child of our first parents Adam and Eve on account of their disobedience to

God. Original sin is the flesh's desire against the spirit's and came with the loss of original justice that had once been given to Adam and his race but which was forfeited through the disobedience of sin.

The second sacrament is confirmation, which is performed only by the bishop with holy chrism and a certain verbal formula. Its effect is to strengthen faith with the Holy Spirit.

The third sacrament is penance, which is, before all else, the tearful resolve that one will not sin intentionally again. Now penance has three aspects: contrition of the heart, confession of the lips, and making satisfaction. Contrition is the genuine and heartfelt sorrow for one's sins; it should be profound because of the offense to God's grace and covenant, and on account of the pains of hell to which sinners are obliged because of their sins. Confession is a full rendering of one's sins before a priest, and it ought to be complete so that everything which comes to mind may be revealed. Confession also ought to be personal and confidential, to prevent penitents from lying and to encourage them to reveal their own sins and not those of another. The penitent should confess with a heartfelt sorrow and a real determination not to sin mortally again and to hope all the more in God's loving kindness. Without these things it is not true confession, nor is it helpful toward salvation. Satisfaction is the performance of good works for the amendment of sins, and these good works include fasting, pilgrimages, almsgiving, and prayer. Fasting and pilgrimage counteract fleshly desires, almsgiving the desires of the world, and prayers an arrogant spirit. Penitents should be required to do these in a relative fashion as some are hale while others are weak, some wealthy and others indigent, some work while others have leisure. It is important that restitution be required of all those who hold on to property that does not belong to them and which they are obliged to return, either immediately or as soon as they can. As St. Augustine says, the sin is not remitted until restitution is complete. Confessors need to be careful about requiring the restitution of goods belonging to the executors, heirs, or neighbors of penitents if such cases arise. But if restitution is impossible, penitents should pray all the more for those whose goods they have or else they should seek pardon from the latter without breaking the seal of confession. It is also important to know that every mortal sin had an automatic penance of seven years, though the actual penance should be moderated depending on the number of sins and the judgment of the confessor. Those who confess many of these mortal sins ought to be given penance for the rest of their lives. Still, penances ought to be harsher in the first years and lighter in the latter if they are to be carried out properly. Everyone ought to know that whenever they ponder their sins, they should be heartily sorry and beg God's pardon with a strong resolve to sin no more. After the penance has been given, the priest should have the penitent recite the *Confiteor* word for word in his or her own language and then the priest may say the *Misereatur,* etc. Finally, he grants the penitent absolution in these words: "By the authority of God and the blessed Apostles Peter and Paul and with the authority and power granted to me, I absolve you of all the sins you have confessed with a contrite heart as well as those you would have confessed had you remembered them. All the good things you will do and the difficult things you will endure are your penance. May the Passion of our Lord Jesus Christ and the merits of his saints strengthen you for the remission of all your sins and for life eternal. Amen." Confessors should be careful not to interfere in cases reserved to the bishop or his penitentiary or when someone is under a sentence of general or particular excommunication, except in danger of death. Nor should they impose penance on the diseased or gravely ill, but urge them to be sorry for their sins and to accept an appropriate penance, and absolve them in the manner described above for their quick healing. If the penitent is an excommunicate and is absolved for fear of death, when the person has recovered, the priest should order the excommunicate to seek absolution from a higher authority. Indeed, the effect of the sacrament of penance is the remission of every sin.

The fourth sacrament is the eucharist, which is the Body and Blood of our Lord under the appearances of bread and wine; only a priest may celebrate this sacrament and with single-grain bread and unsoured wine. The bread is changed into the Body of Christ through the power of these words in the canon of the mass: "this is my Body"; and the wine is changed into blood through the words that follow: "this is the chalice of my Blood, of the new and eternal covenant, the mystery of faith, which is for you," etc. This sacrament is given to the laity only in the form of bread and not in the form of wine because of the danger in spilling it. When the sacrament is given to the sick, it should be emphasized to them that this is truly the Body of Christ, born of the Virgin, who died on the cross and is here under the form of bread and should be adored before they receive it. The sacrament should not be given to the sick because they might vomit or to those who are delirious; neither should it be given to children who have no idea of its power nor to widely-known and public sinners until their penance is equally manifest. The effect of this sacrament is that it feeds the soul and joins it to God, it strengthens virtue and, when devoutly received, takes away venial sins; but mortal sin renders one unworthy to receive it.

The fifth sacrament is holy order. There are four minor orders which an acolyte possesses and three sacred orders, namely the orders of subdiaconate, diaconate, and priesthood. And in each order worthily received through the laying on of hands by the bishop, a spiritual grace is given for ministry in accordance with the office of those ordained. The effect of this sacrament is a special power given by God.

The sixth sacrament is matrimony, and matrimony is the legitimate joining of a man and a woman by the pronouncement of these words: the man says to the woman, "I take you as my spouse." When these words refer to a future event, this is a betrothal and not a marriage. There is a three-fold effect to matrimony, namely, faith, offspring, and sacrament: faith, since both are bound to give their bodies over to each another faithfully; off-spring, since they ought to intend when having sexual intercourse to bring into this world sons and daughters for the honor and worship of God; sac-rament, in that matrimony represents the joining of Christ to his church. By means of this sacrament, a man and woman are freed from the mortal sin that arises from sexual union, so long as the bounds of marriage are not exceeded.

The seventh sacrament is extreme unction, given to the sick when they are gravely ill by the anointing of the body and the recitation of certain words. The effect of this sacrament is the alleviation of physical infirmity if it frees the soul and the remission of venial sins. If one who is sick asks for the sacrament devoutly, it should be given lest that person fall sick again.

It is important to note that baptism, confirmation, and holy orders may be received only once in life, but the other sacraments may be taken more often. Indeed, the eucharist ought to be taken frequently and penance should be continuous since all of us are sinners and after baptism, penance alone can take away sins.

Here ends the treatise on the things a priest ought to know.

○ No. 72. A pastoral compendium: an excerpt from William of Pagula's *Oculus sacerdotis* (*The Priest's Eye*) (c. 1320–23).

Liber Secunda (*Dextera pars oculi*), chap. 1; Hatfield, Hertfordshire, Hatfield House MS 290, fols. 43v–47v. Trans. JS.

The priestly office and how a priest should instruct his parishioners

There are many priests yet there are few priests—many priests in name, but few in deed.[4] There are many priests in name since nothing in this life,

---

[4] Citations of canon law follow almost every sentence in this text. All these references are omitted here.

especially in these times, is easier, more agreeable, and more acceptable to men than to perform the office of bishop or priest; but in the sight of God, nothing is more wretched, sadder, and damnable if it is done indifferently and for adulation.

Yet there are few priests in deed since nothing in this life, especially in these times, is harder, more burdensome, or perilous than the office of bishop or priest; but nothing is holier in the sight of God if one soldiers on and does his duty in the way Christ commands. And according to a sermon of St. Ambrose, due to the disordered and undisciplined lives of many priests, the holy sacrament of the Redeemer is daily heaped with scorn by those who should be vicars of the apostles and sons of Peter but are instead companions of Judas and followers of Antichrist. In order for there to be more priests in deed, they should study holy scripture with great diligence according to the Apostle Paul in his letter to Timothy where he says, always stay dedicated to "reading [the scriptures], in exhortation, and in teaching" [1 Tim. 4:13]. Priests should know holy scripture and at least the major canons of the church; all their effort should be put to preaching and teaching; they should edify everyone with their knowledge both about the faith and about good behavior; and they are bound to mold their subjects with the food of God's word according to how he inspires them, lest they are deservedly blamed because of their idleness. And so a pastor of the church is told: "diligently apply the cure of souls to those over whom you happen to be in charge. Know the state of their souls and each one's deeds; if you discover any vice in them, be mindful to correct it quickly. For you will not always have the power to feed the Lord's sheep, but you will gain an eternal crown if you feed them well in your time," as it says in the gloss upon Proverbs 27 ("Be diligent to know the countenance of thy flock" [Prov. 27:23]). And according to the words of St. Ambrose in one of his letters, nothing is more dangerous for a priest in the eyes of God or so base in the eyes of men than to see the truth and not openly proclaim it.

It should especially be the duty of priests to harm no one and to be useful to everyone. For insofar as they set examples of behavior that warrant perdition, they warrant punishment. Thus it is necessary that they carefully guard themselves as much from sin as from wickedness, since when they commit these things they are not the only ones who die from them. St. Augustine says that everyone who lives evilly in the sight of those over whom he is in charge as much as kills them.

They ought to, indeed they are bound to, obey absolutely the canons, mandates, and constitutions of bishops and superior prelates, because many things are enjoined in the canons and in various provincial constitutions that parish priests, by virtue of obedience, are obliged to announce publicly and also preach to their parishioners. Certain priests, as much out of negligence as ignorance, neither explain nor preach the things that they are bound to; they are therefore disobedient and as a consequence deserve to be punished.

Priests cannot excuse themselves due to their ignorance of the law, since no priest may ignore the canons of the church nor do anything which opposes the rules of the fathers of the church.

And they are especially obliged to know the penitential canons and provincial and synodal statutes. It is absolutely contemptible and dangerous for the church's prelates and parish priests, who are given the governance of souls as representatives of their King, to utterly ignore these things—just as it would be disgraceful for a lawyer to be ignorant about the law he practices or for any worker to neglect looking after his duties. St. Jerome says that it should be considered a priest's duty to respond when asked a question about the law: if he is a priest, he should know the Lord's law. But Jerome argues that if a priest does not know the Lord's law, he is not the Lord's priest since it is the duty of his priest to know the law and to answer questions about it. Yet today there are many priests who neither know God's law nor learn it. Carefree in their idleness, they are keen on feasting and drinking; they covet worldly things—they reek of them; they busy themselves in the streets, but rarely in church; they are slow to inquire about the sins of their parishioners, but quick to hunt the tracks of hares or other wild animals; faster at rounding up their hounds than gathering together the poor, they would sooner offer bread to a dog than to a poor man; they have more people serving them at the dinner table than at the Lord's Table; they want servants and maids attending them, not clergy. These are the sort of men whose bedchamber is better furnished than their church, whose dinner table is better adorned than their altar, whose goblet costs more than their chalice, whose surcoat is finer than their chasuble, whose shirt is more delicately woven than their alb. See how the gold is dulled, the brightest color faded, and how the bricks of the temple are scattered at the head of every street, as Hugh of St. Victor says. Priests should not behave this way; rather, what they do not know they should learn. For even a blind man can see that it is necessary to learn since, if it is better for someone to teach than to learn, it is better to learn than to be ignorant, as St. Augustine writes in one of his letters; and the man who is ashamed to undergo education for a short spell will remain ever after shamefully foolish. It is obvious that any workman who wishes to do well the job given him needs the proper tools for that job; otherwise, as it is plain to anyone considering it, he cannot accomplish his job or duty properly. Exactly the same holds true for the church's prelates and parish priests who, in assuming the job of teaching God's people, need to own and know at the very least the penitential canons and provincial and synodal constitutions. If they do not have these due to negligence and carelessness, they should be accused. If they have these and rashly do not observe them, they should be reproved and also rebuked. Priests also should perform the divine office faithfully and with good intention; as it says in Galatians, "let everyone test his own work" and diligently examine his reason for doing it; "and so he will have glory in himself only" and in God who is in him [Gal. 6:4].

They especially ought to be of good conscience and lead a pure life; thus, Proverb 21 says "the perverse way of a man is strange: but as for him that is pure, his work is right" [Prov. 21:8]. And priests should be pure not only inwardly but also outwardly in order to honor God and support Christ. Thus, Proverb 24: "Prepare thy work without, and diligently till thy ground" [Prov. 24:27] and Matthew 5: "Let your light shine before men, in order that they may see your good works and give glory to your Father in heaven" [Matt. 5:16]; and so those close to you are instructed and enlightened by your good works. Thessalonians 4: "so that you may walk becomingly towards outsiders" [1 Thess. 4:12]; he who does good works will have eternal life. Ecclesiasticus 14: "Every excellent work shall be justified: and the worker thereof shall be honored therein" [Ecclus. 14:21] and Romans 2: "Glory and honor and peace shall be awarded to everyone who does good" [Rom. 2:10]. And "the presbyters who rule well" in their lives and learning should be "held worthy of double honor" [1 Tim. 5:17] by their subjects: spiritually their subjects should obey them and outwardly they should tend them their goods. For good and faithful stewards should be rewarded not only with high honor, but also with material possessions so that they are not distressed by their lack of finery but take delight in their devotion to spiritual things, as Augustine says in his gloss on 1 Timothy, chapter 5.

For parish priests to rule well in this regard they should be discerning, knowing how to bind and loose sins, lest, out of ignorance, the blind take it upon themselves to lead others and they both fall into the pit. Hence the verse: "If a blind man guide a blind man . . . " [Matt. 15:14].

First the leader falls into the pit and then the follower. Their eyes are covered in sin so that they are blinded, and their backs are always bent. For when the leaders who bear all their sins are blind, those following them are easily led astray. Therefore, prelates and priests should strive to slough off ignorance from them as if it were some disease. For, according to Augustine, he who is ignorant will be disregarded, by which he means those who have an aptitude for learning but do not apply themselves to it.

Therefore, so that no prelate or parish priest, by claiming ignorance, will excuse himself in any way from knowing about these things, everything that the canons and provincial councils particularly order them to explain to their parishioners and preach in church is contained briefly and easily in this modest summary.

First, a parish priest should frequently explain to his parishioners on Sundays the English words for the baptismal ritual so that they can baptize someone who is in danger of dying. They should know this formula and be able to use it. The ritual for baptism consists not only in the action of baptizing but also in the order of the words spoken, through which this sacrament is divinely instituted. Here is what should be said while baptizing someone: *Ich cristen the in the name of the fader and the sone and the holi gost*, or similar words in the vernacular using the local dialect. And they should immerse the child in water one to three times or sprinkle the water on it. And people who baptize a child with these words should take care that the child is not baptized a second time as some foolish women do, since someone doing this in effect crucifies Christ twice. Still, the exorcism and catechism should be said over a child baptized by a layman, and the child should be anointed by the priest out of respect for the rituals of the church, because exorcism and anointing have been and still are effective in preventing the devil from harming the baptized child. Nor should anyone wonder why the devil is adjured to depart the body of the baptized child and do it no harm even though he is no longer in it, because this is the sense of the words "depart from him," that is, "you may have no power to do harm."

If someone immerses a child in water three times and says, *In the name of the Father, and of the Son, and of the Holy Spirit,* but fails to say *I baptize you,* the child is not baptized. Understand that the ritual formula for baptism prescribed by the church must be strictly observed. And no one may be baptized in any other liquid than water.

Second, a priest should explain to his parishioners that not only a priest but any other cleric or even the child's own father or mother—with no impediment to their marriage—may baptize in an emergency; the effect of baptism is still imparted to the child. And if a baby is baptized by a layman, the priest should supply those parts of the rite omitted.

Third, the priest should warn his parishioners that children born eight days or less before Easter or Pentecost should be reserved to be baptized on the Holy Saturday before Easter or on Pentecost if baptism can be delayed without endangering them. But children born at other times of the year may be baptized sooner or later according to their parents' wishes.

Also, the priest should warn his parishioners that the men and women who stand as sponsors for children at baptism are responsible for them before God. Thus their sponsors should always admonish them to guard their chastity, love justice, and maintain charity; above all they are obliged to teach them the Creed and the Lord's Prayer.

Those who stand as sponsors by receiving the child from the baptismal font should not also sponsor them at their confirmation unless necessity demands it.

Also, priests should warn their parishioners not to put their little ones in the same bed with them so that they will not accidentally roll over on them or suffocate them and thereby be found guilty of homicide. Nor should they carelessly restrain them in their cradles or leave them unattended day or night because of the danger that the baby's mouth might be covered by the bedding even for a short time which could easily prove fatal. It is the custom in some places for women who have overlain their children through negligence to go to the bishop on Ash Wednesday to be confessed. If their sin is widely known then they are enjoined public penance; if their sin was kept secret, they are given private penance.

A priest also should warn his parishioners and effectively persuade them to take care to have their children confirmed by a bishop within five years of birth if they have the opportunity to see the bishop. If they neglect to do this they should be forbidden entrance to the church until they have their children confirmed. But according to canon law, those to be confirmed should have reached the age of majority and should fast before coming to confirmation. They should be warned to confess their sins first so that, thus purified, they may be worthy to receive the gift of the Holy Spirit.

He should also explain to them that a spiritual consanguinity is created between a child's godparents and real parents, and between the godparents and the child, both at baptism and at confirmation; because of this relationship, they are prohibited from marrying one another.

Therefore, so that a parish priest ignorant of canon law can understand among which people a spiritual affinity exists because of baptism and confirmation, he should realize that such a spiritual relationship is created between ten people through baptism. Namely, between the baptized child and the person who sponsored it at baptism, between the baptized child and the children of its sponsor, between the sponsor and the wife he had carnal relations with before he was made sponsor, between the sponsor and the mother [and father] of the baptized child, between the baptized child and the one who baptized it, between the baptized child and the children of its baptizer, between the baptized child and the baptizer's wife (with whom the baptizer had previously had carnal relations), between the baptizer and the baptized child's father, and between the baptizer and the baptized child's mother. Thus, there are ten kinds of spiritual affinity established through baptism. This affinity is an impediment to contracts of marriage made between these people and it annuls contracts already made.

Likewise, know that the same kinds of affinity are established by confirmation (the anointing of the forehead). Namely, between the confirmed child and the one holding or sponsoring it before the bishop confirming it, between the confirmed child and the children of its sponsor, between the confirmed and its sponsor's wife, between the sponsor and the confirmed child's father, between the sponsor and the confirmed child's mother, between the person confirming and the confirmed child, between the confirmed child and the children of the one confirming it, between the confirmed child and the wife of the one confirming it, between the one confirming it and the confirmed child's father, and between the one confirming it and the confirmed child's mother. Thus, these are the cases forbidden because of spiritual affinity: ten cases through baptism, ten through confirmation. Any one of these cases prevents a marriage between these people from being contracted and annuls one if it has been contracted.

But baptism or confirmation does not prevent marriage from being contracted between people other than the ones just mentioned nor does it annul ones already contracted, customs to the contrary notwithstanding.

Also, he should explain that if legitimate consent is exchanged through words of the present tense between a man and a woman for the purpose of contracting marriage, even though no trothplight or oath has been exchanged nor has there been carnal consummation, nevertheless it is a truly legitimate marriage. And if one of the parties afterwards contracts a second marriage, even if that marriage is carnally consummated, the couple should be separated and the first marriage should be corroborated.

And he should explain that all carnal relations between a man and a woman outside of legal marriage are a mortal sin. Also, he should warn them that boys and girls over the age of seven should not sleep together in the same bed because of the danger of fornication or, if the girl is the boy's sister, incest.

He should explain that marriage should be solemnized with a priest, legitimate witnesses, and banns announced before the members of parish on three prior solemn days. And if a parish priest or any clergyman, regular or secular, dares to be present at a clandestine marriage or fails to prevent one when he has the power to, he should be suspended from office for three years. Also, he should announce frequently that a man having carnal relations with his wife or another woman should do nothing to prevent his wife from conceiving a child; if he does this, he sins more seriously than if had committed adultery.

He should also tell his parishioners that since human nature is always prone toward evil, every person is flawed by sin. For the path of man inclines towards pleasure and in his nature he mirrors the vices. Some men and even some women ejaculate semen or sperm in various ways either while sleeping or while awake.[5] Thus, anyone to whom this happens, either while sleeping or awake, is bound to confess it to his confessor, saying whether he did this willfully or with pleasure, since it can happen in many and various ways. Then their confessor should tell those confessing it how serious and detestable this sin is. Since sperm or semen can be ejaculated in various ways, he should tell him that in doing this he sins more seriously than he would by having sexual relations with his mother or sister.[6] But a priest should not tell everyone the ways that people can sin against nature, since—as bishops' penitentiaries[7] know well enough—these days there are many people who believe that in many cases a sin against nature is not really a sin, which is a deplorable state of affairs. Thus a priest can confidently tell his parishioners that they should be aware that anyone who ejaculates semen knowingly and willingly in any manner other than the normal way with his wife sins gravely, and he should tell his confessor how he did this.

He should warn them that no game warden or bailiff should hold scot-ales[8] or collect or make someone else collect the garb tithe; if he does this he is ipso facto excommunicated because he has violated the Charter of the Forest[9] and anyone violating the Charter of the Forest is ipso facto excom-

---

[5]The existence and nature of female sperm was a matter of lively medical and theological debate in the later middle ages. While Aristotle had denied the possibility, the ancient physician Galen believed that women could produce a "female seed." The influential thirteenth-century theologian Albertus Magnus endorsed the Galenist camp, arguing that women were capable of nocturnal emissions of sperm. See *A History of Women in the West*, vol. 2, *Silences of the Middle Ages*, ed. Christiane Klapisch-Zuber (Cambridge, Mass., 1992) pp. 54–58.

[6]The idea here is that the natural end of sexual intercourse is the procreation of children. Any emission of semen outside of intercourse foils this end.

[7]William of Pagula spoke from experience; he was appointed penitentiary for part of his own diocese of Salisbury in 1321.

[8]See note 5, p. 93.

[9]The royal forests were vast tracts of woodland and pasture spread across England meant for the sport of the king, who rigidly safeguarded his rights to the wild animals (venison) and timber (vert) within them. The Charter of the Forest (1217, with subsequent reissues) developed those clauses in the Magna Carta that restrained the more tyrannical royal abuses of this forest land.

municated. (This is made explicit both in the Charter and in the general excommunications issued by Archbishop Boniface of Canterbury and his suffragan bishops in the great hall at Westminster [in 1258].)

He ought to announce this statute in church frequently: each of the faithful, when they reach the age of discretion [i.e., fourteen] and so are able to commit sins, ought to confess all their sins to their own priest at least once a year and fulfill the penance given to them. And at Easter they should receive the Body of Christ, unless at the counsel of their priest they have been advised to abstain from receiving at this time for some reasonable cause. If they do not do this, they are to be forbidden entrance into the church while they are living and denied Christian burial at their death.

If for some justifiable reason a parishioner wishes to confess his sins to a priest who is not his parish priest, he should first seek and obtain license from his parish priest when that priest is otherwise unable to bind or loose him from his sins.

A priest should explain that pregnant women, because of the danger of death that threatens when they are giving birth, should go to confession so that they will be prepared in such an emergency to receive the eucharist. For it is unseemly for a priest to stay with them too long while they are in labor.

And a priest should frequently teach his people that when he elevates the saving Host during the celebration of mass, they should reverently genuflect if they can comfortably do so, and they should be able to say these words: "Hail, salvation of the world, Word of the Father, true host, living flesh, fully God, truly man," or "Glory to you, Lord, who was born of the Virgin, etc.," or the Lord's Prayer. They should say these same things when they see the saving Host, the Body of Christ, as the priest is carrying it to the sick. Both coming and going, the priest, decently dressed, should openly and honorably carry the Host with all reverence and honor in a clean linen cloth held before him, always being preceded by a lamp representing the splendor of eternal light; by doing this the faith and devotion of everyone may be increased. Prelates should gravely punish violators of this mandate.

The parish priest should teach his parishioners that when the Body of Christ is given to them at Easter or some other time, they receive both Christ's body and blood under the appearance of bread, and that it is Christ, fully and truly man, who is contained in the sacrament. He also should teach them that what they drink from the chalice is not a part of the sacrament but only ordinary wine or wine mixed with water that is given to them to drink to help them swallow the host more easily; for only the celebrant is allowed to drink the blood under the appearance of consecrated wine.[10]

He should instruct them that when the sacrament is in their mouth, they should not crush it too much with their teeth; instead they should gently chew it, swallowing it completely so that no particles get stuck between their teeth and remain there. Parishioners should be urged to look freely and frequently upon the Body of Christ. The priest should announce to his parishioners that whoever yearns to see the Body of Christ will merit the following according to St. Augustine in his book *The City of God:* he who sees it will get whatever food he needs; on that day too, his idle words will be forgiven, unwitting oaths canceled; on that day he will not lose his sight; on that day he will not meet with sudden death; on that day, he will not grow older while he hears the mass; angels will guard the footsteps coming and going of whoever sees the Body of Christ or who even is on his way devoutly to church.

He should warn them that they should not knowingly protect or shelter in their houses or villages anyone they know to be, or who obviously is, a thief.

He should admonish his parishioners to pay tithes faithfully on all goods legally acquired. Unless they do this completely and lovingly many bad consequences will follow, according to Augustine, who says that it is a transgression against divine command since tithes were instituted by God, not man. Secondly, in past times men paying tithes of all their goods had abundance; but now because they do not faithfully and willingly pay their tithes, they are compelled to tithe. The third reason is so that God does not send forth locusts nor stir up plagues that destroy the crops. The fourth is that what Christ does not get, taxes will. But they who faithfully pay their tithes are rewarded fourfold. The first reward is an abundance of crops; the second is bodily health; the third is indulgence for sins; the fourth is an everlasting reward.

He should also teach his parishioners how they should faithfully give to God and to his holy church tithes from all their goods, since many people have been found to tithe badly due to ignorance. Thus, so that henceforward they will not sink down into a pit of such danger out of ignorance, the priest should inform his parishioners and tell them that, because quarrels, disputes, scandals, and great animosity once arose between rectors of churches

[10] By the twelfth century the practice of offering the chalice with consecrated wine to the laity had faded.

and their parishioners due to the many different customs for claiming tithes, Boniface, former Archbishop of Canterbury of good memory—with the consent and assent of all his suffragan bishops and the whole clergy at the Council of Lambeth—decreed and ordered that through the whole province of Canterbury there should be a uniform rule for seeking tithes.

[*Here William of Pagula inserts almost verbatim Archbishop Boniface's mid-thirteenth-century Statute on Tithes. See No. 87 below.*]

The priest should publish and announce those days which are feast days and those which are days of fasting.

Likewise, a priest ought to admonish his people that magical practices and incantations cannot remedy any sort of human sickness or cure sick, lame, or dying animals. Instead, such things are the snares and traps of the ancient enemy by which that treacherous enemy works to deceive the human race; and he who violates this, if he is a cleric, should be degraded; if a lay person, he should be anathematized.

And he should warn his parishioners that none of them should loan money, wine, oil, grain or anything else by usury. If a cleric does this he should be suspended from his office and his benefice. If a lay person does this, he shall be excommunicated until he makes suitable restitution. Usury is when someone receives more in repayment of a loan than he lent.

Also, he should warn them that if anyone receives land or dwellings as a pledge for the loan of some amount of money and he then recovers the whole amount or its equivalent value from the proceeds of that land or the dwellings, after he has deducted his expenses he should return the land to the person who borrowed from him, because a creditor is obliged to credit all the profit that he received from the possessions pledged to him into the debt for the principal; if he refuses to give it back, it is considered usury and he should be compelled to make restitution through ecclesiastical censure.

And he should warn his parishioners both that they should be hospitable and that they should not sell their goods to travelers at a higher price than they could receive at market.

Also, he should warn them that no one should wait to sell his goods at a higher price, since if he does this on purpose it is deemed usury; and when he goes to confession he should be strongly persuaded that he is bound to make restitution for profit he has received due to having delayed the date of sale.

Note that usury is contrary to the teaching of the Old Testament. And so when the prophet asks, "Lord, who shall dwell in thy tabernacle" [Ps. 14:1], he answers, "he who does not lend out his money with usury" [Lev. 25:37]. It is likewise contrary to the gospels where it says, "lend, not hoping for any return" [Luke 6:35]. It is also contrary to the prohibitions of all the saints. And it is contrary to the constitutions of the church. Thus, he who commits usury is a damnable sinner. It also violates civil law.

And note that, according to St. Ambrose, usurers are called robbers. According to St. Augustine they are called crucifiers of the poor. Also they are called minions of filthy lucre driven by avarice. They are called thieves, because they steal their souls from God. They are called the devil's children, not by birth but by joining in his work through sin alone. They are called accursed; John Crysostom says that usurers should be cursed more than any other sinners. This is why usury is forbidden both in the Old and the New Testament, since if usury were allowed, all sorts of evils would follow from it. In particular, since the rich would care more for usurious profits than agriculture, there would be such a dearth of food that all the poor would starve to death. For, although they could get land for farming, they could not get the animals and tools necessary to farm it. Since these poor people would have nothing and the rich would lack nothing—partly because of their greed and partly safeguarded by the profits of their usury—then food would cost so much that the poor could not afford it. This is usury's greatest and most serious danger.

Also, another reason is that it is hardly possible for someone indebted to a usurer to survive for long without falling into poverty, which is an especially dangerous condition unless the desire for poverty is given to someone as a special gift from God.

Many other evils arise from usury, for in lending and loving money, idolatry can scarcely be avoided. For "where thy treasure is, there also will thy heart be" [Matt. 6:21]. For these reasons, therefore, usury is forbidden in both testaments.

Also, the priest should publicly announce to his parishioners three times yearly in church that those men who wish to enjoy the privilege of the clergy should wear a decent tonsure and have the crown of their head suitably shaved, especially in the presence of their ordinaries and in their churches and in congregations of the clergy. Nor should they be ashamed to bear the mark of that man who, obedient even unto death, deigned to wear a crown of thorns for them so that they could share in his resurrection. Whoever would presume to disobey this warning, ashamed to bear the sign of the Savior impressed upon his brow, will beseech the Savior's help in vain, since he deserves to lose that privilege which, after he received it, he betrayed by abusing its dignity.

And the priest should publicly explain the meaning of the Creed to his parishioners on one of the days of Lent.

Also, he should announce to his parishioners that they should enter the church humbly and devoutly and should stand there quietly and respectfully, since this is how you behave even in the presence of a temporal lord. And they should hold in great reverence that name above every name, given to no one else on earth, from which mankind receives salvation, namely, the name of Jesus Christ who saved his people from their sins, and about which it is said that at the name of Jesus Christ all creatures in heaven, earth, and hell bow down [Phil. 2:9–10]. Therefore, each and every person when he hears that glorious name of Jesus, especially during the celebration of mass, should genuflect deep in his heart by striking his breast and bowing his head. He should listen to the divine office with great presence of mind and he should offer up devout prayers.

They should also be admonished that they should not cause a quarrel, disturbance, assault, nor hold a conference in the church or graveyard, nor secular courts or gatherings; nor should they have disputes, fights, conversations, or anything else that could disturb divine services or offend God, so that an opportunity to sin does not arise in the very place where people ought to beg forgiveness for their sins.

And he should warn his parishioners that they should not conduct business in the church or graveyard nor, in particular, should they allow fairs or markets to be held there; and lay people should not be allowed to hold their courts or any sorts of judicial actions there; and there should be no dishonorable dancing in the church or graveyard nor any singing of improper songs as is the custom during the vigils of certain saints' feast days; no games should be played there nor should rocks be thrown nor should they do any other things which could lead to the violation of the church or the graveyard.

He should announce to them that, without the other's consent, a husband or wife may not take a vow of chastity or a vow to make a pilgrimage or to fast (except for the vow to go to Jerusalem), since a man and a woman are not judged according to the same standards. But a husband should be careful that he does not consent to his wife's vow; in fact he should immediately oppose it if he wishes. For once he has given his consent to her vow, she is obliged to fulfill it, since he has not opposed it. But a husband does not sin by revoking his wife's vow because it is within his rights; power over her body rests with him, not her. For if you abstain from sexual relations with your wife without her consent, you are granting her license to fornicate, and her sin will be blamed on your abstinence.

Finally, a parish priest should announce frequently on Sundays and other solemn feast days during the celebration of mass, the articles of general excommunication issued at the Council of Oxford and the Council of Lambeth.[11]

And note that there are many crimes for which someone incurs excommunication ipso facto; these cases are noted in the *Speculum prelatorum,*[12] Part Two, title 21.

✎ No. 73. *Quicumque vult:* the Athanasian Creed from the *Sarum Breviary.*
Breviarium ad usum insignis ecclesiae Sarum, ed. Francis Proctor and Christopher Wordsworth (Cambridge, 1879, reprint 1970), pp. 46–47. Trans. JS.

Whosoever wishes to be saved must above all maintain the Catholic faith. Unless someone keeps that faith whole and inviolate, without a doubt he will be damned for eternity. And this is the Catholic faith: that we shall adore one God in the Trinity and the unity of the Trinity. And the persons of the Trinity are not mixed together nor are they separated in substance. One person is the Father, another is the Son, another is the Holy Spirit. But the divinity of the Father, the Son, and the Holy Spirit is one, equal in glory, coeternal in majesty. As the Father is, so is the Son and the Holy Spirit. The Father is uncreated, the Son is uncreated, the Holy Spirit is uncreated. The Father is infinite, the Son is infinite, the Holy Spirit is infinite. The Father is eternal, the Son is eternal, the Holy Spirit is eternal. But they are not three eternal beings; they are one. In the same way, they are not three uncreated and infinite beings, but one uncreated and infinite being. Similarly, the Father is omnipotent, the Son is omnipotent, the Holy Spirit is omnipotent. But they are not three omnipotent beings; they are one. Thus there is our Lord the Father, our Lord the Son, and our Lord the Holy Spirit. But there are not three Lords, there is only one Lord. Just as we are obliged by Christian truth to profess that each person singly is God and Lord, so Christian belief forbids us to say that there are three Gods or three Lords. No one made the Father, nor was he created or begotten. The Son comes from the Father alone; he was not made or created, but begotten. The Holy Spirit was not made, nor created, nor begotten from the Father and the Son; rather, he proceeds from them. Therefore, the one Father is not three fathers; the one Son is not three sons; the one Holy Spirit is not three spirits. And in this Trinity there was nothing before nor after, nothing more nor less. But they are completely three persons, coeternal and coequal with themselves. To

[11] See No. 83.
[12] I.e., William of Pagula's own *Mirror for Priests,* a massive pastoral compendium combining both the *Oculus sacerdotis* and his handbook of canon law, the *Summa summarum.*

sum up everything that has been said above: both the Unity and the Trinity, the Trinity and the Unity should be adored.

Whosoever wishes to be saved must believe this about the Trinity. But it is also necessary for eternal salvation to believe faithfully in the incarnation of our Lord Jesus Christ. It is therefore orthodox for us to believe and profess that our Lord Jesus Christ, the Son of God, is both God and man. He is God begotten before all ages from the substance of the Father; he is man born into the world from the substance of his mother. He is perfectly God and perfectly man subsisting with a rational soul and with human flesh. Measured according to his divinity, he is equal with the Father; measured according to his humanity, he is less than the Father. Although Christ is God and is also man, he is not two beings; he is one being. But he is one not through the conversion of his divinity into flesh, but through his godhead assuming humanity. He is completely one not through a mixing of his substance, but by the unity of his person. For just as he is one man with a rational soul and flesh, Christ is one God and man. He suffered death for our salvation and descended into hell; on the third day he rose from the dead. He ascended into heaven and sits at the right hand of God the Father Omnipotent. From thence he will come to judge the living and the dead. At his coming all people will rise with their bodies, and they must give account for all their deeds. And those who have done good will go into eternal life; those who have done evil will go to eternal fire.

This is the Catholic faith which unless someone believes it faithfully and firmly he cannot be saved. Glory be to the Father.

ᐸᐤ No. 74. The priest in his cure: excerpts from "A York Priest's Notebook" (late 1470s).

Roy M. Haines, *Ecclesia Anglicana: Studies in the English Church in the Later Middle Ages* (Toronto: University of Toronto Press, 1989), pp. 163–77. Trans. WJD.

[*Memory devices such as rhymed verses were a commonplace in practical handbooks such as this one. In most cases where they occur here, they have been rendered in prose.*]

The Sacrament of Penance

Penance is the remorse for wicked things done and the pious resolve not to commit them again. Penance has three parts, namely contrition, confession, and satisfaction. Contrition is heartfelt sorrow willingly taken on for one's sins with the resolve to confess, make satisfaction, and refuse to commit sin again. Confession is the open declaration of all of one's sins before a priest. Satisfaction is recompense for the injury or loss incurred according to the judgment and direction of the law. And this sacrament takes away venial and mortal sin.

The Invocation of Saints

The eight intercessors: Saints Denis, Blaise, George, Christopher, Katherine, Martha, Margaret, and Agnes.[13]

Questions

Why does the priest turn five times during mass? Because Christ showed himself five times on Easter Sunday, first to Mary Magdalene, for it was fitting that he who came into the world to save sinners should first reveal himself to a sinner. Still, others say that he appeared first to his mother, though this is untrue, but rather, what people would like to believe.

What did Christ write with his finger on the ground when the woman [caught in adultery] was brought before him to be accused? Jerome says it was these words: "Earth accuses earth."[14] And when the woman's accusers saw what Christ had written they knew that their own sins were exceedingly great and they fled. Augustine says that no one can know the heavenly mysteries except the one who sees or senses through Christ. If a person is sick, no one else knows what that sickness is except the one who feels it. Hence, John says, "I saw the ancient writing which could not be put into human speech."[15]

Lucifer's Fall

God created ten orders of angels in heaven and he created an angel named Lucifer in his own image. And Lucifer was arrogant for all his beauty and said, "Who is like me?" And then a tenth of all the angels believed that Lucifer was first among all and went with him. And then Michael and the other angels said against them: "Who is like our God?" Now Lucifer, who was created in a day, in that same day fell to hell with all his angels. And so God created us to take their place in heaven. Thus says Ezekiel, "All who were

[13]With the exception of Martha and Agnes, these saints are numbered among a group of special intercessors very popular in the middle ages known as the "Fourteen Holy Helpers."

[14]John 8:6. The obscure quotation is derived from Jerome's "Dialogue against the Pelagians," (2.17) where he says that Jesus was writing down the sins of the woman's accusers. Jerome cites as his authority the prophet Jeremiah: "they that depart from thee, shall be written in the earth, because they have forsaken the Lord" [Jer. 17:13].

[15]2 Cor. 12:4 should read, "And he heard the ancient words which could not be put into human speech" (as in Haines, p. 164).

damned shall be saved." For which reason anyone gives and should give a tenth of his goods; for, as it is said, if you have not tithed, you will, which is to say, you will fall with Lucifer, etc.

Priestly Function: A Schematic Approach to the Mass

Things to ponder before mass	—when setting out to celebrate, one's first thought should not be on	—vainglory
		—shame
		—routine
	—what you should strive to do	—worship God and his saints, reverence Christ and contemplate his love, give aid to the whole church
Further things	—what outcome you should desire	—an increase in love, the indivisibility of union, the hastening of the vision of God
What ought to come before mass	—a general confession, pure, sincere and humble; forgetting all worldly cares	—of sins committed: in thought, word, and deed
		—sins of omission: through negligence, ignorance, contempt
	—fervent prayer	—bewailing wretchedness, imploring mercy, displaying tears
Before the canon of the mass there should be due consideration	—much for the place	—for the altar makes the place holy
	—more for the vessels	—that is, the chalice and paten, finely-wrought from gold and silver
	—most for the substances	—bread made from wheat and good wine
During the canon of the mass great care should be taken	—much regarding the signs	—so that the hands are correctly placed
	—more regarding the words	—so that the words are not mispronounced

	—most regarding the intention	—so that the mind does not wander
When touching Christ, there should be the greatest reverence, etc.	—much	—because of the restraint of a noble heart
	—more	—because of the restraint of a nobler soul
	—most	—because of the restraint of noblest divinity
After mass there should be	—thanksgiving for what has taken place	—the forgiveness of sins, the granting of favors, and the promise of reward
	—longing for what is to come	—the removal of ills, the abundance of honors, the fulfillment of all yearnings
	—regard for the present in	—mindfulness, devout prayer and godly action
The eucharist: commemorates Christ. It revives the inner life and refreshes the spirit. It increases devotion and diminishes temptation. It confers grace and virtue and remits sins. It is a defence against the devil. It brings new hope and quickens love. It gladdens the angels and opens up the Kingdom of God. It enlightens the mind, nurtures faith, kindles hope, and strengthens charity.	—But those who receive it with awe —with appropriate regard for the Divine Judge —will be assured of salvation —faithful in love	

Illicit Marriages

What people ought to know in cases regarding the solemnization of matrimony when excommunication is incurred ipso facto and when, in other cases, it is not. First of all, those who contract marriage knowing that there is an impediment, even if no one objected when the banns were published, are excommunicated. Also, betrothed couples who solemnize a marriage without the publication of banns are excommunicated even if a priest blessed the marriage. Also, a couple is excommunicated when an impediment, which becomes apparent in the publication of banns, remains unresolved. The same holds for those who force a priest under threat to solemnize a clandestine marriage. Also, when a priest neglects to publish the banns for three separate solemnities, and then solemnizes the marriage and afterwards an impediment is discovered. Also, when a couple acts against the interdict of the church, etc. . . . .

Woman and Man
What is woman? A man's confusion, an insatiable beast, constant anxiety. A constant losing battle, a house of storms, an obstruction to a man's chastity and the shipwreck of purity, the vessel of adultery, a costly strife, the worst creature, the heaviest weight, a deadly viper, humanity's slave.

What is man? The spirit incarnate, the struggling soul, its dwelling for a short time, the spirit's shelter, the model of the human form, life's observer, a deceiver of the light, a devourer of life, in constant motion, the slave of death, a traveler en route, a host.

Aides Memoires
What are the church's sacraments? There are seven:

1. baptism
2. confirmation
3. penance
4. eucharist
5. extreme unction
6. orders
7. marriage

Which ones may be received more than once and which not?
Four may be taken over and over again and these are found in the word "meup": marriage, eucharist, unction, and penance. Three may be received only once and these are found in the word "boc," which means baptism, order, and confirmation. "Boc" are not conferred twice but "meup" may be received many times. Why can these four be received more often than the other three? Because there is a special character in these three which is not found in the other four.

What is a character? A character is an imprint of the soul through baptism and, according to [Pope] Innocent, is a certain disposing quality that illuminates the soul so that grace may be received. Some call this quality or clarity sanctity since it readies the soul for sanctification. John Damascene says that character is the guardian of the soul because it constantly looks after the soul and prepares and readies it for the grace by which the soul itself is safeguarded.

Which sacraments are required and which are voluntary? Five are necessary and they are baptism, confirmation, eucharist, penance and extreme unction.

The Decalogue
Believe in one God lest you worship vain gods before him;
Make the sabbath holy; render honor to parents; be not a murderer, an adulterer, a thief, a false witness; desire not the spouse or property of another.

Articles of Faith
These are the articles: that God is one and three; that Christ was born a man, suffered, was buried, and rose, that he ascended and judges and rewards, that all will rise, and that he established the holy sacraments.

The Seven Corporal Works of Mercy
There are seven corporal works of mercy. The first is to feed the hungry; the second is to give drink to the thirsty; the third to clothe the naked; the fourth to give refuge; the fifth to visit the sick; the sixth to free captives; the seventh to bury the dead.

The Seven Spiritual Works of Mercy
There are seven spiritual works of mercy. The first is to give and the second to ask for good counsel; the third to correct the wicked of their evil deeds and urge them to good; the fourth to subdue counsel that damns or destroys; the fifth to dismiss wicked things when they arise; the sixth to endure evil in deed and word; the seventh to pray to God with all of one's heart.

The Seven Gifts of the Holy Spirit
There are seven gifts of the Holy Spirit given from of old: wisdom for the patriarchs, insight for the prophets, counsel for the apostles, fortitude for the martyrs, learning for confessors,[16] piety in virgins, and fear of the Lord in rulers.

[16] Here the term denotes confessors in the broader sense, those who have witnessed to the faith with their lives.

The Five Senses
The five human senses are all found in this verse:
> Taste, smell, hearing, touch, and sight
> are senses five to mortals true and right.

The Seven Deadly Sins
The seven deadly sins are found in this verse:
> Pride, anger, sloth,
> Gluttony and greed,
> Envy, lust are deadly sins,
> So Christians all take heed.

Further Questions
Why does a priest sing three masses on Christmas Day, more than any other day of the year? In response it should be stated that the three masses represent the three ages from the beginning of creation: the first mass is sung at night and represents the time from Adam to Moses; the second mass, sung in the morning, signifies the time from the Mosaic law to the coming of the Lord; the third mass signifies the time of the New Covenant and Christ's resurrection up to the Day of Judgment.

Why are bells not rung from Holy Thursday to the Easter Vigil? The reason is that the bells represent the apostles, who though many, did not dare speak for fear of the Jews when Jesus was crucified.

Why does the priest stand at the middle of the altar during the sacrifice of Christ's Body rather than at any other place? The answer is that it represents Christ's death when he suffered for all Christians from the middle of the cross.

Why do people not eat meat during Lent or on Friday or Saturday but eat fish instead? Because fish live in the water and the Lord never cursed the water but, rather, the earth on account of Adam's sin.

What is the mass? It is the song of the saints, the slumber of the dead, and the consolation of the living.

What are the grades of the church? There are seven, namely porter, lector, exorcist, acolyte, subdeacon, deacon, and priest. The porter gets his name from "the one who opens," for he is to stand at the doorway to welcome the faithful. The Lord was a porter when he broke the gates of hell. The lector takes his name from "reading" and his duty is to proclaim the law of the Lord. The Lord was a lector when he opened and read from the law of Moses and spoke to his disciples. The exorcist gets his name from "I exorcise," which means to conjure. The Lord was an exorcist when he banished seven demons from Mary Madgalene. The acolyte gets his name from the one who carries the cross. The Lord was an acolyte when bravely he bore the cross. The subdeacon comes from the subminister of the law. The Lord was a subdeacon when he changed water into wine. The deacon is called from "dia" which means two and "conus" which means grade as one having two grades. The Lord was a deacon when he washed his disciples' feet. A presbyter is like a "prebens" or gift for others. The Lord was a presbyter when he fed his disciples, saying, "take and eat this bread."

Riddles

> When will the world end?
> When the old lack wisdom [Wisd. of Sol. 4:8–9],
> The people lack devotion,
> The wealthy are without charity,
> The poor without humility,
> Marriages lack fidelity,
> The clergy lack sanctity,
> Women their shame,
> Earthly lords their justice,
> Churchmen their learning,
> And religious their obedience. . . .

On Transubstantiation

> There appears on the altar flesh from bread created.
> That flesh is God and anyone who denies it is godless.
> The bread is changed, but its outward appearance remains the same.
> It is not a change the senses can perceive.
> The true substance is hidden. Why? Because were it apparent
> You would be awestruck and afraid to eat.

What Man Should Have

A man ought to have:

> Fear of God and longing for God
> Obedience and reverence toward his pastor
> Concern and help for his neighbor
> Discipline and care for those under him

Temperance and holiness regarding his own person.
His sins belong to the Devil whose torments are eternal.

Six Examples of Martyrdom
Here are six clear examples of martyrdom:
Chastity in youth
Good cheer in old age
Generosity in poverty
Abstinence in abundance
Patience in times of trial
Humility and worthiness in prayer.

The Priestly Ideal according to St. Augustine
Attend well, for according to St. Augustine the priest should be careful that his eyes, when they take everything in, do not linger on things that are base. And his tongue, which by uttering the right words can bring God's Son from heaven to earth, should say nothing that is false, against God, or harmful to anyone. His hands which touch the Blood of Christ should not be sullied with any evil deed.

If Christ's tomb was made glorious by the presence of his body which lay there for a while, how much more glorious and worthy ought the bodies of those priests be who carry within themselves daily the body of the Risen Lord. And just as the breasts which suckled the infant Christ were holy, so too should be the mouth that eats his Flesh and Blood.

Beware, then, as St. Augustine says, how vile it is when someone whose mouth has received the eucharist of Christ sings a lusty or amorous song. Priests should live in such a way that no one could justly condemn them. It is especially fitting that those whose order and status require it should live the purest lives and display an abundance of sanctity. It is to such as these that scripture refers: "be holy as I myself am holy."[17] Yes, they ought to be holy who have submitted themselves to divine worship, who have been consecrated to the sacred altar of Christ and ordained for the celebration of the eucharist.

The Priestly Ideal according to St. Gregory[18]
Pope St. Gregory openly proclaimed in his preaching that:

[17] Lev. 19:2; 1 Pet. 1:16.
[18] What follows is a series of Latin puns easy to remember on the qualities which priests should espouse and shun.

A priest ought to be holy, wholly freed from sin
A provider, not a plunderer; a look-out, not an assassin
Wise in judgment, just in counsel
Devout in choir, chaste in bed
Resident in his church, sober at table
Prudent in learning, pure in conscience
Truthful in his preaching, fervent in prayer
Humble before his people, steadfast in adversity
Possessed of many virtues, a soldier in good works
Wise in confession, fearless in preaching
A shining mirror where deeds match words.

Christ's Sacrifice on the Cross

Look upon me, sweet friend, and see the sorrows I bore for you.
None did I bear for myself. I was crucified unjustly,
Nailed here, stretched out on the cross for you.
Indeed, it is true, I bear the pain of your sins
So that you will not have to suffer. Your sins have pierced me
    to death.
And so, from this moment on, you will not die if you choose to
    live in me.
Try as you might, you cannot render fitting thanks
For my anguish is your great reward.

The Mass

These are the materials used in the sacrifice of the mass: single-grain bread, nothing else; pure wine, not vinegar; pure water mixed with wine but not so much as to dilute the wine; a male serving as priest; the intention of consecrating the eucharist and of doing so with real faith in the sacrament; a consecrated chalice, made of silver or gold, along with a good paten; an altar which has been blessed and a clean altar cloth; two palls clean and blessed; two, or at least one wax candle; a priest who has fasted and is free from mortal sin; a cleric to assist the priest, etc. . . . .

Marriage

Cases allowing the dissolving of marriage vows: leprosy, insanity, holy orders, kinship, the absence or loss of virginity, minority of age, loss of the male organ, heretical beliefs, and apostasy may absolve partners entirely and nullify future vows.

Virginity

In the eyes of the church, the life of the virgin is the mark of the highest virtue next to God. It may be likened to the life of the angels, the friendship of saints, the mistress of virtue, joy's lady, the light of the path of salvation, the font of virtue. It is the crown of faith and charity's right hand. Nothing should be required of us save to live as virgins or to die for virginity.

Cases Reserved for the Bishop

The one who commits incest, murder or sacrilege;
who does violence to his parents or commits sodomy,
a breaker of vows and a sorcerer,
one who commits breach of faith, an arsonist, one who overlays a child,
a blasphemer, and one who is thoroughly unchaste.

St. Dorothy's Protection

In any house where there is an image or the name of that glorious virgin and martyr, Dorothy, no child shall be stillborn, no fire or theft shall trouble it, no one shall die an evil death but, when they do die, they shall have their fill of the bread of angels.

B. Sacraments, Rituals, and Preaching

ᖇ **No. 75. Excerpts from the Sarum rite of baptism (fourteenth century).**
Manuale ad Usum Percelebris Ecclesiae Sarisburiensis, ed. A. Jeffries Collins, Henry Bradshaw Society 91 (1960), pp. 31–32, 35–38. Trans. JS.

Blessing of the Font

When the font needs to be cleaned and refilled with fresh water, which should be done often due to the fouling of the water, then the following litany should be recited and the font blessed in the following fashion. Note that the baptismal water should not be changed for the sake of the high station of some powerful person unless it has been fouled.

Note that the holy water in the fonts should not be sprinkled through the church on Easter Eve or Pentecost, but only other water blessed as usual as on other Sundays.

Keep in mind that holy water should be sprinkled around the fonts but not the water from the fonts, whether or not it has been blessed with holy chrism. For in the early decrees of the holy fathers Popes Clement and Paschasius one finds that the water in the fonts is used only for baptism and purification, and not as water used for aspersion. Thus, every priest should take care that this water touches only those whom he is baptizing, for it is not necessary for those already baptized to be baptized again. For this reason, let the foolish sprinkling [of baptismal water] by the presumptuous priest cease both on the eves of Easter and Pentecost and on all other days as well since the Roman Church has forbidden all Christians to do this on pain of major excommunication.

The litany begins in this manner:

[Text in Middle English] "Godfathers and godmothers and all that are here about, say in worship of God and Our Lady and the Twelve Apostles an 'Our Father,' a 'Hail Mary,' and the Creed that we may so administer this sacrament that it may be to the pleasure of Almighty God and to the confusion of our ghostly enemy and to the salvation of the soul of this child.

"Godfathers and godmothers of this child, we charge you that you charge its father and mother to keep it from fire and water and other perils until the age of seven years, and that you teach it or have it be taught the 'Our Father,' 'Hail Mary,' and the Creed according to the law of all holy church, and that in all good haste it be confirmed by my lord [the bishop] of the diocese or his deputy, and that its mother return the chrism-cloth at her purification, and wash your hands before you depart the church."[19]

[*Omitted here is a litany of the saints and the service for blessing the font.*]

Concerning Baptism

Then the infant should be carried to the fonts by those who are going to receive it in baptism [i.e., its godparents], who hold it over the fonts in their hands. Let the priest put his right hand over it and ask its name. Let those who are holding it respond, N. Then let the priest say: "N., do you renounce Satan?" Let the godfathers and godmothers answer: "I renounce him." Again the priest: "And all his works?" Reply: "I renounce them." Again the priest: "And all his pomps?" Reply: "I renounce them."

After this, let the priest touch the infant's breast and between its shoulders with holy chrism and make the sign of the cross with his thumb, saying:

"N., I anoint you" (*on the breast*) "with the oil of salvation" (*between the shoulders*). In Christ Jesus our Lord may you have eternal life and may you live forever. Amen."

Then, when he has asked its name, let them answer: "N." Again the priest: "N., do you believe in God the Father Almighty creator of heaven

---

[19]The chrism-cloth, essentially a baptismal gown, was meant to protect those spots on the infant anointed with chrism. The mother's purification, or churching, occurred thirty to forty days after her child's birth. The godparents were warned to wash their hands to remove any of the holy chrism they may have touched when handling the anointed infant.

and earth?" Let them answer: "I believe." Again the priest: "Do you believe in Jesus Christ, his only Son, our Lord who was born and suffered?" Let them answer: "I believe." Again the priest: "Do you believe in the Holy Spirit, the holy Catholic Church, the communion of saints, the forgiveness of sins, the resurrection of the flesh, and life everlasting after death?" Let them answer: "I believe."

Then let the priest ask the infant's name, saying: "What do you seek?" Let them answer: "Baptism." Again the priest: "Do you wish to be baptized?" Let them answer: "I do wish."

Then let the priest take the infant, holding it sideways in his hands and, asking its name, let him baptize it by immersing it three times and invoking the Holy Trinity only, so saying:

"N., I baptize you in the name of the father," (*and let him immerse the child once with its face turned toward the north and its head toward the east*) "and of the Son," (*and let him immerse it again, turning its face to the south*) "and of the Holy Spirit. Amen" (*and let him immerse it a third time, turning its face toward the water*).

Then, taking the infant from the priest's hands, let the godparents raise it from the font. After it is raised up from the font, let the priest take some chrism with his thumb, saying: "The Lord be with you," and "Let us pray." Prayer:

"Almighty God, Father of our Lord Jesus Christ who has made you be reborn through water and the Holy Spirit, and who gave you remission from all your sins," (*here let him anoint the infant on the top of its head in the shape of a cross with the chrism on his thumb*) "himself anoints you to eternal life with the oil of salvation through his same Son, our Lord Jesus Christ."

After this, let the infant be wrapped with the chrism-cloth, and then the priest asks its name and says:

"N., accept this white gown, holy and immaculate, which you should present at the judgment seat of our Lord Jesus Christ in order to have eternal life and to live forever. Amen."

It is permissable to anoint the chrism-cloth a second time with chrism and put it on another person to be baptized, but that cloth should not be used for ordinary purposes; it should be returned to the church and kept for use in the church.

Next, asking its name, he should place a burning candle in the infant's hand, saying:

"N., accept this torch, burning and flawless; guard your baptism, keep the commandments, so that when the Lord comes to the wedding, you can hurry to him together with the saints in the heavenly hall in order to have life everlasting and to live forever. Amen."

If a bishop is present, it would be fitting for the child to be confirmed immediately and then receive communion if its age calls for it, with the priest saying:

"May the Body of our Lord Jesus Christ guard your body and soul for life everlasting. Amen."

If it is an infant, the father and mother should be enjoined to protect the child from fire, water, and all other dangers until the age of seven; and if the father and mother do not do so, the godfathers and godmothers are bound to do this. Also, the godmothers should be enjoined that they are to teach the infant the "Our Father," the "Hail Mary," and the Creed or have them so taught, and that the chrism-cloth should be returned to the church, and that the child is to be confirmed as soon as the bishop comes within seven miles of those parts.

Next, let this following gospel be recited over the infant if it is fitting, for according to doctors, it is especially effective against falling sickness.[20]

ᴗ No. 76. The Canon and Order of the Mass according to the York Use.

The Lay Folks Mass Book, ed. T. F. Simmons, EETS o.s. 71 (London, 1879), pp. 104–17.

Canon of the Mass

Let the priest with his hands together bow himself and say: Thee therefore most merciful Father, through Jesus Christ, thy Son, our Lord, we humbly pray and beseech:

Here let him raise himself and kiss the altar, and making a cross over the chalice (let him say):

That thou wouldest hold accepted and bless these gifts, these offerings, these holy undefiled sacrifices, which first of all we offer to thee for thy holy catholic church, which do thou vouchsafe to keep in peace, to watch over, to knit together and govern, throughout the whole world, together with thy servant our Pope and our Bishop N., and our King N., and all right believers, and maintainers of the Catholic and Apostolic faith.

Here the Commemoration of the living.

Remember, O Lord, thy servants and handmaidens, N. and all here standing around, and all faithful Christians, whose faith is known and devotion noted by thee; for whom we offer unto thee, or who are offering unto

---

[20] I.e., epilepsy. The gospel citation is Mark 9:16–28, the story of Jesus casting out a spirit from an epileptic boy.

thee, this sacrifice of praise, for themselves and all theirs, for the redemption of their souls, for the hope of their salvation and safety, and unto thee, eternal God, living and true, are rendering their vows.

Eugenius appointed the seven [words or crosses]. And whilst speaking, let him somewhat touch the chalice, and say:

This oblation therefore of our service as also of thy whole household, we beseech thee, O Lord, that having been reconciled thou wouldest accept; and wouldest order our days in thy peace, and ordain that we be delivered from eternal damnation and numbered with the flock of thine elect; through Christ our Lord. Amen.

Which oblation, do thou, we beseech thee, O God Almighty, vouchsafe to render altogether blessed, counted, reckoned, reasonable and acceptable, that it may be made unto us the Body and Blood of thy most beloved Son, our Lord Jesus Christ.

Pope Alexander appointed [the Qui pridie*]. With head bowed over the linen cloths (let him say) at taking up the host:*

Who on the day before he suffered took bread into his holy and most honoured hands, (*Here let him raise his eyes*) and with his eyes raised up towards heaven, unto Thee, O God, his Father almighty, giving thanks to Thee, he blessed and (*Here let him touch the host*) broke and gave to his disciples, saying, Take and eat ye all of this, for this is my Body. In like manner after supper, taking also this most excellent cup into his holy and most honoured hands, and likewise giving thanks unto Thee, he blessed and gave to his disciples, saying, Take and drink ye all of this, for this is the cup of my Blood, of the new and everlasting covenant, a mystery of faith, which shall be shed for you and for many for the remission of sins:

Here the priest covers the chalice with the corporal.

As oft as ye do (*or* offer) these things; ye shall do them in memory of me.

Here the priest spreadeth abroad his arms after the manner of a cross.

Wherefore, also we thy servants, O Lord, and also thy holy people, in memory as well of the blessed passion of the same Christ, thy Son, our Lord, as of his resurrection from the dead, and also of his glorious ascension into the heavens do offer unto thy excellent majesty, of thine own gifts, albeit given unto us,

Here let him draw back his arms and make the sign of the cross
a pure, a holy, and undefiled sacrifice, the holy bread of eternal life, and the cup of everlasting salvation.

Upon which do thou vouchsafe to look with favourable and gracious countenance, and hold them accepted, as thou didst vouchsafe to hold accepted the offerings of thy righteous servant Abel, and the sacrifice of our forefather Abraham, and that holy sacrifice, the pure offering, which thy high priest Melchizedek did offer unto thee.

We humbly beseech thee, Almighty God, command that these things be carried by the hands of thy holy Angel, to thy altar on high in the sight of thy divine majesty, that as many of us as of this partaking of the altar shall have received the most sacred Body and Blood of thy Son, may be fulfilled with all heavenly benediction and grace, through the same Jesus Christ our Lord. Amen.

Remember also, O Lord, thy servants and handmaidens N. who have gone before us with the sign of faith, and sleep the sleep of peace; unto them, O Lord, and to all that rest in Christ, we entreat that thou wouldest grant a place of refreshing, light, and peace; through the same Christ, our Lord. Amen.

Unto us sinners also, thy servants, that hope in the multitude of thy mercies, vouchsafe to grant some part and fellowship with thy holy apostles and martyrs, with John, Stephen, Matthias, Peter, Felicity, Perpetua, Agatha, Lucy, Agnes, Cecilia, Anastasia, and with all thy saints, unto whose company do thou admit us, not weighing our merits, but freely granting pardon, we beseech thee; through Christ, our Lord, by whom all these good (*creatures*) thou, O Lord, ever createst, sanctifiest, fillest with life, blessest, and bestowest upon us.

Through him and with him, and in him is unto thee, God the Father almighty, in the unity of the Holy Ghost, all honour and glory, world without end. Amen.

[Here Ends the Canon]

Let us pray. Admonished by healthful precepts and informed by the divine instruction, we are bold to say:

Our Father, which art in heaven, Hallowed be thy Name. Thy kingdom come. Thy will be done, As in heaven, so on earth. Give us this day our daily bread. And forgive us our debts, As we forgive our debtors. And lead us not into temptation;

The people. But deliver us from evil.

The priest. Amen.

Deliver us, we beseech thee, O Lord, from all evils past, present and to come; and inasmuch as there is interceding for us the blessed and glorious ever-virgin mother of God, Mary, and thy blessed apostles Peter and Paul and Andrew, with all thy saints.

Here let him take the paten and kiss it: he makes a cross therewith on his face, [and] *breast: from the crown of the head down to the breast, on the right across to the left, saying:*

Favourably give peace in our days, that we, being succoured by the help of thy merciful kindness, may both be free from sin, and safe from troubles;

And let him say: Through the same, our Lord.

And let him break the Body into three pieces.

Jesus Christ thy Son, who liveth and reigneth with thee, in the unity of the Holy Ghost, God, world without end. Amen.

The peace of God be with you always.

And with thy spirit.

O Lamb of God, that takest away the sins of the world, have mercy upon us.

O Lamb of God, that takest away the sins of the world, have mercy upon us.

O Lamb of God, that takest away the sins of the world, grant us thy peace.

Let him put the third piece into the Blood and say:

May this all-holy mingling of the Body and Blood of our Lord Jesus Christ be unto us and to all that receive, health of mind and body, and a healthful preparation for laying hold on eternal life, through the same Christ our Lord. Amen.

Let him give (to himself) *to kiss the chalice and the corporal, and* (that), *risen up, he might give the* Pax *to the ministers, saying:*

Receive the bond of peace and charity that ye may be meet for the most holy mysteries of God.

Let us pray.

O Lord, holy Father, Almighty everlasting God, grant us to receive this Body and Blood of thy Son the Lord, our God, that we may be worthy thereby to obtain remission of all our sins and to be replenished by thy Holy Spirit; for thou art God, and beside thee there is none other, but thou only, Who livest and reignest God, world without end. Amen.

The Priest for himself.

May the partaking of thy Body and Blood, O Lord Jesu Christ, which I unworthy, am daring to receive, come upon me neither unto judgment nor unto condemnation, but for thy pity's sake may it be profitable unto me for defence of soul and body; who with God the Father and the Holy Ghost livest and reignest God, world without end. Amen.

O Lord Jesu Christ, Son of the living God, who of the will of the Father, and with the co-operation of the Holy Ghost, hast by thy death given life to the world. Deliver me by this thy holy Body and Blood from all my iniquities, and from all that is evil in me; and make me to be obedient to thy commandments, and never suffer me to be for ever separated from thee; who with God the Father and the same Holy Spirit livest and reignest God, world without end. Amen.

At taking the Body.

The Body of our Lord Jesus Christ be unto me an everlasting medicine unto eternal life. Amen.

At receiving the Blood.

The Blood of our Lord Jesus Christ preserve me unto everlasting life. Amen.

At receiving the Body and Blood.

The Body and the Blood of our Lord Jesus Christ preserve my body and my soul unto everlasting life. Amen.

When the priest has purified the vessels.

What we have taken with our mouth, O Lord, may we receive with a pure mind; and from a temporal gift (2 Cor. 4:18) may it be made unto us an everlasting remedy unto eternal life. Amen.

May this communion, O Lord, cleanse us from guilt and make us to be partakers of the heavenly remedy, through Christ, our Lord. Amen. . . .

The Postcommon or Prayer after the Communion.

May the receiving of this sacrament, O Lord God, be profitable unto us for the health of body and soul; and also the confession of the eternal Holy Trinity, and of the same undivided Unity, in which Thou livest and reignest, for ever and ever.

The deacon. Let us bless the Lord.

At other times. Depart, the congregation is dismissed.

After *Ite, missa est,* the priest standeth in the midst of the altar and so blesseth the people.

The missal appoints the prayer *Placeat tibi* to be said by the priest, and adds other devotions for priest and clerks, beginning with the canticle *Benedicite omnia opera* (the Song of the Three Children), as an anthem, and ending with the collect, *Deus qui tribus pueris.*

❧ No. 77. Annual confession: *Omnis utriusque sexus.* Fourth Lateran Council, c. 21 (1215).

Decrees, Tanner, p. 245.

21. All the faithful of either sex, after they have reached the age of discernment, should individually confess all their sins in a faithful manner to

their own priest at least once a year, and let them take care to do what they can to perform the penance imposed on them. Let them reverently receive the sacrament of the eucharist at least at Easter unless they think, for a good reason and on the advice of their own priest, that they should abstain from receiving it for a time. Otherwise they shall be barred from entering a church during their lifetime and they shall be denied a christian burial at death. Let this salutary decree be frequently published in churches, so that nobody may find the pretence of an excuse in the blindness of ignorance. If any persons wish, for good reasons, to confess their sins to another priest let them first ask and obtain the permission of their own priest; for otherwise the other priest will not have the power to absolve or to bind them. The priest shall be discerning and prudent, so that like a skilled doctor he may pour wine and oil over the wounds of the injured one. Let him carefully inquire about the circumstances of both the sinner and the sin, so that he may prudently discern what sort of advice he ought to give and what remedy to apply, using various means to heal the sick person. Let him take the utmost care, however, not to betray the sinner at all by word or sign or in any other way. If the priest needs wise advice, let him seek it cautiously without any mention of the person concerned. For if anyone presumes to reveal a sin disclosed to him in confession, we decree that he is not only to be deposed from his priestly office but also to be confined to a strict monastery to do perpetual penance.

∾ No. 78. A popular manual of confession from the diocese of Exeter.

The *Summula* for the diocese of Exeter (1240 and 1287). *Councils and Synods,* pp. 1060–77. Trans. JS.

Summula *of the Synod of the Diocese of Exeter*[21]
"The Most High hath created medicines out of the earth" [Ecclus. 38:4]. The Most High is he of whom the church sings, saying: "You alone, Lord Jesus Christ"; and he is the physician about whom the psalm says: "Have mercy on me, O Lord, for I am weak; heal me, O Lord" [Ps. 6:3]. Look—if people have been wounded physically they crave the presence of a doctor. But Origen says: "As many times as someone sins, so often is his soul wounded"; and the Blessed Ambrose says that there is no one sadder than

---

[21]Though the *Summula* was long attributed to Bishop Peter Quinel, recently Joseph Goering and Daniel Taylor have shown that it was written almost half a century before, in 1240, by Quinel's predecessor Walter Cantilupe. Quinel reissued it in 1287. Here we translate Cantilupe's main text but preface it with Quinel's introduction. See Goering and Taylor, "The *Summulae* of Bishops Walter de Cantilupe (1240) and Peter Quinel (1287)," in *Speculum* 67 no. 3 (July 1992): 576–94.

he who pricks his conscience on the sharp blade of sin. Perhaps someone might ask, "How can this be true, since I don't feel this type of injury?" Origen answers that, "When physicians wish to cut into patients or cauterize them they give them some potion to drink which makes them fall into a deep sleep so that they can operate on them and they will feel nothing." Similarly, we are performing an operation to repair those earthly desires which render us so senseless that we do not feel how bad the wounds to our soul are. Because of these injuries, Christ, who is the best physician, must be called in since a doctor is not needed for those who are healthy, only for those who live badly [Matt. 9:12]. Of this doctor, Ambrose says, "Hear me, earthly man; I have found a physician who abides in heaven and prepares medicine for the earth. No one can heal my wounds except he who does not feel his own." Thus Christ is the best physician: he gives us relief from our pain through contrition, and through confession we receive a purgative; he recommends a healthful diet through our keeping of fasts; he orders therapeutic baths through our outpouring of tears; he prescribes bloodletting through our recollection of Christ's passion. But what is this medicine?— Penance. Augustine says, "Penance not only cures past injuries, it also does not let the soul be further wounded by sin." But some people say: "We will find mercy and will do penance later, because the Lord says, 'I do not wish the death of sinners'" [Ezek. 18:23]. Augustine answers them by saying, "No one should linger in his sins in the expectation of mercy, nor should he wound himself now expecting a future cure; for he who promises pardon for the sinner does not promise that there will be a tomorrow." From what has been said it is clear that the triune God—Father, Son, and Holy Spirit—is the physician, and the sinner offends this Trinity through sin. For sin is death and penance is the medicine that, through its three parts, namely, contrition, confession, and satisfaction, appeases the wrath of the Trinity which the sinner offends by sinning.

Therefore, I Peter, priest of Exeter, reflecting on these things in my heart and sympathizing with the shortcomings of secular priests hearing confessions—whose ignorance, sad to say, I have all too often experienced—assign the present brief summary to them which they should know for their benefit and that of those going to confession.

[1] The Ten Commandments.

A criminal ought to make satisfaction not according to his wishes but instead according to the wishes of the one he has offended. In fact, wishing to deal with us more mercifully, the Lord placed the priest between himself and us as a judge whose will we ought to follow in this regard and who actually wants to favor our side—as if, since he is surrounded by human frailty, he knows how to have compassion for those who are ignorant and who sin. But in order for him to know what he should prescribe for us, we are obliged to confess everything, since he cannot study our consciences for himself. And since the multitude of sins can be boiled down to the transgression of these Ten Commandments, both penitents and confessors are obliged to know them. These are the Ten Commandments: [1] You shall not adore false gods but you shall adore and serve only the Lord your God. [2] You shall not take the name of your God in vain. [3] Remember that you should observe and keep holy the sabbath day. [4] Honor your father and your mother. [5] You shall not kill. [6] You shall not commit adultery. [7] You shall not steal. [8] You shall not speak false witness against your neighbor. [9] You shall not covet your neighbor's house. [10] You shall not desire his wife, nor his servant, nor his ox, nor his ass, nor anything that is his.

[2] The First Commandment.

Therefore the penitent must reflect on the first commandment and examine himself to see if he has transgressed it; namely, whether he has rendered the worship due only to God to demons or other creatures—for instance, by practicing magic (that is, by resorting to incantations, as is common when something is stolen, or by using a sword or a basin, or by writing out names, sealing them in a mud plaster, and placing them in holy water, and similar things). Or perhaps he has resorted to omens (trying to divine the future), or has practiced divination—as sorcerers do—or has consulted sorcerers for these purposes, or has sacrificed to demons, as some wretches do for the sake of women with whom they have fallen foolishly in love.

[3] The Second Commandment.

Next he should see if he has transgressed the second commandment, which is, "you shall not take the name of your God in vain"—for instance, by wavering or faltering in his faith in any way. Since perhaps they cannot know everything that they are expected to believe, people who are unlearned should be taught to keep their hearts fixed and steadfast; in other words, they should believe what the church believes and they should do Christian acts. For according to Augustine, it does not suffice for you to accept the name of Christ if you do not perform Christian acts. Thus, the Apostle says, "we entreat you not to receive the grace of God in vain" [2 Cor. 6:1]. Furthermore, he should see whether he has perjured God's name, especially while gazing upon or touching holy objects, which often happens at courts of assizes; in this regard teach them about the evils of perjury. Or whether he has sworn oaths without reason, especially by swearing on the head or limbs of Christ, which people do from habit, ignoring the wisdom of Solomon who said, "Let not thy mouth be accustomed to swearing," etc. [Ecclus. 23:9]. He should also see whether he has broken his promises.

[4] The Third Commandment.

Next let the penitent examine whether he broke the third commandment which is "remember to observe the sabbath day"—by not doing manual labor or committing sins that particularly involve physical effort on Sundays or feast days. These three preceding commandments are God's due; the following seven concern one's neighbors.

[5] The Fourth Commandment.

Fourth, he should consider if he has violated the fourth commandment, which is "Honor your father," etc. This means not only one's carnal father, but also one's spiritual father. One violates this commandment either by striking one's parents (that is, father or mother) or by inflicting injury on them with abusive words or deeds. Or if perhaps they are poor, if one does not come to their aid insofar as one reasonably can. Or if they are dead, if one does not aid them with almsgiving and prayers, or by having someone pray for them. (But a priest should not demand masses for the dead which will be celebrated by him or by an associate who will return any payment for such masses to him.)

[6] The Fifth Commandment.

Next let the penitent consider whether he has broken the fifth commandment, which is, "you shall not kill"—either by attacking someone with the intent to kill or wound him, or by giving counsel or aid to others or ordering others to kill someone, or, for instance, by willfully hating someone even to the death (since he who hates his brother is a murderer), or by withdrawing necessary aid from someone (because even if you have not struck him, you have murdered), or killing someone spiritually by wrongful actions or the example of your words.

[7] The Sixth Commandment.

The sixth point to consider is whether he has violated the sixth commandment, which is, "you shall not commit adultery"—either by actual adultery, or by fornication, or by polluting one's flesh against its natural use, or by committing incest. For the word "adultery" here prohibits every illicit act of copulation. This is covered more fully below.

[8] The Seventh Commandment.

Next he should see whether he has broken the seventh commandment, which is, "you shall not steal"—either by secretly carrying away what does not belong to you, or by pillaging or extortion, as bad lords do, or by cheating or defrauding anyone through deceit, or by usury (which is selling something for more than it is worth). Finding something and not returning it is also stealing, since if you do not return what you have found, you are un-justly seizing it. One also steals by fraudulently calculating or measuring weights or by not paying tithes or other payments that one owes.

[9] The Eighth Commandment.

Eighth, he should see whether he has violated the eighth command-ment, which is, "you shall not speak false witness against your neighbor"; namely, by swearing falsely in court—especially in marriage cases and cases where perjury would lead to the death or disinheritance of someone.

[10] The Ninth Commandment.

Next he should consider whether he has transgressed the ninth com-mandment, which is, "you shall not covet your neighbor's house," etc., be-cause it is a mortal offense not only to steal something from your neighbor but even to desire it, to the extent that someone covets something which he would wrongfully steal given the power and opportunity to do so, and if he believed he could do it with impunity.

[11] The Tenth Commandment.

Finally he should consider whether he has broken the tenth command-ment, which is, "you shall not covet your neighbor's wife"—since it is not only someone who does the deed itself who commits adultery, but even any-one who consents with his rational will to do it. It is just as the Lord says in the gospel: "anyone who so much as looks with lust at a woman has already committed adultery with her in his heart" [Matt. 5:28]. This is how the tenth commandment differs from the ninth: the ninth commandment forbids de-siring another's property; the tenth commandment forbids the desire to abuse someone. Thus, if someone desires to have someone else's wife or ser-vant as a possession or to exercise dominion over them, this pertains to the ninth commandment. But if someone desires only to abuse them, this would pertain to the tenth commandment.

[12] The Seven Deadly Sins.

Since the tree of the vices with its loaded branches is no more clearly revealed than when its very roots are uncovered, I think it fitting to call to mind its roots. There are seven deadly roots of sin, which are to be explained frequently to people.

[13] The First Root.

Of course the first root is pride, from which every wicked offspring of the vices takes its origin. The types of this root may be noted in the follow-ing fashion, without prejudice to the opinion of my betters. The first is dis-obedience, such as when a sinner scorns the commandments of God or does forbidden things. The second type is boasting, as when a sinner says or claims that he is by nature good when in fact he gets his goodness from some other source, or when he says that he is bad because of someone else when in fact it is his nature to be bad. Third, there is hypocrisy, such as when a man pretends to be good when he is not, or when he hides the bad in him so that he appears to be good. The fourth type of pride is contempt for one's neighbor, as when, for instance, a poor man makes light of or disparages his neighbor's property in order to appear as good or even better than his neighbor. The fifth is arrogance, such as when a sinner compares his own evil to the greater evils of others so that his own faults appear less. The sixth is impudence, as, for instance, when a sinner is not ashamed of the patently evil thing he does. The seventh is self-exaltation, such as when, for instance, someone broadcasts—even glories in—the evil that he has done.

Now pride has many sources. For instance, a person's natural gifts; in other words, when a man is proud of his natural endowments—so that because of his physical build, he is strong; or because of the accident of birth, he is wellborn; or because of the way he looks, he is considered handsome; or because of a fluent tongue, or even because he has a nice voice, he is deemed eloquent—as are certain lawyers and even laymen who argue before secular judges. Nobility is also a source of pride, if one is born of a great family; children, too, lead to pride, if one has many of them, or they are comely, or are good sons or daughters. Pride also finds a source in temporal possessions, as when a man takes pride in having great wealth or rich clothes, houses, lands, a large income, or many vassals or servants, or fine horses, or when he outranks others in his temporal possessions. Pride also has a source in gratuitous reward, that is to say those things that come from grace. For instance, when a man is proud because he is wise or even because he is a good scholar [clericus] or a legal advocate, or a good artisan or farmer; or he takes pride in his virtue, because he believes himself to be good and despises sinners; or he is proud because he has gained men's favor or has a good reputation or ecclesiastical dignity or status. One should prescribe a variety of penances to correspond to all these many varieties of pride.

[14]   The Second Root.

The second root of the vices is sloth, which is a kind of apathy of body and a melancholy of the spirit and mind. Sloth is why a man meditating about God without devotion accomplishes nothing. He prays without devotion; he reads and sings the divine office with no sense of the delights of heaven, concerned only with getting to the end of it any way he can. Due to sloth a man becomes so indifferent that he provokes God to vomit him out like lukewarm water [Rev. 3:16]. Sloth makes a man fainthearted so that he will not undertake anything for God; it makes him timid, so that he dares

not suffer for God's sake, neither wearing a hairshirt, nor keeping discipline
or fasts, nor going on pilgrimages. It makes a man so negligent that if he
begins to do anything good, without fail he gradually gives it up. It makes
a man so remiss that he will not exert himself; and so he lets himself, or his
church, or his subjects, or his neighbors be injured, which, with due effort,
he could have prevented. Such is the case with prelates, lords, princes, and
laymen. From sloth is born lethargy, which makes a man despair of finishing what good he has begun. It makes a man sluggish, desiring rest beyond
all measure. Sloth also engenders a weariness of life, which makes this second root extremely deadly. From sloth murmurings against God rise up;
thus a priest should work hard to teach remedies against it—namely, images
of eternal rewards, and the recollection of death (not only earthly death but
also spiritual death) and of eternal suffering. For the slothful will pass, as
Job says, "from the snow waters to excessive heat" [Job 24:19]. And so a priest
ought to teach them to pay attention to the examples of the saints, especially
to the Passion of our Lord Jesus Christ who died for us, leaving us an example so that we can follow in his footsteps who had no sin. A priest should
teach them similar things.

[15] The Third Root.

The third root is envy, which makes someone rejoice at others' misfortunes and grieve over their success. From envy arises slander, by which
someone cheerfully disparages another's good qualities by speaking evilly
of them, and exaggerates someone's bad qualities as much as he can. Envy
also makes a man willingly listen to slander and slanderers.

[16] The Fourth Root.

Wrath is the fourth root, which makes someone so furious, deranged,
or savage that he seeks revenge against and harms his neighbor. Sometimes
wrath makes someone blaspheme against God and his saints. It makes
someone too ready to strike or provoke his neighbor, hurting his good name
and bearing it off. Sometimes it also makes someone commit murder. And
yet sometimes wrath is good, as for instance when it makes someone rise up
with honest restraint against a neighbor's or his own sin.

[17] The Fifth Root.

Greed is the fifth root. It is the immoderate love of material possessions.
It is a mortal sin when it holds such sway over someone that for the sake
of getting or keeping material things, that person has no fear of breaking
one of God's commandments. So that, for example, to acquire possessions
someone chooses to worship idols, or perjure himself while touching holy
objects, or to dishonor his parents, or to commit murder, adultery, or fornication, or to bear false witness. From greed rise up fraud, theft, and robbery.

A greedy person does not pay his debts, or fulfill his promises; he does not return things entrusted to him, nor does he give aid to the needy. He lays up his treasure with thieves, and with moths and rust [cf. Matt. 6:19]. Greed makes someone a simoniac when he buys or sells something spiritual or something connected to the spiritual, such as the right of patronage or of foundation. It makes someone commit sacrilege when he steals something holy from a sacred place, or a secular thing from a sacred place against the will of the lord, or a holy thing from a secular place. It makes a man into a usurer when someone makes an agreement to receive payment above his proper share for lending someone something over a length of time, though he pretends it is another kind of contract. Greed, as the saying goes, makes a man a cheat and a robber when he secretly carries off his neighbor's property without his consent or through fraud. It makes a man ambitious; in other words, he craves possessions and honors too much.

[18] The Sixth Root.

The sixth root of the vices is gluttony—an immoderate fondness for eating and drinking. A man labors under this vice when he eats or drinks so much that the natural and regular workings of his body and mind are impeded by food and drink, to the extent that he frequently and willingly does this. In this vice there are five kinds of sin, as described in this mnemonic:[22] eagerly, lavishly, too much, too fondly, too meticulously. Eagerly means when someone is preoccupied by or always waiting for dinnertime. Lavishly means one is too opulent in preparing one's meals. Too much means when one eats more than is called for. Too fondly means when one eats food voraciously. Meticulously means when someone is too painstaking over the delectable foods and drink he has prepared for him. A vice related to greed is self-indulgence, which is when someone eagerly pursues sensual pleasures, for instance, clothing that is too luxurious, soft beds, and pleasure baths.

[19] The Seventh Root.

The seventh root is lust, which consists of adultery; that is, when a married man has sex with someone else's wife or also with a widow, or when a married woman has sex with someone else's husband or with a widower. It likewise consists of incest; that is, when someone has sex with a woman related to him by blood up to the fourth degree, or with an in-law (that is, a blood relative of his wife), or even with a relative of a woman whom he has previously defiled by illicit intercourse. Lust also involves sacrilege when it is committed with someone in religious orders or someone ordained (namely,

---

[22]I.e., *versum*, not reproduced in the translation.

a subdeacon or above). Lust consists also of the vice of sodomy; that is, when anyone, man or woman, has sex against nature with any creature. It consists of impurity, which is when anyone willingly pollutes himself during the night. It likewise embraces nocturnal emissions when these happen because one's habits—namely, drunkenness or licentiousness—overrule one's reason. Lust also consists of abuse; that is, when anyone has sex with a woman in disregard of its proper purpose, even if she is his wife.

Therefore, each of these roots and the things that arise from them (and more if he knows them) should be reviewed with the penitent just as has been said. And so he should be confessed of all those sins into which he has fallen.

[20] The Circumstances of Sins.

Just as it is proper for a person to undress completely to show his bodily wounds to a doctor or a surgeon, since confession is the healing of injuries done to the soul it is proper for someone to reveal all his inner wounds to his spiritual doctor—in other words, all those circumstances and everything which could aggravate the sin in any way. The circumstances of sin can be noted in this mnemonic [versum]: Who, what, where, by whose aid, why, how, and when.

[21] Therefore the penitent is obliged to confess what he did not in general terms but as specifically as he can. Thus, if he committed adultery it does not suffice for him to say that he fornicated or that he had a lapse of the flesh; he is hiding his sin through this sort of generality. Furthermore, a priest would not know what penance to prescribe for him since a greater penance should be done for adultery than for simple fornication. Someone truly penitent should greatly hate sin. He who greatly hates something calls it by the foulest name he can; that is what the penitent should call his sin provided that he is speaking truthfully. Thus, it does not suffice for someone who has killed a parent to say that he has merely committed homicide. The same is true for other circumstances of sin. He who commits incest with his sister should not just say that he has committed incest.

[22] Next one should find out who it was that committed the sin. This does not simply mean that the sinner should give his name, but rather that he should describe his status or his character, saying, for instance, "I am a bishop," or "I am a priest," and so on for the other sacred orders; or "I am a monk of such and such an order," or "I am a nun or an anchoress," since these conditions make the sin more serious. For it is worse for a bishop to commit fornication than for an ordinary cleric, worse for a cleric than a lay person, worse for a member of a religious order than an ordinary secular priest. And if someone sinned while he was a bishop or a priest or any of

the other above mentioned statuses, it is not adequate for him to say "At one time I sinned"; rather he should say that he sinned while in one of these holy orders. In the same way a penitent should say whom he sinned against. Thus, if perhaps he struck a priest it is not sufficient to say he struck a cleric. If someone sinned with a nun, a married woman, or a relative it is not adequate unless he completely describes the degree of consanguinity or affinity, and whether he sinned with an in-law. But a man should not reveal the name of the woman with whom he sinned nor should a woman reveal the name of the man; they should not even hint at the name—for instance, by mentioning some peculiarities or distinguishing marks which would make it obvious to the priest who he or she was. For we ought to confess only our own sins, not another's, since each one of us is responsible for so greatly increasing sins instead of diminishing them.

[23] Next, where the sin was committed should be examined, since if some-one committed murder or an act of lust or some other sin on sacred ground it is more serious than if he sinned in a secular place. Thus, many things are deemed sinful if they happen in a church or some other holy place—for ex-ample near relics—that would not be considered sinful if they happened elsewhere.

[24] After that, he should examine with whose help the sin was committed. For example, if someone killed a man with the aid of clerics or members of religious orders whom he dragged along with him, he has sinned more gravely than someone who did this alone or even with the help of laymen.

[25] Added to this is why someone sinned. Thus, someone sins more seri-ously who kills a man out of avarice (that is, to acquire the other person's possessions or inheritance) than someone who kills in order to gain venge-ance for some wrong done to him or to ward off a violent attack. In the same way the priest should examine why deeds that appear at first glance to be good were done. Take for example going to church or doing acts of charity; if the motive for these acts was to gain glory or people's praise, they are to be considered sins rather than goods.

[26] Consider also how the sin was committed. For example, if someone killed a man, it is less sinful if he did it quickly by beheading him with a sharp sword than if he slowly tortured him, hacking him to pieces with a dull blade, quartering him alive limb from limb. Also in sins of lust and other sins there are many scurrilous inventions and many improper prac-tices, even between married couples, which it is disgusting to mention or describe. Still, a penitent is obliged to confess such things carefully. In these matters a priest should be discerning enough that if the penitent does not confess to such practices, the priest will ask him about them. Nevertheless,

he should not bring up particulars but talk instead in generalities. Thus, if the penitent has sinned against nature or by using some such scurrilous practice, he will surely know what the priest is asking him. But if he clearly does not know what the priest is talking about, the priest should not say anything more about such matters, because, as one of the saints says: Reciting a catalogue of sins drags many people into sin. An ignorance of sins guards the innocence of many. A priest should also question married people about such matters.

[27] A penitent is obliged to confess when he committed his sin, since someone sins more gravely who sinned during one of the greater feast days than during one of the lesser ones. And he sins more gravely who sins during a time of fasting (for instance, Lent or Advent or the vigils of saints) than someone who sins at another time. Someone sins more gravely who sins often than someone who sins only a few times. Thus a sinner should say with Hezekiah, "I will recount to thee," Lord, "all my years in the bitterness of my soul" [Isa. 38:15]. For the sinner should reflect on how he has behaved from the very beginning of his life, thinking over every year of his life he can remember, considering what he did during which years, on which days, and in what places (for place is the beginning of memory). By remembering places we can frequently recall to mind things we had forgotten, and by doing this we will be able to record the number of times we committed the sin which we are confessing. Number and length of time greatly increase [the gravity of] sins.

[28] The Circumstances of the Sins.

A sinner should next recall those circumstances surrounding deeds which appear to be good. For if you say, "What did you do?" and he says "I had intercourse with a woman," having intercourse with a woman is not completely bad, but it is bad if it occurred outside of marriage. To be married is not bad, but for a monk or someone who has taken a vow of chastity it is bad. To plow a field, or to weave, or to do similar work is not bad; but to do this in places where it is forbidden or during holy times is bad. To kill the king of enemies fighting against your land is not bad, but it is bad if a person in religious orders does this since such people are not allowed to spill blood. Also, just as above with the circumstance of "why," where something could be considered bad which otherwise would not be bad (for instance, someone being very generous in order to gain empty glory), here too circumstances can make something bad which otherwise would not be. For example, eating is not bad, but eating too greedily is.

[29] Contemplation.

A penitent ought to recall his thoughts—in other words, whether he

contemplated his evil actions before doing them. Contemplation leads to pleasure which, if it is lingering, is bad; that is, if it leads to consent, meaning that someone consents that he wants to commit a mortal sin even though he does not actually do it. Nevertheless, while contemplation impels someone toward sin, it does not defile that person until he takes pleasure at the thought of the sin, which is a venial sin. But when contemplation reaches the point where one consents to sin, then in fact it becomes a mortal sin.
[30] Words.

Next one should turn to words, because the tongue is the font of all sin, just as the blessed James and also Solomon says: the soul lives or dies by the tongue [James 3:6; Prov. 18:21].
[31] Works.

Finally we should consider our deeds, as was said, doing this in respect to each part of the body and each of the senses, seeing whether we have sinned through our feet, our hands, our eyes, our ears, and so on with every other part of the body. For so it is written: "The just man is first accuser of himself; his friend cometh and shall search him" [Prov. 18:17]. Thus, if a penitent omits any of these things, by a careful examination the priest ought to make good the omissions.
[32] Cases in which a penitent must be sent to the bishop.

Since there are certain sins for which an ordinary priest must send a penitent to the pope or a bishop for absolution, we have had them added to this tract. When a priest hears such sins in confession he should send the penitent to the bishop or his penitentiary so that they can decide whether the bishop may grant absolution or whether he must send the penitent on to the pope. These are the people who must be referred to the pope to receive absolution: [1] those people (clergy or laymen) who strike members of the clergy, members of religious orders, or lepers who are gathered in a sanctified community; [2] arsonists who burn dwellings; [3] violators of churches; [4] sorcerers and those making offerings to demons or adoring anyone other than God; [5] those people knowingly and purposely in contact with people excommunicated by the pope; also someone accused and excommunicated by the pope or a bishop; [6] forgers of papal letters or those procuring false letters from someone, and those knowingly and purposely using forged letters; [7] those who bear false witness; [8] someone promoting a supposititious heir; that is, someone who makes another his heir, thereby disinheriting others;[23] [9] those who kill their own child by incautiously suffocating

---

[23]"Suppositious" suggests a fraudulent heir, but was sometimes synonymous with "illegitimate."

[i.e., overlaying] it;[24] [10] coin-clippers;[25] [11] those who impede a papal legate; [12] someone who betrays his lord, the king, or someone else; [13] someone falling into the divisiveness of heresy; that is, a heretic or one who supports heretics; [14] a simoniac, that is, someone who buys or pays for some spiritual thing, or someone who sells a spiritual thing or even something connected to a spiritual thing; also someone who procures something to be paid so that he or someone else gets something spiritual—for example, an ecclesiastical benefice or holy orders; [15] a plunderer of sacred things; [16] a schismatic, that is, someone withdrawing from the unity of the Roman Church; [17] encroachers on church property; [18] those who help the Saracens by supplying them with arms or other prohibited things; [19] usurers; [20] judges who make statues against the liberty of the church or who support those who do; [21] those who celebrate divine services while under suspension; [22] those who, because of lust, commit enormities against nature.

If this sort of sinner cannot be induced to confess to a bishop or his penitentiary, the priest should go to the bishop, inform him of the sin, and obtain the authority to absolve the penitent himself. But these sinners, as has been said, should be sent to the bishop so that he can absolve whomever he can absolve; those he cannot absolve the bishop should send to the pope to obtain absolution.

[33] Instructing penitents.

Keeping these points for examination in mind, the discerning priest should supply what the penitent has ignored by asking questions with discretion. However, a priest wishing to absolve a penitent should consider if the penitent is a Christian, that is, does he have faith. Once he has ascertained this, he should teach the penitent the articles of faith which he does not know. Then he should teach him to have bitter contrition in his heart for his sins. But his contrition should be appropriate to his sins (lest his grief become uncontrollable). He should have contrition which perseveres with the intention of always abstaining from sin. And he should have general contrition for all those things he has done and not done, and this especially because they have offended God. Then the priest should take care to advise him that he must make a truthful confession in his own words, exposing all the circumstances, and totally revealing everything he did wrong; he should do all this for the sake of God. Then the priest should admonish him to make voluntary and complete satisfaction for his sins: in secret for secret

---

[24] Since families usually shared a pallet (beds were for the well-to-do), babies sleeping next to their parents would sometimes be inadvertently smothered; but such an "accident" could be a cover for infanticide.

[25] Coin-clippers shaved the edges of coins, which diminished their weight (and value) and allowed the clippers to pocket the shavings.

offenses, openly for public offenses. The priest should advise him that the satisfaction must be sufficient for all his sins. All of this is on God's behalf. [34] Enjoining penance.

In assigning penances a priest should be aware that there are three types of sins: some are sins of the spirit, such as pride, wrath, envy, and sloth; others are sins of the flesh, such as gluttony and lust; others, still, are a combination of both, such as greed and avarice. Against sins of the spirit, prayers, acts of humility and compassion, and similar things should be prescribed. Against intermediate sins, generous almsgiving and the practice of works of mercy should be enjoined. And against sins of the flesh, mortification of the body through fasting, scourging, and pilgrimages should be prescribed. There are, however, certain experts who teach that for all sins prayers, almsgiving, and mortification of the flesh (through fasting, scourging, and pilgrimages) should be enjoined. They conclude this perhaps because they believe that every sinful act has some element of pride whose spiritual corrective is prayer; and perhaps this is the sort of demon which is not cast out without prayer and fasting. In every sin there is also something that the eyes desire which almsgiving is especially effective against. And every sin also has some desire of the flesh connected with it against which scourging the flesh is effective. Whoever thinks about this subtly will clearly see the point these experts make. Nor will we criticize this theory except to suggest that a priest should enjoin the most appropriate medicine for a sin based on whether the sin is more spiritual, or carnal, or intermediate. Whoever is unable to give material alms should at least give spiritual ones, for instance, by showing compassion. He should have the intention of giving material alms when the opportunity presents itself. A priest should also teach the penitent remedies for any types of spiritual sins according to how God inspires him from the authority of scripture. We say this, for we have chosen not to burden this handbook with them at this time.
[35] Penances are arbitrary.

Since there is such a diversity of sinners that it is said that penance is arbitrary, these things should be borne in mind: The condition of the penitent—whether he is of servile status or free. Also the penitent's gender—that is, male or female; and his estate, rich or poor; and his age, young or old; and his order—that is, whether he is a cleric or a layman. If he is a cleric, in what order is he? The penitent's temperament should be considered: whether his humor is sanguine, phlegmatic, choleric, or melancholic.[26] Also

[26]Medieval physiology and psychology were based on the assumption that all matter, humans not excepted, was a mixture of the four elements—earth, water, fire, and air. The four humors—cold, wet, hot, and dry—were the basic matter of the body; whichever humor predominated in a person determined that person's temperament or character.

the condition of his body—whether he is sick or healthy, weak or strong. A priest should consider these things and, using his discretion, adjust the quality or the quantity of the prescribed penance based on them.

[36] Sick penitents.

A priest should observe the following when dealing with penitents who are sick. If someone is near death or otherwise seriously ill, the priest should not enjoin penance on him. Instead, he should explain to him the penance he would prescribe were the penitent healthy. It is allowed for a penitent's friends to receive penance on his behalf; however, the sins of the dying person are not to be revealed to them, unless he himself insists on this. The priest should oblige a sick penitent that, if he recovers, he should go to the church to receive his penance. Then the priest should absolve him, advising him that, with his soul made ready, he should subject himself to the divine will, accepting it either for death or for health. And he should advise him about everything that he has decided he should do to save his soul. However, what may profit the sick person if he dies, is that the penance which his friends agreed to do for him may be relaxed through divine clemency. Likewise, in those cases in which penitents who should be sent to a bishop for absolution are near death, an ordinary priest may absolve them. Nevertheless, they should be enjoined that if they recover they should go to the bishop to fulfill the penance he assigns them.

[37] The Articles of Faith.

These are the articles of faith which a priest is obliged to teach a penitent. They are written here as certain men have recorded them: God is one in essence and has three persons: the Father, the Son, and the Holy Spirit. He is without beginning, without end, and he created everything from nothing. The Son of God assumed flesh from a virgin and was born, truly God and truly man, from her with her virginity intact. This son of God and the virgin was crucified, died, and was buried in order to redeem us, not out of necessity but by his own will. This person—both God and man—rose from the dead in a glorified body after the resurrection; all of us will also rise from the dead. This Jesus Christ, both God and man, ascended into heaven in his full manhood and will come again to judge the world. And faith in the sacraments and their effects is necessary, namely: baptism cleanses us from original sin and also cleanses adults from actual sin (though an adult must be contrite to be cleansed of actual sin). Confirmation strengthens the Holy Spirit in a baptized person. True penitence removes actual sin, both mortal and venial. The sacrament of the altar is the real Body and Blood of Christ, true God and true man; and this sacrament fortifies a penitent against actual sin by reconciling and sustaining him to keep him from lapsing into sin. The collected holy orders confer the power of celebrating divine services and the sacraments. Marriage which has been legitimately contracted removes mortal sin from acts of reproduction between a man and a woman. The last anointing alleviates physical and spiritual pain. Also, a priest should teach a lay person to know and believe the Creed, at least in the vernacular; and a lay person should know the Lord's Prayer (that is, the *Pater noster*) and the salutation of the Blessed Virgin Mary (that is, the *Ave Maria*). He should also admonish a lay person to guard himself carefully lest he lapse into sin; and he should frequently come to confession at least three times a year, as the synodal constitutions mention. And if perhaps he slips into sin, as soon as he has done so he should hurry to a priest. After the priest instructs the penitent in these things, he should absolve him and send him away in peace. Still, may he do better if the Lord has inspired him to do better.

[38] This treatise should be kept in every church in the various parishes, under the penalty of a one mark fine (or more or less, depending on the capacity of the negligent priest to pay) payable to the local archdeacon, which we entrust to the archdeacon's judgment under threat to his soul; but we reserve the right to punish him if he is found negligent in this matter. For any sort of negligence he shall pay at least two marks to the fabric [fund of the cathedral of] St. Peter in Exeter or to the bishop. And every priest should learn the material in this handbook and know it; otherwise, when they are examined about this, those who do not know it will be expelled.

Pray for the bishop Peter—living and dead—and whoever does this, let them enjoy an indulgence of forty days. Amen.

∾ No. 79. The penitential canons from the *Summa* of Hostiensis (Henry de Susa) (1253).

Hostiensis, *Summa* (Lyons, 1537), fols. 283r–v. Trans. JS.

[*Hostiensis extracted these canons from Gratian's* Decretum, *which he cites at the end of each canon; these citations are omitted here.*]

In order for a priest to be more careful in dispensing penances, noted here are those cases for which a specific penance or penances are imposed according to the canons. For a priest is obliged to know the penitential canons; otherwise the title "priest" scarcely suits him.

1. The first canon says that if a priest commits fornication he shall do penance for ten years. . . .

2. The second canon says that if a priest has carnal knowledge with one of his spiritual daughters—namely, a woman he has baptized or has sponsored in baptism or whose confession he has heard—he ought to

do penance for twelve years and also be deposed from his office if the crime is made public. A bishop who commits such a crime should do penance for fifteen years. The woman involved in this matter should surrender all her possessions and give them to the poor and spend the rest of her life serving God in a convent.

3. He who sins against nature, if he is a cleric, should be deposed or else he should enter a monastery—if he seems reformable—in order to do perpetual penance. But if he is a layman he should be excommunicated and cut off from the company of the faithful until he makes worthy satisfaction.

4. A priest who is present at a clandestine marriage is suspended for three years; and if the crime is carried out, he should be more seriously punished. . . .

5. He who breaks a simple vow should do penance for three years.

6. He who celebrates mass while excommunicated should do penance for three years and should abstain from wine and meat.

7. He who unjustly accuses another of a capital crime should fast for forty days on bread and water and then do penance for seven years; this is if the accused is executed. But if the accused is punished only by having one of his limbs amputated, the accuser shall do penance for three years.

8. Anyone who has sexual relations with his spiritual daughter or godmother should do seven years of penance and likewise she who consented to this.

9. He who contracts a marriage with someone already betrothed to another should give her up and fast for forty days on bread and water and then do seven years of penance.

10. He who has sexual relations with either of his two godmothers or his godsisters—whether his wife is alive or not—should do at least seven years of penance, though he ought to do more.

11. [A priest] who commits premeditated homicide should be deposed without hope of reinstatement and should do penance for seven years.

12. A priest who commits involuntary homicide should do penance for [five] years.

13. He who commits homicide on account of an avoidable situation should do penance for two years; but if the situation was unavoidable he is not held responsible for the sin. But it is true that since this is a sin, it would be good for him to do penance in order to show his conscientiousness and innocence to the churc'. If anyone commits homicide while insane he should not be punished. But a priest who carelessly strikes someone while disciplining him and so kills him should be deposed. He who kills a thief who has been captured and bound should be deposed.

14. He who commits matricide should do penance for ten years following the very harsh procedure prescribed in Gratian. . . . But he who kills his wife should be punished even more severely. Someone who does this or someone who kills his lord should never again ride a horse or ride in a carriage. A greater penance is imposed on one who kills his wife not because it is a greater sin than killing one's mother but because men are more prone to kill their wives than their mothers.

15. A perjurer should fast for forty days on bread and water and then do penance for seven years following; but he should ever after do interior penance.

16. He who uses false weights and measures should fast thirty days on bread and water.

17. If anyone does solemn public penance and then "returns to his vomit" [Prov. 26:11], he should do penance for ten years.

18. He who has sexual relations with a nun or a woman vowed to God should do penance for ten years, and likewise the woman should do penance following the established form.

19. A priest who celebrates mass and does not take communion should do a year's penance and in the interim should not celebrate mass.

20. A priest who clothes a dead cleric in altar vestments should do penance for ten years and five months; a deacon, for three and a half years.

21. He who commits sacrilege by violating a church, or accepting the holy oil or the chalice with sinful hands, or some other similar sacrilege, should do penance for seven years, the first two of which he should not enter the church. Up until the fourth year he should not distribute communion. For three days a week he should abstain from wine and meat.

22. If parents break the betrothal of their children they should be forbidden communion for three years. But if the betrothal is made a second time and the children marry, both parents are excused from ecclesiastical punishment, but not from guilt of having disobeyed.

23. He who takes as a wife a woman whom he has polluted through adultery should do penance for five years.

24. He who publicly blasphemes God or his saints should do penance for seven weeks.

25. A priest who reveals by word or sign what was told to him in confession [is to be deposed from his office according to the ancient law, and he should spend the rest of his life wandering in ignominy as a pilgrim.][27]

[27] This phrase added from the canons as they were printed in the *Corpus Juris Canonici* (Lyons, 1679), cc. 1255–64.

26. He who has been forced to commit perjury, if he is a free man, should fast on bread for forty days and then do penance for seven years; if he is of servile status he should do penance for three years.

27. He who commits perjury while swearing in the hands of a bishop or over a consecrated cross should do penance for three years. If the cross is not blessed, he should do penance for one year. If he is forced to do this or does it unwittingly and then later discovers his perjury, he should do penance for three periods of forty days.

28. He who knowingly swears falsely or compels another to do so should do penance for seven years.

29. He who, in saying the canonical hours or other divine offices, ignores the customary rite of his metropolitan church should be deprived of communion for six months if this happens because of his contempt for the rite.

30. A bishop who, without just cause, ordains a cleric who is unwilling to be ordained or is inwardly reluctant should be completely suspended for one year.

31. A bishop who ignores correcting the sale of the sacraments should do penance for two months; a priest should do four months; a deacon, three; subdeacons and others should do penance according to the discretion of the judge.

32. Someone practicing sorcery should do forty days of penance.

33. Someone who practices astrology should do two years of penance.

34. He who negligently spills a drop of the consecrated wine on the ground, should lick up what has spilled with his tongue and scour the flooring. If there was no flooring, the ground where it dropped should be scraped up, burned, and the ashes concealed inside the altar. The priest should do penance for forty days. If the chalice drips on the altar, the minister should suck up the drop and do penance for three days. If the drop soaks through the top altar cloth to the one underneath it, he should do penance for seven days; if it soaks through to the third cloth, he should do nine days of penance; if to the fourth, twenty days. The minister should wash the cloth on which the drops fell by putting the chalice underneath it and pouring water on the cloth three times and then drink the water or conceal it within the altar if it is too tainted to be consumed.

35. If anyone vomits up the eucharist because he is drunk or has overeaten, if he is a lay man he should do forty days of penance. If he is a cleric, he should do penance for seventy days; if he is a bishop his penance should be ninety days. But if he vomits the eucharist because he is sick, he should do penance for seven days.

36. He who kills a priest should do penance for twelve years.

37. He who willingly burns a house or a field should restore all that was lost or burnt and do three years' penance. And the canon says that if he did this out of hatred or revenge he should be excommunicated; he cannot be absolved until he makes compensation. Furthermore, as a penance he should be compelled to go in God's service on crusade to Jerusalem or Spain for a full year. If any bishop or archbishop relaxes this, the penalty shall be restored and he shall be suspended from episcopal office for a year. Today those who have been so denounced are only able to be absolved by the Holy See.

38. He who unknowingly gives communion to a heretic should do penance for a year; he who knowingly does this should do penance for seven years. He who unknowingly allows a heretic to say mass should do penance for forty days. But if he allows this out of respect for the heretic he should do penance for a year. If he allows this in order to subvert the faith, he should be condemned as a heretic unless he does penance for ten years. And if anyone leaves the church and takes refuge with heretics, and leads others to do the same, he should do penance for twelve years: three years outside the boundaries of the church, six years among the members of the church, two years without receiving communion.

39. He who unwittingly has sexual relations with two sisters or with a mother and her daughter or with an aunt and her niece should do penance for seven years. However, if he did this knowingly, he should remain forever unmarried.

40. He who commits bestiality should do penance for more than the standard seven years; and similarly for incest.

41. The patron of a church who allows church property to become dilapidated should do penance for one year.

42. He who purifies his house with magic and incantations should do penance for five years.

43. When a mouse nibbles the consecrated Host, the priest should do penance for forty days. If he loses the Host, he should do thirty days penance. If he carelessly leaves it lying about even though nothing bad happens to it, he should be suspended from office for three months.

44. He who refuses to swear to keep peace with his neighbor should do penance for one year and restore peaceful relations with him.

45. Usually seven years of penance are given for perjury, adultery, and homicide. The same amount is given for fornication but not so severe a penance is enjoined.

46. He who knowingly rebaptizes someone—if he did this because of the vice of heresy—should do penance for seven years, fasting on bread and

water on the fourth and sixth days of the week for three periods of forty days. But if he did this for the sake of health, that is to say, in order to be healed, he should do penance for three years. And someone who has been baptized or confirmed twice should be put under the jurisdiction of the church and should consider taking on the religious life.

And though a priest should pay careful attention to all the circumstances surrounding a sin, he should give principal weight to the status of the penitent.

∾ No. 80. The rite of marriage from the *Sarum Manual* (fourteenth century).

Manuale ad Usum Percelebris Ecclesiae Sarisburiensis, ed. A. Jeffries Collins, Henry Bradshaw Society 91 (1960), pp. 44–59. Trans. JS.

At the start let the man and the woman stand before the priest and the people at the door of the church, the man to the right of the woman and the woman to the left of the man.

(Know that even though betrothal and marriage can be contracted at any time, since it is done privately by consent alone, nevertheless the customs of wives and the solemnity of the wedding prevent it from being done at certain times; namely, from Advent until the eighth day after the Epiphany [January 6], and from the third Sunday before Ash Wednesday until the eighth day after Easter, and from the Sunday before the Ascension [forty days after Easter] until the octave of Pentecost. On the eighth day after the Epiphany, however, nuptials may be licitly celebrated because there is no prohibition against this even though this is not allowed on the eighth day after Easter. Similarly, nuptials may be licitly celebrated on the Sunday after the feast of Pentecost since Pentecost does not have an eighth day.)

Then the priest should ask about the banns, saying these words in the vernacular: "Behold, brothers, we have come here before God and all his angels and saints in the sight of his church to join together the bodies of this man and woman"—(*Here let the priest look at the couple.*)—"so that, no matter what they have done before this, from now on they may be one flesh and two spirits in faith and in the law of God earning eternal life together. Therefore I admonish you that if there is anyone among you who can say anything about why these young people should not be married, let him reveal it now."

Let this same warning be made to the man and the woman so that if something was done secretly by them, or they are aware of something, or know anything about why they themselves are unable to be married, they should then reveal it. If anyone wishes to propose some impediment, show caution in proving it. The wedding should be postponed until the truth of the matter can be discovered. If no one wishes to propose an impediment, the priest should inquire about the bride's dower; namely, her bridal array, which is described as the ring or the money or anything else given to the bride by the groom. (This gift is called the subarray chiefly when it consists of the gift of the ring; and then it is popularly called an espousal gift.) The priest shall not pledge or consent to the exchange of faith between the man and the woman until the third announcement of the marriage banns. He should announce the banns in church during the mass when the greater part of the people are present on three separate solemnities (so that between each one solemnity there are at least two week days).

The priest should set a suitable date within which he who wishes to and is able may put forward some legitimate impediment to the marriage. And if those contracting the marriage are from different parishes, the banns should be announced in both of their parish churches.

If they are from the same parish, all of the banns should be announced in that church. That priest who dares to be present at the wedding of those contracting marriage before the three solemn announcements of the banns incurs the penalty of a three-year suspension from office.

Similarly, a parish priest who makes little effort to prohibit clandestine marriages in his parish should be suspended from office for three years; he should be more seriously punished if the magnitude of the fault requires it. Clandestine marriages are forbidden for two reasons: first, so that fornication will not be committed by someone expecting to be married. Second, so that those legally married will not be unjustly separated. For frequently in a secret marriage, one of the partners will have a change of mind and leave the other partner, who lacks proof of the marriage, destitute and without remedy of restitution. Thus, priests should frequently warn their parishioners not to make a mutual vow except before public and trustworthy people appointed for this. And any priest, secular or regular, who without the license of his diocesan presumes to solemnize or be present at a marriage outside of the parish church or a chapel having parochial rights attached to it from ancient precedent, will be ipso facto suspended from office for a year.

Then the priest says in the vernacular to the man in the presence of all: "Will you have this woman as your wife to love, honor, and hold her, and to protect her in health and in sickness just as a husband should do for his wife? And for her sake will you leave all others and cling to her alone for as long as either of you shall live?"

The man responds: "I will."

Next the priest says this to the woman: "Will you take this man as your husband to obey and serve him, and to love, honor, and protect him in health and in sickness just as a wife should do for her husband? And for his sake will you leave all others and cling to him alone for as long as either of you shall live?"

The woman responds: "I will."

Then let the woman be handed over by her father or friends. If she is a maiden her hand should be ungloved; if she is a widow, it should be gloved. The man should receive her in God's faith and in her service, just as he vowed before the priest, and he should take her right hand in his right hand. And the man should make an oath to the woman by thus saying after the priest in words of the present tense: "I, N., take the, N., to my wedded wyf to have and to holde fro this day forwarde for bettere for wers for richere for pouerer; in sykenesse and in hele tyl dethe us departe if holy chyrche it woll ordeyne and therto Y plight the my trouthe." (*He removes his hand.*)

Then the woman should say after the priest: "I, N., take the, N., to my wedded housbonde to have and to holde fro this day forwarde for better, for wors, for richer, for pouerer, in sykenesse and in hele, to be bonere and buxom[28] in bedde and atte borde tyll dethe us departhe if holy chyrche it wol ordeyne and therto I plight the my trouthe." (*She removes her hand.*)

Then the man should put silver, gold, and a ring on a plate or a book.[29] The priest should ask whether or not the ring has been blessed before. If he says that it has not, the priest should bless the ring with these words by saying "The Lord be with you" and then "Let us pray." (*Prayer.*)

"Creator and conserver of the human race, giver of spiritual grace, bestower of eternal salvation, send, Lord, your blessing upon this ring— (*Look at it.*)—so that she who wears it will be armed with the power of heavenly defense, and may it bring her to eternal salvation. Through Christ our Lord, etc."

"Let us pray. Lord, bless † this ring—(*Look at it.*)—which we have blessed in your holy name so that whoever shall wear it may dwell in your peace and endure in your will, and live and wax and wane in your love, and increase the length of their days. Through Christ our Lord, etc."

Then let him sprinkle holy water on the ring.

But if the ring was previously blessed, then immediately after the man places it on the book, the priest takes it and gives it to the man, who takes it in his right hand with the three main fingers. Holding his wife's right hand with his left, he should say after the priest:

---

[28]Obedient and kind.

[29]See the wedding sermon in No. 85 for the symbolic meaning of these rituals.

"With this rynge, I the wed and this gold and silver I the give, and with my body I the worshipe and with all my worldely cathel I the endowe." And then the husband should place the ring on his wife's thumb saying, "In the name of the Father." And then on the second finger saying, "and of the Son." And then on the third finger saying, "and of the Holy Spirit." And then on the fourth finger saying, "Amen." Let him leave the ring on that finger because according to medical art there is a special vein that leads from there to the heart. The ringing sound of the silver stands for the inner love which should always be fresh between them.

Then they should incline their heads so that the priest can say a blessing over them:

"May the Lord bless you, who made the world from nothing. Amen."

[*The ceremony continues with a verse from Psalm 67:29–31 and other prayers omitted here.*]

Here let them enter the church and go to the foot of the altar. As the priest enters with his servers, let him say this psalm.

[*Psalm 127 and other prayers follow.*]

Then, when the groom and bride have prostrated themselves before the foot of the altar, the priest should ask those people present to pray for them saying:

"Our Father.[30] And lead us not into temptation. But deliver us from evil. Save your servant and your handmaiden. God my hopes are in you. Send them your aid, Lord. And look down upon them from Zion. Be for them, Lord, a tower of strength. From the face of the enemy. Lord hear my prayer. And let my cry come unto you. The Lord be with you. And with your spirit. Let us pray." (*Prayer.*)

"May the Lord bless you from Zion so that you may see how good Jerusalem is all the days of your life; and may you see the sons of your sons and peace upon the land of Israel. Through our Lord Christ. Let us pray.

"God of Abraham, God of Isaac, God of Jacob, bless † these young people and sow the seed of eternal life in their minds so that whatever they learn of profit to them, this they will desire to do. Through Jesus Christ your Son, the redeemer of mankind. Who lives and reigns with you, etc. Let us pray.

"Look down from heaven, Lord, and bless † this accord. And just as you sent your holy angel Raphael to Tobias and Sara, the daughter of Raguel, so deign, Lord to send your blessing † upon these young people so that they may remain in your will and endure in your care, and live and prosper and grow old

---

[30.]The following are the first lines of several familiar prayers and psalms.

in your love, and may be worthy and peaceful and increase the length of their days. Through our Lord Christ. Let us pray." (*Prayer.*)

"Look favorably, Lord, on this your servant—(*Look at the husband.*)—and upon this your handmaiden—(*Look at the wife.*)—so that they may receive a heavenly blessing † in your name, and may see unharmed the sons of their sons and the daughters of their daughters all the way to the third and fourth generation, and may they persevere in your will. And may they come in the future to the heavenly kingdom. Through Christ. Let us pray." (*Prayer.*)

"May the almighty and eternal God, who by his power created our first parents Adam and Eve and joined them together in their holiness, sanctify and bless † your hearts and your bodies, and join you together in true partnership and love. Through Christ."

Then he blesses them saying.

"May almighty God bless you † with every heavenly blessing and may he make you worthy in his sight. May he abundantly pour forth his grace upon you. And may he teach you with the word of truth so that you may please him both in body and in mind. Through our Lord."

When these prayers are finished (which are said over them while they are prostrate before the foot of the altar) the priest should lead them into the presbytery; that is to say, between the choir stalls and the altar in the south part of the church. The woman should stand to the right of the man—namely, between him and the altar. The nuptial mass should then begin. . . .

After the *Sanctus* [of the mass] let the groom and bride prostrate themselves in prayer at the foot of the altar. Extended over them is a cloth that four clergy hold by its four corners to form a canopy, unless one of them has been previously betrothed or blessed. Then they should not have the canopy over them nor should the sacramental blessing be said, as explained below. . . .

When night arrives and the husband and wife retire to their bed the priest should come and bless their room saying: "The Lord be with you. Let us pray." (*Prayer.*)

"Bless † Lord, this chamber and everyone dwelling in it that they may live in your peace and endure in your will, and that they may live and grow old in your love and the length of their days may be multiplied. Through the Lord."

Next the blessing of the bed begins with "The Lord be with you. Let us pray."

"Bless † this bed, Lord, (*Look at it.*) you who neither sleeps nor nods. You who guarded Israel, guard your servants sleeping in this bed from all imaginary illusions of the Devil; guard them while they are awake so that they will think upon your commandments while they sleep and will feel you in their dreams; may they be strengthened through the help of your protection here and everywhere. Through the Lord."

Next make a blessing over them in the bed up to the "Let us pray." Blessing:

"May God bless † your bodies and your souls, and may he give you blessing as he blessed Abraham, Isaac, and Jacob. Amen."

Another blessing with the "Let us pray."

"May the Lord's hand be upon you, and may he send his holy angels to guard you all the days of your life. Amen."

Another blessing with the "Let us pray."

"May the Father, Son, and Holy Spirit bless † you who is three in number but one in Godhead. Amen."

After doing these things, sprinkle them with holy water, and so depart and leave them in peace.

∾ No. 81. "Seven Questions to Be Asked of a Dying Man" (c. 1400).

John Mirk, *Instructions for Parish Priests*, ed. Edward Peacock, *EETS* o.s. 31 (1902), pp. 69–71. Modernized by WJD.

Here follow seven special interrogations a curate should ask every Christian person who is gravely ill.

First: Do you believe fully all the principal articles of faith as well as all the holy scriptures in all things according to the teachings of the holy and true doctors of Holy Church and forsake all heresies and errors and opinions condemned by the church? And are you happy to die in the faith of Christ and in the unity and obedience of Holy Church? The sick person answers, yes.

Second: Do you know how often, in what ways, and how grievously you have offended the Lord your God who created you from nothing? For Saint Bernard comments in the "Canticle of Canticles," "I know well that no one can be saved who does not know himself." It is from this knowledge that a person knows the Mother of health, that is humility, and also the fear of God which is the beginning of wisdom. And so it is the beginning of the soul. The sick person answers, yes.

Third: Are you sorry in your heart for all the sins you have committed against the high majesty and love and goodness of God and of all the goodness that you did not do but might have done, and of all the grace that you have rejected, not only for fear of death or any other pain, but rather for love of God and righteousness? For you have displeased his great goodness and kindness and due order and charity by which we are bound to love God above all things. Do you ask forgiveness of God for all these things? Do you also desire in your heart to know every offense you have committed against God and to have special repentance for them all? The sick person answers, yes.

Fourth: Are you resolved to amend your life that you may live longer and never commit mortal sins intentionally again? . . . And do you pray that God give you the grace to continue in this purpose? The sick person answers, yes.

Fifth: Do you forgive fully in your heart anyone who has done you harm or caused you grief either in word or deed for the love and worship of our Lord Jesus Christ from whom you hope to have forgiveness yourself? And do you ask for the forgiveness of others whom you have offended in any way? The sick person answers, yes.

Sixth: Would you have all things in your possession given back as much as is possible . . . and prefer to leave and forsake all your worldly goods if you cannot make satisfaction in any other way? The sick person answers, yes.

Seventh: Do you believe fully that Christ died for you and that you will never be saved except by the merit of Christ's Passion, and do you thank God as heartily for this as you can? The sick person answers, yes.

Then let the curate invite the sick person to recite the "Into your hands," etc., mindfully, if able. And if not, let the curate recite it on behalf of the infirm. And whosoever can truly and of good conscience without any falsehood answer yes to all these articles and points noted above, that one shall forever live in heaven with Almighty God and with his holy company where Jesus brings both you and me! Amen!

↷ No. 82. Miscellaneous blessings (fourteenth century).

Manuale ad Usum Percelebris Ecclesiae Sarisburiensis, ed. A. Jeffries Collins, Henry Bradshaw Society 91 (1960), pp. 63–64, 66–67, 69–70. Trans. JS.

Blessing for Seed
Blessing for seeds with "The Lord be with you," and "Let us pray." Prayer: Almighty and eternal God, creator of the human race, we humbly beseech you that you bless with a heavenly blessing this seed which we will sow in our fields, and that you deign to make it grow and bring it to maturity so that your right hand may be praised throughout the whole world. Through our Lord, etc. *Then sprinkle holy water on the seed.*

Blessing for Fruit
Blessing for Orchards on St. James' Day [July 25] with "The Lord be with you,"
and "Let us pray." Prayer:. . . . We beseech you Almighty God, to bless this
fruit from the new trees so that we who are wounded by the just sentence
of death from our First Parents who ate the fruit from the Tree of Death
may be made holy and be blessed in all things through the light of your only
son, God, the Redeemer, and with the blessing of our Lord Jesus Christ and
the Holy Spirit; and, with the snares of the ancient evil tempter averted by
the solemn remembrance of this day, may we eat healthily from the many
fruits sprouting from the earth. Through the same Lord. In unity with the
same. *Then let the priest sprinkle it with holy water.*

Blessing for Bread
Blessing for bread on Sundays.[31] *First let the priest read the Gospel according
to John: "In the beginning [was the word]," etc., and then say these words:*
"Blessed be the name of the Lord." *Response:* "Now and forever." *Then let
the priest say,* "The Lord be with you," *and* "Let us pray." *Prayer:* Bless †
Lord, this creature, bread, just as you blessed the five loaves in the desert, so
that all eating from it may have health in body and soul. In the name of the
Father and of the Son. *Then let him sprinkle holy water on the bread and
distribute it.*

Blessing for the Eyes
*A blessing for weak eyes can be done in this manner if necessity requires it and
someone requests it out of piety. First, let the person genuflect before the altar.
Then let the priest say,* "The Lord be with you," *and* "Let us pray." *Prayer:*
Lord Jesus Christ, you who opened the eyes of the man born blind, clear the
eyes of this your servant, making his (her) vision keen, ample, fit, and able
in your service by the power of this sacrament and through this the sign of
your holy cross. *Here let the priest sign the eyes of the sick person with the sign
of the cross using his corporal and then let him fan his eyes with it saying,* In
the name of the Father and the Son and the Holy Spirit. Amen.

Blessing for the Sword of a New Knight
*The blessing for the sword of a new knight is done in this way. While the knight
genuflects before the altar, let the priest first say without singing,* "The Lord be

---

[31]This is not the consecrated bread of the altar, but, since lay people took communion only a
few times a year, the bread blessed and given to them in its place.

with you," *and* "Let us pray." *Prayer:* Lord, protector of all who hope in you, attend to our prayers and grant that this your servant, who with sincere heart aspires to gird himself with his first sword so to be a knight, may be protected in all things by the helmet of your strength. And just as you handed victory to David and Judith over the might of the enemy of your people, by your aid let him everywhere be the victor over the fierceness of your enemies, and let him rush to the protection of Holy Church. Through Christ our Lord. Amen. *Then let the priest sprinkle the knight, girded with his sword, with holy water; and let the knight depart in the name of the Lord.*

◌ No. 83. The "Great Cursing": articles of excommunication from York (late fourteenth century).

Manuale et Processionale ad Usum Insignis Ecclesiae Eboracensis, ed. W. G. Henderson, Surtees Society 63 (1875), pp. 119–22. Modernized by JS.

[*This list, from a manuscript written c. 1403, is a compilation of excommunications the core of which date back to the Council of Oxford of 1222.*]

Anathemas

[1] To begin, God and Holy Church curse all those who break or disturb the freedoms of Holy Church; and all who are against the peace, rights, or state of Holy Church, or who assent thereto in deed or counsel; and all who deprive Holy Church of its rights, or make of Holy Church, which is holy and sanctified, a lay fee.[32]

[2] Also all those who knowingly or willingly tithe falsely, and do not give to God and Holy Church the tenth part or tenth penny of everything lawfully acquired in profit or merchandise, or from any other craft, deducting only the necessary expenses and costs from the thing that produces profit, but not balancing the profits from one thing against the losses of another.

[3] Also all those that do not give their holy tithes of the fruit of the earth, or of cattle, or of any other thing that renews during the year, without deducting expenses.

[4] Also all those who with evil will toward the parson, the parish priest, the clerk, or any other minister of Holy Church withhold oblations, rents, offerings, or any other thing that ought to be given to Holy Church.

[5] Also all those that hinder, break, or disturb the privilege of Holy Church; that is to say, if a man flees to a church or churchyard [for sanctuary], anyone who prevents him or drags him out, or procures or assents to this.

---

[32] I.e., a fief held in return for secular services.

[6] Also all those that commit sacrilege; that is to say, take any holy thing out of any holy place, or anything that is unhallowed out of any holy place.

[7] Also all those that purchase letters in any lord's court that prevent a case about rights from being determined or judged.

[8] Also all those that disturb the land.

[9] Also all those that draw blood from any man or woman in violence or in any other felony in a church or churchyard, so that the church or church-yard is placed under interdict, or suspension, or is polluted.

[10] Also all those that are against the king's rights.

[11] Also all those that wrongfully sustain war against the king's peace.

[12] Also all robbers and raiders or slayers of men, except in self-defense.

[13] Also all those that are against the king's Magna Carta, which is con-firmed by the court of Rome.

[14] Also all those that knowingly bear or procure false witness, especially in a matrimonial case in or out of any court whatsoever.

[15] Also all those that bear false witness in order to interfere with a legiti-mate marriage or any man or woman or to disinherit anyone of land, rent, tenements, or any other chattel.

[16] Also all false advocates that for payment put forth false exceptions and quarrels in order to undo a legitimate marriage.

[17] Also all those who for payment or favor or for any other reason mali-ciously deprive another man or woman of his or her good name and put them into wicked repute, or cause them to lose their worldly goods or hon-ors, or wrongfully make them undergo purgation for which they were never before defamed.

[18] Also all those that maliciously disturb or hinder a lawful patron from making rightful presentation to a church, or who procure such by word, deed, or false inquest, or by other means.

[19] Also all those who maliciously refuse the royal order to seize an excom-municated man who has been under sentence for forty days without seeking remedy; and all who disturb the captors with judgments or false inquests.

[20] Also all those that take payment to break peace, where there should be love, or that maintain contention or strife with word or deed; they may not be absolved until they have returned the payment to whom they took it from.

[21] Also all who bear away or by force wrongfully carry off or waste the houses, manors, farms or any other movable or immovable goods of parsons or vicars, or of any other men of Holy Church against the will of their agents; they may not be absolved from this cursing until they have made restitution to them who were wronged.

[22] Also all those people who carry off with violence from inside churches or from houses of religion anything put there as a warranty or for safekeeping; and all who procure or assent thereto.

[23] Also all witches and those that trust in them.

[24] Also all those who lay violent hands on a priest or cleric except in self-defense.

[25] Also all who give counsel or help against Christian men to the Saracens.

[26] Also all women who destroy their pregnancy or children with potions or other craft.

[27] Also all those who with malice wrongfully accuse any man of fathering their children.

[28] Also all those that willfully lose their children or leave them in a field, or in a town, or at the church door, or in any other place, leaving them succorless.

[29] Also all makers of false money and their associates.

[30] Also all those that clip good money to their advantage.

[31] Also those who falsify papal bulls or counterfeit the king's scales.

[32] Also all those who buy or sell using false measures or weights; that is to say, they buy with one and sell with another.

[33] Also those who falsify the king's standards.

[34] Also all those who maliciously prevent a man or woman, married or unmarried, from making a lawful testament, and those who hinder the execution of a lawfully made testament.

[35] Also all those that knowingly and willingly perjure themselves out of love or hatred in order to cause any man to lose his goods or his honor.

[36] Also those who burn churches or men's houses in peacetime.

[37] Also robbers and raiders who steal any man's goods openly or secretly by day or by night, entailing the death of good men.

[38] Also they that knowingly hold any man's goods that have been inquired after openly in church.[33]

[39] Also all felons and their maintainers.

[40] Also all conspirators and perjurers in assizes and in any other court.

[41] Also all those that put forth any false complaints against the rights of the church, the king, or the realm.

[42] Also all those that withhold or put in any other place, against the will of the parson or his parish priest, offerings made in the church, the churchyard, a chapel, oratory, or in any other place within the Province of York, unless they have permission to do so.

---

[33] Priests commonly used the pulpit to inquire about people's lost property.

[43] Also all those that are loath to turn over due goods in fraud of Holy Church, or to avoid their debts, and all that counsel thereto or help.

[44] Also all those that hinder prelates or ordinaries of Holy Church from holding consistories, sessions, or chapters for making inquiries necessary for the health of the soul into sins or excesses.

[45] Also all heretics that do not believe in the sacrament of the altar, which is God's own body in flesh and blood in the form of bread, and in the other sacraments that concern the health of man's soul.

[46] Also all usurers, that is to say, if a man lends his chattel or goods to another in order to make profit from the contract for the loan. For if there were any usurers in a city, it should be placed under interdict, preventing the sacraments from being administered there until the usurers were ejected from the city.

These are the points of the Great Cursing that our holy fathers, popes, and archbishops ordered to be published at least three times during the year: that is to say, the first or second Sunday of Lent; some Sunday before or after Maudlintide,[34] as is best; and also some Sunday in the Advent before Christmas; and this is the practice of Holy Church throughout Christendom.

∾ No. 84. Pope Innocent III [1198–1216] on preaching: from the preface to a collection of his sermons.

Patrologia Latina 217, c. 313. Trans. WJD.

The preacher should have wine and oil, flail and grain, fire and water using each rightly in its place. But the preacher needs first to look after the teaching of the faith and instructions for living, from the foundation to the building itself, strengthening what he says with authority, reason and example "like a three-ply rope hard to unravel" [Eccles. 4:12]. However, since the dust of vainglory often clings to the feet of preachers, the preacher ought to shake the dust from his feet and wash them as well in the water of compunction until he is entirely cleansed. If he does not, when he preaches to others he makes himself a reprobate [1 Cor. 2:1–5]. Would that I myself did what I say a preacher should do; but I am so hindered by the rush of cases, so snared in the nets of administration, that I end up giving a little bit of myself to each and every thing. So much so that I am not even allowed to meditate, hardly permitted to breathe, and my interior life seems to me completely distracted. But, lest I neglect entirely spiritual duties on account of temporal demands which weigh upon me greatly in these wicked times and which require all the more my office of apostolic service, I have con-

---

[34]I.e., the feast of St. Mary Magdalene, July 22.

ceived and dictated some sermons to the clergy and people, some in Latin, some in the vulgar tongue, which you urged me to do in your petition conveyed through our mutual son, Brother Nicholas, my chaplain and your monk; these I have endeavored to send your grace, asking and imploring in Christ Jesus that you commend me spiritually in your prayers to the Just Judge and the Heavenly Father.

ᥐᴗ No. 85. A selection of late fourteenth-century sermons.

Middle English Sermons, ed. Woodburn O. Ross, *EETS* o.s. 209 (1940), pp. 61–65 (Easter). *Myrc's Festial: a Collection of Homilies,* ed. Theodor Erbe, pt. 1, *EETS* extra series 96 (1905), pp. 289–97 (wedding and burial). Modernized by JS.

A. An Easter Sermon

"*Qui manducat meam carnem et bibit meum sanguinem, in me manet et ego in eo.*" "*Et ideo revertar unde exivi*" [John 6:57; Matt. 12:44].

Worshipful sirs, these words that I have chosen to say to you at this time are the words of Christ himself, written in the gospel for this day. For your understanding, this is what they mean: "Whoever this day eats my flesh and drinks my blood worthily, he shall dwell in me and I in him forever; and therefore I will go back to the place that I came from."

In these words two things may be understood: first, a man must consider what he is receiving [in the sacrament of the altar]. Second, every man and woman must well consider how perilous it is for them to presume to receive the worthy Lord when they themselves are unworthy. The scripture passage concludes this way: "*Qui enim manducat et bibit indigne, iudicium sibi manducat et bibit*"—that is to say, "whoever eats and drinks me unworthily thereby takes on his own doom and damnation" [1 Cor. 11:29].

Thus I find in chronicles that there was once a good woman who had mortally hated a poor woman for more than seven years. This woman, though lacking charity, on Easter Day had received the Holy Sacrament during this whole time. Finally her spiritual father called this good woman to him and said that she must forgive the poor woman her trespasses or else he would withdraw her right to receive the sacrament that very day. Lacking resolve, she said, "I will do as you bid me." And so out of worldly shame more than respect for God she forgave the woman her trespass, for she would not be without her communion rights on Easter Day. When the Easter service was ended and all the people had received communion, neighbors came with the poor woman to the good woman's house to cheer her and thank God that the two of them were at peace. But then this wretched women said, "Are you sure that I forgave this woman with my heart as I did with my mouth? If I did so, I hope that I may never pick up this bit of straw at my feet." Then she stooped down to pick it up and the devil strangled her on the spot. Thus, any of you who settle a dispute with another, be sure that you do so without feigning, and let your heart and your tongue agree. Then I may truly verify and say that you are in perfect love and charity. If you do the reverse, I will conclude with the words of Christ: "*Qui enim manducat et bibit indigne, iudicium sibi manducat et bibit*—whoever eats my flesh, etc."

Concerning the second reason, I also spoke of how perilous it is for a man to receive the Blessed Sacrament. For many people receive it and give little thought to what they have done; within two or three days after Easter, they turn again to their sin and their wretchedness, soon forgetting the Blessed Lord that they received such a little while before. So I counsel you to follow the advice of St. Paul, who said, "*Caritas fraternitatis maneat in vobis*—love and the charity of brotherhood be among you" [Heb. 13:1]. You should maintain these after Easter is over just as you should before during the holy time of Lent; and continue to do so ever after so that the devil will have no interest in or power over you.

I read and find that there was once a Christian clerk who was holy and devout. He had a brother sworn to him who was a Jew. This Christian clerk, as the chronicle records, during the holy time of Lent would part from his brother the Jew and go to the church of God for reconciliation, that is to say, to confess his sins once each week[35] so that he could worthily receive the Blessed Sacrament—may it be worshipped!—on Easter Day. One time this Jew saw this Christian clerk going toward the church and he asked him where he was going. He said, "I am going toward God's house, there to purge and cleanse myself of my sins so that on Easter Day I can worthily receive the Holy Sacrament for the salvation of my soul." Then the Jew asked his brother, "Is that your Sabbath day?" "Yes, truly," said the Christian clerk. The Jew said, "Good brother, when you've been to God's house and have received the Lord there, come again and meet me here in this same place and tell me how it stands with you." "Truly," said the Christian clerk, "I will." Then this Christian clerk went into the church of God and there found his spiritual father ready with the Holy Sacrament. With great meekness and humility he received the blessed Lord. When the service was done, he hastened back to his sworn brother the Jew, as they had agreed. And as he went by the way he saw a great company of Jews loitering and waiting where his brother had told him to meet him. He was dreadfully afraid and he asked God to be his help and succor. And suddenly an angel came from heaven

---

[35]Far in excess of the annual confession required by canon law.

and comforted him and bade him not to fear for God would defend him. So he went boldly forth to his brother the Jew. As soon as they saw him they took him, and bound him hand and foot, and asked him where he had been. He humbly answered them and said, "I have been at the temple of God, and there I received the blessed Lord Christ Jesus who made both you and me." Then they said, "Tell us where in your body you have put him." [*The text continues in Latin.*] They cut his body down the middle and removed his intestines, his liver, his diaphragm, and finally his heart. But they were unable to hold his heart and it fell flat upon the ground. And then a bright flash cleaved his heart in two and in the middle of it there was the body of the Lord in the form of bread. And none of the Jews were able to look at it nor could they move. And when high mass ended Christians came out of the church. They found the Christian clerk lying dead, his heart cleft down the middle and at its center the body of the Lord in the form of bread. And it changed into the shape of a little boy one cubit tall who stood on the heart and said, "I am the bread of life who descended from heaven. Whoever eats my flesh and drinks my blood worthily, he shall dwell in me and I in him. And so I will go back to the place that I came from, just as I first was." And the dead man's heart leapt back into his body just where it had been, and also his intestines, liver, diaphragm, and so forth. Thus his body was restored to life. All of the Jews believed in God and were baptized. [*The text returns to English.*] So then many thousands were turned to Christ's faith through this glorious miracle, as is clear in Acts 3, the tenth chapter.

Thus, to conclude all these aforesaid matters: God give us grace to receive his blessed Lord this day and to put him in our heart as this Christian clerk did, we to abide with him and him with us, so that we may come to that endless joy and bliss among the saints of heaven, rejoicing there with them and they with us, to see that glorious face of Christ Jesus—may God grant us such a sight!—who died for us on the rood tree. Amen.

B. A Wedding Sermon

As you all see, a man and a woman have been wedded together as the law of Holy Church instructs. May God by his goodness give them his grace so that they may maintain this sacrament that they have received so that God may be satisfied and they will be esteemed in heaven and on earth. But since there are many who receive this sacrament without understanding what it involves, I will now briefly show you what it is so that you may in the future fear God all the more and better keep your way of life. Thus, you should know that this sacrament is holy: first, for making a good beginning; second for good living; and finally for a good ending. For they who take heed of what duty they take up at the beginning and then take care to keep it while they are alive shall finally come to the bliss that is without end.

They should know that this sacrament was not first founded by earthly man but by the Holy Trinity of heaven. Father and Son and Holy Ghost made it in the earthly paradise, which is a place in the east so high that Noah's flood came nowhere near it. In this place there is so much joy and bliss that no tongue can describe it nor heart conceive it. And since this way of life was made in that happy place, Holy Church allowed it to be made here on earth with mirth that is holy in itself and without villainy. Here, then, is how it was made: After God had made this earth and everything in it by his will for man, then, at last, he made man. Thus, when man was made, he found everything ready at hand and obedient to him. And then the Holy Trinity said, "Let us make man in our image!" [Gen. 1:26]. That is to say, man, by his imagination and his virtue is like God in soul but not in body. Thus, all the virtues that a man has come out of his soul into his body. Then God brought Adam into paradise and made him its keeper. And it is full of trees bearing fruit all year long; there is nothing like it in the world. Then, in the middle of paradise God set one tree that surpassed all the others in beauty and virtue. This tree God reserved only for himself so that anytime Adam saw it, he should be reminded of God. For when a man is prosperous he forgets God and himself unless he is aided by grace. Then God said to Adam: "Eat of all the trees in Paradise except this one; eat not of it on pain of death" [Gen. 2:16–17]. And this same warning was passed on by Adam to Eve. Then God said: "It is not good for a man to be by himself" [Gen. 2:18]. Here began the form of the words of the wedding of man and woman.

Thus, by God's command a man should take on a wife of like age, like condition, and like birth. For when these things are in accord, things are likely to fare well; otherwise, they are not. With this in mind the priest should ask them on their oath whether they are related to each other within the forbidden degrees of marriage or not, whether either of them is es- poused to another person, and whether they are both fully willing to live together and keep the obligations he will lay on them.

As a sign of this, angels, by God's bidding, brought all sorts of creatures before Adam. But since there was no creature like Adam, God made him sleep, and suddenly his spirit was taken up into heaven and there he saw everything that would happen to him and his offspring. Meanwhile, God took one rib from Adam's flesh and said, "Make it a woman, flesh of flesh and bone of bone." Then God woke Adam and put the woman before him and gave her to Adam.

And the priest does likewise when he gives the woman to the man. Then the man puts silver and money on the book that bears an image of a man as a token that he intends to beget children that are God's image, in order to restore the number of the angels.

Then Adam took the woman and said, "This is now bone of bone and flesh of flesh" [Gen. 2:23], for a man shall leave father and mother and draw to her as a part of himself. And she shall love him and he her, truly together; they shall be two in one flesh: for their child is one flesh of father and mother. Then afterwards, the woman, by the teaching of the fiend, with her hand took fruit of that tree that was forbidden and ate from it. She gave it to her husband Adam, which shows that she loved her husband more than God.

Therefore the priest blesses a ring, that symbolizes God who has neither a beginning nor an end, and puts it on her finger which has a vein running to her heart, symbolizing that she shall love God over all things and then her husband.

Then, when they had broken God's warning, suddenly by God's bidding an angel drove them out of paradise into this world to follow their livelihoods with travail and sickness, and the woman to bear her children with woe and pain.

Therefore, the priest takes them by the hand and brings them into the church (which is God's house) as those who have sworn an oath to live by God's law and to follow his commandments. And so he sets them before the altar as if before God's own face. The ceremony that was just said was for the Holy Trinity. As a sign of this, the priest then begins the mass of the Trinity.

Since Adam and Eve were naked, God had mercy on them and clothed them with pelt, that is, a cloth made of dead beasts. And so there is a cloth held over the couple, teaching them to have death and the cover of their grave in mind, and thus, out of fear, to avoid evil and do good.

And inasmuch as the woman sinned more than Adam, the priest reads more over the woman than over the man. Afterwards, the man kisses the priest and then kisses his wife, signifying that there is complete peace and accord of love between God and them, and so there ever shall be while they maintain the way of life they have taken upon themselves. To show you what punishment they are worthy of who break this way of life, I'll tell you this example.

I read that there was an old knight who wedded a young lady. But since this old knight did not please her to her liking she took another younger knight who was their neighbor. After they had long lived in sin, they both died suddenly. Now there was a man who made charcoal in a field near the lord's estate. He made a great fire of coals and then lay by it all night long in order to keep an eye on it. Then, before midnight, he saw a woman coming as fast as she could, crying mightily in fear. After her there came a man all in black, riding on a black horse, and wielding a sword in his hand. He chased this woman all around the coal fire and at last he caught her; he chopped her all to pieces, threw her into the fire, and rode away. The next night the coal-man saw the same thing, and the night after that too, so that he was so afraid that he went to his lord and told him that he dared not dwell there any longer. Then the lord said, "Go once more and I will join you this night and with the might of God I shall find out what they are." So the lord went there and when the other rider came and chopped the woman in pieces and cast her into the fire, this lord took him by the bridle and conjured him to tell him who they were. Then he said, "I am such and such a man, and she such and such a woman I had, unbeknown to her husband. And each night I must slay her and burn her in this fire because she was the cause of my sin. And I ride here on a devil that looks like a horse, and this saddle burns hotter than any earthly fire. Thus we shall both do until we are helped by some good man." Then the lord asked, "What may be your help? Tell me and it shall be done." Then he told him how many masses must be said for them and what sorts of almsgiving. The lord did as he promised them and they were helped. Thus is marriage holy in its beginning.

It is also holy in living. As a sign of this, Christ and his mother Mary and his disciples were called to a wedding between John the Evangelist and Mary Magdalene.[36] By his presence he made marriage holy, which it is now, as I have said before. As a sign of this, after the mass the priest is asked to the wedding banquet. He comes and blesses their food and their drink, just as Christ, with his blessing, at the request of Our Lady turned water into wine. To show you the power of a priest's blessing I'll tell you this story.

A group of fellows had taken a stein of ale to drink in an arbor. The priest of that town would have joined them, but since he had not yet sung mass he told them to go along and he would come when he had done. One of them said to him, "Sir, bless the drink before you go." Then he said, "God bless it, and so do I, *In nomine Patris, et Filii et Spiritus Sanctus. Amen.*" And suddenly the stein burst into pieces and there was a great toad at the bottom of the stein. Everyone held up their hands to God and thanked him for saving them from poisoning with his blessing.

---

[36] Medieval legend picked these two as the wedding couple at Cana [John 2:1–11].

Wedlock is also holy at its ending, for those that keep it well in their lives shall be taken in at the great wedding that shall happen after Doomsday when God and Holy Church shall be wedded together for everlasting bliss.

Thus, near Northampton there was a an eleven-year-old child who was sick with a pestilence and was in a coma. But when he woke, he spoke many wonders. There was a man nearby who had a lover unknown to his wife and to everyone else. The man decided to go and speak with this child. As he went forth he met a devil who looked like his lover; he kissed her and rode on. When he reached this child he asked him how he was. Then he said, "I am well, sir, but you are very ill, for you keep a mistress against God's law. You think you kissed her on your way here, but it was a devil resembling her, and with that kiss it has set a chancre on your lip that will eat into your heart unless you repent." But this man took his words for a fantasy and the chancre spread, ate into him as the boy said, and killed him.

Therefore, each man and woman should beware that they keep that high oath that they made before God and all his saints; for whoever breaks it, they shall not escape without vengeance.

C. A Sermon for the Burial of the Dead

Good men, as you all see, here is a mirror for us all: a corpse brought to the church. God have mercy on him for his mercy and bring him unto his everlasting bliss. But, good men, you should understand that this corpse is brought to the church for three principal reasons.

The first is to show us that he was meek and obedient during his life to God and to Holy Church. But since he knew that he oftentimes did wrong against God through pride, as we all do, therefore at his death he bequeaths his soul into God's hands and his body to Holy Church, putting himself wholly into God's mercy to do with his body and his soul whatever his will shall be. For no man shall ever be saved who is not meek to God and to Holy Church. This is the first reason why his corpse is brought to church: just as a mother does not forsake the child who is obedient to her, so Holy Church receives each man who will obey and acknowledge his guilt with a purpose of amendment.

The second reason is that mankind was made of the slime of the earth; that is, by nature he stinks. Therefore man's flesh, even though it is not so fair or sweet while it lives, as soon as it is dead begins to stink and turn into the foulest carrion there is. When a man dies he soon takes on the smell of death. Therefore it is brought to the church to be put in earth that is hallowed; for each corpse is earth and comes from the earth and lives on the earth and is, in the end, buried in the earth. And he has a white sheet on

him to show that he has been cleanly shriven and cleansed of his sins by his
heart's contrition and by the absolution of Holy Church. His head is laid
toward the west and his feet toward the east so that he will be more ready
to see Christ who will come out of the east at Doomsday; thus he will rise
up facing Christ. He also has a wooden cross set at his head, showing that
he has the full right to be saved by Christ's passion, who died for him on a
wooden cross. There is another cross made of candle wax laid on his breast,
showing that he died burning in charity to God and man. For all those who
die in full charity shall have help and part of all the prayers of Holy Church
in all the world. Those that die without charity shall have no part of the
prayers of Holy Church. There is also a food bowl laid by him instead of a
staff to show that he is going to his final home; but this staff is broken to
show that therein there is no defense; he must accept, for better or worse,
what he deserves. Then earth is cast on him and the door shuts on him forever and so everlasting farewell be to him and his works. So that devils will
have no power in his grave, the priest sprinkles it with holy water and goes
on his way. It often happens that devils have the power to trouble a corpse
which has not had the full sacraments of Holy Church; I can demonstrate
this with an example.

   I find that there were three brothers fighting in a town and all three were
slain. Two of them had all the proper burial rites, but the third did not. They
were buried together inside the church. Then a devil came, took the corpse
that had not received the last anointing, entered into it, went into the town,
and began making many cries which made men aghast. It did this for a long
time. Now there was a hermit in the town who lived in the church. He was
saying his prayers just before midnight when by the light of the moon he
saw the fiend approaching like an ape. And when the fiend reached the
grave, the corpse rose up out of it and the fiend entered it and went forth as
it had been doing. When the fiend approached him, the hermit conjured
him by the power of him who died on the cross for mankind, that he should
tell him why he had more power over that corpse than any other. The fiend
said to him, "This corpse did not receive the last anointing; therefore I have
power over it. But his soul is safe. Thus, I do this not to harm his soul but
to make others sin against him who think that he is other than he is, so that
I may hold these sins against them at Doomsday, telling how they treated
their neighbors as they should not have, in violation of God's commandment." Then the hermit ordered him by virtue of God's passion to leave off
and to tempt God's people no more. And so he ceased. This is the second
reason why this corpse is brought to the church.

   The third reason is so that it can be helped by the prayers and sacraments of Holy Church. For a long time, as John Beleth[37] reports, the common people were buried at home in their own house; but there was so great and violent a stench from the corpse that they couldn't bear it. Then, by common assent, they made a place outside the town and buried the corpses there; rich men were buried on hilltops or in rocks under hills. But nothing was done to succor them after death, and so souls often appeared to their friends complaining bitterly that they had no help. Thus churches are blessed by holy bishops, who allowed them to make churchyards and bless them, and bring everyone to Holy Church so that all should have part of the prayers of the mass and of Holy Church.

Therefore we pray intently for all whose bodies rest inside the church or in the churchyard, and all who are brought to the church. For as often as their friends see their graves they shall remember them and pray for them. But for all the prayers that have been offered for the help of men's souls, the mass is the chief and principal succor for all souls. For any particular soul, the mass that he loved most in life helps him the most when he is dead. So if a man or a woman loves the mass of the Trinity, or of the Holy Ghost, or of Our Lady, that mass will most help them when they are dead. For the common help of all Christian souls, after the mass, the psalms of the psalter and especially the seven [penitential] psalms with the litany are sung; for they are aid against the seven deadly sins, with the prayers of the saints that are called on for help. Also *Placebo* and *Dirige* with the nine lessons, the *Laudes*, and the requiem mass nourish souls and make them strong to suffer their pain with more patience.

The joy of Our Lady also gives them great succor and refreshment; this is what a spirit said that came and spoke openly to a prior in the hearing of many others that were called there to hear the spirit speak. And if a spirit has received all rites of Holy Church, when it first leaves the body Our Lady is ready to comfort it against the attacks that demons make on it by showing it all the sins it has committed, yelling at it, and threatening to drag it to hell with them. But then Our Lady is ready—blessed may she be!—and she rebukes the demons and says this to them: "I am God's Mother, and I pray my Son that he give this soul a place in heaven. I am also the Empress of Hell, and I have power over you demons; therefore, I command you to harass this soul no longer. Go your way and let him have rest. I am also Lady of all the world, and therefore I grant this soul the help and succor of all the prayers that are said in Holy Church, and of all the prayers of all the saints of

[37]The twelfth-century theologian and liturgist, author of an influential book, *Summa de ecclesiasticis officiis*, whose allegorical stories made their way into many medieval sermons.

heaven. Then the demons go flying away yelling, for they cannot do their will. Thus you shall know, good men and women, that for these three reasons corpses are brought to Holy Church to be buried. Therefore, each man and women who is wise, make yourself ready. For we all shall die and we know not how soon.

6
↶

Managing the Cure

*H*istorian John Moorman once described the English parson as a man who "divid[ed] his time between the calls of his spiritual and natural sheep."[1] He drew this apt image to underscore how the parochial benefice straddled two worlds: as an office with cure of souls its end was spiritual; but it also encompassed land and buildings, the income generated by them, the revenues owed to it by the parish's inhabitants, and the outlays of money needed for its upkeep. So however spiritual-minded the curate may have been, he was also a man inevitably bound by very practical, daily, economic responsibilities. And whatever spiritual boon his parishioners got from him, they were equally linked to him in an intricate, and often antagonistic, economic relationship.

The parish church itself was a potent symbol of this intertwined association. By custom enshrined in law, a rector and his parishioners were mutually responsible for its furnishings and its upkeep (No. 86). Inventories of church goods colorfully demonstrate just how many things a pastor and his people had to acquire to provide the basics for celebrating Christianity's rituals (No. 89). The mutual recriminations over who failed to provide what to the church, or who let what fall into ruin, suggest how strictly rector and people took their obligations toward furnishing the church and how jeal-

---

[1] J. R. H. Moorman, "The Medieval Parsonage and Its Occupants," *Bulletin of the John Rylands Library* 28, no. 1 (March, 1944): 5.

ously they guarded their rights. In fact, lay people's concern to have a voice in their parish's financial management led, by the late thirteenth century, to the development of the office of the churchwarden. Often holding his post jointly with other parishioners, he was a layman who supervised his church's routine fiscal affairs. Typically, he was responsible for the upkeep of the church's fabric, for purchasing candles, books, and sacred vessels, for distributing the coins collected in the poor box to needy parishioners, and for managing the income from the church's rents and legacies. Churchwardens' accounts of their parish's revenues and expenditures are invaluable documents for reconstructing the daily ebb and flow of the parish economy (No. 90).

In addition to their duty to furnish the church, all adult parishioners were bound by the *jus parochiale,* or parochial duty, that legally obliged each of them to make a variety of regular payments to their rector (No. 88). Tithes were the most cumbersome exaction they faced; they were as inevitable as (and probably even more onerous and annoying than) our modern income taxes. The tithe—from the Old English word for a tenth—was the rector's claim to a tenth of almost every conceivable thing a parishioner produced. He collected the greater (or garb) tithe on every kind of grain; the lesser tithes were gathered from everything else, natural or man-made, that parishioners or their animals produced. There were tithes on hay, fruit, vegetables, and herbs; a tithe of the tenth lamb, the tenth calf, the tenth kid, piglet, chick, and gosling; tithes on milk and eggs and honey and wool; tithes on the fish the parishioners caught, the birds they snared, the bees in their hives, the acorns they shook from a tree; tithes from everything they wove, or milled, or baked, or forged, or cobbled, or hammered together— tithes, in fact, on every penny they earned (No. 87). One audacious Glastonbury parson went so far as to demand, in vain, the tenth child from one of his fecund parishioners.[2] And just to make sure that nothing was forgotten, when parishioners died, their rector claimed a mortuary—usually their second-best beast—as compensation for any unpaid tithes. Most English parishes were rural, but even in town parishes, urban workers, artisans, and merchants were bound to tithe the profit of their commercial labors and whatever victuals they coaxed from their small garden plots. The curate John Mirk, who wrote a pastoral handbook for priests in English, barely mentioned tithes in it, explaining that he thought it an "idle thing" to elaborate on the subject since even a priest who was a fool knew how to ask for

---

[2] J. Z. Titow, *English Rural Society, 1200–1350* (London: George Allen and Unwin, 1969) p. 55, n. 36.

his tithes. Priests prodded parishioners who balked at tithing—and many did balk—with the threat of excommunication.

Even after all the tithes were reckoned, collected, and stored in the parsonage's tithe barn (or sometimes, to the parishioners' ire, in the church itself), the curate's hand was still open. Altarage was the term for all the other customary offerings that parishioners had to pay: a few pennies at the four major festivals of the year (Christmas, Easter, the church's dedication day, and the feast of its patron saint), a few more pennies for weddings and funerals and churchings, money for the blessed bread on Sunday, perhaps some eggs or cheese at Easter, more pennies still if you wanted the chantry priest to teach your child the ABCs. It must have seemed an endless drain on an already threadbare purse. And it was inescapable. Worse still, pastors were set in economic rivalry with their parishioners. The curate's glebe was usually at least slightly larger than his parishioners' plots, and he owed no tithes and no service to his manorial lord since the glebe was freehold. His livestock pastured side by side with that of his fellow villagers, and sometimes illegally grazed in the churchyard, always at the complaint of his parishioners. His annual revenues from tithes and other offerings, and from the produce of his own farmland, typically placed him among his village's well-to-do. His spiritual social status, derived from his sacerdotal anointing and office, was thus bolstered by real economic clout.

Keeping track of what was owed, what was paid, and what was spent—the domestic economy of the benefice (No. 91)—was the practical side of the *cura animarum* that mixed God with mammon in ways that might seem to tarnish the pastoral ideals embodied in, for instance, Chaucer's Poor Parson. The mix, of course, was unavoidable; curates had to eat. But the prospect of a benefice that turned a profit surely lured some men toward a clerical career. When curates conceived of a benefice chiefly as a source of income, non-residence was the worst result: an absent pastor could leave parishioners in the spiritual lurch. Pluralism, where a man held more than one benefice, was the major cause of non-residence. It was an abuse denounced throughout the middle ages, but papal dispensations and legal loopholes ensured that the practice never totally stopped. Some pluralists, with their hands in many parochial pots, managed to amass amazing incomes (No. 43). Likewise, the practice of exchanging churches, where incumbents swapped parishes with each other, was another abuse widespread by the fourteenth century. Though many pastors traded benefices for innocent reasons (for example, to secure a pension, to move closer to their birthplace, or to escape quarrelsome parishioners), the possibility of trading up to a more lucrative benefice clearly spurred some exchanges. Certainly lay patrons knew how to advertise vacant benefices with an eye to the market. The description of a living in the patronage of the rich and famous Norfolk Pastons was couched in the language of the savvy realtor rather than of someone looking for the best candidate to occupy a spiritual office (No. 93).

But wealthy benefices were rare and always in the hands of well-connected or noble rectors. Many smallholder peasants scrabbled a bare existence out of the ground, and in a little rural parish even a curate's claim of a tenth of all produce didn't really amount to much. One property assessment assembled in 1291 for a papal tax suggests that the income of the average English parochial benefice was around £10 a year; maybe as much as half of this was eaten up by living expenses, procurations, synodal fees, pensions, and taxes.[3] Where the rector was an ecclesiastical corporation and a vicar bore the parish's cure, the income from the greater tithe was gone; by the fifteenth century, about one-third of the 9,000 or so parishes in England had been converted into vicarages. Working under the theory that the ox that treads the grain shouldn't be muzzled, at the turn of the thirteenth-century the Fourth Lateran Council had ordered that a decent portion of a parish's income had to be assigned to its vicar—a step so significant for ensuring their livelihoods that one historian has called it "the Magna Carta of the parish priest."[4] A few years after the Lateran Council, the Provincial Council at Oxford calculated that an equitable wage for an English vicar should be at least five marks (£3 6s. 8p.) a year (No. 96). Still, many vicars and even rectors lived at or below the borderline of poverty, scraping by only with help from their superiors (No. 97).

If rectors and vicars from poor benefices were often strapped for funds, the lives of the unbeneficed clergy were more precarious still. Salaries for hired or "stipendiary" priests—the majority of the secular clergy— were notoriously low, but prelates were reluctant to acknowledge just how poorly paid these clerical workhorses were. In 1350, Archbishop Simon Islip, appalled at what he perceived as unbridled greed in men who should live simply, blasted those chaplains who seemed to be shopping their spiritual services to the highest bidder in the wake of the Black Death, which severely battered the clerical ranks and created a seller's market (No. 99). A generation later Archbishop Simon Sudbury grudgingly admitted that perhaps his assistant clergy were due a raise (No. 100). The account book of household expenses obsessively kept by a chantry priest in Dorset in the middle

[3] J. R. H. Moorman, *Church Life in England in the Thirteenth Century* (Cambridge: Cambridge University Press, 1945), pp. 136–37.

[4] R. A. R. Hartridge, *A History of Vicarages in the Middle Ages* (Cambridge: Cambridge University Press, 1930), p. 21.

of the fifteenth century suggests how comfortably—or not—an assistant priest could live on his statutorily-fixed salary of seven marks a year (No. 92). Charity alone sustained the lives of others less fortunate (No. 98).

Medieval currency is notoriously hard to translate into values that make much sense by twentieth-century standards. By contrast, inventories of the items bequeathed in the last wills of parish priests offer a more concrete sense of the comparative worth of these men (No. 94). Deathbed testaments, ironically, help bring these men vividly to life. We see them solicitous for their souls but also anxious to distribute what they owned, whether a little or a lot, to best effect for themselves, their churches, their families, and their friends. The contrast between a poor chaplain's testament (No. 95A) and that of a rector whose father was the Earl of Suffolk (No. 95G) sharply reminds us just how diversified a group of men the secular clergy were.

While the economic gulf between a rich pluralist rector and a hired chaplain could be as vast as that between a baron and a cotter, it is important to remember that during the middle ages, priesthood offered the surest path to social advancement. A man like Robert Grosseteste could spring from humble Suffolk peasant stock and, sheerly through talent in the clerical arts both intellectual and spiritual, end up as the bishop of Lincoln and the most renowned pastoralist and natural philosopher of his day. Of course, Grosseteste's meteoric ascent hardly represents the typical priest's career path; he was not even ordained until he was past fifty. Even so, the clerical life (secular or regular) was the only vocation that drew men from almost every medieval social class, from the younger sons of lords at the pinnacle of society, to members of the lower nobility and gentry, to merchants' and artisans' sons, sons of the yeomanry, and large numbers of men born and raised as peasants in England's countryside. Even villeins' sons, once they had won their manumission, could enter the clerical ranks. Only men at the lowest margins of society—beggars, vagabonds, professional criminals—were practically barred from service.

Although priests came from widely varied social backgrounds, the typical rural curate's manse, whether rectory or vicarage, was hardly different from the houses of his better-off villagers. It was a plain thatched cottage of timber-framed wattle and daub or perhaps of stone, depending on the local abundance of building material. All but the best houses had just a few rooms sparely furnished: a main parlor, a solar or loft bedroom, a detached kitchen, a privy or garderobe, perhaps a servant's room, and a cellar and pantry. Usually there were a few outbuildings as well: a barn or two for storing tithes of grain and hay, a stable, a dovecote, maybe a brewhouse or bakehouse. But there was great latitude here. Wealthy resident rectors lived much better, in parsonages that were only slightly inferior to the local manor house; poor unbeneficed chaplains lived much worse, probably lodging in a tiny room rented from some parishioner. When vicars depended on absent corporate rectors to maintain the parsonage, or when a non-resident plural- ist held the benefice, the manse might be in poor repair. But when bishops ordained a vicarage, they often took pains to stipulate that the vicar's house be well-built and suitably maintained. Usually the parsonage would be large enough for the curate and a few of his assistant clergy to live together. In towns, curates lived in parsonages built near or attached to their church. Their assistant clergy either lived with them or squeezed into rented rooms in the long, narrow, gabled townhouses of their urban parishioners.

In the typical parish, besides the curate there were also several assistant clergy: a few chaplains (one perhaps to serve an outlying chapel-of-ease), a deacon or two, a parish clerk. A curate usually also had a servant living with him to do the housework and tend his livestock, especially his horse. Some- times this was a young boy, or page; other times, despite the strict and re- peated warnings of canon law, a priest hired a village woman as a house- keeper, which was apt to set tongues wagging even when the arrangement was completely innocent. Only female relatives—a mother, a sister, an aunt—usually raised no suspicions living in the parsonage.

A curate might also share his house with his wife or concubine, though this was an exception that provoked the full weight of a bishop's judicial wrath. The eleventh-century Gregorian reforms redoubled the church's ef- forts to bind all the upper clergy (subdeacons and above) by the rule of celi- bacy; but local churches never entirely stamped out marriage or cohabita- tion among Europe's clergy. It is impossible to speak in exact numbers about the problem. Still, while the records do not imply that clerical concubinage was rampant (despite the twelfth-century prelate Gerald of Wales' exagger- ated alarm that "nearly all" of England's clergy were married), they do sug- gest that it was a continuing concern. The practice was harder to uproot in some pockets of the land—Wales and parts of Norfolk, for instance—where long-ingrained custom tolerated married clergy. Visitation records convey the impression that parishioners were willing to turn, if not a completely blind eye, at least a myopic one to their curate's private life so long as he remained discreet and so long as he left the parish women alone. They showed no tolerance for notorious fornicators and adulterers; but a priest living quietly and respectably with his companion—traditionally called his *focaria* or "hearth-mate"—raised little complaint.

Always looming over the domestic affairs of the clergy was the king. Relations between the English church and state flipped between calm and controversy throughout the middle ages; but we are not concerned here with

those grave moments of confrontation between Crown and Canterbury—
Henry II and Becket, John and Stephen Langton—that regularly erupted.
These episodes are the compelling stuff of narrative history, but oddly
enough, they seem to have had little long-lasting impact on the lives of the
parish clergy. Ordinary clergy were touched by less history-making but
more onerous events, from their perspective. Though the king and his court
were distant figures, parish priests' pockets still felt the royal pinch. When
kings needed money, which was always, the clergy were an easy mark. Taxes
soaked from the English clergy, no less than the laity, were often cloaked as
contributions needed for pious crusades or national defense (No. 101). Beyond the apparently quenchless needs of the Exchequer, there were always
questions over law. Dispensing justice was a sure way to make money in the
middle ages, and no monarch was thrilled at the church courts that sat side
by side with his own tribunals, constantly clashing with them over jurisdiction and constantly sidetracking coin that could have gone to the royal
purse. The prelates of the English church frequently lodged their complaints
to the king over royal or secular infringements of the church's privileges.
Just as frequently, kings affected concern and hedged. Finally, responding to
clerical grievances aired the year before in Parliament, Edward I issued the
writ *Circumspecte agatis* in 1286—a milestone in relations between Church
and Crown insofar as it clearly spelled out the general jurisdiction of the
church's courts (No. 102). Notice that almost all of the issues it covers pertain not to the weighty fiscal and theoretical questions that were soon to
set the earth quaking across the Channel between Philip IV of France and
Boniface VIII; instead, they involve the quotidian concerns of parish life.

☙ No. 86. Duties of rectors and parishioners for the care of the church (c. 1295–1313).

Councils and Synods, pp. 1385–86, 1387. Trans. JS.

[*This decree, which exists in several versions and draws on older pro-
nouncements on the subject, is usually attributed to Archbishop Robert
Winchelsey (1293–1313). Whatever its origin, it circulated widely and was
treated as an archbishop's authoritative and binding word. We translate here
one popular version of the text, adding the final paragraph from another version of the statute.*]

Decree of the lord Robert of Winchelsey, recently archbishop of Canterbury, concerning the provision and upkeep of church furnishings:

This was the decree of the lord Robert, recently archbishop of Canterbury, made during his provincial visitations, to be observed perpetually
among rectors and their parishioners.

In order for parishioners to be clear about their obligations regarding

church furnishings so that there will be no further misunderstandings between them and their rectors, we notify them that parishioners are obliged
to provide the following items: a chalice, a mass book, the principal set of
vestments (namely, a chasuble, an alb, an amice, a stole, a maniple, a girdle,
and two altar cloths for the main altar); also a processional cross, a funeral
cross, a censer and an incense boat, a lamp and a small bell for use when
carrying the Body of Christ to the sick, a Lenten veil, a banner for the rogation procession, two hand-bells for ringing when the dead are carried to
the church, a funeral bier, a holy water vat, a pax-board, a candle-holder for
the Paschal candle, bells for the bell tower and ropes for them, and the baptismal font with a lockable cover. Parishioners are responsible for repairing
the nave of the church: its length and breadth, its inside and outside, including its altars, images (especially the principal image in the chancel), and
windows; they are obliged as much by law as by custom to fence the churchyard. We desire that each of these items be the responsibility of parishioners
forevermore. It is incumbent on the rector or the vicar by due law and custom to look after other things pertaining to the upkeep of the interior and
exterior of the church's chancel as well as anything not expressly listed here.

[*Another version of the statute concludes with this paragraph:*]

Furthermore, parishioners should be compelled to provide the following items: a lectionary for matins, an antiphonary, a gradual, a psalter, a
book of sequences, an ordinal, a manual, a choir cope with all its appurtenances, a frontal for the main altar, three surplices, one rochet, a decent pyx
for the Body of Christ, and repair of the books and vestments whenever they
happen to need mending.

☙ No. 87. Tithes and oblations: statute of Archbishop Boniface on tithes (1249–69).

Council and Synods, pp. 792–97. Trans. JS.

[*This statute, though it seems never to have been formally enacted, was
known widely throughout England during the later middle ages. It is generally,
and probably accurately, attributed to Boniface of Savoy, Archbishop of Canterbury (1243–70).*]

Quarrels and disputes, scandals and great animosity arise between rectors of churches and their parishioners because of the many different customs for claiming tithes which various parishes have. Therefore we desire
that in every church in our archdiocese there should be one uniform way
for claiming the tithes and the revenues of churches.

[1] First, we desire that tithes of produce should be paid wholly with
no subtraction; expenses should not be deducted. The same applies to tithes

of fruit trees, of all types of seeds, and of garden herbs unless parishioners wish to make suitable compensation for such tithes. Further, we wish that tithes of hay—whether it grows in large meadows, small ones, or in open fields—should be exacted and expediently paid.

[2] From the increase of animals—namely, lambs—we wish that six halfpence should be paid in tithes for the first six lambs born or fewer. The seventh lamb or over should always be given as a tithe; but the rector of the church who takes the seventh lamb should return three halfpence in compensation to the parishioner from whom he took that tithe. If he takes the eighth lamb to be born, he should pay a penny back to his parishioner. If he takes the ninth lamb he should pay another halfpenny; if he so wishes, the rector of the church may wait another year until he takes the tenth lamb. But if he postpones taking it for a year, then in the second year he should always choose the second-best lamb, or at the least the third-best since he postponed taking another lamb during the first year. This is how the tithe of wool is to be interpreted. But if a sheep produces some young during the winter and some during summer the tithe should be divided. Similarly, if anyone buys or sells a sheep during the middle of the year and is sure of the parish it came from, the tithe of that sheep should be divided, just as if it came from two domiciles. But if he is uncertain where it came from, that church should collect the tithe within whose boundaries the sheep are found during shearing time. Regarding the tithe of dairy products, we desire that the tithe should be paid while those products last. Namely, the tithe of cheese should be paid when the cheese is in season; the tithe of milk should be collected in the autumn and winter, unless parishioners wish to make suitable compensation for those tithes and this is convenient for the church.

[3] From things produced by a mill we wish that tithes should be exacted and paid according to the value of the products, unless parishioners must pay a fine to their lord for the value of these products.

[4] We order that tithes must be faithfully paid from pastures and grazing land, both communal and private; this should be reckoned according to the number of animals and the number of days they are at pasture, if this is expedient for the church.

[5] We order that tithes must be exacted from fishponds and beehives, as well as from all other goods fairly acquired which reproduce themselves during the year, as is required.

[6] We further order that tithes must be paid from the goods of artisans and merchants, from the profits of business, from the work of carpenters, smiths, weavers, brewers, and all other wage earners; namely, they should pay tithes from their wages, unless the wage earner wishes to pay

instead some tithing penny to the fabric or the devotional lights in his church if the rector agrees.

[7] When seeking the mortuary [from a deceased's estate], we desire that the custom of the province with jurisdiction over the church should be observed; but in seeking to collect it, the rector of the church (or the vicar or the annual chaplain) should keep God in mind.[5]

[8] Since there are many people who do not wish to pay tithes, we order that parishioners should be admonished once, twice, and a third time that they should faithfully pay their tithes to God and his church. But if they do not change their minds, they should first be forbidden to enter the church and then, if it becomes necessary, they should be compelled by the threat of ecclesiastical censure to pay their tithes.

[9] Rectors of churches, or their vicars, or annual chaplains who, putting aside the fear of God on account of either the fear or favor of men, do not effectively claim their tithes according to the above rules, shall be punished with suspension until they pay a fine of one half mark of silver to the archdeacon for their disobedience.

∞ No. 88. The *jus parochiale:* customs of the diocese of Salisbury (c. 1228–56).
Councils and Synods, pp. 510–15. Trans. JS.

[*These chapters, never officially issued, survive in a single manuscript; still, they give a good impression of the general obligations, spiritual and temporal, imposed on parishioners and their ministers.*]

These are the customs followed in the bishopric of Salisbury.

[1] First, it is customary to pay tithes on all things that are replenished during the year; namely, tithes of grain and hay which are due to parsons or vicars at harvest time, and tithes of all types of fruit from gardens and yards, and from all seeds produced in fields, gardens, and yards, all of which are due to said parsons or vicars in their season. And if there is any uncultivated land which, when it is cultivated, will be sold for pasture, the said parsons or vicars should receive a tithe of the money from the sale; similarly, they should receive a tithe of the money from the sale of any meadow put to pasture which is sold.

[2] Likewise, they should receive a tithe of mare's foals, of calves, lambs, piglets, and goslings, all of which should be collected for the whole

---

[5]The fifteenth-century commentator William Lyndwood construed this to mean that the rector should consider the relative wealth of the estate and whether he would cause hardship "by seeking the best item from among the few things a parishioner has." (*Provinciale,* III.16, s.v. "habeat," p. 196.)

year during the week before Easter. They should receive one penny for a foal and a halfpenny for a calf. They are due a full tenth of all cheese and butter, of linen and of wool. And if someone has so few mother cows or sheep that he cannot make cheese, he should pay according to the custom of the parish: in some places in the diocese, one penny for the cows; in other places, a penny and a half; he should pay one penny for every four sheep. And if someone has only seven lambs, then he should give the seventh as a tithe; similarly, he should pay his seventh fleece of wool or his seventh goose if has no more than that. And if someone happens to have the sheep of his neighbor in his care, he should pay a full and complete tithe of lambs, as if these sheep were his own, even though they may belong to several other men. The same holds true for the tithe of all his fleeces. Foals, calves, goslings, piglets, and lambs should be tithed wherever they are born. And if there are wandering cows or sheep pasturing in one parish by day and sleeping at night in another parish where they are actually domiciled, and if these animals winter in the parish where they pasture, the parson of the parish where they pasture and the parson of the parish where they sleep should split the tithe of cheese, butter, and wool. And if someone's sheep dies or is killed after the feast of St. Martin [November 11], he should pay a tithe of the fleece of the dead animal just as if it were the tithe of wool. And no parishioner should presume to sell his sheep or remove them in any manner from his parish after the feast of St. Martin unless he has first paid the parson his tithe of wool. If a sheep from one parish happens to be shorn in the parish of another parson, he shall receive that sheep's tithe of wool, unless something reasonably prevents this.

[3] A parson or vicar should receive tithes from the handiwork of artisans, carpenters, cobblers, weavers (both male and female), skinners, fishermen, fowlers, and every other type of workman, from the profits of business, from honey, from windmills, water mills, and fulling-mills, from dovecotes, from cider, and from everything else from which the church customarily receives tithes.

[4] Parishioners of every parish are obliged to make due offerings four times a year (at Christmas, Easter, the day of the solemnization of the parish church, and the dedication day of its patron saint). Every married person holding any kind of land must offer a halfpenny. All other persons, man and woman alike, should also make an offering on these days unless their poverty excuses them. During Lent everyone must go to confession and offer whatever they wish, unless their poverty excuses them. Likewise, on Good Friday all parishioners should come to give veneration to the Cross and offer there whatever they wish. No one should dare to receive the Body

of Christ at Easter without first going to confession and venerating the Cross.

[5] Espoused women and women who have recently given birth should go to the church with a lit candle and, accompanied by other women, make an offering of the chrism-cloth of their newborns. The chrism-cloth must not be given away or put to any other use except for its use in church.

[6] Upon the death of any landholder, the parson or vicar shall receive from the deceased's property the second-best draft animal (the deceased's lord receiving the best animal). And if it should happen that there are not enough animals for this, the deceased's executors are obliged to make satisfaction to the parson or vicar from the goods of the deceased's estate, as his resources allow, before implementing any other terms of the deceased's testament. The same applies in carrying out the terms of the testament of a married woman and of all other parishioners, man or woman. The parish chaplain should be appointed chief executor so that he can diligently provide and arrange that a portion of the goods which concern the deceased is distributed according to form.[6]

[7] Unless the parish chaplain has agreed otherwise, trentals and other anniversary masses should not be celebrated in any other church except the one to which the deceased parishioner for whom the masses are being said belonged.

[8] The parson is obliged to see that the chancel of his church is in good condition and has a good roof. Both the altar tabernacle and the chrismatory should have locks. The corporals should be made of fine linen cloth. He should also provide suitable cruets for the wine and water, a censer, candlesticks, and a lamp and a bell to be carried before the priest to light his way on his visits to the sick. The parson or vicar is obliged to provide two processional candles. Parishioners are obliged to see that the nave of the church is kept in good condition and has a good roof, and that the bell tower has a good roof and is secure against all danger. They should also provide the bells and the bell cords, a crucifix, crosses and images, a silver chalice, a missal, a silk chasuble, suitable books, and all other types of vestments belonging to the altar. They should provide the processional banners, the Lenten veil, the baptismal font (which must be suitable and have a lock), and the small bells rung ahead of the funeral procession on its way to a burial. The chaplain of the church should see to it that the altar cloth and all

---

[6]This suggests the one-third portion of an estate that, according to English custom, was to be spent doing pious works on behalf of the deceased's soul. Another third went to one's spouse, the final third to one's children.

the other linen that belongs to the altar are clean and suitable. If it happens—God forbid!—that the chalice or the books or the vestments are stolen or otherwise lost, the parson or the vicar or the chaplain or whoever is responsible for this negligence shall pay for their replacement. The parishioners shall also see to it that their church graveyard is well-fenced and free from nettles and other harmful weeds. Parishioners are obliged to provide the Paschal candle and the other candles used in the chancel, as well as sufficient lights for use during the whole year at matins, evensong, and mass. They are also bound to provide the blessed bread and candles every Sunday of the year in every church in the Christian world.

[9] The parson and vicar should also see to it that they live in an adequate and decent house and have an honest servant who causes not a hint of suspicion. They should offer hospitality and charity insofar as their resources allow; and they should maintain residence, never being away from their domicile for more than a day without the permission of the bishop or the archdeacon.

[10] People shall not dare to go to confession or communion anywhere other than in their own parish without license of their curate.

[11] Parsons and vicars of churches must pay synodal fees, namely, fifteen pence. Every chaplain customarily gives the archdeacon twelve pence at Christmas. The archdeacon, if he so wishes, shall visit every mother church once a year, and the parson or vicar shall treat him decently and entertain him.

[12] The summoner should not cite anyone in any parish unless he has a chaplain or clerk as a colleague who will offer truthful testimony as to the justice of the citation.

[13] Parsons or vicars should appoint a poor clerk pursuing his studies to the benefice of the holy water clerk.[7] And he is obliged to come to the church on every service day to perform his duties, which is why he is given said benefice.

[14] Weddings should not be held in any church until the marriage banns have been officially announced three times. Nor should there be any excommunication pronounced in the church until three warnings have been given.

[15] Note that the general excommunication ought to be pronounced three times during the year in every church.

[16] Parsons, vicars, and parochial chaplains should give canonical obedience to the lord bishop and his archdeacon.

---

[7]The *aquabajulus.* See No. 22.

[17] There should be two learned and discreet inquisitors and two chaplain confessors to whom priests, vicars, and chaplains should make their confessions during Lent or at another time if it is necessary. They should be men who know how to discern between a leper and a leper, etc. [Lev. 13].

[18] We order that there should be no other holidays from farming and work—without which the earth cannot be cultivated—except the following, which we mark out of reverence for the saints and which priests should announce to their parishioners for celebration: the Nativity of the Lord [December 25] and the four days after it, the feasts of the Circumcision [January 1], the Epiphany [January 6], the Resurrection, the Ascension, and Pentecost,[8] every Sunday, the feasts of the Glorious Virgin,[9] of the Apostles,[10] and of the Evangelists,[11] the feasts of the Holy Cross [Good Friday, September 14, May 3], of St. Michael [September 29], of St. John the Baptist [June 24, August 29], of St. Lawrence [August 10], the translation of St. Thomas [of Canterbury, July 7], the feasts of St. Martin [November 11, July 4], St. Nicholas [December 6], St. Mary Magdalene [July 22], and St. Catherine [November 25], the feast of the dedication day of their parish church, and also the feast of the particular saint in whose honor each church was constructed.

∾ No. 89. A parish church's contents (c. 1368).

Archdeaconry of Norwich Inventory of Church Goods, temp. Edward III, ed. Dom Aelred Watkin, Norfolk Record Society 19, pt. 1 (1947), pp. 76–77. Trans. JS.

[*This inventory was first made at a parish visitation in 1368 and then supplemented in later years.*]

Parish of SALLE [Church of Saints Peter and Paul]
Its valuation: 40 marks.[12] Payment for the Synod of St. Michael: 10 d.; for the Easter Synod:[13] 10 d. Procuration[14] fee 7 ½ d.
Ornaments: One ordinal. Three antiphonaries. Lesson-book for the season

[8] Respectively, Easter, the seventh Sunday after Easter, and the Thursday following the fifth Sunday after Easter.
[9] e.g., the Nativity [September 8], the Immaculate Conception [December 8], Annunciation [March 25], Assumption [August 15], Visitation [July 2], etc.
[10] e.g., Peter [August 1 and, with Paul, June 29], Paul [January 25, June 30], Andrew [November 30], Barnabas [June 11], Bartholomew [August 24], James [July 25], John [December 27], Mathias [February 24], Matthew [September 21], Philip and James [May 1], Simon and Jude [October 28], Thomas [December 21, July 3].
[11] Matthew [September 21], Mark [April 25], Luke [October 18], John [December 27].
[12] Total annual income of the benefice from all sources.
[13] These synodal fees were customary payments made to the archdeacon by those who were called to attend his synods (councils).
[14] See the glossary for this and for descriptions of the various books and vestments mentioned in the inventory.

and saints festivals in two volumes. Four psalters. One martyrology together with the penitential canons and the legatine statutes.[15] Two manuals. One processional. Three missals. Three graduals with books of sequences. Lesson-book for the season and the saints in one volume. Four suits of vestments with a tunic and a choir cope. Seven altar-cloths. Three towels. Six corporals. Two altar frontals and one for the gospel lectern. Two silver chalices with spoons[16] and one pewter chalice. Four cruets. Lamps in the chancel. A lantern. A censer. Six surplices. Two rochets. A Lenten veil. Two funeral palls. A portable cross. Two portable altars. A pyx for the eucharist, a chrismatory, and a locked baptismal font. Two handbells. Three ceremonial banners. Two pewter candlesticks. A ladder for the rood-loft. Also one missal and one suit of vestments. Also two suits of vestments. Also one missal and one large breviary. Also one complete suit of vestments of silk decorated with gilded beasts sewn with green velvet edging with gilded stars and crescents—a gift from Sampson Bussell [d. 1361]. Also one chalice given by the same person.

Also one suit of vestments of red-colored gold with two albs, tunics, dalmatics, stoles, maniples, and choir copes, and one altar-frontal matching the vestments, donated by the parishioners.

Also two red-colored striped copes donated by the parishioners. Three vestments given by Sir John Luttyng [d. 1400], chaplain, to be used at the common altars in the church. One new gradual given by William Belys.

Also one good breviary. One large missal. One suit of vestments in cloth-of-gold, viz. one chasuble, alb, maniple, stole, amice donated by Sir John Holweye, the recent rector [1375–1401].

Also three processional books donated by Agatha Melman. Also one cross of gilded copper and two bronze candlesticks donated by the said Agatha.

Also one gilded silver censer donated by Agatha Melman. Also two silver cruets donated by Ralph Hewode. Also one book called *Pars Oculi*.[17] Also one embroidered bench-cover with two cushions, which set was donated by Ralph Boleyne and others. Also two copes of red silk with blood-red cloth-of-gold edging.

Also one book called *Orgeneboc*[18] donated by John Holweye, chaplain.

[15]Penitential canons were lists of prescribed penances for sins; see above, No. 79. The legatine statutes were canons issued at general church councils for all of England by the papal legates Cardinal Otto in 1237 and Cardinal Ottobuono in 1268.

[16]The spoons were used to add a few drops of water to the altar wine before its consecration.

[17]See No. 72.

[18]Presumably not a book of organ music but a book of *organum* or prick-song—music for several voices that was written down, or "pricked," as opposed to improvised.

No. 90. Churchwardens' accounts: St. Mary at Hill parish church, London (1493–94).

The Medieval Records of a London City Church (St. Mary at Hill), A.D. 1420–1559, ed. Henry Littlehales, *EETS* o.s. 128 (London: Kegan Paul, 1905), pp. 195–99. Modernized by JS.

This is the account of us, Robert Howtyng and William Overay, wardens of the goods and rents belonging to the church of Saint Mary at Hill in London, from Michaelmas [September 29] of the year 1493 to Michaelmas of the year 1494.

First, we charge us with the old debts that we have received within this year of our account:
First, received of Thomas Mowse, capper: 12s.
Also, of John Mowse, clerk: 20s.
Also, received of Master Remyngton, alderman, for timber that was in the great churchyard: 16s.
Also, received of John Smyth, haberdasher: 10s.

Sum total: 58s.

Also, we charge us as well with the church's rental properties and the rents belonging to the chantries [in the church]:
The church rents: £15 15s. 6d.
Also, [John] Nasyng's chantry: £9 8d.
Also, Rose Wrytell's chantry: £6 13s. 4d.
Also, Richard [Goslyn]'s chantry: £8 12s. 8d.
Also, John Causton's chantry: £18 4s. 4d.
Also, John Bedham's chantry: £13 6s. 8d.
Also, Master William Cambridge's chantry: £10.

Sum total: £81 13s. 2d.

Also, we charge us with the [parish] clerk's wages and with certain money received for the beam-light[19] (received during 4 quarters of the year) within the said year: Sum total: £6 7s. 10d.

Sum total [debts, rents, and wages]: £90 19s.

Also, we charge us with the money that we received [from parishioners] at Easter for [their] paschal [communion]. Sum total: 10s. 5d.
Also, we charge us with certain incidental receipts received within this said year of our account:

---

[19]The candles burning before the church's main cross on the rood screen.

First, received for burying a man from Dartmouth who died in William
   Olyvere's house: 3s. 4d.

Also, from [John] Mascall for burying a Breton: 3s. 4d.

Also, received from [the assistant priest] Master John Redy at various times:
   10d.

Also, received from Master Smarte for the 2 tapers burned at his wife's anniversary mass: 4d.

Also, for burying a stranger who died at Dann's: 12d.

Also, for burying William Graye: 13s. 4d.

Also, for burying John Condall's wife: 13s. 4d.

Also, for burying Thomas Andrew's wife: 2s.

Also, received from Master Smarte in money he found in the church: 4d.

Also, received from [the clerk] Robert Debenham in money that he found
   in the church, along with a penny that Robert Howtyng found: 5d.

Also, received for burying Harry Kellowe: 13s. 4d.

Also, received for [ringing] his knell: 3s. 4d.

Sum total: £3 5s. 4d.
Sum total of all the charges this year is: £94 4s. 4d.

The discharge [i.e., expenses].

Here follows the payments that belong to the church as well as to the chantries:

First, paid to the abbot of Waltham for a quitrent[20] going out of the tenement of John Weston for a whole year at Michaelmas last passed: 38s.

Also, paid to Robert Fyherbard and Godfrey Oxinbryge, wardens of the
   parish of St. George's in Botolph [Lane], in London, for a quitrent going
   out of the tenement of John Weston for a whole year at Michaelmas: 20s.

Also, paid to the prior of Christchurch, in London, for a quitrent going out
   of the tenement of John Weston for 2 years at July 8, last passed: 16s.

Anniversary masses kept at the cost of the church.

Weston. Also, paid for keeping the anniversary mass of John Weston on
   April 19 to priests and clerks: 3s. 8d.

Also, paid for the anniversary mass of Master John Badmere, kept November 23: 3s. 6d.

The first year, also, paid to the fellowship of Holmes College, founded in St.
   Paul's [cathedral], for the anniversary mass of Sir John Mortram, which

---

[20] A payment made in lieu of some required service.

must be kept at the expense of the church for the term of 20 years, each
year to pay to the said fellowship of Holmes College: 6s. 8d.

Sum total: £4 7s. 10d.

The costs of the clerks' wages and the morrow mass.

Also, paid to Robert Debenham, clerk, for the whole year's wages past at
Michaelmas: £4 13s. 4d.

Also, paid to Sir John Plummer for celebrating the morrow mass for a whole
year at Michaelmas: 20s.

Also, paid to Sir John Plummer in partial payment for £7, which he lent for
the repair of the new house in the priests' alley: 20s.

Sum total: £6 13s. 4d.

Expenses for the choir and other necessities done in the church.

First, for [Christmas] holly: 3d.

Also, to a child who sang the treble part to help the choir during the Christmas holidays: 12d.

Also, for nails: ½d.

Also, for wine on Christmas Day: 4d.

Also, spent while agreeing on the clerk's wages at the water-bailiffs': 2d.

Also, wine for Candlemas Day [February 2]: 5d.

Also, for palms, box, and flowers on Palm Sunday: 8d.

Also, for bread and wine on the same day: 8d.

Also, paid for scouring the latten candlesticks: 2s.

Also, for a quarter of coal: 4½d.

Also, for nails and hooks: 1½d.

Also, paid to [William] Paris for a ceiling piece for St. Stephen's altar: 4d.

Also, paid to Paris and Reignolde Bull[21] for keeping watch at the [Easter]
sepulcher:[22] 6d.

Also, for bread and wine on Holy Thursday: 4½d.

Also, for garlands on Corpus Christi Day: 3d.

Also, on the same day for bread and wine for the priests and the clerks: 6d.

Sum total: 8s. 1d.[23]

Sum total [of clerk's wages, morrow mass, and church expenses]: £7 17d.

[21] Both William Paris and Reignolde Bull were almsmen—two of the three poor men provided
a weekly wage of 4d. from a legacy made in 1472. They did odd jobs around the church.

[22] A temporary tabernacle, symbolic of Jesus' tomb, in which the pyx with the host was kept
away from the main altar from Good Friday until Easter.

[23] Correctly, 6s. 2d. This error affects the next sum total.

Also, paid for carrying 4 torches on the same day: 8d.

Also, for rose garlands on St. Barnabas' Day [June 11]: 2s. 1d.

Also, for bread, wine, and ale the same day: 20d.

Also, paid to [choirboys] Bowyer and Pye as a payment: 3s. 4d.

Also, paid to another singer who came with them as a payment: 8d.

Also, paid for birch [boughs] at Midsummer's Day [June 24]: 4d.

Also, paid for 2 loads of rushes for [spreading under] the new pews: 3d.

Also, paid for the underpinnings of Mistress Atclyffe's pew: 6d.

Also, to Paris and William Ellmys for cleaning the same pew: 4d.

Also, to Paris and another man for cleaning the churchyard and setting up the frame[24] over the porch on the eve of Palm Sunday: 6d.

Also, paid to William Paris for 2 hinges for the table as you go into the rood loft: 4d.

Also, paid for a mat for the shriving pew: 3d.

Also, paid to Richard Welles, mason, for underpinning the new pews, enclosing the [baptismal] font, and for making the altar and the wall over Master [Robert] Revell's tomb, for 10 days for him and his laborer: 10s. 10d.

Also, paid to William Horne and his man for 6 days' labor in making the steps, leveling the ground, and paving the same ground in St. Stephen's chapel:[25] 6s. 6d.

Also, paid to the suffragan [bishop] of London for blessing St. Stephen's altar: 10s. 4d.

Also, for a thousand bricks for St. Stephen's altar and for the wall over Master Revell's tomb: 5s.

Also, paid to the king's almoner for the offense of ringing the [church] bells against the king: 4s. 10d.

Also, for making the crosses on the reredoses: 4d.

Also, paid for nails: 4d.

Also, paid for 80 paving-tiles: 18d.

Also, spent for cutting out the vestments that Master Marowe made: 8d.

Also, paid to the women who made the orphreys when Master Remyngton was there with certain [people] of the parish with him: 8d.

Also, paid to Mascall for 28 paving-tiles: 8d.

Also, paid for 3 dozen candles: 3s.

Also, paid to [John] Russell for nails: 5d.

[24]From this small stage, several men of the parish, costumed in wigs and false beards, performed a brief drama of biblical prophets predicting the coming of the Messiah.

[25]The testament of parishioner William Cambridge, a local grocer, bequeathed the yearly income from most of his rental property to construct this chapel to be the site of his chantry.

Also, paid to sir parson for blessing the vestments: 12d.

Also, paid to Robert the clerk for mending the vestments and copes at various times within this year: 6s. 4d.

Also, paid to Hugh Materson, smith, for certain things done in the church and the church's rental properties as appears in his bills: 16s. 9d.

Also, paid to Constantine the carpenter for making all the new pews and for enclosing the font: £6 13s. 7d.

Also, paid for nails: 13d.

Also, paid to Master Smarte for a fother[26] and a half of lead that the church owed him: £5 19s.

Also, paid to Master Remyngton for a piece of line for the sanctus bell, price: 12d.

Also, paid to Thomas Mondes for nails: 19d.

Also, paid to the raker for carrying away the rubbish: 12d.

Sum total [of other church expenses]: £14 6s. 10d.[27]

Expenses for wax [paid] to the wax-chandler.

Also, paid to Roger Middilton for making 150 lbs. of wax [into candles], and for making the Paschal candle, and decorating the 4 tapers at Corpus Christi-tide, and for burning 2 tapers at an anniversary mass: 10s. 8d.

Also, paid to Walter Develyn for a quarter of wax on March 22, price per pound, 6d. Sum total: 14s.

Also, paid to John Derham on March 29 for a quarter of wax, price: 16s.

Sum total [of the 2 quarters of wax]: 30s.

Sum total [of all the wax]: 40s. 8d.

Sum total [of church expenses and the wax]: £16 7s. 5d.

[*The account continues with itemized expenses for the repairs to the various rental properties of the church and its chantries, omitted here.*]

☙ No. 91. A parish budget: the accounts of the parish clergy of Hornsea (1483–84).

EHD IV, No. 449, pp. 749–54.

Receipts of the vicar of Hornsea from the feast of St. Mark, 1483, as appears below.

Lambs. In the first place, for tithes of lambs received by the hands of Dom John Wylson, chaplain, as appears by bills made by diverse persons	16s.	
Wool. Also received from the price of six stones, price per stone 3s.	19s.	4d.

[26] A unit of measurement. As applied to lead, now equaling 19½ cwt.

[27] Correctly, £16 17s. 4d. This error affects the final sum total.

Also received from Dom John Wilson, parochial chaplain for various offerings and other perquisites this year		13s.	4d.
Also received from the same John for tithes of piglets this year		7s.	6 ½d.
Also received from the same John for tithes of chickens, hens (2s. 10d.) and geese (3s. 1d.) this year		5s.	11d.
Also received from the same for flax and hemp this year		8s.	4d.
Also from the same for farm of land and holding there this year		31s.	6d.
Also from the same for tithes of eggs this year			16d.
Also from the farm of the chapel of Riston this year	£10		
Sum total	£15	3s.	3 ½d.

Payments made and discharged this aforesaid year as appears below.

First, paid for bread and wine bought for celebrating masses this year			9 ½d.
Also paid for oil and chrism this year			5d.
Also paid in expenses twice in general chapter		2s.	1 ½d.
Also paid for repair done this year as appears by bills		4s.	6 ½d.
Also paid to the parochial chaplain for his salary this year	£5		
Also paid to Master John Proketour, the vicar, on various occasions	£8		
Total	£13	7s.	10 ½d.
So there remains		35s.	5d.
From this was paid for two synods		4s.	
And thus remains net this year		31s.	5d.

The first receipt of the parochial vicar of Hornsea from the feast of St. Mark the Apostle and Evangelist to the same feast next following, 1483–84, as above.

First, from the pardoner of the blessed Mary of Bethlehem[28]	4d.
Also [Another 4d. from the same pardoner later, 4d. from the pardoner of St. John the Baptist, Leicester, 4d. from the pardoner of St. Thomas de Urba, Rome, 3d. from St. Thomas of Akers and 4d. from the pardoner of St. Anthony]	
Also from the purification of the wife of John Major	1 ½d.
[Also 3s. from twenty-four other cases of purification]	
Also on the day of the wedding of John Ladeson	4d.
[Also 2s. 8d. from eight other weddings]	
Also on the day of the burial of the wife of Thomas Horsman	6d.
[3s. 4d. from eight other burials—six were wives and two men]	
Also from the wife of Robert Heweston [reason unspecified]	6d.
Also from Robert Perkyn for half a goose	2d.
Also from Richard Byrke for 4 chickens and hens	4d.

---

[28]These pardoners seem to have paid a licensing fee to sell their indulgences in the church or its precincts. See glossary.

Tithes of lambs of Hornsea, A.D. 1483

    First, from Robert Calyngerth for three lambs, price   2s.

    [21 ½ lambs from fifteen people, making 24 ½ in all, at 8d. a
        lamb which should have made 16s. 4d. in all, but in fact
        the total was]   16s.   8 ½d.

Tithes of wool of Hornsea in this year

    Also from Peter Loyne   9 hides

    [28 hides from seventeen people]

    Sum of 6 stones of wool, price the stone 3s.

                        Sum total   19s.   4d.

Memorandum of piglets in this year

    First, from Joan Watson, 1 piglet, price   4d.

    [23 piglets from twenty-three persons, but tithes varying, 4d.
        3 ½d. or 3d.]

                        Total   7s.   5 ½d.

Memorandum of chickens and hens with other revenues this year

    First, 3 ½ dozen chickens and hens, price 10d. a dozen   2s.   10d.

    Tithes of geese of Hornsea this year—14 geese, price the
        goose 2 ½d.   3s.   1d.

From hemp and other crops this year

    First from Newbegin   2s.

    Also from Southgate   5s.

    Also from Hornseaborton   8d.

    Also from Northorpe and Southorpe   8d.

                        Total   8s.   4d.

From apples tithed this year

    Memorandum of apples and pears by estimation   14d.

    Memorandum of the farm of land and holding for the whole
        year   31s.   4d.

                        Total   45s.   11d.

        Sum total of the church of Hornsea this year £5   3s.   2d.

Receipts of the chapel of Riston in the aforesaid year as appears £14   7d.
    by the bills of Walter Ryppon parochial chaplain of the same
    chapel from all the fruits, receipts, and revenues this year

Sum total of the church of Hornsea and chapel of Ryston this year £19 3s.   9d.

Expenses made through the whole year as above.

Also for the general chapter at Hornsea with other expenses   12 ½d.

Also for bread and wine bought for the whole year   9 ½d.

Also for hay bought for the thatch   2s.

Also for drawing of the same   3d.

Also for thatching of the same   12 ½d.

Also for a general chapter at Michaelmas at Hornsea   13d.

Also for the repair of a louver[29]   4d.
Also for walls plastered   6d.
Also for nails bought   2d.
Also for the repair of the window in the hall   3d.
Also paid to Henry Wyndyll for oil and chrism for the sick   5d.
Also paid to Master John Sherparowe   £3   6s.   8d.
Also for repairs at Ryston this year   47s.   10d.
Also for the visitation of the archdeacon   10s.
Also for the synod   4s.
Also for riding to York twice   5s.
Also for the general chapter at Easter   12d.
Also for bread and wine at Ryston   15d.
Also to the parochial chaplain of Hornsea   £5
Also to the parochial chaplain of Ryston   7 marks
Also to the synod of Ryston   12d.
Also for oil and chrism   4d.
Also for the archdeacon's breakfast   5s.

                                    Total £16   18s.   3 ½d.

Receipts of the church or chapel of Reston from the feast of St. Mark the
Evangelist, A.D. 1483 by the hand of Dom Robert Wod, parochial chaplain
of the discreet man Master John Proctour incumbent of the said chapel.
Oblations with other tithes, as shown.

First, for various oblations made in the choir of the said chapel
    this year   23s.   11d.
And for Lenten tithes this year from various persons received by
    the hands of Thomas Wright   31s.   8d.
And for various lesser tithes received by the said Thomas this year   7s.   8 ½d.
And for tithes of flax and hemp this year   4s.
And for tithes of hay this year   24s   4d.
And from William Robynson for the farm of lands   2s.
And from Henry Sutyll for the farm of one bovate of land per annum 14s.
And from the same Henry for the farm of one garden   4s.
And from Thomas Harup and Thomas Story for the tithes of
    grain of Wodhous handed over this year   20s.
And from Richard Rouston for the farm of one strip   6d.
And from the mortuary of Thomas Tidman   8s.
And from the mortuary of Thomas Holpe   13s.   4d.
And from Thomas Wryght for the tithes of lambs on various occasions 13s. 3 ½d.
And for tithes of wool this year   16s.   8d.

                            Total £9   3s.   5d.

[29] An opening in the roof for the hearth smoke to escape. It had a hood to stop the rain falling
into the room.

Sale of grain

And from William Byrsay, baker of Beverley, for the price of 10 quarters and a half of corn		42s.	
And from John Cramer for 5 bushels, price		2s.	4d.
And from Thomas Hall and his partner for a quarter of corn mixed with other grains, price		2s.	10d.
	Total	47s.	2d.

Barley and drage[30]

And from Robert Clark for 10 quarters, price		23s.	4d.
And from Olfrid Standeld for seven quarters, price		16s.	
And from Geoffrey Storry for a quarter, price		2s.	4d.
And from William Chaplane for half a quarter, price			14d.
And from John Cramer for a quarter and two bushels, price		2s.	11d.
And from William Swyre for a quarter, price		2s.	
And from Thomas Serll for a quarter and a half and one bushel of drage, price		3s.	9d.
And from Thomas Stirtway for half a quarter, price			13d.
And from Thomas Smyth for 2 bushels			6d.
And John Stevenson for half a quarter, price			12d.
And William Birthan for 3 bushels, price			10d.
	Total	54s.	11d.

Rye

And from Thomas Wryght for 6 bushels, price		2s.	6d.
And from John Hall for 1 bushel, price			5d.
And from William Swyre for 3 bushels, price			14d.
And from Thomas Smyth for 1 bushel, price			5d.
And from John Stevenson for one bushel, price			5d.
	Total	4s.	11d.

Peas

And for the price of 6 bushels sold by Thomas Wryght			20d.
And from the same Thomas for the price of 10 quarters, price		20s.	
	Total	21s.	8d.

Straw

And from William Sawyer for 14 thraves[31] of straw, price		7d.
And from Ralph Wryght for 20 thraves		10d.
And from the same Ralph for [18] thraves, price		9d.
And from Thomas Smyth for 12 thraves		6d.
And from John Kale for 14 thraves, price		7d.
And from William Wencelagh, for 10 thraves		5d.
And from John Stevenson for 6 thraves, price		3d.

[30] Drage was a mixture of barley and oats.
[31] Twenty-four sheaves make one thrave.

And from William Burthan for 8 thraves, price			4d.
And from Thomas Stirtwan for 42 thraves, price			21d.
Total		6s.	10d.
Sum Total	£15	18s.	11d.

From which was paid to the parish chaplain	£5		
Also paid to the sacristan of the collegiate church of St. John of Beverly	£3	6s.	8d.
Also paid for the Easter and Michaelmas synods			12d.
Also for oil and chrism			4d.
Also for two general chapters		[2s.]	

Total paid	£8	10s.	
And thus remains net	£7	8s.	11d.

☙ No. 92. Daily expenses of a small clerical household: the account book of Munden's chantry, Bridport (1456–57).

EHD IV, No. 445, pp. 736–40. With additions from *A Small Household of the XVth Century*, ed. K. L. Wood-Legh (Manchester: Manchester University Press, 1956), trans. JS.

[*John Munden founded the chantry in 1361. This ledger was compiled by William Savernak, one of its chaplains. Around sixty-seven years old when he was appointed to the chantry in 1452, he died in 1460. Annual expenses in 1456–57 for the household and the chantry totalled £25 4s. 6d. At the time of the dissolution of English chantries (1545–47), the annual income of Munden's chantry was £12 9s. 6d. Section totals in the original manuscript are not always accurate, but these errors are neither noted nor corrected here. Italicized and bracketed entries are newly added to the translation.*]

A.D. 1456. *Fourth year [beginning at Michaelmas]*
First week. Bread 12d. Ale 13d. Meat 10d. Fish 1d. Almonds 3d. At the table, 2 workmen for 3 days, 2 carpenters for 4 days.

Total, 3s. 3d.

Second week. Bread 8d. Ale 10 ½d. Meat 13d. A little pig 5d. Fish 7 ½d. At the table, 2 workmen for 1 day. Also at one meal John Bedescom, William Olever, Richard Marchel, Thomas Clerk, Peter Eno.

Total, 3s. 7d.

Third week. First, for bread 9d. Also ale 12d. Also meat 10d. Also fish 6d. At the table, 2 carpenters for 5 days.

Total, 3s. 1d.

Fourth week. Bread 6d. Ale [*10*]d. Meat 10d. Fish 6d. Oaten flour 3d. Also in candles 1d. At the table, 3 workmen for 2 days.

Total, 2s. 11d.

Fifth week. Bread 6d. Ale 8d. Meat 8d. Fish 4d. Coarse salt 2d. At the table, 1 workman for a day.

Total, 2s. 4d.

Sixth week. Bread 6d. Ale 8d. Meat 8d. 6 chickens 7d. Fish 5d. Mutton ½d. Candles 1d. For the diet of 1 workman for a day.

Total, 2s. 11d.

Seventh week. Bread 6d. Ale 8d. Meat 7d. [*Fish 3d.*] Oaten flour 3d.

Total, 2s. 3d.

Eighth week. Bread 7d. Ale 9d. Meat 10d. Fish 5d. Coarse salt 2d. Candles 1d. 8 chickens 6d. At one meal 3 priests, 1 workman for 2 days, 1 thatcher for 1 day.

Total, 3s. 2d.

Ninth week. Bread 6d. Ale 8d. Meat 8d. Fish 6d. At table, John for 1 day.

Total, 2s. 4d.

Tenth week. Bread 6d. Ale 8d. Meat 6d. Fish 3d. Almonds 1 ½d. Candles [1d].

Total, 2s. [*1*] ½d.

[*Eleventh week. Bread 5d. Ale 7d. Meat 7 ½d. Fish 3d. Oaten flour 3d. Candles 1d.*

Total, 2s. 2 ½d.]

Twelfth week. Bread 6d. Ale 8d. Meat 6d. Fish 4d. Candles 1d.

Total, 2s. 1d.

Sum total of the first quarter, 32s. 3d.

[*Detail for the weeks of other quarters is omitted here.*]

[*Sum total of the*] second quarter, 36s. 5d.

[*Sum total of the*] third quarter, 39s. 3 ½d.

[*Sum total of the*] fourth quarter, 40s. 2 ½d.

Sum total of diets for the whole year, £7 8s. 2d.

Expenses of the house of the fourth year with gifts and wages

Paid to John Clek for cleaning out of dove-cots for a day, 2d. Paid to John David for pruning of vines, 2d. Paid for one hook called a "hach houke," 3d. Paid to Henry Carpenter for the cutting of three feet called "shorveet," for a day, 3d. Also paid for four quarters of lime, 2s. Also, paid to John Cleek for making a [path to] the chapel, 2d. Paid to Henry Carpenter for renewing one screen partition in the kitchen and for putting one foundation timber in the chapel, for 4 ½ days, 14d.

Total, 2s. 8d.

Cost of upkeep and cleaning of the dove-cot

Paid to William Bocher for 1 quarter of peas, price 2s. 6d. Also to John Clek for cleaning out the dove-cot for a day, 2d.

Total, 2s. 8d.

Purchase of fuel

Paid for 1 quarter of coal, 3d. Paid for 2 dozen bundles of ash wood, 3s. 6d. Paid for 12 bundles of wood, 18d. Also for 12 quarters of coal, 3s.

Total, 8s. 3d.

Cost of the barn of Edward Tracy

Paid to Henry Carpenter for making of one gable for 2 days, 6d. Also paid to John Clek for wattling per day, 2d.

[*Total, 8d.*]

Wages for sawyers

Paid to Richard [Henry] Carpenter for sawing of 300 "peperel bords," price of 100, 16d. Also paid to the said Henry for squaring the "peperel," 4d. Also paid to 2 sawyers for one day, 6d.

Total, 4s 10d. With purchase of wood 2d.

Waldych

Paid to Henry Carpenter for the repair of the door of the penfold, for half a day, 2d.

[*Total, 2d.*]

The cost of the tenement of John Keet

Paid to Henry Carpenter and his assistant for a day and a half, 8d. Also for board nails, 2d. Also to John Clek for wattling for a day, 2d. Also paid to 2 workmen for making one part of a wall called a mud wall, for a day, 4d.

Also for a cart-load of stones for making one oven, price with the carriage, 8d. [*Also paid to John Clek for wattling for half a day, 1d.*] Also paid to Edward Tracy for 7 bundles of straw with carriage, 2s. 11d. Also to the thatcher with his assistant for 5 days, 2s. 1d. Also for one bundle of straw with carriage, 5d. Also for pitch, 1d. Also for spars [hazel pins to keep thatch in place], 4d.

Total, 7s. 11d.

Cost of one cottage of Bradpole

Also paid to Henry Carpenter and his assistant for 1 day, 5 ½d. Also paid for hinge-bands with hooks for a door, 5d. Also for 3 pairs of hinge-bands for windows, 3d. Also for 150 nails called board nails, 10 ½d. Also for 50 door nails, 2d. Also paid for 2 keys, 4d. Also paid to Henry Carpenter for 6 days, 18d. Also to his assistant for 6 days, 15d. Also for 2 staples, 1d. Also for 1 pair of door hinges, 3d. Also paid to the tenant of the said cottage for wattling a wall with twigs and daubing it, 3s. Also paid to Hugh for the table of the said carpenter for 14 days, 21d.

Total, 10s. 4 ½d.

Chapel

Paid for bread, 1 ½d. Also for one pound of wax and one pound of wick with the making, 10d. [Several other entries for bread and wax, and also rushes.] Also for a cord for ringing the bells, [4d.] Also paid to Henry Carpenter for the repair of a screen partition, for a day and a half, 5d. . . . Also paid to Richard Birrwe for wine, 2s.

Total, 8s. 8d.

Hall

Paid for rushes, 1d. [Plus five other items for rushes.]

Total, 5 ½d.

Kitchen

Paid for the repair of one pitcher, 1d. For the repair of one spit, 2d. Also paid to John Forcy for a cord for drawing water, 2d. Also paid to Henry Carpenter for the repair of a screen partition for 3 days, 9d. Also paid to Cleek for wattling and daubing and sparmaking for 2 days and a half, 5d.

Total, 19d.

Pantry

Paid for a cupboard, price 16d.

Total, 16d.

Issues of rents

Paid to the bailiff of Bradpole for Christmas term, 7 ½d. Also paid to the said bailiff for the terms of the Annunciation and St. John the Baptist, 15d. Also paid to the collector of John Roger for annual rent, 3s. 1d. Also paid to Matille Wodewale for the annual rent, 6s. 8d. Also paid to the bailiff of Bradpole for St. Michael [i.e. at Michaelmas], 7 ½d. Also paid to the bailiffs of Bridport for the annual rent of Munden, 9d. Also paid to the bailiffs for the tenements of William Burgeches and for the tenement of Henry Barber, 6d.

Total, 13s. 6d.

Fee

Paid to Bedescomb, 6s. 8d.

Total, 6s. 8d.

Gifts with wages

Paid to John Bedescom for the court held at Bridport, 3s. 4d. [This entry is cancelled.] Also to two serjeants of Bridport, 2d. Also for wine given to the bailiffs on Monday after the feast of Michaelmas, 10d.

Total, 4s. 4d.

Stipends with gifts and wages

Paid to William Wontchacer for service of 2 weeks, 10d. Also to John Stalbridge for the service of 9 weeks, 3s. Also to John Lyly for the service of one week, 6d. Also paid to John Lyly for the term of the Annunciation, 6s. 8d. Also paid to John for the term of St. John the Baptist, 6s. 8d. Also paid to the washerwoman for the whole year, 16d. Also paid to the parish clerk for the four terms of the year, 8d. Also paid to John Lilyng for the term of St. Michael, 6s. 8d.

Total, 27s. [...]

The fourth year. Cost of the garden

Paid to John Clek working in the garden for 3 days, 6d. Also paid for 22 stakes for supporting the branches of a vine, 5d. Also paid for a spade for digging the garden, [4d.] Also paid to John Clek for supporting the vine with stakes, for 1 day, 2d. Also paid to John David for pruning the vine, 2d.

Total, 19d.

The cost of the tenement of William Webbe

Paid to Henry Werthbroke for 6 days, 18d. Also paid to William his servant, for 6 days, 15d. Also paid for the carriage of timber, 7d. Also paid to Henry Carpenter, for 2 days, 6d. Also for bread and drink, 4d.

Total, 4s.

The cost of William Brownye

Also paid to Henry Cok for 4 bundles with carriage, 16d. Also paid to 2 workmen to make a wall, for 2 days, 8d. Also to 1 workman for making 1 wattle and for applying daub for 2 days, 4d. Also paid to Henry Cok for 3 bundles of straw, 13 ½d. Also paid to one thatcher with his servant for 3 days, 15d. Also paid for a bundle of hazel broaches [for securing thatching], 4d. Paid to a thatcher and his servant for one day, 5d. Paid for 2 bundles of straw with carriage, 8d. Also paid to one thatcher per day for making spars, 5d. Also to one thatcher per day for making spars, 2d. Also for one bundle of straw with carriage, 4d.

Total, 7s. ½d.

Cost of the tenement of John Huchynys in Bradpole

Paid to Philip de Bothlyngton for 4 cart-loads of stone, 14d. Also paid to John Huchynys for the making of 10 ½ perches of mudwall, 2s. 4 ½d. Also paid to John for the clearing of the footing of the base of the old wall, 6d. Also paid to John Boleyne for the base of the wall, taking for one perch as an assessed payment, 6d., and so taking altogether, 4s.

Total, 8s. […]

Loss of revenue for which he seeks to be allowed

First from the rent of William Burgeches, 4s. 6d. Also from the rent of Henry Barber, 8s. Also from the lower court, 5s. 4d. Also from the rent of Agnes Gurci, 4s. Also from 6s. 8d. of Benytte. Also from the rent of John Huchyn de Bradpole, 5d.

Total, 28s. 11d.

Fourth year. Expenses of the tenement of William Burgesches

Paid to Henry Cok for 8 bundles of straw, 2s. 8d. Also paid to John Clek and John Prior for the repair of a wall for 2 days, 8d. Also to John Clek, 2d. Also for one cart-load of rods with the mowing, hoeing, and carriage for making one "blade" [?cornfield], [3s. 4d.] Also paid to Hugh the thatcher for the thatching and making of a "wake" [?length of thatch] of half of the outside of the house at the assessed payment of 3s. 4d. Also for a bundle of hazel broaches, 4d. Also paid for a staple for the door of the barn, 1d.

[*Total, 10s. 7d.*]

The cost of the tenement of Henry Carpenter

Paid to a thatcher and his servant for 2 days, 10d. Also paid to Henry Cok for 2 bundles of straw with carriage, 8d. Also for hazel broaches, 3d.

Total, 21d. with Henry Whythebrok

Necessary expenses
Paid for parchment and paper, 8d.

Total, 8d.

Stock
Paid for cheese bought, 14d.

Total, 14d.

Purchase of timber
Paid to John Stroude for 4 cart-loads of oak with carriage, 7s. 6d. Also paid to John Hulbrond for a cart-load of timber, 2s.

[*Total, 9s. 6d.*]

Cost of the tenement of Henry Barber
Paid to Henry Wythbrok for the repair done in a new window and in the solar for a day, 3d. Also paid for a door nail, 1d. Also paid to John Cleek for the plastering of the gable wall, for a day 2d. Also paid for sending hay with earth, 1d. Also paid to Henry Carpenter for making of a chimney for 6 days, 18d. Also paid to a thatcher and his servant for a day, 5d. [*Also for a lock with a key, 4d.*] Also for the repair of a lock, 1d. Also for one bundle of straw with carriage, 5d.

Total, 3s. 4d.

Purchase of lime
Paid for three quarters, 18d.

Total, 18d.

∾ **No. 93. Prime real estate: the Paston's parsonage at Oxnead parish (1478).**
The Paston Letters, ed. James Gairdner, vol. 5 (London, 1904), pp. 325-26. Modernized by JS.
[July 31, 1478]

The commodities of the parsonage and the value of the benefice of Oxnead [in Norfolk]
My new parson of Oxnead, when he is instituted and inducted, at his first entry into the church and benefice of Oxnead must, by ancient custom long continued in the diocese of Norwich, pay 14 marks to the bishop of Norwich for the first fruits of the said benefice. For this 14 marks, if the new parson is clever and has favor with the bishop's officers, he shall have days of payment to pay the said 14 marks in fourteen years—that is, a mark a year until it is paid, providing that he can find sufficient means to be bound by obligation to the bishop to honor his days of payment.

And the church is but little, and is reasonably pleasant, and repaired. And the dwelling place of the parsonage is adjoining to the [*lacuna in manuscript*] well housed and repaired, halls, chambers, barn, dovecote, and all houses of office.

And it has a dovecote worth 14s. 4d. a year.

And it has two large gardens with fruit, adjoining the place and the churchyard, the fruit of which is worth 26s. 8d. yearly.

And there belongs to the said parsonage in free arable land, pasture, and meadow adjoining to the said parsonage, 22 acres or more, of which every acre is worth 2s.; to rent, £3 4d.

And Justice William Paston, when he first came to dwell in the manor of Oxnead, paid £24 to the parson then there for the grain growing on the parsonage's lands and for the tithes, in grain only, when it was brought into the barn.

And the same year the parson had all the altarage and other profits besides the said, £24.

It is yearly worth, as the world goes now, £10.

And it is but an easy cure to keep, for there are not past twenty persons to be yearly given communion.

The parsonage stands by a fresh riverside.

And there is a good market town called Aylsham within two miles of the parsonage.

And the city of Norwich is within six miles of the parsonage.

And the sea is within ten miles of the parsonage.

And if a parson came there now, and was presented, instituted, and inducted, he should have by the law all the crop that is now growing on the parsonage's land (which was winnowed and sown at the old parson's cost) as his own goods, and also all the tithe of all manner of grains of the manor, lands, tenants' lands, towards his charges of the first fruits. And if it was collected, the crop now growing would be worth the value of his first fruits.

He who holds this benefice, if he is a poor man, might have license to be in service besides.

The bishop ought not to claim the value of this [current] crop for the arrearage of the first fruits that Sir Thomas Everard, the last parson of Oxnead, owed to the bishop when he died. For the said Sir Thomas Everard was bound to the bishop by an obligation for the first fruits, and the said Sir Thomas Everard, to defraud the bishop and other men that he owed money to, gave away his goods to certain persons, which persons took away the said goods and also the doors and windows of the parsonage. And it is thought that both the bishop and the patron might take action against the said persons [to reclaim the missing property].

[*Five days after this document's date, Agnes Paston, the church's patron, presented Richard Lincoln, who had a degree in theology, to the living of Oxnead.*]

∾ No. 94. A country parson's goods: inventory of the movable property of a deceased priest (1439).

EHD IV, No. 442, pp. 733–35.

1439. Sale of the goods of John Grene, late Rector of Castle Combe, by Richard Carpenter, chaplain, and William Blackman.

By William Porter for one chest	2s.	
By the same for 1 white coverlet	2s.	
By William Benett for 2 coverlets and one vest	5s.	
By Richard Hollwey for 1 gown	2s.	
By the same for one gown	2s.	
By William Benett for 11 towels	4s.	
By William Parker for 1 green gown	8s.	6d.
By the same William for 1 pair sheets	2s.	
By the same William for 1 sheet	2s.	4d.
By Richard Hollwey for 3 sheets	6s.	4d.
By the same for a doublet of worsted	1s.	
By the same Richard for one vestment with appurtenances for the use of the church	20s.	
By the same Richard for 26 lb. of wax	9s.	
By Geoffry Tayllor for one blanket	2d.	
By Richard Hollwey for 3 "dorelokks", 9d; 5 other "dorelokks"	2s.	5d.
By the same for a pair of "dorebands"		6d.
By the same for other iron articles [*ferramentis*]		4d.
By the same for 1 basin [*pelves*] with a washtub [*lavatorio*]	2s.	8d.
By the same for 3 powder platters	1s.	10d.
By the same for three sheets and a table-cloth	2s.	
By Richard Dighton for 1 tester	2s.	
By Richard Hollwey for 2 napkins, 2 towels, 2 sheets, one being of raynys,[32] two yards of canvas	20s.	
By the same for one *legend* and one *manuall*[33]	6s.	8d.
By Thomas Donan for 4 tables		8d.

Sum total, 104s. 9d. from which the expenses of Richard Carpenter and William Blackman for the sale 10s., and so remains to be paid to the lord, £4 14s. 9d.

---

[32] Fine linen, so called, from Rennes in Brittany.

[33] Service books.

Item, by Edward Jones for one silver-gilt bowl	53s.	4d.
By the same for one dozen of spoons	33s.	4d.
By the same for two silver bowls	26s.	8d.
By the same for a silver belt	6s.	8d.
By the same for three "fethyr bedd"	26s.	8d.
By the same for timber	40s.	
By the same for 1 two-horse cart	3s.	4d.
By the same for tiles [*tegulis*]	5s.	
By the same in money in gross	1s.	11d.

Sum of the whole, £10 5s. 7d., of which was paid to John Peryncourt for satisfaction to the lord of the debt of John Grene, late Rector of Castle Combe, 20s., and so remains £9 5s. 7d.

[*The inventory continues with these articles, which appear not to have been brought into the account:*]

Richard Carpenter, the lord's chaplain, for 1 spoon	1s.	8d.
By the same Richard for 1 silver-gilt seal with a white stone hanging from it (He says he has not got it)	2s.	
By William Blackman for three gold rings	6s.	8d.
By Thomas Yong for 1 pair of [blank]	[*sic*]	
Item, memorandum, that by the statement [*per relationem*] of the tenants the three gold rings were of the value of	30s.	
Item, there remain in the hands of Richard Carpenter and William Blackman £20 from the goods of the Rector of Castle Combe above mentioned, etc.		
Item, from certain pieces of velvet and satin by the statement of Thomas Yong, clerk	106s.	8d.

[*Besides these, other articles seem to have been abstracted fraudulently before the sale (probably by friends or creditors of the deceased), for in a subsequent page occurs the following entry:*]

Memorandum, that John Parker of Dursley, in the county of Gloucester, husbandman or chapman, William Porter of Castle Combe, in the county of Wilts, fuller, and John Seman, of the same place, weaver, and William Porter, also of the same, weaver, by force of arms, on the [blank] day [blank], had taken away goods and chattels of John Grene, late Rector of Castle Combe, to the value of [blank].

ℂ No. 95. Priests' last wills (1370–82).

Norfolk Record Office, Norwich, Norwich Consistory Court Wills, *Register Heydon*. Trans. JS.

A. John Palfreyman, chaplain of Mildenhall. *Reg. Heydon*, fol. 184v.

In the name of God. Amen. I, John Palfreyman of Mildenhall, chaplain, establish, ordain, and make my testament on March 10, 1380 in this fashion: First I will my soul to God and to the Blessed Virgin Mary and all the saints, and my body to be buried in the church of Blessed Mary of Mildenhall. Also I bequeath 12d. to the high altar of that same church. Also 2s. to the fabric of that church. Also 6d. to both the parish chaplains there. Also 3d. to both the parish clerks of the church. Also I give and bequeath the rest of my goods to my sister Denise, William Sopere, and John Claver; and I appoint, ordain, and establish the same Denise, William, and John as my executors to dispose of these for the good of my soul.

B. Robert, perpetual vicar of St. Margaret, Crimplesham. *Reg. Heydon,* fol. 192.

In the name of God. Amen. I, Robert, perpetual vicar of the church of St. Margaret, Crimplesham, make my testament in this fashion on the sixth day before the ides of March [March 10] 1380. First I leave my soul to God, the Blessed Virgin Mary, and all his saints; and my body to be buried wherever it pleases God. Also I leave two candles worth eight pounds of wax to be burned during the elevation of the host. Also I give and leave 10s. for mending the picture of the holy Virgin Mary at the side altar. I give and leave the rest of my goods to my executors for them to distribute for the sake of my soul however they best see fit, and I appoint these men my executors: William, perpetual vicar of the church of Stow; Stephen Talbot of Crimplesham; and Ralph Clerk, of the same place.

C. Theodoric de Colonia, rector of Melford. *Reg. Heydon,* fols. 9r–v.

In the name of God. Amen. I, Theodoric of Colonia, rector of the church of Melford, being of sound mind and good memory, make my testament in this fashion: First I will my soul to God and to Blessed Mary and to all the saints; and I will my body to be buried in the church of Saint Mary at Bury. Also I leave all the new fruits coming from my church of Melford for my executors to divide into four portions: I leave one portion to be spent for my funeral. And the second portion is to be distributed among my poor parishioners. The third part is for doing work on the church bell. And the fourth portion is for doing work on the chancel. Also I leave one black horse to Richard Gosenile. Also I leave one cow and one horse to Richard Stansted. Also I leave three cows to John Boughed and his wife. Also I leave three cows to Lawrence Porterese and his wife. Also I leave one cow to Stephen Attehol. Also I leave two cows to William Kok. And if there is anything left from my possessions after my debts have been paid and above and beyond what has been bequeathed in this testament, I leave it to my executors to dispose of in a manner would be willing to report before God, and as seems most expedient to them. In witness of this I appoint and ordain these men as my executors: Master Ralph de Neckton, public notary; John

Boughed of Melford; and Richard Gosenile, my servant. In witness of this
I have affixed my seal to the present testament in the presence of these wit-
nesses specially called for this matter: Sir Robert Stabler, chaplain; and John
Coteler. Done at Bury Saint Edmund's on the feast of the finding of the Holy
Cross [May 3] in the year of our Lord 1371.

D. Ralph Chylton, perpetual vicar of Brooke. *Reg. Heydon,* fol. 6r.

In the name of God. Amen. I Ralph, perpetual vicar of the church of
Brooke, vigorous of mind, establish my testament in this fashion: First I bequeath my soul to God and to Blessed Mary and to all the saints, and my
body to be buried in the parish church of Brooke. Also I bequeath to my
parishioners too proud to beg, two quarters[34] of barley. Also I will to my
brother John Reyd two bushels of barley. Also I will to my sister Joan two
bushels of barley. Also I will to my parishioners ashamed to beg, four bushels of beans. Also I will to John de Chilton of Sudbury four bushels of malt.
Also I will to Alice Cristen two bushels of barley. Also I will to Richard
Calworth two bushels of barley. Also I will to Richard Howyster two bushels
of peas. Also I will to Agnes Brid one bushel of wheat. Also I will to Matilda
Le Anller one bushel of wheat. Also I will to Richard Roche two bushels of
peas and one of barley. Also I will to the [votive] lights of the Blessed Mary
of Brooke one ewe and one hog. Also I will the rest of all my goods to the
free disposition of my executors so that they will do and ordain as seems
best to them in order to profit God, Blessed Mary, and all the saints, and for
the salvation of my soul. I appoint these men to be the executors of this
testament: Robert, parson of the church of Howe; Henry Barel; and John
Kibert. Done at Brooke on March 3, 1370. In witness of the present document, I have affixed my seal.

E. William Ernald, rector of Carleton Rode. *Reg. Heydon,* fol. 121v.

In the name of God. Amen. Seven kalends May [April 25] in the year
of our Lord 1375, I, William Ernald, rector of the church of Carleton Rode,
ill in body but still of sound mind, make my testament. First I recommend
my soul to God my savior, to the Blessed Virgin Mary, and to all the saints;
and I leave my body to be buried in my chancel.[35] Also I desire that during

---

[34] A quarter usually equalled eight bushels.

[35] According to the eighteenth-century Norfolk antiquarian Francis Blomefield, he was "buried in the midle [*sic*] of the Chancel in 1375; his stone lies now at the Enterance [*sic*] his effigies in
a Priest's Habit in his Desk, with a Book lying before him, & a Cross standing before, remains in
Brass, but the Inscription is lost." *An Essay towards a Topographical History of the County of Norfolk*
(Lynn, 1769), vol. 3, p. 83.

my funeral exequies there should be five candles made from twenty pounds of wax around my bier. Also I desire that my funeral expenses should be handled by my executors in every particular. Also I leave one half mark for repairs to the said church. Also I leave 2s. for the repair of the chapel of the Blessed Mary standing in the said village. Also I leave to my brother Adam, one horse called Brok. Also I leave one book called *Pars Oculi*[36] to my chaplain John. Also I leave Peter of Boxstead my bed in which I am lying. Also I leave two bushels of barley to John Bridylsmyth. Also I leave four bushels of barley to William Nichol. Also I leave all the rest of my goods to Sir Roger, perpetual vicar of the church of Rockland; Robert Brid, citizen of Norwich; William Wodehirde; and Adam Ernald whom I ordain and appoint my executors so that they will distribute these goods among the poor as seems best to them for the sake of my soul.

F. William Cadyman of Quidenham, chaplain. *Reg. Heydon,* fol. 198v.

In the name of God. Amen. In the year of our Lord 1382, on the eighth kalends of May [April 24], I, William Cadyman of Quidenham, chaplain, make my testament in this fashion: First I commend my soul to Almighty God, Blessed Mary, and all the saints; and I leave my body to be buried in the graveyard of the church of St. Andrew, Quidenham. Also I leave 2s. to the high altar. Also I leave 12d. to the [votive] light of Blessed Mary in the chapel of the said church. Also I leave 12d. for sustaining the light of St. Anne in the other chapel. Also I leave 2s. for the repair of the church of Knettishall. Also I leave 12d. for the light of Blessed Mary there. Also I leave 2s. for the repair of the church of All Saints, Garboldisham. Also 2s. for the repair of the church of Gasthorpe. Also 2s. for the repair of the church of Riddlesworth. Also I leave four bushels of barley to support the guild of the Holy Trinity of Quidenham. Also I leave four bushels of barley to support the guild of St. John. Also I leave one lamp to burn in honor of St. Anne, mother of Blessed Mary in Quidenham, with three rods[37] of arable land to sustain this lamp. Also I leave one complete suit of vestments for feast days together with a chalice to the altar of St. Anne's chapel. Also I leave to Brother John Kokerel of [Caistor?] one trental of masses. Also I leave 40d. to Roger Cook of Quidenham, chaplain. Also I leave 30d. to John Kec of the same place. Also I leave four bushels of barley to William Rathe of Knettishall. Also I leave four bushels of barley to William, son of John Spoyle. Also I leave 6d. to Roger, parish clerk of Quidenham. Also I leave 6d. to

---

[36] Part of William of Pagula's important fourteenth-century pastoral manual. See No. 72.
[37] A rod equals one-quarter acre.

Richard, son of Thomas Wattessone. And anything discovered from the rest of my goods and chattels not mentioned or bequeathed in this testament I leave to my executors William Cadyman, Thomas Apekyn of Garboldisham, and Nicholas le Wand of Eccles; and I entreat them for God's sake to dispose of my goods for the sake of my soul and the souls of my father and mother, and for all the souls of the faithful departed for whose sake I am indebted to pray.

G. John de Ufford (c. 1341–75), rector of Hingham and prebendary of Salisbury and Lincoln. *Reg. Heydon,* fol. 118r.

In the name of God. Amen. In the year of our Lord 1375 on the 10th of August in the town of Cambridge, I, John de Ufford,[38] rector of the church of Hingham in the diocese of Norwich and prebendary of the churches of Salisbury and Lincoln, make my testament in this fashion: First I bequeath my soul to God, to the Blessed Mary, and to all the saints, and my body to be buried in the chancel of the church of St. Andrew, Hingham, in the southern part of the chancel. Also to the high altar of the same church I leave one vestment given to me by my lord and father, the venerable Lord Robert of Ufford, Earl of Suffolk, namely: one chasuble with two tunicles and one cope with a matching amice; one alb with an amice, stole, maniple, and girdle, and one gilded tablet given to me by the Lady Margaret, my mother, Countess of Suffolk, with my bible. Also I leave ten silver pounds for preparing and making certain decorations next to the altar. Also I leave to the altar of St. Mary in the same church a suit of priest's vestments of red-striped material, namely: one chasuble, two albs with two amices, two cloths, and two curtains cut from them, and with two towels for that altar and one chalice with a missal. Also I leave five pounds for building a bell tower for the church. Also I leave ten pounds for repairs to the chancel of the [prebendal] church of Sleaford. Also I leave five pounds to the high altar of the [cathedral] church of Salisbury. Also I leave to John Panton, chaplain of Lafford, 100s. which he has owed to me for a long while for the old rectory given to him to rent, and one lined robe. Also I leave 20s. to Sir Ralph Leronthon, my vicar at the church of Lincoln. Also I leave to William Hengham one suit of priest's vestments with one full set of bed-clothes bought from the executors of my lord the Earl of Suffolk, namely of green and white

[38]John de Ufford, the third son of the Earl of Suffolk, one of the great barons of England, was perhaps the earliest paying student at Gonville Hall, Cambridge, to which he later donated a window and where he ultimately gained a master's degree. Instituted to Hingham in 1359, he was papally dispensed in 1360 to hold this benefice though underage. From 1366–68 he was the archdeacon of Suffolk.

worsted mixed with quilt, and also the *Book of Sentences*.[39] Also I leave to Robert, my chamberlain, the red bed on which I am lying along with its bedclothes. Also I leave to Sir John, my chaplain at Hingham, one robe plus 10s. Also I leave to the assistant chaplain of the church of Hingham one robe plus 6s. 4d. Also I leave 6s. 4d. and a shirt to my clerk, John; and a shirt to his associate. Also I leave 40s. to be distributed among the poor of Hingham. Also I leave 30s. to be distributed among the poor of Sleaford. Also I leave to Master Richard de Pulham my commentary. Also I leave to Master William Pysehale the text of [Aristotle's] *Metaphysics* with one commentary on that book. Also I leave to Master William Elmham a text of [Aristotle's] *Physics*. Also I leave to Master Walter Harlyng one book called "Aquinas on the *Physics*." Also I leave to Master Henry Compston [pseudo-]Aristotle's *The Rule of Princes*[40] with [a book] *Pastoralibus* contained in a small volume. Also I leave to Master John Tynmewe [a book of] the Master of History.[41] Also 40s. to the nuns of Campisse. Also I leave 40s. to my sister, the Lady Matilde, who is a nun at Campisse. Also I leave 40s. to the University of Cambridge. Also I leave 20s. to the nuns of Cambridge. Also I leave to Sir Robert Hardeneth the old coverlet with a tester of double worsted and a dressing-gown which are in my study. Also I leave 40s. to Sir John Pyeshale. Also I leave two marks to Sir Robert Sutton. Also regarding my burial, I wish, ordain, and dispose that it should be as follows: namely, my body should be buried as has been said as quickly as is decently possible. It should be accompanied by four or five candles containing eight to ten pounds of wax apiece and by four paupers holding four torches in their hands and dressed in white gowns purchased at my expense. In regard to holding a banquet on the day of my burial, I wish to have one but it should not be extravagant, and what is left over from it I wish to be distributed among the poor at the discretion of my executors. And I make and appoint the executors of this testament to be Sir John Pyeshale; Master Robert Sutton, rector of the church of Rollesby; Stephen Dunmowe; William Hengham, rector of the church of Stonham Aspall; to which people I particularly leave all my autumn harvests and incidental revenues from my church of Hingham, and also all the autumn harvests of my prebendal church of Sleaford, and all incidental revenues with their rights and appurtenances of any kind whatsoever that pertain to the said church; and also all produce, rents,

---

[39] By Peter Lombard (d. 1160); the standard textbook of medieval theology.

[40] *De regimine principum*, a spurious Aristotelian work, though the title might mean the genuine Aristotle's *Politics*.

[41] I.e., Peter Comestor (d. c. 1179). The book in question is probably his *Historia scholastica*, a compendium of biblical history and legends.

and incidental revenues together with all rights and appurtenances that will accrue this year to my prebend called "the major part of the altar" in the said church. My executors should arrange and dispose of the rest of all my goods that are left unpledged in this testament in a way that best aids my soul. Done in the abovementioned year, day, month, and place. In witness of this I have appended my seal to this testament after it was folded up.

◌᷎ No. 96. The annual wage for vicars: Council of Oxford, c. 21 (1222).
Councils and Synods, p. 112. Trans. WJD.

Abundance often breeds neglect and indigence beggary, to the scandal of our order. We, therefore, choosing the middle course, command that an estate which has a farming value of at least five marks be assigned to the perpetual vicar (i.e., its rent value should be at least five marks), except in those parts of Wales where vicars should be content with less because of the poverty of the churches. Let the bishop, after careful consideration of the church's value, judge whether the parson, the vicar, or both are to bear the charges of the church, provided that the archdeacon remains content with one procuration,[42] either from one or both.

◌᷎ No. 97. A bishop augments a vicar's meager holdings (1357).
Reg. Trillek (Hereford), pp. 252–53. Trans. WJD.

To all concerned, etc. John, etc., greetings. When we were recently visiting the deanery of Leominster in our diocese and, within it, the parish church of Eardisland appropriated to the abbot and convent of Lyre in the diocese of York, . . . we found that the place originally assigned by those religious to the perpetual vicar of the church is so narrow and hemmed in that the vicars of the church have not had sufficient space to walk about or to grow leeks, vegetables, and other herbs for their soup or other necessities of the house. While the church's property is ample and spacious enough, it must be said that the vicar's wage and land drawn from the area, estates, and income of the said church are neither just nor adequate. Thus, in the same church, one portion is poor and wanting, while another is excessively wealthy. And yet, in the words of the Apostle, the one who serves the church and altar ought to live sufficiently from it and have those things that are necessary for himself. Wishing, as we are bound, to correct this fault, this injustice, absurdity, and error and to turn these to the good and just, we assign, order, and grant with apostolic and episcopal authority and by these letters a certain portion of the rectorial lands of the church behind the monks'

[42]See glossary.

grange from the enclosure walls to the southern wall of the grange, including a bit of land belonging to the monks on the western side, a narrow stretch to the north, and a pathway on the eastern part. This courtyard which the vicars of this church have been wanting to this day, we grant to the current vicar who manages and supports the cure of this church and to his successors in the vicarage. The said religious and all other appropriate persons have been advised legally and properly on this matter. From this point on, any persons who act against these rights in any way, either with respect to the said religious or anyone else, and impede or disturb our decision, order, and grant regarding this place, incur, ipso facto, major excommunication. We state this canonical warning in these letters. In testimony of which we append our seal, etc. Given at Colwall on the 24th day of November, in the year of our Lord 1357, etc.

‿ No. 98. Charity for a poor priest (1290).

Reg. Sutton (Lincoln), vol. 3, p. 30. Trans. JS.

Oliver, [by the grace of God, bishop of Lincoln,] etc., to every rector, vicar, and parochial chaplain whatsoever in our diocese, sends greetings, grace, and blessing. With brotherly feeling and sympathy we offer you evident proof of the misfortunes and miseries of William of Hanslope, a poor priest who has been greatly burdened both by the various hardships that befall someone of his age and by certain other infirmities. In the Lord we advise and exhort you all on behalf of the said William that if this same poor man should visit your area seeking relief of his poverty and assistance in getting the necessities of life, you should welcome him out of pious regard for his status; and for the sake of charity you should explain his situation with kindness and support to your parishioners at mass during feast days, allowing them to apply what they will charitably donate to him in this regard for the remission of their sins. Given at Sleaford August 7, 1290, the ninth year of our episcopacy.

‿ No. 99. Exorbitant charges of chaplains: Archbishop Simon Islip's *Effrenata* (1350).

Reg. Trillek (Hereford), p. 157. *Bishop's Register*, pp. 191–94. Revised by JS.

. . . Simon Archbishop, etc., to our venerable brother, Ralph, [bishop of London,] etc., greetings, etc. The unbridled cupidity of the human race would so break forth from its innate wickedness that charity would be banished to the ends of the earth, unless the power of justice crushed its attempts. A very common complaint has brought home to us and potent experience (that guide of all things) shows that the priests who now survive—neither mindful that the Divine Will has preserved them unmerited from the dangers of the recent pestilence[43] so that they may carry out the ministry committed to them on behalf of the people of God and public usefulness, nor ashamed that other workers, even laymen, wickedly and perniciously hold up their insatiable avarice as an example—do not care about the cure of souls (which deserves to be preferred over all other cures by ministers, especially ecclesiastical ones, and to which when anyone is brought against his will, if he obeys humbly, he is able to boast the greater merit). They fail to exercise the cure of souls and to support the burdens of their cures by mutual charity. Utterly abandoning them, they turn instead to celebrating annual masses and doing other exceptional duties so that they can more boldly renew their old insolence. Dissatisfied with their appropriate and accustomed stipends, they demand excessive pay for their services so that in exchange for simple and undemanding work they can obtain for themselves more money than they could as curates. Consequently, unless their unreasonable appetites are restored to an equitable measure, then— both because of the increasing number of annual masses and because the amount of their stipends is unregulated—many, indeed most churches, prebends, and chapels both of our diocese and of yours and of the whole of our province will remain completely destitute of the service of priests; and curates for the sake of the same kind of profit will eagerly seek similar employment, altogether neglecting their cures, which deeply grieves us. Wishing therefore to restrain with suitable remedies the insatiable desires of such priests because of the aforesaid dangers and the other serious losses which our further indulgence might increase, we request and exhort your fraternity in the bowels of Jesus, that, thinking above all of the perils of souls and the aforesaid causes, you soundly provide from among the better and more suitable chaplains in whomever's service (other than a curate's) they may be found for the care of each parish church, prebend, and chapel to which a cure of souls is attached, according to their need. And not excepting their relatives, or their supporters, or those acting in their service against our ordinance, or any similar person rashly violating our ordinance, you shall canonically constrain by any ecclesiastical censures even the chaplains themselves (and anyone else celebrating in our diocese, whoever or wherever they may be) to be content with a reasonable salary. And if anyone rebelling against you attempts to transfer to our diocese or to that of one of our brother bishops, we wish and command that, when the procedure has been

---

[43] The Black Death, which arrived in England in 1348, taking a particularly hard toll on the clergy.

completed, you or they will make known by letter his name and surname
either to us or to that bishop into whose diocese he has moved. For we wish
to proceed against those who thus come into our diocese according to your
procedures or those of our other brothers, and to carry out the censures
brought against them according to our power. We similarly require and order these things to be done and carried out in everything by our brothers
each in his own diocese. To make our intention clear to you concerning the
amount of salary, we wish in our said diocese that the chaplain of a church,
prebend, or chapel with cure of souls be content with a salary of one mark
of silver more than that which was previously the customary pay of the
priest ministering in the same cure; also we wish that the salary of any other
stipendiary priest be subjected to the common assessment customary in former times. Furthermore we command and enjoin you that you inform us
clearly and distinctly by letters of notification about your actions and their
circumstances regarding each single article aforesaid before the feast of the
Blessed Virgin Mary. Know that after the lapse of the aforesaid feast, in accordance with the nature of the business and the requirement of the law, we
intend to do whatever our office obliges in this regard concerning the appeal
of anyone who complains to us about your negligence or that of other
brother bishops or their suffragans. And we wish you to make known this
our present mandate to all our brothers and suffragans, and to enjoin them
to inform us before the aforesaid feast about what they shall have done in
this matter in letters having this form. Given at Mayfield, 27th May, A.D.
1350, the first year of our consecration. . . .

❧ No. 100. Archbishop Simon Sudbury raises chaplains' wages (1378).
EHD IV, No. 728, pp. 728–29.

Simon by divine permission Archbishop of Canterbury, Primate of All
England, and legate of the Apostolic See, to our venerable brother William,
by the grace of God Bishop of London, greeting and brotherly love in the
Lord. . . . A common complaint is soundly made to us, and experience of
things shows us, that priests of the present time, of our city, diocese, and
province of Canterbury, are so tainted with the vice of cupidity that they
are not content with reasonable stipends but claim and receive excessive
wages. These greedy and fastidious priests vomit from the burden of excessive salaries of this kind, they run wild and wallow, and some of them, after
gluttony of the belly, break forth into a pit of evils, to the detestable scandal
of all clergy and the pernicious example of clerics. And although the Lord
Simon Islepe [Islip] of good memory, lately Archbishop of Canterbury, our
predecessor, while he was alive, established and ordained with the counsel

and assent of his brethren, that chaplains celebrating anniversaries, and other clerics not having the cure of souls, ought to be content with an annual stipend of five marks [£3 6s. 8d.] and parish priests and chaplains and others having such a cure should be content with six marks annual wage [£4]; any cleric not obeying this statute to be liable to the penalty of suspension from his office ipso facto. We, however, having considered the character of the times, with the counsel and advice of our brethren and suffragans, on the 16th day of November in the year of the Lord underwritten, assembled for this purpose in a certain room in the precincts of the monastery of Saints Peter and Paul at Gloucester, ordained and established the salaries of the chantry and parish priests to be received henceforth in our said city, diocese, and province of Canterbury under the form given below.

In the name of God, Amen. We, Simon, by divine permission Archbishop of Canterbury, Primate of All England, and legate of the Apostolic See, by the counsel of our brethren and suffragans establish that whoever shall celebrate masses for the souls of the departed shall be content with seven marks [£4 13s. 4d.] a year, or food with three marks [£2]; but those who have a cure of souls shall be recompensed with eight marks [£5 6s. 8d.] a year, or food and four marks [£2 13s. 4d.]. No one is to charge more by any agreement, unless the diocesan of the place first orders it to be done otherwise with those who have the cure of souls. If any clerk shall presume to give or receive more against this our constitution, he shall incur the sentence of excommunication ipso facto, and shall not be absolved from this except by the diocesan of the place. . . . Therefore we commission and order you firmly that you should transmit all the foregoing to your subordinates to be published quickly and to demand due execution of them as soon as possible. . . . Given at Lambeth, so far as the sending out of these presents is concerned, on 26th November, 1378, and the fourth year of our translation.

☙ No. 101. The clergy summoned to Parliament (1295).

Documents Illustrative of the History of the English Church, ed. Henry Gee and William Hardy (London: Macmillan, 1896), pp. 85–86.

The king to the venerable Father in Christ, Robert, by the same grace archbishop of Canterbury, primate of all England, greeting. As law most righteous, established by the prudent foresight of holy princes, enjoins and ordains that what affects all should be approved by all, it is in such wise, as is most clear, that common dangers may be met by remedies taken in common. You are doubtless well aware, and it is now, we believe, spread abroad through all the countries in the world, how that the King of France has treacherously and surreptitiously deceived us in regard to our land of Gascony by wickedly withholding it from us. And now, not content with the treachery and wickedness aforesaid, he has, in order to attack our realm, collected a very large fleet and a numerous retinue of soldiers, with whom he has already invaded our kingdom and the inhabitants of the same, and proposes to blot out entirely from the earth the English tongue, if his power correspond to the abominable design of the sin he has conceived, which God avert; because weapons foreseen do the less injure, and your interest, as that of all your other fellow-citizens in the realm, is at stake, we command you by the faith and love whereby you are bound to us, firmly enjoining that on the Sunday next after the Feast of St. Martin in the winter [November 11] next to come, you be present in person at Westminster, forewarning the prior and chapters of your church, the archdeacons, and all the clergy of your diocese, causing that these same prior and archdeacons, in their own persons, and the said chapter by one, and the same clergy by two fit proctors, having full and sufficient authority from the chapter and clergy themselves, to be present with you, by all means, then and there to discuss, ordain, and do with us and the other prelates and nobles and other inhabitants of our realm, in what manner we are to meet such perils and evils devised. Witness the king at Wengham, the 30th day of September [1295].[44]

Cℒ **No. 102. Royal protection for the clergy: the writ *Circumspecte agatis* (1286).**
EHD III, No. 60, pp. 462–63.

The statute about the lord king's prohibition begins. Edward by God's grace king of England, etc. to Richard de Boyland and his fellow justices greeting. Act circumspectly in the matter of the lord bishop of Norwich and his clergy, not punishing them if they have held a plea concerning those things which are purely spiritual, that is concerning corrections which prelates impose for mortal sin, namely for fornications, adulteries and such like, for which sometimes corporal punishment is inflicted, sometimes a money penalty, especially if he who is convicted of such is a free man; also, if a prelate punishes for an unenclosed cemetery, a church without a roof or not properly provided with ornaments, in which cases no penalty can be inflicted other than a money penalty; also, if a rector claims a mortuary in places where mortuaries have customarily been given; also, if a rector claims from his parishioners oblations, [or] due and accustomed tithes, or a rector

---

[44]King Philip the Fair had used a feudal pretext to seize Gascony from Edward in 1294. At the parliament, the clergy agreed to pay a tenth of their revenues as a war tax, even though they had paid a remarkable half just the year before.

brings an action against a rector about tithes lesser or greater, provided a quarter of a church's value is not claimed; also, if a prelate claims from a rector a pension due to him as advocate of a church: all such claims are to be made in a church court. With regard to laying violent hands on clerks and in a cause of defamation it was granted on another occasion that a plea concerning these things should be held in court Christian, provided money is not claimed but the action is for correction of the sin; also with regard to breach of faith, provided the action is for the correction of the sin. In all the aforesaid cases and the like the ecclesiastical judge has cognisance, notwithstanding a writ of prohibition, even if it is delivered. Given at Paris, in the fourteenth year of our reign.

7

Life and Manners

Church officials and parishioners alike were always interested in how their clergy bore themselves in behavior and manner of life. In the evaluations that had to occur by law before a cleric was ordained or promoted to a benefice, examiners sought some assurance that the man before them not only possessed the right qualifications of skill and learning but also that he could be relied upon to be a moral leader for his community—that he was spiritually worthy, as far as anyone could be, of his office. A local pastor's moral life was often, whether he wished it so or not, the most effective means of educating his flock, for good or ill. And the people he led in prayer, whose homes he visited, whose sickbeds he was summoned to, and whose tithes he required were rarely indifferent to the relative disparity between what their pastor preached and how he lived.

How a pastor lived in the later medieval centuries was not something that can be described in a generalized fashion. If the documents and records in this book have indicated anything, it is that medieval clerics were a motley group, as varied in their background and character as the places of their birth and the range of activities they were expected to engage in. This was not because church leaders valued such diversity—the constant appeals in doctrine and canon law to standards of clerical behavior and excellence of life reveal something else entirely—but because medieval bishops tended to be practical men who realized that parish life was local life. And this would be the case until the fathers at the Council of Trent (1545–63) decreed the founding of seminaries where clerical aspirants would obtain a far more

standard pastoral education and where men would be formed into a more
common clerical culture. In the medieval centuries, pastors were far more
likely to reflect the diversity of their background, upbringing, and the pastoral opportunities acquired in the narrow orbit of the parish.

It is important not to overstate this point or to view medieval clerics
as men who were willfully variant, often moving against the established
boundaries of acceptable behavior and expectation. Certainly there were
standards to which church leaders often summoned their clergy. But the
standards were not always completely clear or even agreed upon. Within the
guidelines fixed by church law, often quite generous, bishops were allowed
to moderate the behavior and activity of their clerics as they saw fit, always
with a mind to viewing the local church much on its own terms. After all,
who were better able to interpret the finer details of canon law or the broad
proscriptions of church teaching than local ecclesiastical officials?

In spite of the variety (or, perhaps, because of it), there were numerous
ways in which the church sought to affirm the good work of its pastors and,
similarly, to bring those who had wandered from the path back to the fold.
With the gradual centralization of ecclesiastical authority that really begins
our period, the church devised various ways to enforce discipline and restore
order among the clergy and people. Episcopal mandates often carried personal reprimands and the threat that, without conversion, the cleric might
be deposed from office or have his income sequestered. Some ecclesiastical
court was nearly always in session, and bishops and archdeacons issued numerous citations for wayward clergy to appear. Some of these, after arraign-
ment and while awaiting trial, spent a dismal length of time in an episcopal
jail (No. 106).

The failings of the clergy inevitably fell within that generous variety
provided for in the seven deadly sins, but the commonplace accusations usually had to do with some activity that threatened the peace of the local
church or gave rise to scandal: the various shades of heresy, clerical ignorance, embezzlement, misuse of church resources and lands, sporting about
in secular dress, hunting or being drunk in public, and sexual misconduct
(Nos. 106–110).

There is certainly no lack of these kinds of references in the records that
survive from the period. Bishops' registers and court documents, ecclesiastical and secular, are rife with such accusations and judicial processes. But
while there is no reason to believe the clergy were a uniformly saintly lot,
neither were they, as a group, as tainted as the records suggest. There is no
doubt that many, if not most, medieval pastors carried on their work re-
sponsibly and to good effect; they taught and preached ably enough, admin-

istered the sacraments with care, met strangers with hospitality, helped build up their own community, practiced the "art of arts." But when this happened, it was hoped for, even expected, so it did not often warrant the intervention of some authority or the need to make a record against some future judicial process. In other words, misdeeds were far likelier to be recorded when discovered than commendable pastoral actions. The records that survive to tell us the most about medieval clergy were administrative records, legal and official, that addressed a constant need to oversee communities, rein in dissenters, manage property, and defend rights. These are well represented here as a way of understanding with some detail the moral lives of medieval clergy; but we also include the fewer and more modest references to those men who worked their cures well and successfully without the kind of celebrity captured by their more notorious brothers (Nos. 103, 104).

The life and manners of medieval clergy were not shaped solely by the personal morality of individual pastors. There were larger influences that inevitably bore on the way curates carried out their duties. Times of crisis always test the soul, and medieval pastors were not immune to the ravages of plague, famine, and war that touched their lives directly and elicted from them some response, heroic or cowardly. The flight of clergy from parishes during the high season of plague in the mid-fourteenth century is well-known. There were many pastors as well who remained with their parishioners, tending the dying and burying the dead. Their own deaths, often in great number, strained the limits of pastoral provision and required bishops like Zouche of York to suspend the usual restrictions of minority and illegitimacy in order to find the necessary clergy for vacant parishes (No. 111). The bishop of Bath and Wells summoned the faithful of his diocese to the sacrament of penance as a necessary preparation for death and if no priest was available to absolve them, they were to confess to any baptized man or woman (No. 112). Though England had escaped the more direct ravages of its prolonged and costly war with France, the English clergy were bent under the incessant demands from the Crown for clerical subsidies to finance the war effort. Steady ecclesiastical demands for taxes only compounded the problems facing medieval pastors and their people. It was rare and against canon law, but on occasion when the need was keen, clergy could be ordered to take their place as fighting men along with every able-bodied person in a community. In 1415, the king summoned a clerical muster to defend the kingdom and the church from enemies foreign and domestic (No. 114).

Social and religious divisions took their toll as well. Two priests, one an Oxford theologian, the other a parish priest from Kent, clamored for reform in the church and the kingdom. John Wyclif's cries for radical religious reform won him the friendship of magnate and commoner alike, but his ideas also threw parish communities into discord and division (No. 109). John Ball's fiery preaching finally put a voice to years of social and economic anxieties, directing an army of impoverished workers against their landed neighbors (No. 110). No doubt, it was hard to foster unanimity in parish communities with such forces at work.

A portrait of medieval pastors in their daily lives is inevitably a mosaic of impressions and details drawn from a great variety of documents and stories. But one sort of record which reveals the parish clergy as flesh-and-blood individuals capable of steady leadership or scandalous sin is the visitation register, a compilation of documents stemming from the official inquiry of a bishop or other ecclesiastical authority into the life of a particular region within the diocese. The canonical visitation was an indispensable means of providing a reform-minded administrator with the information needed to bring errant sheep, clerical, religious, and lay alike, back to the fold (No. 115). From the early thirteenth century on, bishops were required by canon law to visit their dioceses at least once every three years, whether or not a dispute or crisis warranted it. But the visitation was also useful in that it allowed for episcopal intervention at any time and in any place. A bishop might commit himself and his retinue of advisors, scribes, and knights-at-arms to visit the entire diocese; or he might limit his attention to an unruly parish or religious house of bad repute. The inevitable result of the visitation, no matter how extensive the region visited, was a broad, horizontal view of the moral and religious activities of the people and institutions canvassed.

The procedure that accompanied a visitation began with a *littera admonitionis,* a warning that such an event was about to occur, and very often, the publication of common questions that those to be visited could expect to hear and answer (No. 116). Visitations could comprise an evaluation of the physical condition of the church and its lands, the moral condition of clergy and parishioners, or both (Nos. 117, 118). During the course of the inquiries, scribes would take notes of the depositions, often in the vernacular language used in the interrogation, and then later winnow out gossip and summarize and translate the credible assertions into Latin for preservation until the sins recorded had been confessed, the damages paid, and the crime absolved. Since these records amounted to lists of personal sins, there was no need to keep them after the transgression had been absolved. Fortunately for students of church history, some of these visitation records survive and they reveal with unusual clarity—if only for a moment in a parish's history—the moral and religious lives of medieval clergy and their parishioners. Their survival, however, was often more a matter of accident than design.

Another important aspect of these visitations is their inclusiveness. Not only do they reveal much about how the parish clergy and parishioners carried on their personal and workaday lives, but they show, directly or indirectly, the full exercise of the bishop's pastoral ministry. The visitation was a liturgical and sacramental event which the bishop regularly opened with a sermon (usually on some aspect of sin and conversion). Because of its liturgical context, the visitation could also entail the celebration of the sacraments of confirmation and holy orders. During a visitation, the bishop was engaged in every aspect of his office as preacher, teacher, and judge. The occasion was perhaps the only and often the best means at his disposal to observe, affirm, and correct the lives of souls in his keeping. As the reader will see, the bishop and his assistants, listening to the depositions of sworn witnesses offering graphic and sometimes comical descriptions of what their clergy and neighbors were supposed to have done against God, the church, and one another, had an opportunity to uncover any number of transgressions in parishes scattered across the diocese. But the news was not always bad. There were times when the bishop found a local church in good order, its curate managing the parish confidently and well, and its parishioners generally devout and conscientious in their prayer and work. Whether or not the witnesses from such a parish had much to offer by way of detail in this regard, the scribes noted tersely and without ornament, "they say that all is well there."

How much was good or ill in medieval parishes, we will never know for certain. What we do know is that medieval clerics, like their counterparts in other periods of Christian history, were men of diverse background, character, and accomplishment, and that these qualities were bound to affect their identities and labors as pastors.

A. *Personalities*

∽ **No. 103. Three priests in *The Book of Margery Kempe* (1430s).**
The Book of Margery Kempe, ed. Sanford Brown Meech and Hope Emily Allen, *EETS* o.s. 212 (Oxford, 1940). Modernized by JS.

[*Margery Kempe (c. 1373–c. 1440), townswoman of Bishop's Lynn and self-proclaimed mystic, dictated her remarkable autobiography to the priest who served as her spiritual counselor.*]

A vicar once came to this creature asking her to pray for him and find out whether it would be more pleasing to God for him to leave his cure and his benefice or keep them, since he thought that he was of little good to his parishioners. When this creature was at her prayers she called to mind this matter and Christ said to her spirit: "Bid the vicar to keep his cure and his benefice, and to be diligent in preaching to and teaching his parishioners in person. Sometimes he should have others teach them my laws and my commandments so that he will never be at fault. And if they are never the better for it, he shall have his reward none the less." And so she gave him this message as commanded and the vicar kept his cure. . . . [chapter 23, p. 53]

Once it happened that a young man came to this priest [her amanuensis], whom he had never seen before, complaining to the priest of the poverty and trouble he had fallen into through misfortune. He explained his misfortune, saying that he too had received holy orders to be a priest. But once he was too hasty defending himself, though he didn't choose to do this—he had to or his enemies would have killed him. He struck one or two of the men who, he said, were [consequently] either dead or likely to die. And so he had fallen into an irregular life and could not perform his priestly orders without dispensation from the Court of Rome. For this reason he fled from his friends and dared not return home for fear of being seized for their deaths. The priest believed the young man's words since he seemed an amiable fellow, good-looking, well behaved and of good countenance, sober in speech, and priestly in his manner and dress. He took compassion on his misfortune, proposing to get him some friends to help relieve the young man's distress and comfort him. He went to a noted citizen of Lynn, a mayor's equal and a merciful man, who had been quite sick for a long time. He told him and his wife, a very good woman, about the young man's troubles, trusting that they would give him fitting alms for the young man, as they had often done for others on whose behalf he asked. The creature about whom this book is written happened to be present and heard how the priest pleaded for this young man and how he praised him. She was strongly moved in her spirit against that young man. She said that they had many poor neighbors who, they well enough knew, had great need to be helped and relieved. It was more charitable for them to help those that they knew to be of good disposition and their own neighbors instead of strangers whom they didn't know; for while many outwardly speak and present themselves well before people, God knows what their souls are like. The good man and his wife thought that what she said was right and therefore they gave him no alms. At that point the priest was not pleased with this creature, and when he met with her alone he said how she had prevented him from getting any alms for the young man, who was a well-behaved man in his opinion and he admired his disposition. The creature said, "Sir, God knows what his disposition is, for, as far as I know, I've never seen him. But I understand what his disposition could be. Therefore, sir, if you follow my advice and my intuition, let him choose to help himself as well as he can and don't meddle with him, for he shall deceive you in the end."

The young man always went to the priest, flattering him and saying that he had good friends in other places who would help him if they knew where he was—and quickly too—and they also would thank those people who had supported him in his distress. The priest, trusting that it would be as this young man told him, lent him money with good will in order to help him. The young man asked the priest to excuse him if he didn't see him for two or three days; he would be gone for a little while, but he would come back shortly and bring him the borrowed money right well and truly. The priest, having confidence in his promise, was content, wishing him love and farewell until the day he promised to return.

When he was gone, the aforesaid creature came to understand through a feeling in her soul that our Lord would show that he was an untrustworthy man and would not come back. To prove whether this feeling was true or false, she asked the priest where the young man he had praised so much was. The priest said that he had gone a short distance away and he trusted that he would come back. She said that she suspected that he would see him no more, and he never saw him again. Then he repented that he had not followed her advice.

A short while after this happened, there came another lying rascal—an old man—to the priest and offered to sell him a breviary, a good little book. The priest went to the aforesaid creature and asked her to pray for him and find out whether God willed that he should buy the book or not. While she prayed he encouraged the man as well as he could and then he went back to this creature and asked how she felt. "Sir," she said, "don't buy the book from him, for he is not to be trusted; you'll find that out if you meddle with him."

Then the priest asked the man if he might see this book. The man said that he didn't have it with him. The priest asked him how he came by the book. He said he was the executor of the estate of a priest who was related to him, and he had charged him to sell it and dispose of it for him.

"Father," the priest said (out of respect), "why do you offer me this book rather than to another man or another priest, since there are so many more prosperous and richer priests in this church than I? And I well know that you've never known me before now."

"In truth, sir," he said, "I don't know you, but I have good will toward you. Also, it was his will, who owned the book before, that if I knew any young priest who I thought serious and well-disposed, he should have this book before any other man for less cost so that he might pray for him. These reasons move me to come to you rather than anyone else."

The priest asked where he was staying. "Sir," he said, "but five miles from this place at Pentney Abbey."

"I've been there," said the priest, "and I've not seen you there."

"No, sir," he said again, "I've only been there a little while, but now I have a livery there, God be thanked."

The priest asked him if he could take a look at the book and see if they could reach an accord. He said, "Sir, I hope to be here again next week and bring it with me. And, sir, I promise you that you shall have it before any other man if you like it."

The priest thanked him for his good will and so they parted. But the man never came to the priest again, and then the priest knew well that the aforesaid creature's feeling was right. [chapter 24, pp. 55–57]

One time, when the aforesaid creature was in contemplation, she hungered sorely for God's word and said, "Alas, Lord, with as many clergy as you have in this world, would that you send me one who could fill my soul with your word and with readings from Holy Scripture; for I think that my soul is so hungry that all the clergy who preach cannot satisfy it. If I had enough money, I would daily pay a gold noble to have a sermon every day, since your word is dearer to me than all the gold in this world. Therefore, blessed Lord, have pity on me since you have taken away the anchorite who was my single solace and comfort and who many times refreshed me with your holy word." Then our Lord Jesus Christ answered her in her soul saying, "Someone shall come from far away who shall fulfill your desire." And, many days after this answer, there came a priest new to Lynn who had never known her before. When he saw her walking down the streets he was greatly moved to speak to her and he asked other folks what sort of woman she was. They said that they trusted God that she was a very good woman. Afterwards the priest sent for her, asking her to come speak with him and with his mother, for he had rented a room for his mother and himself and they lived there together. Then the said creature went to find out what he wanted and to speak with him and his mother, both of whom were very friendly to her. Then the priest got a book and read about how our Lord, seeing the city of Jerusalem, wept over it, rehearsing the misfortunes and sorrows that would befall it, since it knew not the time of its visitation [Luke 19:41–44].

When the said creature heard read how our Lord wept, she wept bitterly and cried aloud, though the priest and his mother didn't know the cause of her weeping. When she stopped, they rejoiced and were happy in the Lord. Then she left them. When she had gone, the priest said to his mother, "I wonder why this woman weeps and cries so? Still, I think she is a good woman and I greatly desire to speak more with her." His mother was very pleased and advised him to do so. Afterwards the priest loved her and trusted her greatly and blessed the time that he had known her; for he found great spiritual comfort from her which prompted him to read much good scripture and many doctors of the church which he would not have read had she not been there. He read to her many a good book of high contemplation and other books, such as the Bible with the doctors' commentaries on it, St. Bridget's book [*Heavenly Revelations*], [Walter] Hilton's book [*Scale of Perfection*], [pseudo]-Bonaventure's *Prick of Love,* [Richard Rolle's] *Fire of Love,*[1] and other such books. Then she realized that it was a spirit sent from God that had said to her, when she had complained of a lack of reading, "Someone shall come from far away who shall fulfill your desire." Thus, she knew by experience that it was a very true spirit. The aforesaid priest read books to her for the better part of seven or eight years, greatly increasing his own knowledge and merit; and he suffered many evil words because of her love, since he read her so many books and approved of her weeping and crying. Afterwards he received a benefice with a large cure of souls, and on account of this he was glad that he had read so much before. [chapter 58, pp. 142–44]

No. 104. A vicar's good behavior praised (1346).

Reg. Trillek (Hereford), p. 35. Trans. WJD.

From John, etc., to all the faithful in Christ who receive this letter, health in him who is the way, the truth, and the life. Our Savior, who is the very essence of the truth, was born and came into this world as a witness to give testimony to the truth, to holiness and merit for all the faithful, but in particular, to church leaders to whom he promised life eternal for the declaration of that truth. He gave them an example to work zealously for the spreading of that truth.

Here we have noted for your community that the reverend Ralph de Bridge, vicar of the church of Bridge Sollers, is a good and upright man, that he has not been suspended or excommunicated, and has not been taken to court for any reason. These things we have learned from the testimony of

[1] These last four were contemporary mystical treatises.

sworn witnesses. He has also been steadfast in residing in his vicarage ever since his appointment as vicar and has celebrated the liturgies in a praiseworthy manner. In whose testimony, the seal, etc. Given, etc.

∾ No. 105. Episcopal prisons: Constitutions of Archbishop Boniface, c. 29 (1262).

Councils and Synods, p. 684. Trans. WJD.

With a special injunction we ordain that every bishop have one or two prisons in his bishopric (he is to see that it is large enough and secure) for the safekeeping of criminous clerics under canonical censure, that is, caught in a crime or convicted of it. And if any cleric be so incorrigibly wicked that he would have suffered capital punishment had he been a layman, we judge such a cleric to life in prison. But we decree that the ancient laws be observed with regard to those who do not transgress willfully, or in a premeditated fashion, but by chance, through anger or madness.

∾ No. 106. Complaint of the parishioners of Burmington against their chaplain (1484).

Registrum Annalium Collegii Mertonensis, 1483–1521, ed. H. E. Salter, Oxford Historical Society 76 (1923), pp. 33–34. Modernized by JS.

[*Merton College, Oxford had appropriated the parish of Wolford in the diocese of Worcester and its chapel of ease, Burmington, in 1266. In return for Burmington's tithes, the college's warden and senior fellows were obliged to appoint and support its chaplain. The account below records [1] Thomas Cocsey's letter to the college in support of the parishioners of Burmington; [2] the parishioners' articles of complaint against their college-appointed chaplain; [3] a copy of the college's investigation and dismissal of most of the same complaints two years before; and [4] the college recorder's note about the Burmington parishioners' longstanding recalcitrance.*]

[1] On the same day [March 19, 1484] we [the warden and fellows] received the following letter from Thomas Cocsey, Esq.: "Reverend Sirs, I commend me to you, etc., informing you that recently your parishioners and my servants of the town of Burmington with many other honest men of the country came to my place at Milkot to inform me of the great burden and trouble they have experienced through the meanness of their chaplain Sir Thomas Dyar of the said town. According to their report, the said Sir Thomas is not good and virtuously disposed in his living as a priest should be who has such a cure; and do not doubt that many have told me that they will testify to the same hereafter and give proof if the case requires. Notwithstanding that I trust in God that you and I shall hereafter find at more leisure some means

to make them amicable and friendly and to make a concord between them so that unity and peace may be had according to right and conscience; nevertheless I desire and pray you that it would please you—knowing how they both stand in this trouble—to send some honest priest or curate on to your cure of Burmington so that your parishioners and my poor servants may receive the sacraments of Holy Church during this holy time of Lent as Christian people ought, praying you heartily to do this at my request just as I would gladly do for you or any of yours if you requested me in any similar case; and Jesus preserve you, amen. Written at Milkot, the Tuesday after Saint Gregory's day [March 12].

Unto Master Doctor Fitzjames, warden of Merton College of Oxford and to all masters and fellows of the same be this delivered. Your beloved friend Thomas Cocsey, Esquire."

The following articles were put forward before Thomas Cocsey, Esq. by [Robert] Tole, parishioner of Burmington and certain other men from his neighborhood against Sir Thomas Dyar, the chaplain there. Since it appears that the said Thomas Cocsey has no jurisdiction in that place, he wrote the above letter to the college asking the college to intercede in order to bring peace between the two parties:

[2]   "To Master Cocsey,

Show your poor petitioners and servants, the parishioners of Burmington, how that one Sir Thomas Dyar of the said parish when he first arrived from the parish of Barton and proposed to be our priest, we understood his disposition and his previous administration of the parish of Barton to be such that we refused to take him as our priest and to let him dwell among us unless he bound himself by a pledge of forty pounds guaranteeing his good behavior and administration of the parish. Nor would he undertake any duties wrongfully, nor engage in any brawling, nor trouble any members of the said parish under pain of the fine stated above. It is his obligation to attest for his behavior as is specified in the said contract. It now happens that the said Sir Thomas desires to enact other duties and would bring in wrongful customs to the said parish—things that his predecessors before him never did, asked, or took from the said parish church of Burmington. First, the said Sir Thomas tends to take away and bear off small wax candles [from the church] to his place and burn them. He also sells them, and takes them to his own dwelling. [He also takes away] all manner of votive offerings given to the saints in the said church, to wit: tapers, candles, silver or any wooden ornaments whatsoever which are meant to maintain the said votive lights in worship of God, Our Lady, and all the saints. And moreover, the said Sir Thomas orders the churchwardens not to meddle with any of the votive offerings belonging to the church. And also, last Candlemas the said Sir Thomas argued with the parishioners both before and after mass about unblessed candles that were offered in the nave of the church before the images there that the parishioners had a devotion to, in addition to their offering that day. Also there is another complaint: the said Sir Thomas has more cattle grazing in the parishioners' common pasture than he ought to. Furthermore, the said Sir Thomas has openly said before all the parish what Robert Tole told him in confession. Furthermore, the said Sir Thomas will have the tenth penny for a calf if it is sold and three pence for a cow or else he will deprive them of their rights[2] as parishioners. [He did this to] one John Culper of the same parish last Easter who had sold a calf, and he made him pay the tenth penny for the calf and three pence for the milk of the cow, or he would not give him his rights contrary to our previous custom as far back as we can remember to pay no more but three pence and a half for a cow and a calf, and two pence and a half for a heifer and a calf. And furthermore, the sister-in-law of the said Sir Thomas, who lives in the house with him as his servant, has reported and said in the presence of John Hasting and certain other members of the parish that Sir Thomas wished to have her own sister in a sinful way. The parishioners are much aggrieved by these and other faults. And in order for the said parishioners to have their legal rights peacefully, as reason and conscience ask out of reverence for God and for charity, as it please your mastership to redress this grievance, so will the parish abide. Also the said Sir Thomas takes the tapers from the nave of the church in order to set them on the high altar and go in procession with them at the parish's expense. For the parson or his deputy ought to provide these lights, not the parish; this is the custom in every place."

[3] Regarding these articles, the warden and senior members responded that John More, Doctor of Canon Law and official of the Lord Bishop of Winchester, elected impartially by the consent of both parties, rendered his findings and judgment between the warden and his associates on one hand and the parishioners on the other: the said warden and his associates or their proctor are not liable for damages and should make no counter-claim concerning the articles about which the parishioners complained, excepting the complaints about Sir Thomas' infamous desire for the woman and about the candles in the church. This finding and judgment was given at Stow, June 3,

---

[2] I.e., the curate refused to allow them to receive Easter communion.

1482 as it appears of late under seal of the said official in our treasury. And so the said parishioners departed from us with shame, awaiting the arrival of the warden there.

[4] Note that on February 11 in the fourth year of King Edward's reign [1465], through an inquiry at Burmington made before the lord king's Escheator [who confiscated vacant fiefs], it was discovered through sworn jurors that the chapel of Burmington is and has been annexed to the parochial church of Wolford in the diocese of Worcester since time out of mind; and that this chapel was constructed by a certain lord of the village of Burmington whose name is unknown. This lord went to the Roman Curia to seek permission to build this chapel in order to avoid the danger that occurred when the bodies of the dead being taken for burial were carried across a certain stream running between Wolford and Burmington (with the understanding that the rights of the mother church of Wolford would always be upheld). Before this chapel was built, the village of Burmington was and still is part of the parish of Wolford. Because the parishioners of Burmington are terribly rebellious against their curates and especially against the church of Wolford, I have inserted the preceding information [into the register] so that it will be plain to everyone that the said village of Burmington is only a chapel, as is sufficiently clear in our register concerning the inquiry noted above. I fear that the reason why these people of Burmington are always so bitter and always going to extremes is because they love neither God nor the church.

◌ No. 107. Lawsuits (fifteenth century).

C. Trice Martin, "Clerical Life in the Fifteenth Century as illustrated by Proceedings of the Court of Chancery," *Archaeologia* 60, pt. 2 (1907): 353–78. Modernized by JS.

A. An elderly priest falsely accused of child molesting.

Piteously complaining, your humble petitioner Sir William Barbour of London, priest of the age of seventy-six years, pleads to your good lordship that one William Garrard of London, a draper, three years past urged and desired your said petitioner to instruct and teach one Elizabeth Garrard, then seven years old, kinswoman of the said William Garrard, as he said, the Our Father, Hail Mary, and Creed with further learning as at that time he taught thirty other young children. And so your petitioner did, thinking that Garrard was an honest man. And within four weeks afterward, Garrard of his crafty and malicious mind, alleged and said that your petitioner had molested the said Elizabeth and thereupon he commenced an action before the sheriffs of London against your petitioner. Whereupon twelve men were charged to investigate, who then acquitted your petitioner of the charge. And, gracious lord, now lately Garrard out of his malice has commenced an action of breach of law in the aforesaid matter before the sheriffs of London against your petitioner, and has craftily set up an inquest, which he intends to pass against your petitioner, a poor man, to his utter destruction unless your gracious lordship pleads for him in his behalf. May it therefore please your lordship that a writ of *certiorari*[3] be directed to the sheriffs of London, commanding them by the same to bring before your good lordship in the King's Chancery the cause of the arrest of your said petitioner, there to be adjudged by your good lordship according to good conscience. And he shall ever pray to God for your grace long to endure. [pp. 359–60]

B. Parishioners attempt to blackmail a priest.

Your poor and devoted petitioner Sir William Pierson meekly beseeches your good and gracious lordship that one Agnes Coll, wife of John Coll, a tiler, being associated with certain evilly-disposed persons, came to the house of your petitioner and spoke to one of his servants, desiring to speak with his master. And thereupon your said petitioner came out of his house into the churchyard to find out what she wanted. Then she desired to speak with him inside his house, and after she got inside she left and said nothing to him at the time, but she said she would soon come again. And then she went to her evilly-disposed associates and asked them to come with her to your said petitioner's house and wait at his door until she went inside. And they did so, your petitioner not knowing about this or imagining anything wrong, as God knows. And when Agnes had come into his yard, she desired to see his rooms, but your petitioner denied her and said no, asking her to say what she wished there in his yard, for she should not come into his rooms. And then she took your petitioner by the arm and said that she had come to inquire about five shillings that her husband owed him. And thereupon the evilly-disposed people that she was associated with looked in at his door and said, "You dishonest priest, what are you doing with that woman?" And with that they approached him and said that if he did not give them a great reward they would send him to prison and utterly shame him. And he would in no way agree to give them anything, but he sent for his neighbors who lived around him to relate the incident to them. And then the accusers departed from your petitioner and would not stay there since

---

[3] A writ which transferred a case from a lower court to a superior court when a petitioner claimed that he could not receive impartial justice in the lower court.

they could not have their way. But then they went to John Coll, husband of
Agnes, and made him affirm a charge of breach of law before the sheriffs
of London against your petitioner, of which he was acquitted. And now the
said John has affirmed another charge of breach of law against your petitioner before the said sheriffs and has declared against him alleging that he
tried to take from his wife his goods and chattels to the value of six marks
and to his damage £100, which as God knows is utterly false. And as a consequence a jury has been summoned for the inquest to which some of the
said evilly-disposed people associated with Agnes at the time have been appointed, and so propose to condemn your petitioner for the aforementioned
sums, against all right and conscience, and to his uttermost undoing unless
your gracious lordship pleads for him in his behalf. Therefore, may it please
your lordship carefully to consider the aforesaid matter and to grant a writ
of *certiorari* to be directed to the sheriffs of London, etc. [pp. 358–59]

C. Broken promises over a pious bequest.

Your poor petitioners Richard Joy and Henry Joy of the town of South-
wold in the county of Suffolk, executors of the testament of John Joy,
meekly beseech your good and gracious lordship that the said John by his
last will bequeathed to the honor of Almighty God and the adorning of his
church £12 to make a chrismatory for the church, which money lately rested
in the keeping of your said petitioners. To perform the said good deed they
had communication with one Sir John Hopton, their vicar, who promised to
purvey to the church a chrismatory that none could match in Suffolk. And
afterwards the vicar bargained with a goldsmith at Cambridge and agreed,
as he said, to give £28 to the goldsmith for the chrismatory. Thereupon he
wrote with his own hand to your beseechers describing the contract, and
showing furthermore that he had four sufficient men who guaranteed that
the goldsmith would carry out the contract. And since the vicar wrote furthermore in his letter that he had bought sixty ounces of broken silver at
three shillings an ounce, and also that the goldsmith needed to have some
money in hand, he asked your beseechers to send him by his servant, bringer
of the said letter, £8 12s. 4d., promising to answer them for it, as appears in
greater detail in the same letter, which we are ready to produce in evidence.
Trusting this promise and the letter, and out of the good zeal they had for
the church in this matter, your beseechers delivered to his servant the said
£8 12s. 4d., which money went solely to the hands of the vicar, as the same
servant will testify before your lordship. Now it happens that the appointed
day for making and finishing the chrismatory is past for over a year or more,
and your beseechers have many times requested the vicar to deliver them

the chrismatory ready made or else to return to them the £8 12s. 4d., but he has refused and still refuses to do so. And inasmuch as your beseechers do not have an indenture of the contract for the delivery of the said money to the vicar or any other bond sufficient to demand the money according to the common law, they are without remedy unless your gracious aid is showed to them in this behalf. May it please, therefore, your gracious lordship in augmenting the honor of God's church and so that hereafter lay people there may be gladder and more willing to help the ornaments of the said church, to grant a writ of *subpoena* directed to the said vicar, etc. [pp. 370–71]

D. A parish priest caught with stolen goods.

Sir William Paule, parish priest of the church of St. Andrew in Holborn in the suburbs of London, piteously pleads before your good and gracious lordship that on the 12th day of February, the first year of the reign of our sovereign lord the king that now is, three persons evilly disposed came into the church yard of the aforesaid church studying the same for a felony. And one of them then and there cast over a fence attached to the parsonage set within the churchyard, a wallet otherwise called a bag, in which was contained a partially gilded, footed cup with a cover, a footed, gilded cup made from a coconut with a cover, a piece of silver flatware, and a mazer with a narrow band. This wallet or bag and the goods in it thus cast over the fence came by information to the notice of your said petitioner by way of one Thomas Bermingham, a cloth-shearer, who lives next to the parish church of St. Andrew, through whom the wallet or bag and goods came into the possession of your said petitioner and nothing else. Immediately afterwards there came one Thomas Fereby of London, a goldsmith, to your petitioner, saying that the goods were his, feloniously stolen from him by the said three persons. Whereupon your said petitioner, believing Thomas, delivered to him on the 13th day of February, the year abovesaid, at the church of St. Andrew in Holborn, the wallet or bag and the goods aforesaid. Then and there he was completely satisfied and content with the matter. But since that time Thomas has said and still says that he is missing many other goods— more than were contained in the aforesaid wallet or bag—which your said petitioner never had or saw, as he will answer before Almighty God. The said Thomas has caused diverse necromancers to search for the whereabouts of these goods, and they have concluded, so he says, that your said petitioner has the goods with him, which is not at all true. And now Thomas has brought a charge of breach of law against your said petitioner for the goods delivered to him by your said petitioner as described above as well for the other goods as alleged, which never came into his possession. He alleges in the same charge that your said petitioner with force and arms took all the said goods out of the possession of the said Thomas in the parish of St. Peter in Cheapside, to his hurt and damage of 100 marks; and he intends by the same charge and by might and power to have your said petitioner condemned to pay great sums of money against all right and good conscience to the uttermost undoing of your petitioner unless your good lordship pleads for him in his behalf. Therefore, may it please your good and gracious lordship carefully to consider the aforementioned matter and to grant a writ of *subpoena* under a certain punishment to be contained in the same to be directed to the said Thomas Fereby at a certain day as it shall please your good lordship to set, and then and there to have an injunction from your good lordship that he nor any other person for him proceed any further in this action against your said petitioner, until the time when it is duly examined before your good lordship in right and good conscience. And this for the reverence of Almighty God and in the way of charity.

The Answer of Thomas Fereby to the petition of William Paule
The said Thomas says that the matter contained in the petition is a matter determinable before the common law and not in the Court of Chancery. By way of answer he says that it is true that on the 12th day of February, as described in the petition, three evilly-disposed persons took and bore away the goods specified in the petition and diverse other goods and plate taken from the dwelling house of the said Thomas Fereby in the Cheapside of London into the said churchyard. With the same Thomas Fereby immediately in pursuit of them, the evilly-disposed persons saw that they could in no way escape the same Thomas, so they wound around and cast all the plate and goods over the fence within the aforesaid churchyard attached to the dwelling house of the said William Paule. Since the goods and plate were within the closed and locked fence, Thomas Fereby could in no way get at them without the permission and consent of William Paule. Whereupon Thomas Fereby, perceiving and knowing his goods and plate to be cast over the fence and closed up behind the same, as before stated, asked William Paule to allow him to go within the fence to fetch and have his goods. But William for no request nor desire would allow Thomas to do so, but William—more like a miscreant than a Christian priest—untruly affirmed and said to Thomas Fereby and to many other credible persons both by the Holy Sacrament that he had used and by the holy mass and by many other great oaths, not more serious, that the plate and goods were not cast within the fence. And before William would allow Thomas Fereby or any other per-

son on his behalf to come within the fence to fetch his goods, William and Thomas Bermingham wrongfully took the same goods and plate and divided them between them. And afterwards Thomas many times expended great persistence and labor to his great hurt, cost, and charge, to William and Thomas Bermingham to deliver to him his goods and plate. And they refused to do that, swearing by as great oaths as Christian men might ever hear that they had no part in the matter. And after that, about the 18th day of February, the goods specified in the petition were found in the dwelling place of the aforesaid William buried in the ground at the foot of his bed, as it shall be sufficiently proved before your lordship. All of these matters Thomas Fereby is ready to prove as this court will allow, and he prays to be dismissed out of this court with his reasonable costs and damages for the wrongful vexation of him. [pp. 371–73]

E. An abused vicar.

Your humble and faithful petitioner Sir John Hickson, priest and vicar of Wisborough Green in the county of Sussex, piteously pleads before your lordship that after he was instituted and inducted into the said benefice, he required and demanded that those who bore office or were ministers within the said church should swear obedience to him in accordance with the provincial constitutions, as your lordship well knows and understands. And because of that, various of his parishioners took displeasure against him; namely, William Lutman, John Napper, Walter Milner, Richard Hifold, Richard Shudde, and John Chaper, saying that your said suppliant would bring new customs and practices among them; and so they moved and excited certain ministers within the church not to make their oath of obedience. For this reason the ministers were cited [to appear before an ecclesiastical court], and at their appearance before their Ordinary they were ordered to give their obedience to your suppliant as their curate and to be ruled by him in all things and observances concerning the ministering of divine services within the said church. For this reason the said persons began to treat maliciously and intrigue against your suppliant and aroused others of the parish to do the same. And also, the parishioners and many others of the parish claimed to make their regular entrance into the church by a door in the chancel, notwithstanding that they had diverse doors into the church in the nave of the church, and they tried to compel their curate to be bound to let them in and out the door in the chancel, as if they were the parish clerk, saying that it had been the custom for as long as they could remember for them to do so. And because your suppliant refused to allow this, they intrigued and plotted the utmost that they could do to the rebuke and de-

struction of your suppliant; so much so that when the church was robbed
and despoiled, the said persons alleged and affirmed that your suppliant had
knowingly and willingly assented to the same, even though—as God knows
and as he has openly and lawfully cleared himself of the charge—he was
never guilty, as appears more plainly in his letters of purgation and procla-
mation. And the said persons have labored at various seasons in various
court sessions held in the county to have your suppliant indicted for the felony. The persons who had to make judgment in this matter, weighing in
their conscience that no evident proof could be showed or argued in the
matter, in no way could find your suppliant guilty of the said offence. And
the said persons, seeing that they could not obtain their malicious ends by
that means, pleaded before a justice of the peace of the county for a warrant
both for surety of the peace and for suspicion of felony which was insufficient. And by virtue of the same, the said persons, when your suppliant
had administered divine services and holy bread to them one Sunday, and
as he knelt before the altar offering his intercessions and prayers, laid violent
hands on him and restrained him and treated him so roughly that in the
same place they drew blood from him (because of which many of them
were excommunicated and remain so). And so with outrageous violence
they drew him out of the church and rashly set him openly and shamefully
in the stocks; and after that, with his arms bound by a cord like a thief, they
led him to the king's jail at Gifford where, by their untrue allegations, he
was treated as a thief and lay in great duress of imprisonment through
which he acquired unbearable costs and charges. Whereupon, my lord [the
earl] of Arundel, understanding the ungodly and unlawful demeaning
caused by the said persons, sent to the jail in all good haste for the deliver-
ance of your suppliant, on whose authority he was released. And after that,
by the command of my said lord, the matter was committed to the authority
of certain worshipful gentlemen; that is to say, Edward Berkelay, Philip
Lowes, James Byne, and Thomas Bartolot. But the parishioners, understanding that the said gentlemen were fully disposed to order that certain money
be given to your suppliant in compensation for the manifest injury and
wrong that was done to him, refused to abide by the order, choosing rather
to abide by the determination of the common law. But your suppliant is not
in the position to go to court with them, seeing that they have such great
riches and also that they have engrossed and influenced the region to abide
by their intent so that if the matter should go to court, your suppliant shall
never prevail against them. Therefore may it please your gracious lordship,
benignly considering the aforesaid matters, to direct writs of *subpoena* to
each one of the said persons, commanding them to appear before your lord-

ship at a day to be fixed to answer to these matters, and at their appearance to provide by your wisdom such sharp punishment and reformation therein as they may take notice and fear to do or attempt any such things thereafter, so that your suppliant may live and rest in peace according to the laws of the church and of the realm. And this for the love of God and in defense of his church, seeing that your said suppliant does not know where to have remedy in this matter except from your lordship. And he shall heartily pray to God for the preservation of your lordship during his natural life. [pp. 363–65]

∾ No. 108. A citation to unchaste clerks (1423).

Reg. Spofford, p. 35; Bishop's Register, p. 124.

Thomas [bishop of Hereford], etc. to John Berewe and William Stowe, notaries public, etc. Borne by public rumor there has come to our ears a lamentable and far too scandalous insinuation that certain clerks of our diocese beneficed and unbeneficed who have been infected by the crime of incontinence publicly and wickedly are keeping for love suspected women in their houses wherefore they incur most wickedly by the deed itself sentences of suspension and excommunication shown by the sacred canons provided for the purpose. We, indeed, who are not able by right of our office in accordance with justice to pass over with closed eyes so great a habit of offending without great danger to our conscience, and lest such heinous sin should be left unpunished and that the punishment of such might be an example to others, command you forthwith that all such delinquents the names of which are written on the back of these present orders be cited by our authority as ordinary, etc., to appear before us or our commissioners in this matter to answer and further to receive what is just. Given on the last day of December, in the year of our Lord written above.

B. Crises

∾ No. 109. A priest confesses to Lollardy (1429).

Heresy Trials in the Diocese of Norwich, 1428–31, ed. Norman P. Tanner, Camden Fourth Series 20 (London, 1977), pp. 94–97. Trans. JS.

In the name of the Lord, Amen. Before you, reverend father in Christ and lord, Lord William [Alnwick], by the grace of God, Bishop of Norwich, I, your subject, Robert Cavel, parochial chaplain of the parish church of Bungay [Suffolk] in your diocese, considering and contemplating that prior to now I had frequent communication with notorious heretics in your diocese—namely, with William Whyte, Hugo Pye (both condemned heretics), and with other known heretics—in their secret schools, from which I acquired perverse and erroneous doctrines, confess that I believed and maintained all the following articles which I adhered to in good faith:

First, that the sacrament of baptism done in water according to the form used by the church should be considered of little or no use since as soon as the soul of an infant is united to its body in its mother's womb it is filled with the grace of the Holy Spirit, which is baptism enough. And when this little child reaches maturity and needs to learn how to understand God's word, this earlier infusion of grace suffices for confirmation.

Next, that verbal confession should be made to no priest, but only to God since he alone forgives sins.

Next, that the remission of sins comes exclusively from God; thus, no priest or man should enjoin penance to a sinner.

Next, that no priest ordained according to the rite of the church has the power of consecrating the Body of Christ at the altar. After the sacramental words are offered by such a priest, unchanged material bread remains on the altar.

Next, that no one is obliged to fast during Lent, ember days, Fridays, and saints' feast days prescribed by the church. It is permissible for any faithful person to eat meat and drink anything with no distinction during these times and days.

Next, that on Sundays and other feast days it is permissible for anyone to do any type of work except for any servile work that in their teachings these heretics declare to be sinful or vices.

Next, that tithes and offerings should be withheld from the clergy and their churches, although this should be done prudently.

Next, that the relics of the saints—namely, the flesh and bones of dead men—should not be venerated by the people in any way. They should not be removed from stinking graves, nor placed in silver or gold containers; those doing this commit idolatry.

Next, that the celibacy of priests and nuns is not commendable; it would be better for them to marry.

Next, that the mutual consent of their love for Jesus Christ suffices to make a marriage between a man and a woman; there is no need for spoken vows to be exchanged nor for any blessing by the church.

Next, that it is not sinful to go against the commands of the gospels.

Next, that no one should fear ecclesiastical censure or excommunication.

Next, that no one should offer prayers to any saint; one should pray to God alone.

Next, that no honor should be shown to any image of Christ, or of the

Blessed Mary, or of any saint. Since trees growing in the forest have more life and power, they should sooner be adored than dead stone or wood carved in the likeness of man.

Next, that if the Passion of Christ was useful and precious, the death of the martyr St. Thomas [Becket] was accursed and is worthless and blameworthy.

Next, that no one should go on pilgrimages, except to the poor.

Next, that it is unlawful to kill anyone, even someone legally guilty of theft or homicide.

Next, that no one should fight over his inheritance or for his country; those doing so lack charity.

Because of these errors and heresies, I, the aforesaid Robert Cavel, have been judicially summoned before you, reverend father; and you, with paternal care, have fully instructed and informed me that the aforesaid articles judicially confessed by me to you—which I believed, held, and affirmed—contain in them notorious errors and manifest heresies which by the determination of the Holy Roman Church are contrary and repugnant. Therefore, wishing to abide by the teaching of Holy Mother Church, and considering that she never closes her bosom to those wishing to return to her, and that God does not desire the death of sinners but rather that they be converted and live [Ezek. 18:23], with a pure heart I detest, despise, and renounce my errors and the aforesaid heresies and any others whatsoever; the aforementioned opinions that I admit before you are erroneous and heretical and are contrary and repugnant to the faith of the Holy Mother and Universal Church of Rome. And since I have publicly proved myself to be corrupted as well as unfaithful through these errors and heresies which I wrongly held, believed, and affirmed, so that I may return at this very hour to my former uncorrupted and faithful self, I promise that I will faithfully preserve in any way whatsoever the faith and teaching of Holy Mother Church. And I renounce and abjure any kind of error and heresy, teaching and opinion which is contrary to the determination and faith of the Holy Roman Church, especially the aforementioned articles or opinions judicially confessed by me before you. And in your presence, with my hand touching God's holy gospels, I swear that from this moment on I will never again hold, believe, or affirm, as I formerly did, any error or errors, heresy or heresies, or any false teaching against the faith of Holy Mother Church and the determination of the Roman Church. Nor will I obstinately defend, either personally or through any third party, any person holding, believing, or affirming errors or heresies. Nor will I give counsel, aid, or favor to heretics or any person suspected of heresy. I will neither believe them nor become acquainted with

them. And if in the future I recognize or discover heretics or anyone suspected of heresy, or favorers, comforters, counselors, or defenders of heresy,
or any persons making secret conventicles or holding contrary or peculiar
opinions at odds with the common teaching of the church, I will endeavor
to give you, reverend father, certain and speedy notice of them. In your absence I will notify your spiritual vicar-general if they are within your diocese, or the diocesans of any other diocese. May God and these holy gospels
give me aid.

In witness whereof, I, the aforesaid Robert Cavel, write here in my own
hand the sign of the holy cross †. And I put my seal on one half of this written
indenture which will remain in your possession in your register. The other half
of the indenture, sealed with your seal, I will keep in my possession to remain
with me for as long as I live. Given at the collegiate church of St. Mary's in the
Fields in Norwich, under your seal on the third day of March, A.D. 1429.

∾ No. 110. A sower of rebellion: the priest John Ball during the Peasants' Revolt (1381).

Thomas Walsingham, *Historia Anglicana*, ed. H. T. Riley, Rolls Series 2 (London, 1864), pp. 32–34.
Trans. JS.

About John Ball, the Priest

Also on that day [Saturday, July 13], [Chief Justice] Robert [Tresilian],
after hearing him confess to the basest crimes, sentenced the priest John Ball
(whom men from Coventry had captured and taken the day before to St.
Albans into the presence of the king, against whom he had so seriously committed high treason) to be drawn, hanged, beheaded, disemboweled, and
quartered (as the common term puts it). His execution was put off until
Monday after Lord William [Courtenay], the bishop of London, intervened
out of concern for the salvation of his soul, and sought that delay in order
for him to do penance.

For more than twenty years he had chased after the common people's
favor more than merit in God's eyes by constantly preaching in various
places those things that he knew won popular approval, disparaging churchmen as well as secular lords. Of course he taught people that they should
not give tithes to their curate unless the person giving them were richer than
the vicar or rector who received them. He also taught that tithes and offerings due the curate should be held back if the parishioners' lives were better
than the priest's. He taught that no one was suited for the kingdom of God
who had not been born of married parents. He also taught the perverse doctrines of the faithless John Wyclif, the opinions and mad falsehoods that he

held, and many other things it would take too long to tell. Due to this, after
the bishops in whose parishes he presumed to teach such things forbade him
to preach anymore in churches, he took it upon himself to preach in squares,
streets, and meadows. He was never let down by his listeners among the
common people, whom he took pains to attract to his sermons by disparaging the church's prelates and by his flattering words.

After he had been excommunicated when he would not desist, he was
put into prison, where he predicted that he would be delivered by twenty
thousand of his friends. Later this happened when the kingdom fell into the
turmoil mentioned above [i.e., the Revolt], and the common people broke
open all the jails and forced the prisoners to leave. After he had been freed
from prison in this manner, he followed them, goading them to do many
wicked things, and preaching that these things absolutely needed to be done.
At Blackheath, where two hundred thousand common people had all come
together, he began a sermon with words like this to poison even more people
with his teachings:

> "When Adam delved and Eve spun,
> Who was then a gentleman?"

Continuing the sermon, he used the words of this proverb, which he
had taken as his theme, to try to put forward and prove the idea that, from
the beginning, everyone was created equal by nature, and that serfdom had
been introduced through the unjust oppression of good-for-nothing men
against God's will. For, if it had pleased God to create serfs, he surely would
have established from the beginning of the world who would be a serf and
who a lord. But they should consider that now is the moment granted to
them by God in which, having cast off the yoke of long-lasting serfdom,
they could—if they wished—delight in the freedom for which they had long
strived. For this reason, he warned them that they should be prudent men;
they should hasten to act right now with a love like that of the good yeoman
tending his fields, rooting out and mowing down the harmful weeds that
are wont to choke the crops: first, by killing the realm's greater lords; next,
by destroying the country's lawyers, judges, and jurors; and finally, they
should snatch from this earth anyone whom they knew would in the future
harm their community. And thus at last they would create for themselves
peace and security in the future if, after the magnates were pulled down,
there were equal liberty, the same nobility, like dignity, and similar power
among them.

When he had preached these and many other absurdities, the common
rabble honored him with such favor that they proclaimed he should be
the next archbishop and Chancellor of the realm; he alone was worthy of

the honor of the archbishopric. The current archbishop was a traitor to the realm and the commons; he should be beheaded wherever in England he could be seized.[4]

In addition, he sent a letter filled with riddles to the leaders of the common people of Essex urging them to finish what they started. It was later found in the sleeve of some man hanged [in punishment] for the turmoil. This is what it said:

"John Schep, sometime Saint Mary's priest of York and now of Colchester greets well John Nameless, and John the Miller, and John the Carter, and bids them to beware of guile in the borough and to stand together in God's name. And he bids Piers Plowman to go to his work, and to chastise well Hob [i.e., Robin] the Robber, and to take with you John Trueman and all his fellows (but none other), and be careful to have one head and no more.

John the Miller has ground small, small, small;
The King's son of heaven shall pay for all.
Beware or you'll have woe,
Know your friend from your foe;
Have enough and say 'Ho!'
And do well, and better, and flee sin.
And seek peace, and keep therein.
And so bids John Trueman and all his fellows."

John Ball confessed that he wrote this letter and sent it to the common people; he also admitted many other things he had done. Due to this, as we have said, he was drawn, hanged, and beheaded at St. Albans on July 15 in the king's presence. His corpse was cut into four parts and sent to four cities in the realm.

∾ No. 111. A petition for special ordinations and dispensations during the Black Death from William la Zouche, archbishop of York (October 12, 1349).
Archivum Secretum Vaticani, Registra Supplicationum 21, fol. 46v. Trans. WJD.

Most Holy Father. On account of the pestilence and deaths of people taking place in the diocese and province of York at this time, it is hard to find adequate numbers of priests for the cure and direction of souls and for administering the sacraments of the church. Your humble petitioner, William, archbishop of York, begs your holiness that he, or any of his suffragans, or any Catholic bishop may for one year hold ordinations to all ranks of clerics, beneficed and non-beneficed, beyond the commonly held

---

[4]Archbishop Simon Sudbury, who was also Chancellor, was seized and beheaded by the London mob on June 14, 1381.

times and the four ember days as often as he sees fit. Also, that he be able to dispense, under apostolic authority, up to forty clerics in the diocese from minority of age (those who are at least twenty-one years old) and illegitimacy so that they may be ordained to any holy order and be promoted to an ecclesiastical benefice, even one with a cure of souls attached and to keep this benefice.

❧ No. 112. A bishop's pastoral counsel during the Black Death: Mandate of Bishop Ralph of Bath and Wells on confessions in time of plague (1349).

F. A. Gasquet, *The Black Death of 1348 and 1349* (London: Bell and Sons, 1908), pp. 93–95.

The contagious nature of the present pestilence, which is ever spreading itself far and wide, has left many parish churches and other cures, and consequently the people of our diocese, destitute of curates and priests. And inasmuch as priests cannot be found who are willing out of zeal, devotion, or for a stipend to undertake the care of the aforesaid places, and to visit the sick and administer to them the Sacraments of the Church (perchance for dread of the infection and contagion), many, as we understand, are dying without the Sacrament of Penance. These, too, are ignorant of what ought to be done in such necessity, and believe that no confession of their sins, even in a case of such need, is useful or meritorious, unless made to a priest having the keys of the Church. Therefore, desiring, as we are bound to do, the salvation of souls, and ever watching to bring back the wandering from the crooked paths of error, we, on the obedience you have sworn to us, urgently enjoin upon you and command you—rectors, vicars, and parish priests—in all your churches, and you deans, in such places of your deaneries as are destitute of the consolation of priests, that you at once and publicly instruct and induce, yourselves or by some other, all who are sick of the present malady, or who shall happen to be taken ill, that *in articulo mortis,* if they are not able to obtain any priest, they should make confession of their sins (according to the teaching of the apostle) even to a layman, and, if a man is not at hand, then to a woman. We exhort you, by the present letters, in the bowels of Jesus Christ, to do this, and to proclaim publicly in the aforesaid places that such confession made to a layman in the presumed case can be most salutary and profitable to them for the remission of their sins, according to the teaching and the sacred canons of the Church. And for fear any, imagining that these lay confessors may make known confessions so made to them, shall hesitate thus to confess in case of necessity, we make known to all in general, and to those in particular who have already heard these confessions, or who may in future hear them, that they are bound by the precepts of the Church to conceal and keep them secret; and that, by a decree of the sacred canons, they are forbidden to betray such confession by word, sign, and by any other means whatever, unless those confessing so desire. And (further) should they do otherwise, let such betrayers know that they sin most gravely, and incur the indignation of Almighty God and of the whole Church. And since late repentance (when, for example, sickness compels and the fear of punishment terrifies) often deceives many, we grant to all our subjects, who in the time of the pestilence shall come to confession to priests having the keys of the Church and power to bind and loose, before they are taken sick, and who do not delay till the day of necessity, forty days of indulgence. To every priest also who shall induce people to do this, and hear the confessions of those thus brought to confess whilst in health, we grant the same by the mercy of God Almighty, and trusting to the merits and prayers of His glorious Mother, of the Blessed Peter, Paul, and Andrew the Apostles, our patrons, and of all the Saints. You shall further declare to all thus confessing to lay people in case of necessity, that if they recover they are bound to confess the same sins again to their own parish priest. The Sacrament of the Eucharist, when no priest can be obtained, may be administered by a deacon. If, however, there be no priest to administer the Sacrament of Extreme Unction, faith must, as in other matters, suffice for the Sacrament. . . . Given at Winchcomb on the fourth ides of January [January 10], in the twentieth year of our consecration [1349].

ᘂ No. 113. Archbishop William Courtenay requests prayers for the general welfare of the realm (1382).

Concilia, Wilkins, vol. 3, pp. 155-56. Trans. JS.

William by divine permission, etc. to his venerable brother, our lord Robert [Braybrooke], by God's grace the bishop of London, sends greetings and brotherly love in the Lord. The fearsome God, by whose commands all are subdued to the power of his will, sometimes punishes the sons of man— whom he loves, tests, and chastises—with various kinds of scourges and tempests while they live on this earth, instead of damning them for eternity. Without a doubt this realm of England will be sunk down by the divisions of war, which exhaust and consume the means of wealth, and by many other misfortunes because of the exceptional pride and the growing vices of its inhabitants and their uncounted sins, and by pestilence and all kinds of storms, which sadly boiled up for a long while in other kingdoms, unless the merciful Lord, in answer to the prayers of the faithful, reins in his wrath, and remembers his mercy. And so our most excellent prince and lord, Lord Richard [II], by God's grace illustrious king of England and France, intently reflecting on these things, zealously implored us in his parliament together with the nobles and the community of his realm also there, that we should order devout prayers to be poured forth through our whole province for the peace of the Holy Church and for his realm, and for temperate weather; and that Almighty God himself in his great mercy will save and protect his kingdom of England from these kinds of misfortunes, pestilences, and tempests, and from sudden death. Therefore, we enjoin and command you, brother, strictly obliging you by our power and authority, each and every of our fellow bishops and suffragan bishops in the diocese of Canterbury, or, in their absence, their vicars general or their deputies, and the guardians of the spiritualities of the diocese of St. Asaph (whose see is temporarily vacant), that with all possible speed you admonish and induce everyone subject to you to beseech the Almighty with pious prayers such as these; and our suffragan bishops and others in priestly orders should celebrate masses in which they specially pray the prayers mentioned below; and they should preach sermons at suitable times and places, and should hold processions weekly on Wednesdays and Fridays; and with humility and devotion they should do any other acts of pious placation so that our Almighty God, pacified by their prayers, may rescue the English people from these misfortunes, show forth the aid of his grace on them, and through his ineffable mercy spare them from the dangers of storms and sudden death. In order to stir the minds of the faithful people of our province more willingly to these prayers, we mercifully grant in the Lord an indulgence of forty days relaxation of the penance imposed on them to all Christians in our province who have true contrition for their sins, and who celebrate the aforesaid masses, make such sermons, or participate in such processions, or attend and pray at such events; the same applies to those who are unable to attend these Wednesday and Friday processions because of distance or some other reason, but say instead five "Our Fathers" and five "Hail Marys." You should see to it that all of the above-mentioned is effectively carried out in your city and diocese of London.

Here follow the prayers we mentioned above:

"God, you who turned away the imminent ruin of the Ninevites through your mercy alone [Jon. 3:1–10], discharging the penance of conversion on them because you are merciful, look down, we beseech you, on your people prostrate in the face of your mercy, and through your mercy do not allow those whom you redeemed by the blood of your only begotten to suffer the punishment of sudden death, through the same Lord, etc. *Secret:*[5] Your church beseeches you, Almighty God, show forth your pacifying grace and

[5] The prayer said in a low voice preceding the canon of the mass.

overcome us with your mercy rather than your wrath, since if you wish to note our iniquity, no creature will endure; but mindful of the wonderful mercy by which you made us, do not let the work of your hands perish, through our Lord, etc. *Post-communion prayer:* Almighty and merciful God, look upon your people subject to your majesty, so that the holy reception of your sacraments may help us lest the fury of fierce death find us, through our Lord, etc." Given at our manor at Lambeth by our personal seal, June 8, A.D. 1382, the first year of our translation.

∾ No. 114. Clerics in the breach: a muster of the clergy (1415).
Reg. Mascall (Hereford), p. 87. Trans. WJD.

On the twenty-ninth day of June [1415], the bishop received a writ from the king that he should muster the clergy of the diocese, regular as well as secular, exempt and nonexempt, and gather and unite them into an effective fighting force as their abilities may allow. They are to be rallied and arrayed in resistance of the wanton malice and infestation of the enemies of Holy Mother Church, the king, and kingdom, under forfeiture of anything they can forfeit. Each and everything pertaining to this letter was put into effect and certified [as such] to the king's chancellor on the third day of July.

[*On August 11, six weeks after Henry V issued this writ, he sailed with his army to France. On October 25, 1415, they defeated the French at Agincourt.*]

C. Visitations

∾ No. 115. Bishop Robert Grosseteste describes his diocesan visitations (1250).
Councils and Synods, p. 265. Trans. JS.

In past times the bishops of Lincoln used to visit the religious houses subject to them in their diocese and to receive procurations from the houses for these visitations. But it is not at present my intention to speak about these customs, both approved and tolerated by long tradition. However, it might be fruitful to say a few words, if I may be permitted, about the new practices I introduced.

After I was raised to the episcopate, I reflected on the fact that I was both a bishop and a pastor of souls, and that I needed to look after the sheep committed to me with all diligence, just as scripture instructs and decrees, lest the blood of my sheep be looked for on my hands at the Last Judgment.

Thus, during my episcopacy I started making a circuit through every rural deanery, ordering the clergy of each deanery to assemble together at a specific day and place and forewarning the people to be present at that same day and place with their children who needed to be confirmed and to hear the word of God and be confessed. When the clergy and people had gathered, as often as not I myself expounded the word of God to the clergy and a Friar Preacher or Friar Minor preached to the people. Afterwards four friars would hear confessions and enjoin penances. And after confirming children on that and the following day, my clergy and I would attend to investigating, correcting, and reforming abuses in accordance with the rules of visitation.

The first time I made one of these circuits, certain people approached me, saying, as if in rebuke for the things I mentioned above, "Lord, what you are doing is new and unaccustomed." And I responded, "Every new thing which creates, advances, and perfects the new man, smashes and destroys the old man; that which is new is blessed and thoroughly pleasing to him who comes to renew the old man by his newness" [cf. Rom. 6:4–6].

◯ No. 116. Questions posed at visitations (1253).

Annales de Burton, ed. H. R. Luard, Rolls Series 36 (London, 1864). Trans. WJD.

[*This collection of inquiries is the most detailed of any that circulated in the middle ages. No extant visitation record, however, indicates that bishops were inclined to ask all of these questions. Rather, these inquiries served as a complete checklist, some parts which were bound to be more useful than others, that visitors could employ as guides for their pastoral investigations.*]

Each year the following inquiries should be made in each and every diocese in the kingdom of England concerning the life and behavior of the clergy and laity.

1. Whether any layman in the parish where he dwells has had sexual relations with any woman outside of marriage.
2. Whether any layman has committed adultery with another man's wife or a woman of any other status.
3. Whether any layman has committed incest or any other kind of lustful sin with his sister, daughter, or any other relation.
4. Whether a layman frequents the house of another person of whatever condition without reasonable cause.
5. Whether the laity are often drunk or frequent taverns or practice usury of any kind.
6. Whether any layman farms the free land of the church.
7. Whether any layman appropriates for his own use church tithes.
8. Whether donations given for candles or other specific uses in the church are used for other reasons by the rector or vicar.
9. Whether laypersons are ordered to take communion and make an offering after mass on Easter.

10. Whether any layperson or anyone of any condition or reputation falls away from the fold with the knowledge of the rector or vicar of the place.

11. Whether any layperson is notoriously proud, envious, greedy, slothful, quarrelsome, gluttonous, or lustful.

12. Whether any laypersons engage in business or play sports in sacred places, hold courts there, and whether these activities are forbidden by the bishop.

13. Whether any laypersons build quintains or hold scot-ales or, when carrying banners on visitations to the mother church, fight for first place.

14. Whether any layman or laywoman entertains the concubine of any man, whatever his status or condition; also, the identity of anyone who runs a house of ill repute.

15. Whether any sick person suffers from want of any sacrament when a priest has been properly summoned but is neglectful in his duties.

16. Whether any layperson or a person of any status dies intestate or without the sacraments because the rector or vicar was neglectful.

17. Whether any churches lack a priest.

18. Whether any churches have yet to be dedicated or whether any have been torn down without the bishop's permission as decreed by the Council of London [1237].

19. Whether Jews are living anywhere they have not customarily dwelled.

20. Whether any layperson has contracted a clandestine marriage, in cases not granted by the law, because church banns had been omitted.

21. Whether any laypersons insist on standing in the chancel with the priest.

22. Whether any layperson has arranged for spiritual services in a chapel without the bishop's permission.

23. In what manner the lay servants or assistants of parsons, abbots, priors, prioresses, and others behave themselves in their granges, houses, or lands.

24. Inquire diligently about how each church is taxed and how much the rector has given in aid to the lord pope.

25. Whether any rectors or vicars or priests are woefully illiterate.

26. Whether the sacrament of the eucharist is carried to the sick in every place with due reverence and in what manner it is reserved.

27. Whether the aforesaid [rectors and vicars] and others in holy orders are incontinent and, if so, how.

28. Whether the archdeacon disciplines those who are incontinent, how often and in what manner.

29. Whether those who were found guilty of incontinence or confessed to it have resigned their benefices willingly or underwent any other form of penance if they lapsed. Also, if any lapsed after penance.

30. Whether any beneficed clerics or men in orders have wives.

31. Whether any clerics frequent the churches of nuns without good reason.

32. Whether any cleric in holy orders has a female relative living with him from which evil rumors may arise.

33. Whether any clerics drink heavily, frequent taverns, or are known merchants, usurers, soldiers, wrestlers, or engage in other vices.

34. Whether any clerics are farming church lands, that is, putting out to farm or receiving in like manner churches or vicarages without the bishop's permission.

35. Whether any clerics are working as sheriffs, secular judges, or administering lands for lay people to whom they must render an account.

36. Whether any rectors negotiate with their hired chaplains to receive pay beyond the stipends granted from the rectors in the form of annual and triennial masses from others.

37. On simoniacs who enter the clergy and are ordained.

38. Whether any parish priest lacks an adequate salary from his rector.

39. Whether any rector or vicar has used church revenues to build in the cemetery or on land owned by the laity or stores tithes on lay property.

40. Whether any of the clergy bear arms, do not keep their tonsure, or wear inappropriate garb.

41. Whether anyone holds more than one cure of souls without dispensation.

42. Whether any rector or vicar is the son of the last incumbent.

43. Whether any priest extorts payment for the sacrament of penance or any other sacrament or levies costly fines.

44. Whether deacons hear confessions or administer other sacraments reserved to the priest alone.

45. Whether any rector or vicar fails to reside in his benefice.

46. Whether any church lacks sufficient and worthy clerics according to its provisions.

47. Whether cemeteries are enclosed, churches worthily built and decorated, and the sacred vessels and ornaments properly maintained.

48. Whether any priests use sour wine in celebrating mass.

49. Whether any beneficed clerics study or teach civil law.

50. Whether cartings are done on Sundays or feast days and by whom.

51. Whether the canon of the mass is recited correctly in every way.

52. Whether any layperson or cleric keeps in his house a cleric's concubine and where the dwellings of concubines are located.

53. Whether any priest celebrates mass twice a day, except when permitted and in his own church.

54. Whether any members of religious orders have appropriated tithes or

churches or anything else of the sort, and whether a pension or portion from the church has been augmented for the religious without the permission of the local bishop.

55. Whether vicars are pretending to be rectors or the other way around.

56. Whether illegitimate men who have not obtained a dispensation hold church benefices or have been ordained.

57. Whether men who have not been instituted by the bishop pass themselves off as rectors or vicars.

58. Whether altar cloths are clean and undyed.

59. Whether the archdeacon corrects laity charged with adultery or other public and notorious crimes and whether anyone has married improperly.

60. Whether there are penitentiaries appointed in every deanery for rectors, vicars, and priests and who they are.

61. Who the priests are who were ordained in Ireland or outside this diocese, where they are from and in what places they have ministered up to this time, and who licensed them to celebrate.

62. Whether there are sufficient episcopal penitentiaries in every archdeaconry.

63. Anything regarding the life and conduct of archdeacons, deans, and the parish clergy as well as the officials and servants of parsons and others.

64. Whether any hermits were instituted without the bishop's consent.

65. Whether any monks or religious dwell on their granges or other lands, how they live their spiritual lives, and what is their reputation.

66. Whether, during an episcopal vacancy, the dean and others have conspired in any way against the newly appointed bishop before his arrival.

67. Whether any archdeacons have received more in the way of procurations than they are entitled to under the new constitution.

68. Inquiry should be made into the activities of the executors of wills and whether they have acted well and faithfully in their testamentary duties; also, whether they paid what was owed to the bishop.

69. Whether markets are being held anywhere on Sundays.

ॐ No. 117. Visitations of parishes in Hereford (1397).

A. T. Bannister, "Visitation Returns in the Diocese of Hereford in 1397," *English Historical Review* 44 (1929): 279–89; 444–53; 45 (1930): 92–101; 444–63. Trans. WJD.

A visitation was made by the reverend father in Christ, John Trefnant, by God's grace lord bishop of Hereford, in the parish church of Burghill in Weston deanery on Monday, the last day of April, in the year of our Lord 1397 and the eighth year of the consecration of the same reverend father.

Brinsop [April 30]. The parishioners say that the chancel roof needs repair under the responsibility of the prior of Llanthony Prima, the rector there. They also say that Margaret Bayliss of Brinsop appropriated a piece of property worth eight shillings per year, reserved by a certain Ralph Terel, lord there, for the chantry of Our Lady in the parish church. Margaret has held the land for fifteen years. They say that Thomas Bayliss built a fence encroaching the cemetery by two feet long or more and that he lives on holy ground, breaking the confines of the cemetery. They say that the baptismal font is not secured, in defect[6] of the parishioners. They say that a certain Thomas Simmons and Matilda, whom he keeps as his wife, are cohabiting illegally and that a certain Sir William Penny, a cousin of the said Thomas within the fourth degree, had relations with Matilda before she married Thomas.

Wellington. The parishioners say that everything is well there.

Burghill. The parishioners were put off until the following Sunday at Wormsley, where they reported that the chancel wall needed repairs, in defect of the rector and vicar. The latter were ordered to repair the chancel before the next feast of St. John the Baptist under penalty of a twenty shilling fine. They also reported that John Watys, a carpenter, committed adultery with Sybil Weston. Harry Daundevyl, a tiler, refuses to live with his wife, fails to love her as a husband ought, and has an adulterous relationship with Matilda, whom he keeps in his house at Pyon. Walter Herring commits fornication with Agnes, recent mistress of William Leper. Davy Elvael is fornicating with Matilda of Wales to whom he is related within the fourth degree of affinity. It is rumored that Davy Matis is fornicating with Isabella Prestone. Also, the same Isabella refuses to bring the holy bread in her turn. They say that Jenkin Watkins, Harry Twiches, Robin Strange, John Kyf-flyhode, Jenkin Cedyche, and Hugyn Hull of Hull are common laborers on feast days and Sundays. They say that Juliana Twiches, Joanna Bolte, Margaret Been, Agnes Copp, and Agnes Scate do not come to church on Sundays and feast days. Also, Cecilia Claver, Helen Strange, Alice Watkins, Joanna, wife of William Watkins, Clemens Wolfe, and Rosa Trigg do not come to church. . . .

Dormington [May 1]. The parishioners say that Richard Hugges, unjustly and against the will of the parishioners, keeps in his care a number of ornaments and other things of the altar and refuses to let the parishioners use them. Richard withholds one measure of corn and eleven bushels of

---

[6]'In defectu,' a common, technical phrase in these documents, translated here in its literal sense as a failure to carry out a canonical responsibility. For parishioners' responsibility to provide a locked font, see No. 86.

oats collected in part for the reconciliation of the cemetery and refuses to restore either the grain or its value. Richard's wife, Agnes, is a common slanderer of her neighbors and a sower of discord in the community, to the harm and danger of the inhabitants there. Margaret Northyn chatters in church, disrupting the divine services. . . .

Weston. The parishioners say that Sir John Pole, who holds a chantry in Weston church and is obliged to celebrate daily there, has not done so and has been absent from the chantry sometimes for a month, other times for three weeks, completely disregarding his responsibilities. They say that the same John made off with two or three cartloads of stones from the church cemetery without the parishioners' permission and refuses to return them. John also took the lock from the baptismal font in the church and the font is now unsealed. They say that John is disobedient to the vicar of the church, his right and proper commands, and chooses not to attend the divine services along with the vicar in the church, but impedes as much as he can church income, offerings, and other revenues. . . .

Worley [May 7]. A visitation was made there on Monday, May 7, in the same year of our Lord. The parishioners say that the breviary in the choir is unbound, in defect of the rector. They say that the rector's wheat is winnowed in the cemetery most inappropriately, etc. [*Added note:* It is forbidden that this be done again.] They say that the rector is obliged to hire a deacon to assist in the church and to care for the books and ornaments of the church. The vicar puts horses, cows, and geese out to graze in the cemetery, in great disrespect, etc. [*Added note:* He denies it roundly.] The parishioners say that the bells are not rung at dawn or at evening on ferial days, in defect of the vicar. Care of the bells and their rope pertains to the vicar, who has refused to do it. [*Added note:* He says that he is not bound to do this.] They say that the vicar has refused the sacraments to Jevan Slefmaker, his parishioner, because he refused to pay him tithes at the vicar's pleasure. The vicar has taken some planks and stones from the church floor. The vicar is absent from the church sometimes for forty days, nor does he find another chaplain to perform divine services, except when other chaplains living there do so out of charity. [*Added note:* The vicar denies it.] They say that the vicar is obligated to provide for each and every chaplain celebrating in the church, bread, wine and candles for services, but he does not. [*Added note:* The vicar says he is not so bound.] They say that the vicar is supposed to have two candles burning before the high altar on Sundays and feast days while high mass is being celebrated, but instead of these candles he burns two tapers. [*Added note:* The vicar says he does his duty.] . . .

St. Weonard [May 11]. The parishioners say that the vicar of Lugwardine is bound to hire two chaplains to assist at services in St. Weonard and one more for the chapels of Treveranon and Penrose, but he has not done this. Also, Sir John, the chaplain there, frequents taverns and talks in his cups, much to the scandal of the locals, etc. The same Sir John is incontinent with a certain Margaret whose surname they do not know. The common consensus is that Sir John is ill-suited and ignorant with respect to the cure of souls.

Garway. The parishioners say that Maurice Pengrych and Rys Duy laid violent hands on a certain Sir William Watkyn, and Thomas Pengrych, Maurice's father, gave them counsel and aid in their actions. Also, Sir Thomas Folyot frequents the taverns inordinately and excessively to the great scandal of the clergy, and he reported the confession of Robert Scheppert, one of his parishioners, in public. John Smyth commits adultery with Alice Willok, his mistress, and he treats his wife badly. Also, Richard, chaplain there, celebrates twice a day, that is, here at Garway and also at Wormbridge and receives a double salary. The same sir is ill-suited for the pastoral care, as he does not know the Welsh tongue and most parishioners there do not know English. Also, Llewelyn ap Jevan ap Madoc and Gladys Bach promised to be married to each other, but did not. Jankyn, a servant of Peter Smyth, fornicates with Johanna Scheppert, and Hugh Walle treats his wife badly, often threatening to kill her and treating her wickedly.

Newton. The parishioners say that the chancel is in bad repair, in structure and in glass, in defect of the rector. The same rector is supposed to find a service book for worship there but has not. Also, Gwenllian Bache is bound to pay 20d. to the fabric of the parish church, left by her husband David Paty in his will; Gwenllian is the executrix of the will and refuses to pay the said pence. [*Added note:* They reach an agreement and the debt is satisfied.]

Castle Goodrich [May 12]. The parishioners there say that the vicarage lies vacant, or so they believe, since neither the vicar nor any other chaplain serves there; the parishioners' souls are in grave danger since they have no curate. They say that the vicar who was there for a time was supposed to hire a deacon for assisting in church and caring for the liturgical books and ornaments, but nothing was done. They say that Thomas, the prior of Flanford, is incontinent with Joanna, John Taylor's wife. Also, the chrism is not changed from year to year. They did not have matins on Easter Sunday last. Sir John Byterlowe celebrates mass twice a day, at Castle Goodrich and at Honsham chapel. John Smith celebrates twice a day, at Castle Goodrich and at Honsham. The same Sir John Smith is incontinent with Maiota Wattakyns, whom he keeps. The same Sir John Byterlowe took a chalice that he had given out of his own possessions for use *in perpetuo* in the church at Castle Goodrich. This same chalice he took from the church, having neither sought nor obtained permission of the parishioners, and has kept it for his own use. Also, the church tithes are not stored in the tithe-barn. . . .

Ganarew. The parishioners there say that the church has been vacant since the death of the last rector, Maurice, and has been vacant for six months or more; consequently the parishioners have gone without the divine services. Also, William Staunton turned the rector's house into a tavern. . . .

Sellack [May 13]. The parishioners say that the parishioners of Sellack who live at Little Dewchurch and at Combe are obliged to visit the mother church of Sellack once a year, namely, on the feast of St. Tysilio,[7] patron of the same church, and to make an offering on that day, but they do not. They refuse to contribute proportionately to the upkeep of the cemetery wall at Sellack. Also, the Sellack parishioners who live at Hentland are held to contribute to the repair of the cemetery wall, but they have not. The Sellack parishioners at Bridstow are bound to do the same, but they do not. Willok Owen de Rytir witholds his parishioner's dues from the church of Sellack and is obliged to contribute to repair work in the cemetery, but he does not do it. Also, the baptismal font is not sealed. The cemetery is not enclosed, in defect of the parishioners. [*Added note:* There is an order that the parishioners make the necessary repairs before the next feast of St. Michael under a penalty of 40s.] . . .

Newland [May 17]. A visitation was held there on Thursday, May 17, in the same year of our Lord.

The bishop of Llandaff, the rector.

The reverend Richard Peer, the vicar.

The reverend Nicholas Mede, chaplain.

The reverend John Follier. He does not have letters of ordination and refers [us] to the register of the lord [bishop] John Trillek.

The reverend William Davy.

[*There follow the names of fifteen parishioners or sworn witnesses whose depositions were taken in the visitation inquiry.*]

Parishioners: William Courte, Jankyn Ely, Thomas Ely, William Roberts, William Geere, Jack Bursch, William Ralffe, Jak Watkyns, Harry Nortone, Jankyn Nortone, Watkyn ap Okel, William Brute, Philip Nychole, Roger Bullynghope, Thomas Drewe.

[7] A popular Welsh monk of the seventh century.

The parishioners say that the chaplain, Sir Walter Hadyrley of Newland, is incontinent with Joanna Sarney of Newland. [*Added note:* Both purged themselves (of the accusation) at Monmouth.] . . .

Huntley [May 22]. The parishioners say that everything is well there [*Added note:* except that Sir William Herte, the rector there, is unchaste with Isabella, whom he keeps in his house.] . .

Westbury [May 22]. The parishioners say that for the last three years John Alayn has not received the Body of Christ at Easter as every parishioner is bound to. [*Added note:* He is corrected and promises to change his ways.] They say that Walter Kadyle treats Ivel his wife badly, shutting her out of his house and refusing her food and clothing and other things a husband owes his wife. She also bore him a son he refuses to support. [*Added note:* (the case) is deferred, under the hope of concord (*sub spe concordie*), to the court at Hereford.][8] Symond Acherhulle treats his wife badly in much the same way. [*Added note:* The man appeared and indicated his readiness to take his wife back as he ought.] Also, John Brasyer and Isabella Vyell, William Vyell's wife, are publicly defamed for committing adultery. Walter Wodemon fornicates with Juliana Arthur. Robin Acherhulle commits adultery with Agnes, wife of Jacob Smith. Richard Robins commits adultery with Joanna, Roger Hickock's wife. The same Richard commits adultery with Elena Hotte, his cousin within the second degree. Dom John Faukener, monk of the monastery of Flaxley, is incontinent with Florence Donne, former parishioner of Rudford, now living there [Westbury]. Sir John Carter, chaplain at Littledean, is incontinent with Juliana Irishe of Blaisdon. Sir Thomas, rector of Blaisdon, is incontinent with Margaret Martin, wife of John Martin. Also, Cecilia Robins, who has not yet been corrected, used to fornicate with John Prestbury, a monk of Flaxley, now dead. [*Added note:* The man is dead; the woman purged herself before (her) vicar.] They say that William atte Mynde, monk, is incontinent with Elena de Plas, also known as Elena at Yate, wife of John at Yate. Dom Richard, abbot of Flaxley, is incontinent with Alice Tiburton of Littledean and has continued in his sin for thirteen years. Elizabeth, wife of William Watkins of Blaisdon, commits adultery with the same lord abbot. Also, Joanna Gosbroke of Gloucester, unmarried, fornicates with the said lord abbot. [*Added note:* The woman is from outside the diocese.] They say that Joanna Kassy, wife of Walter Kassy, commits adultery with the same lord abbot and lives within

---

[8] Evidently, this case was to be taken up in the matrimonial court at Hereford where it could be fully heard. The phrase *sub spe concordie* describes a provision that settlement be reached between the two parties before the case is heard.

the monastic enclosure. The same Joanna commits adultery with Dom John Faukener, monk of the same monastery. Alice Tiburton of Littledean commits adultery with the same Dom John, monk. The same Dom John is incontinent with Lucia, wife of Anelm Kalknase of Littledean. Elena Byllyng fornicates with Walter Hope, a monk there [at Flaxley]. John de Pistrina, servant of the said abbot, commits adultery with Johanna Kassy, wife of Walter Kassy. Elena, wife of Henry Zeynor of Northwood, commits adultery with the said Walter Hope, monk. Agnes Badron, wife of Reginald Taylor, commits adultery with Dom Stephan, monk of Flaxley. Joanna Bude, wife of Thomas Baker of Alvington, commits adultery with Roger Stretton, monk of the same monastery. Also, Isabella Vyell, wife of William Vyell of Frodesley, is publicly defamed with John Brasyor, monk of the same monastery. . . .

Ledbury [May 26]. The parishioners say that the lord bishop is obliged to pay an annual sum for the maintenance of a lamp burning before the high altar from a certain piece of land which he gave up through escheatment; he witholds the 18d. [*Added note:* Let the lord be consulted on this matter.] They say that the master or warden of the Hospital of St. Katherine's is held to hire and maintain in the said hospital for the service of God five chaplains dressed always in the habit as established from the foundation of the said hospital, a white cross on the breast, but he has provided only two chaplains. Also, he is held from ancient [practice] to feed twelve paupers daily, a practice which he has neglected entirely. The same warden farms out to laymen all the hospital's benefices along with lands elsewhere in the diocese. The warden neglects to distribute money to the poor twice weekly. William Davis and his son Thomas swore to support the ordination titles of Master Robert Prys and Hugh Carwy, junior, under penalty of 40s. to be paid to the work of Ledbury church, but they refuse to honor the agreement. Also, William Calwe, having been ordained deacon in Ledbury church, did not contribute to the treasury, for the upkeep of the church's ornaments, as he is supposed to. . . .

Coddington. The parishioners say that the rector is remarkably tepid and indifferent towards the divine service and that his pigs rut in the cemetery. He has broken the cemetery enclosure. He is so frequently absent from the parish that the parishioners have to go elsewhere to have their infants baptized. Everyone knows he keeps a mistress in his house, whose name they do not know. He uses the bell tower as a place to store hay and keep his livestock. He is supposed to provide bell cords but has not. He also keeps certain lands formerly given to the parish for the maintenance of a lamp in the church. . . .

Much Cowarne [May 30]. A visitation was made here on Wednesday, May 30. The parishioners say that the vicar is held to find a deacon for serving in the church, but he has not. They say that the deacon who works there temporarily is supposed to supply bell cords, but this has not been done, in defect of the vicar because there is no other deacon there. They say that Andreas Hope unjustly witholds 4s. bequeathed to the church of Cowarne by John Gesses, recently deceased, whose executor the same Andreas is. John Walsh unjustly witholds 10s. which Roger Gryn, recently deceased, left to the fabric of the same church. John Walsh, recent churchwarden, refused to render payment on the goods of the church received by him from parishioners of Cowarne. Lewis Taylor and Isabel, whom he keeps as his wife, are committing adultery together. The rector is bound to provide a service book for the worship of God in the church, but he has not done so. Also, the rector is obliged to obtain two bushels of grain for making communion bread at Easter but he has not done so.

Ocle Pychard. The parishioners say that all is well there. . . .

Leominster [June 5]. The parishioners say that the rector is bound to hire a cleric for carrying the bell and candle before the vicar when he bears the Body of Christ in visitations to the sick, but he has not done so and has neglected this for three years: by ancient custom, the rector should pay 8s. annually for support of the same cleric. Also, the church lacks a book for the burial of the dead, in defect of the rector. There are two old worn-out books. But during the time of pestilence there were sixteen or eighteen bodies on one and the same day, for which two books were inadequate. Also, the rector's proctor[9] does not allow anyone to communicate in church who has not first paid at least one halfpenny as an offering. [*Added note:* He is forbidden to do this again.] They say that the two antiphonaries and the two graduals in the church are worthless and inadequate for the old priests as they are too faded, in defect of the rector. The vicar's cows graze in the cemetery and so ruin the place that the silk vestments are fouled during processions there. Sir William Crompe is a common merchant of animals and sheep, buying and selling at a profit, and a sharer in the profit of 'Baggeres' who come there.[10] Sir William, the chaplain of the Blessed Virgin Mary, and Sir William Crompe, Sir William Casyn, Sir Richard Pastay, and Sir John Grasley are disobedient to the vicar in the service of God according to the

---

[9] The rector's proctor could be any agent that he appoints to oversee the administration of the parish; if he were a cleric, he could be the farmer of the benefice with certain religious responsibilities.

[10] "Baggeres" were, as their name denotes, laborers who reaped and bundled products ranging from wood to hops and grain.

terms of the constitution.[11] The same Sir William Casyn threatened parishioners working there in the service of the bishop to uncover the faults and failings of wrongdoers, because they discovered his crimes. Sir Walter Goodrich, chaplain, is a common merchant, especially of sheep, whose profit is 5s. for every sixty sheep bought and sold. Also, Sir Thomas Whitbread, chaplain, is incontinent with a certain Alice Taylor.

Docklow. The parishioners say that the vicar of Leominster is supposed to provide divine services for them the two days following Christmas, Wednesday, Thursday, and Friday of Holy Week and the Monday and Tuesday after Easter and the Monday and Tuesday after Pentecost, but he has not done so. [*Added note:* The vicar denies this. The parishioners press their claim.] . . .

Eardisley [June 11]. The parishioners say that the chancel is in need of repair in plaster and other things, in defect of the rector. The same rector is supposed to provide a breviary in the choir for serving God and the church, but he has not done so. The vicar is obliged to hire a cleric to serve God and the church, who knows how to read and sing, ring the bells, and walk before the vicar when he goes to visit the sick and for doing other things, but he has not done so. [*Added note:* All claims against the vicar are deferred under the hope of concord.] They say that Agnes Knetchur and Isabella, servants of the said vicar, ring the bells and assist the vicar at mass, which is against the law of the church. Scandal and suspicion have arisen among the parishioners over the fact that these women live with the vicar. Also, Walter Grobbe died without the sacraments and confession, in defect of the vicar. Roger, Walter Wardroper's son, died in the same way, in defect of the vicar. Richard Bady and Alice Barber died without extreme unction, in defect of the vicar. Also, a certain infant, Thomas Coreyour, was baptized without chrism, in defect of the vicar. The same vicar, when he buried John Boley in the cemetery, stated publicly and within the hearing of those nearby, "Lie there, excommunicate," with great hate, etc. Last Easter the vicar refused to administer the sacraments to Walter Jewe, senior, until he agreed with the vicar on certain tithes which . . . [*half a line blank*]. Also, he refuses to administer the Easter sacraments to laborers in the same parish until they meet his demands for the tithes of their wages. The same vicar celebrated a clandestine marriage between Jankyn Colle and Margaret his wife, who had announced their banns only once. The vicar is a common merchant of various goods,

[11]This constitution is likely from a set of constitutions attributed to Robert Winchelsey, Archbishop of Canterbury, and decreed sometime between 1295 and 1313. Constitution 3 outlines the proper working relationship between parish curates and hired clergy.

grain, and other things, and is a usurer. Also, the vicar celebrates twice in a day. They say that Walter Machin, who dismissed his own wife, commits adultery with Cecilia Besannde. Andrew, Walter Wardrop's son, fornicates with Matilda Carpenter. John, Walter's son, fornicates with Juliana Barron. William Jewe and Juliana Lachar fornicate with each other. Also, the vicar refused to administer the Easter sacraments this past year to Amisie, daughter of John Baker. Mylo Webb fornicates with Alice Syre. Davy Thresser fornicates with Joanna Specerer. The vicar is obliged to provide a lamp burning in the church day and night, but he has not done so. John Baker does not come to church on Sundays and feast days. Isota Lather does not come as well. Also, the vicar swore before the lord bishop that he would hire a chaplain to celebrate in the chapel of Bullinghope, but he has not; therefore he is a perjurer. One chalice was stolen from the goods of the parishioners with a value of 40s., in defect of the vicar who is responsible for its custody. The vicar is supposed to ring the bells before mass every day, but he has not done so. The church linen and cloths are a disgrace. [The vicar] is obliged to provide bell cords for the bells, but he has not done so. Also, Jankyn Baeley and Amisia, his wife, do not live together. They say that John Baker and Margery his wife complained to the bishop's official that the vicar of Eardisley blankly refused to absolve Margery last Lent after having heard her confession unless she paid 12d. for repairing the church's books: so Margery went to Hereford to receive absolution and there confessed her sins and was absolved by Sir John Mawdely. At Easter, Margery went up to the Lord's Table and the vicar refused her the sacraments unless she confessed her sins again to him. Also, during last Lent the vicar refused to administer the sacraments to others if they did not agree to dismiss charges against Richard Wilson Baker for the murder of Walter, John and Margery's son; they dismissed the prosecution. . . .

Almeley. The parishioners say that everything is well there, except that the vicar's wage is too mean to support him and the work he is obliged to do there.

♘ No. 118. Visitations of parishes in Exeter (1301, 1330).

Reg. Stapledon, pp. 109, 111, 337; and *Reg Grandisson,* pt. 1, pp. 572–74. Trans. JS.

Colebrooke, June 27, 1301. Hugh de Copplestone, William de Wottone, Jr., John de Godescote, William de la Come, and William Batin, with other trustworthy men of the parish, legitimately questioned and examined about the articles relevant to the visitation, say that Sir William, the vicar, preaches after his own fashion. Also he explains the gospels to them on Sundays in-

sofar as he understands them. But he does not tell them much about the
articles of faith, the ten commandments, and how to avoid mortal sin. He
also does not say his matins with singing on feast days, and he only celebrates mass every other day of the week. He is defamed concerning the sin
of incontinence with Lucy de la Stubbe, who is married. His house, except
for the hall and one room, is dilapidated and threatens to collapse. When he
first took up residence it was in good repair; now it will take 100s. to repair
it. And the door of the rectory is so far from the [main hall] (which has been
newly extended) that someone knocking from the outside cannot be heard
in the hall. This poses a danger to sick parishioners. . . .

Colyton, July 10, 1301. In the mother church there is one adequate breviary, with a collect-book and a capitularium[12] provided by the vicar, and an
old breviary of no value provided by the parishioners. The antiphonary by
itself is not adequate for such a church. There is a lesson-book complete for
the whole year in two volumes; inserted in it is an antiphonary, although it
does not completely follow local liturgical use. The letters in the ordinal are
too faded. The martyrology with a hymnal, a capitularium, and a collect-
book are adequate enough. The gradual book is good, but it is old and
imperfect. There is a missal well notated with music and clearly written;
another missal has no musical notations. The manual is worthless. The processional book, with some of the sequences, is adequate. There is one large
chalice, partly gilded; another chalice at the altar of the Blessed Virgin is the
same size; there is a third smaller chalice, but it is sufficient. There are five
complete suits of vestments, with one stole missing. The choir cope is adequate; another one is old and worn. There is a tunic with a silk dalmatic.
There are seven frontal cloths and other furnishings for the church. There
are three banners. The Lenten veil is adequate. There are five pairs of corporals with one silk corporal case and another made of wool. There are two
decent, metal processional crosses. There are two small pewter candlesticks
for processions. There is one worn altar cloth and another of no value. There
is a good rochet. There is an ivory pyx securely hanging from the ceiling
over the altar, but it has no lock. The lead chrismatory is not locked. There
are four cruets. There are no lanterns. The chancel lacks a covering.
Synodal witnesses: Richard Libor, Thomas de la Knolle, Thomas de la
Doune, Henry Honte, John de Radyng, and William Roc. Asked about those
things that pertain to the spiritual condition of the parish, they say that Sir

[12]A book of the "little chapters," short responses said by the principal celebrant of the divine
office. All its contents were contained in the collect-book.

Robert [Blond], their vicar, is an upright man who preaches to them insofar
as he knows how, but that this does not seem adequate to them. Further,
they say that his predecessors used to call in the friars to instruct the parishioners in the salvation of souls, but he does not care for the friars, and he
won't admit them when they happen to pass through the parish, nor supply
them with provisions for their travels. They ask that he be rebuked for this.
Also they assert that all the chaplains and clerics of the church lead upright
and chaste lives. The official rent-farmer[13] carries out his duties well. Also
they say that Philip Liver assigned the annual rent of 12d. coming from two
acres of land in equal portion to the [upkeep] of the bridge at Axe, to the
lights in the church of Blessed Mary at Colyton, and to the chapel of St.
Calixtus. This land was farmed out to another tenant who now receives the
rent but pays nothing out from it. Also they say that the predecessors of the
current vicar used to hire a deacon at their own expense to look after the
church and sleep in it in order to guard the books and church ornaments.
He was paid a penny whenever he rang the church bells for the dead or at
weddings. But the current rector dismissed the deacon and assigned his
duties to his holy water clerks [aquabajuli]. Also, four tenants of the glebe-
land, together with the above-named parishioners, say that when the current rent-farmer arrived, an old dilapidated tithe-barn stood in the courtyard which the baliffs tore down since it was about to fall down. It was
valued at 20s., but to rebuild it will cost 40s. The timber and the roofing-
slate from the old building were saved. Also, one barn is about to collapse
due to age. The said rent-farmer built it for the most part from new, and
now it is worth twice as much. Also, in his time, a certain small house col-
lapsed which could not be used and so it was freely allowed to fall into ruin.
Its estimated value was 5s. Also, when he arrived the cider press and its vat
were roofed with old timber which they estimate would cost 2s. They say
that all the dwellings that are now standing are in better repair now than
they were when he took possession of them. But there is nothing which it
would be inappropriate to renovate, except the hall with its rooms and the
kitchen, which lack nothing except a roof. They say that they could rebuild
as good as new part of the barn (which is falling down) along with four
other buildings in the courtyard for eight marks by reusing some of the old
timber in those buildings. Furthermore, they say that the rent-farmer improved the glebe-land by fertilizing it and digging drainage ditches at a cost
of 77s. And the rents of assize together with the vicar's pension are worth
£6 7s., and one carrucate of land not valued.

[13]Not the vicar but the man "farming" the church. See glossary.

[*Note that the following is a visitation of same parish twenty-nine years later.*]

Colyton, 1330. On the following day, July 14, 1330, visitation at Colyton. There are three suitable chalices there, and five suits of vestments, one of which is worn out. Also there is one cope, tunic, and dalmatic donated by Master Benedict [de Pastone?]. . . . [*Manuscript illegible.*] One worn choir cope. Four towels for the main altar, two with colored hems. . . . [*Manuscript illegible.*] One adequate surplice. One worn rochet. There are two adequate missals plus another one. There is a gradual poorly written. . . . [*Manuscript illegible.*] An antiphonary in the other missal, which is not adequate. An ordinal poorly written; it has been badly looked after and is faded. There is no breviary for the vicar. A hymnal, a capitularium, and a collect-book are all badly bound in one volume. There is one adequate altar frontal. There is an ivory pyx for the eucharist, without a lock. The chest for storing the books is adequate. There is an adequate pewter chrismatory with a lock. There is no holder for the Paschal candle. There is a pax-board. Three cruets. A stone water basin. The offering box and the censer are adequate. The incense bowl is inadequate. There is a bowl for holy water. The funeral bier is adequate. The canopy over the main altar is too small and is insufficient. The rest of the ornaments in the church are currently in good condition except the lantern which is missing. The official of the place is sufficiently certified. [Richard Brondiche], the vicar, appeared in person. Sir Robert de Schirburne, the parish chaplain, appearing personally, says that he does not have help for celebrating divine services in the church because the vicar of the parish has been struck with leprosy. He also says that the pastoral care there is well looked after in everything, and he has heard no rumors about sins that need to be corrected. Sir John Knolle, a member of the household of the lord of Courteney, says that the church is poorly administered in divine services because of its defects. The vicar has leprosy. Sir John Gode, parish chaplain of the chapel of Monkton, says that the chapel is badly roofed and about to collapse, and that all the books in it are inadequate. He says that he does not know who ought to be held liable. Inquire into this. William Saunforde, William Frere, John de Yerdecombe, William Scoty-beare, Sr., and Richard Pever, tenants of the said church, say that the rent-farmer, the official, the seneschal, and its other ministers conduct themselves well in all matters. They say that the church has many defects, especially with regard to divine services, because of the vicar who is not up to the task due to his leprosy. Also they say that, this not withstanding, the vicar mingles in common with the parishioners publicly in church whenever he wants, which risks infecting the whole parish. This has caused a

scandal. They say that they are accustomed to have one competent vicar, a
suitable parish chaplain, a deacon, and two clerks serving the church paid
for through the parishioners' donations; the vicar used to hire these people.
But now they have only one chaplain and a clerk, and the vicar refuses to
hire anyone else. Also they say that due to the negligence of the vicar and
the chaplain, the parish lost one Rhenish cloth worth 6s. 8d. They say that
their own failings contributed to the loss. Also, the vicar chose a parish clerk
for himself at his own pleasure, but he did not want to support him. Also,
the parish clerks are accustomed to ring the church bells for curfew and at
the elevation of the Body of Christ during the consecration. They say that
the parish chaplain is an upright person who bears himself well in his pastoral duties as they require. Also, John Prouz [the lord of the manor of Gat-
combe in the parish] does not wish to contribute with the other parishioners
to the church, nor does he do the other things incumbent upon him. Also,
Sir [Hugo] Prouz, knight, now deceased, father of the said John, bequeathed
ten marks sterling to the building fund of the church of Colyton, which his
heirs refuse to pay.

John de Bytelisgate, parishioner of the said church, whose wife died intestate, did not want to allow the official of this jurisdiction, so he claimed,
to be involved in the administration of his wife's estate. Consequently, John,
legitimately rebuked for these faults, said that he wanted us to settle the
matter. After the commissioners heard the case, they enjoined him to make
an honest inventory of his wife's movable goods, and then to distribute
them for the sake of her soul and to render an honest account of this distri-
bution. After he swore to this, they handed over to him the administration
of his wife's estate. The vicar of the parish showed a written petition to the
visitors, attached to this present document, to be explained to the lord dean
and chapter.

Memorandum that Nicholas, the bailiff, proctor of the rent-farmer of
Colyton, acknowledged that his lord, as holder of the rent of Colyton, was
bound in his own name for the sum of £46 payable to the lord dean and
chapter of Exeter [Cathedral] on the due date set by law and custom at the
cathedral's exchequer. The visitors fined him. Also take note that the vicar
of the place is bound for all due and accustomed debts. Such is the ordination of the vicarage.

The dwellings on the glebe. There is one suitable hall there that has a
room with chimney which is repaired. . . . [*Manuscript illegible.*] There is a
suitable kitchen there, but it has no oven. There are two suitable tithe-barns,
the smaller of which was constructed by Sir Adam Carletone. All the other

structures are sufficient. Also, the garden is consumed with age and badly tended. Estimated cost of the defects: [blank].

St. Mary Church with its chapel, 1301. One psalter worn and inadequate with a manual bound in it. Another worthless psalter. A good antiphonary with a collect-book, a capitularium, and hymnal all bound in it. A two-volume lesson-book for the whole year, with a capitularium, collect-book, and hymnal, and an antiphonary. An inadequate ordinal. Adequate synodal statutes.[14] A well-written missal with musical notation. A gradual with a troper collated to the capitularium, but not completely in accord with local liturgical practice. And another gradual, old and decayed. No manual other than the one bound in the psalter mentioned above. Three suits of vestments, only one of which has an adequate chasuble. Only one surplice, old and with holes in it. A less than adequate rochet. Five blessed towels, one of which has a colored hem; six unblessed towels. No pyx for the eucharist, but a box for the offerings. A wooden chrismatory with a lock. No cup for visiting the sick. Two processional crosses that are good enough. Two pewter candlesticks for processions. Five pairs of corporals, with four worn purses for them. A decent small pax-board. An adequate chalice, gilded inside. (Memorandum about the chalice from the ruined chapel of Colyton: the chapel's former parishioners, now divided partly between St. Mary's church and Carswille, hold the chalice and refuse to return it to the mother church [i.e., St. Mary Church]. The parishioners of the mother church seek to have it turned over to them along with the chapel's stock and timber. This is just.) Four adequate cruets. A silk frontal for the main altar in tolerable condition. One window in the south side of the chancel is poorly glazed and lacks a mullion; a second window has a worn mullion and no glass; a third has a mullion, but no glass. Furthermore, the roof of the chancel is in very poor condition. The baptismal font lacks a cover. The nave of the church and the bell tower both need roofing. The troper and the processional book are both very good.

The parishioners say that up until the time of the present vicar they were accustomed to supply the chancel of the church with all its necessities and thereby to be exempt from paying tithes of livestock to the church. But the present vicar, even though he does not pay for the upkeep of the chancel, demands this tithe and forces them to pay it. They say that Agnes Bonatrix bequeathed 5s. worth of barley for the upkeep of the church of St. Mary,

---

[14]Several Exeter churches visited also owned copies of the Cantilupe-Quinel Summula. See No. 78.

which the vicar took and kept. Also, Master Robert le Rous bequeathed a certain sum of money to the church which the same vicar is said to keep for himself. They say that the vicar lets all kinds of his animals into the graveyard, which has left it badly trampled and absolutely filthy. Also, the vicar appropriated for himself some trees blown down in the graveyard by the wind, and he used [their wood] for his own dwellings. They say that the vicar has his malt stored in the church, and he also keeps his wheat and other things there. Because of this, when his servants open the door going in and out of the church, during storms the wind comes into the church and tends to blow the roof off it. They say that he preaches well and carries out all his duties laudably well when he is there. But he often leaves the parish and goes off to Mortenhampstead, sometimes for fifteen days, sometimes for eight. When this happen the parish has no chaplain, except when Sir Walter, the archdeacon's chaplain is there, or when on request one is found from somewhere else. . . .

Glossary of
Ecclesiastical Terms
෴

ABBOT. The head of a monastery, elected by his monks.

ACOLYTE. The highest rank of the four MINOR ORDERS. Also called "colet" (by loss of the initial "a") in England. An acolyte had to be at least fourteen years old.

ADMISSION (to a benefice). The act by which a bishop, after formal examination of a candidate, allows him to occupy his benefice. Compare INSTITUTION.

ADVENT. The period of prayer and fasting beginning on the fourth Sunday before Christmas.

ADVOWSON. The right to appoint a curate to a benefice.

AFFINITY. The spiritual relationship formed between two people; for example, between the man and woman who sponsor the same child at baptism or confirmation. It creates an IMPEDIMENT to the marriage of that man and woman. Compare CONSANGUINITY.

ALB. See VESTMENTS.

ALTAR. The stone or wooden table set against the eastern wall of the CHANCEL on which the MASS was celebrated. A fragment of a saint's RELIC was installed inside the altar stone set into the table.

ALTARAGE. Income to a benefice from various customary fees and offerings. It included offerings from each adult parishioner collected at Christmas, Easter, the feast day of the church's patron saint, and its dedication day; fees collected for announcing banns, performing weddings and funerals, and churching women after childbirth; and offerings in kind such as the leftover BLESSED BREAD each Sunday, candles, cheese, and eggs. The LESSER TITHES were also sometimes counted as altarage. Compare TITHES and GLEBE.

AMICE. See VESTMENTS.

ANATHEMA. Formal canonical punishment through EXCOMMUNICATION. Compare CENSURE.

ANNUAL. A mass offered on the anniversary of a patron's death for the repose of his or her soul.

ANNUELLER. A priest hired to a CHANTRY for an annual wage to say regular memorial masses on behalf of its dead patrons.

ANTIPHONARY. A service book containing the prayers and responses accompanying the CANONICAL HOURS, and sometimes other prayers of the divine services.

APPROPRIATION. The transfer of a benefice, usually to a religious house. That community then became the legal RECTOR of the benefice and received its GREATER TITHES. It was obliged to appoint a VICAR to the benefice to attend to the CURE OF SOULS. Upwards of a third of English parishes had been thus appropriated by the end of the fifteenth century. Compare IMPROPRIATION.

AQUABAJULUS (or HOLY WATER CLERK). A boy or man who had received at least the first tonsure or the first of the minor clerical orders, and who carried the holy water used for sprinkling the congregation during processions. By tradition and synodal law the small payments he received were meant to help finance his education. Compare PARISH CLERK.

ARCHBISHOP. A bishop holding jurisdiction over multiple dioceses gathered together into a PROVINCE. Medieval England was divided into the Province of Canterbury and the Province of York, each ruled by its own archbishop.

ARCHDEACON. An episcopally-appointed officer who oversaw one of the archdeaconries into which a diocese was divided. He was obliged to supervise the parochial clergy in his jurisdiction, INDUCT clerics to their benefices, and hold regular VISITATIONS of his archdeaconry. He also had an ecclesiastical court to which violators were summoned. Compare RURAL DEAN.

BANNS. A church's thrice-repeated public announcement of a couple's intent to marry. Required by the Fourth Lateran Council (1215) in an effort to curtail clandestine marriages. See MATRIMONY.

BAPTISM. The first SACRAMENT, in which a candidate is sprinkled with or immersed in water, thereby washing away original sin and admitting that person into the Christian community.

BENEFICE (or LIVING). The spiritual office of the INCUMBENT and the land, dwellings, and income attached to it.

BENEFIT OF CLERGY. The legal immunities enjoyed by members of the clergy. They included the *privilegium canonis* (benefit of the law), which provided automatic excommunication for anyone physically assaulting a cleric, and the *privilegium fori* (benefit of the court), which exempted clerics from criminal prosecution in secular courts.

BISHOP. A priest consecrated to exercise the highest spiritual and legal jurisdiction over a diocese. Bishops possess unique power to administer HOLY ORDERS and CONFIRMATION, to absolve certain serious sins, to consecrate churches, chapels, and cemeteries, to reconsecrate church buildings polluted by bloodshed, to institute to benefices within their jurisdiction, to grant letters of ordination and licenses for nonresidence, to inspect religious houses and churches in their jurisdiction, and generally to oversee the spiritual welfare and all that pertains to it in their diocese.

BLESSED BREAD. Since medieval parishioners as a rule received the eucharist only two or three times a year in most dioceses, blessed but unconsecrated bread was offered to them at Sunday mass instead.

BOOK OF HOURS. See PRIMER.

BREVIARY. A book containing all the prayers and psalms necessary to recite the DIVINE OFFICE.

CANON. (1) A rule or law, especially one promulgated by a pope. (2) A secular cleric living in community in a secular cathedral or a collegiate church.

CANONICAL HOURS. The eight times set aside for daily prayer by religious and clergy. They are Nocturn (in winter, about 3:00 A.M.), Matins (or Lauds, at daybreak), Prime (about 6:00 A.M.), Terce (about 8:00 A.M.), Sext (about noon), Nones (about 1:30 P.M.), Vespers (or Evensong, about 4:15 P.M.), and Compline (about 6:15 P.M.). Together they equal the DIVINE OFFICE.

CANON LAW. The body of law, collected from scripture, the writings of the Church Fathers and popes, and church councils, that governed all the operations of the Christian Church.

CANON OF THE MASS. (See also MASS.) The central portion of the mass containing the consecration of the EUCHARIST.

CATHEDRAL. The mother church of a diocese and, as such, the bishop's church. It contained his throne, or *cathedra*. English cathedrals were staffed either by monastic clergy whose monastery was attached to the cathedral, or by a community of secular CANONS known collectively as the CHAPTER.

CENSER (or THURIBLE). The small vessel, often shaped like a boat, in which incense was burned during special liturgical services.

CENSURE. Canonical punishment: either EXCOMMUNICATION, INTERDICT, or SUSPENSION.

CHALICE. The cup, usually of silver or pewter, in which the wine was consecrated during mass.

CHANCEL. The eastern end of a church where the altar is situated, often separated from the NAVE by a latticed rail or a ROOD-SCREEN. The church's rector was responsible for its upkeep.

CHANTRY. A spiritual service set up in a church by private, often perpetual endowment by which a priest was hired for a term during which he celebrated daily mass, usually at a side altar, for the repose of the souls of the donors and their families.

CHAPEL. A small auxiliary church within a large parish or a side altar within a church. A chapel-of-ease was erected where distance or the elements prevented parishioners from regularly attending the main parish church. Wealthy members of a parish sometimes built private chapels for their convenience. Chaplains staffed both sorts of chapels, but curates jealously guarded the rights of the main parish church to tithes, baptism, burial rights, etc.

CHAPLAIN. An unbeneficed, salaried priest serving as an assistant in a parish. See PARISH PRIEST.

CHAPTER. See CATHEDRAL.

CHASUBLE. See VESTMENTS.

CHOIR. The part of the church where the clergy and choir sat. It was at the western end of the chancel, dividing the chancel from the nave. Parish churches did not invariably have choirs.

CHRISM. The holy oil used by a priest in baptism and the last anointing, and by a bishop in confirmation.

CHRISMATORY. The small vessel which held CHRISM.

CHURCHING (or PURIFICATION) of women. A ceremony (based in scripture) in which, after giving birth, a woman, wearing a white veil, went to her parish church ostensibly to give thanksgiving for a safe delivery; but in general opinion it was construed as a rite of purification to be performed after a thirty- or forty-day absence from the church.

CHURCHWARDEN. The lay man (or men) chosen to act as the parishioners' representative to the curate, protecting their property interests in the parish church. He was charged with overseeing the general fiscal affairs of the church. Compare PARISH CLERK, AQUABAJULUS, and SEXTON, all of whom were often at least partly supervised by the churchwarden.

CHURCHYARD. The cemetery attached to the parish church. By law it had to be enclosed, kept clean of weeds and trash, and forbidden to all secular activities.

CLERK (CLERIC). The general title for anyone in minor or major orders. The tonsured head was this group's distinctive badge. Compare PARISH CLERK.

COADJUTOR. A cleric appointed to assist another cleric in performing his duties.

COLLATION. A bishop's presentation and institution of a candidate to a benefice in the bishop's ADVOWSON.

COMMENDATION (*in commendam*). The practice by which a man received the revenues of a benefice without being instituted to it. It was declared illegal in 1268, but continued long after that as a favorite way for PLURALISTS to hold more than one church.

COMMISSARY GENERAL. See OFFICIAL.

COMPERTA. The official report of findings derived from DETECTIONS collected at VISITATIONS.

COMPLINE. See CANONICAL HOURS.

CONFESSION. See PENANCE.

CONFIRMATION. The SACRAMENT administered by a bishop through an anointing with CHRISM. Confirmation strengthened the effects of BAPTISM by infusing the candidate with the Holy Spirit. The age for confirmation varied: some thought it should not be administered before the candidate reached the age of seven; others thought it should be given by age three; still others thought it was required soon after birth.

CONSANGUINITY. Blood relationship which is an IMPEDIMENT to marriage within certain degrees of relationship. Compare AFFINITY.

CONSISTORY COURT. See OFFICIAL.

COPE. See VESTMENTS.

CORPORAL. A double linen cloth placed in the middle of the ALTAR and on which were set the chalice and eucharistic bread.

CREED. The basic tenets of Christian belief. Legend claimed that each of the twelve apostles contributed to the APOSTLES' CREED (or Greater Creed), which was the most important creed; all medieval Christians were required to know it by heart. The NICENE CREED (or Lesser Creed) was issued at the Council of Nicaea in 325; it differed only slightly from the Apostles' Creed. The ATHANASIAN CREED (usually known by its Latin incipit, *Quicumque vult,* and ascribed to St. Athanasius) was a summary of beliefs about the Trinity.

CROZIER. The long staff carried by archbishops, bishops, and sometimes abbots as a sign of their pastoral office. Compare MITER.

CURATE. A cleric who had a CURE OF SOULS: the incumbent rector or vicar, or—the most common use of the word—the priest hired either to assist the incumbent or to administer the cure in his absence.

CURE (OR CARE) OF SOULS (*cura animarum*). The spiritual office of the pastor involving celebrating mass, administering the sacraments, preaching, moral teaching, and acts of charity.

DALMATIC. See VESTMENTS.

DEACON. The second highest rank of the three MAJOR or HOLY ORDERS. A deacon had to be at least nineteen years old.

DEAN. (1) The head of a cathedral CHAPTER. (2) See RURAL DEAN.

DECRETAL. A papal letter, usually in answer to a question, that bears the force of law.

DEDICATION. The ceremony at which a church was consecrated. A church's dedication day was annually observed as a FEAST day in the parish.

DEGRADATION. The punitive act by which a cleric was stripped of his special spiritual dignity and clerical immunities and reduced to the status of layman.

DETECTIONS (Latin, *detecta*). The transcript of the answers to questions posed to witnesses during a VISITATION. Compare COMPERTA.

DIGNITY. An official rank and the powers, perquisites, and jurisdiction attached to it.

DIOCESAN. A bishop.

DIOCESE (SEE). The geographical area over which a bishop exercises jurisdiction. The spiritual center of the diocese is the CATHEDRAL church and its precincts.

DIRIGE. Latin, "Direct, [O, Lord]" [Ps. 5:9]. The first word of the MATINS antiphon in the Office of the Dead.

DIVINE OFFICE. See CANONICAL HOURS.

EMBER DAYS (*quatuor tempora*). The four three-day periods (i.e., Wednesday, Friday, and Saturday) of fasting and abstinence that followed the first Sunday in Lent, Pentecost, Holy Cross Day (September 14), and St. Lucy's Day (December 13), during which bishops conferred Holy Orders.

EUCHARIST (or HOLY COMMUNION). The central event of the MASS in which bread and wine are changed into the Body and Blood of Christ through the words of consecration. Unless they were granted special episcopal permission, medieval lay people received communion only a few times a year, usually at Easter, Pentecost, and Christmas.

EXCHANGE. A practice increasingly common by the fourteenth century in which two incumbents swapped their benefices.

EXCOMMUNICATION. The canonical CENSURE that cut an individual off from the spiritual life of the church. In practical terms, an excommunicate could not receive the sacraments or be buried in consecrated ground until granted absolution.

EXECUTOR. The person(s) charged with implementing the provisions of a last will and testament.

EXORCIST. The second highest rank of the four MINOR ORDERS. Also called "benet" in England.

EXTREME UNCTION (or LAST ANOINTING). The sacrament in which the priest anointed a gravely ill or dying person on the eyes, lips, ears, nose, hands, and feet with chrism as a preparation for death. If they were able, those so anointed also received the eucharist which the priest carried with him in a PYX.

FARMING A CHURCH. An economic arrangement whereby a usually non-resident incumbent licensed the collection of the revenues from tithes from his benefice to a local agent (PROCTOR) who paid him a lump sum in return.

FEAST (or HOLY DAY). The celebration day commemorating an event in the life of Jesus, the Virgin Mary, or the saints (e.g., anniversary of a martyrdom, or a TRANSLATION). Some feasts were fixed on a particular date; others—movable feasts—were reckoned as a certain number of days before or after the variable date of Easter. All work, both physical and administrative, was banned on feast days (though plowing was sometimes exempted). According to a decree of Archbishop Simon Islip in 1362, there were ninety-three feast days each year in the province of Canterbury, a number that did not vary greatly from diocese to diocese or from decade to decade.

FERIA. A day of the week on which no feast or solemnity falls.

FIRST FRUITS. The income of a benefice in its first year, in most cases payable by the newly-appointed incumbent to the pope.

FONT. The basin raised on a pedestal in which HOLY WATER was stored for baptisms. By law the font had to have a cover that could be locked to prevent people from stealing the water for magical purposes.

FRIAR. From Latin *frater,* or brother—a member of one of the MENDICANT ORDERS.

FRUITS. Income of a benefice.

GARB. See TITHES.

GIRDLE. See VESTMENTS.

GLEBE. The land legally attached to a benefice. Produce from the glebe was one of the three sources of a rector's income. Compare TITHES and ALTARAGE.

GRADUAL. A service book containing all the music sung by the choir during mass and other ceremonies.

GREATER TITHES. See TITHES.

HERIOT. A customary payment to a manorial lord of a deceased tenant's best animal or its equivalent. Compare MORTUARY.

HOLY ORDERS. See MAJOR ORDERS.

HOLY WATER. Water blessed for use in BAPTISM, general blessings, dedications, purifications, consecrations of objects and buildings, and exorcisms.

HOLY WATER CLERK. See AQUABAJULUS.

HOST. The consecrated EUCHARIST.

IMPEDIMENT. Any obstacle—physical, mental, or spiritual—that prevented someone from being ordained or married. Papal dispensation could remove many impediments.

IMPROPRIATION. The transfer of a benefice to a secular person or corporation. Compare APPROPRIATION.

INCUMBENT. The legal holder of a benefice, whether or not resident.

INDUCTION. The ceremonial act by which a cleric is physically admitted to his benefice and acquires freehold possession of its tithes and glebe. It was usually performed by the archdeacon at the mandate of the bishop. A key often physically symbolized the possessions that the incumbent now controlled.

INDULGENCE. Time remitted from punishment in purgatory, and acquired through prayers and pious acts (e.g., pilgrimage, donations to church maintenance, upkeep of bridges and roadways).

INJUNCTION. A prelate's official order to abide by the law.

INSTITUTION. The act by which a bishop, after admitting a candidate to his benefice, legally appoints him as its RECTOR or VICAR and grants him the CURE OF SOULS over its parishioners. Compare ADMISSION.

INTERDICT. The papal suspension of all sacraments in a country to compel its ruler into obedience.

INVESTITURE. The ceremonial act often accompanying an INSTITUTION by which the holder of a benefice was presented with a ring or (especially on the Continent) a hat called a biretta, which was a symbol of his office.

JURISDICTION. A prelate's power of office and the area in which that power is exercised. Compare DIGNITY.

KISS OF PEACE (or PAX). In the early middle ages, immediately after the consecration at mass the priest and congregation shared a ritual kiss to symbolize their communion in charity. By about the middle of the thirteenth century the ritual changed: the priest now kissed the PAX-BOARD which his clerk then handed to the rest of the clergy and then to the congregation for each of them to kiss in turn.

LAST ANOINTING. See EXTREME UNCTION.

LAUDS. See CANONICAL HOURS.

LECTIONARY. A service book containing lessons—bible stories, excerpts from the Church Fathers, sermons, saints' lives—read during the divine office.

LECTOR (or READER). The third highest rank of the four MINOR ORDERS.

LEGATE. An official deputy of the pope granted special jurisdiction. He was either sent as a temporary ambassador or was permanently resident in a country (e.g., the Archbishop of Canterbury).

LENT. The forty days of fasting that begin on Ash Wednesday and end at Easter.

LESSER TITHES. See TITHES.

LESSON-BOOK. See LECTIONARY.

LETTERS DIMISSORY. Official permission from a bishop to a cleric from his diocese allowing a bishop from another diocese to ordain him to higher orders.

LITANY. A long prayer of supplication or thanksgiving that invokes the Godhead and its attributes, Mary, and the major angels and saints.

LITURGY. The public services of the church, especially the MASS and the DIVINE OFFICE.

LIVING. See BENEFICE.

MAJOR ORDERS (or HOLY ORDERS). (1) Generally, the three highest clerical orders. In ascending rank: SUBDEACON, DEACON, and PRIEST. Major orders imposed the vow of celibacy on their recipients. Compare MINOR ORDERS and ORDINATION. (2) Specifically, the SACRAMENT of HOLY ORDERS or ORDINATION.

MANDATE. An order from a bishop, his deputy, or the pope ordering some course of action.

MANIPLE. See VESTMENTS.

MANUAL. A service book containing the rites for administering SACRAMENTS and SACRAMENTALS.

MARTYROLOGY. A service book that calendars day by day brief histories of the martyrs of the church.

MASS. The principal ritual of Roman Catholicism consisting of scriptural readings, prayers, and the consecration of the EUCHARIST.

MASTER. The title generally applied to any teacher, and especially to one who had begun his career as a master at a university.

MATINS. See CANONICAL HOURS.

MATRIMONY. The SACRAMENT that joins a man and woman in marriage. By the twelfth century the *concubitus* theory, which held that the act of sexual intercourse created the matrimonial bond, was replaced by the consent theory, which held that a couple's exchange of mutual consent to marry formed the bond. Licit marriages could be created without the presence of witnesses—so-called clandestine marriages—but church law denounced such unions and demanded that couples marry before a priest and witnesses or risk ecclesiastical penalty. See BANNS.

MENDICANT ORDERS. The urban religious orders formed in the early thirteenth century that technically owned no property either privately or corporately. They were meant to earn their keep by begging (Latin, *mendicare*). They were usually well-educated at universities or their own schools and excelled at preaching and hearing confession. Individual mendicants were called FRIARS. The largest mendicant orders were the Franciscans, the Dominicans, the Augustinians (or Austins), and the Carmelites.

MINOR ORDERS. The four lowest clerical orders. In ascending rank: PORTER (or DOOR-KEEPER), LECTOR, EXORCIST, and ACOLYTE. Generally these were all received at the same time. Minimum age for the first three orders was seven; minimum age to be an acolyte was fourteen. Minor orders did not impose the obligation of celibacy. See TONSURE. Compare MAJOR ORDERS.

MISSAL. A service book containing all the prayers and rites necessary for celebrating the mass.

MITER. The tall hat worn by archbishops, bishops, and sometimes abbots as a sign of their office. Compare CROZIER.

MOIETY (or MEDIETY). When a church was divided into two benefices, each half was called a moiety and a rector was appointed for each moiety. When a church was divided into three benefices, each third was called a PORTION, and the rector of each was called a PORTIONER.

MONK. A member of a REGULAR communal religious order, especially a member of the non-mendicant regular orders.

MORROW (or MORNING) MASS. The first mass of the day, usually said by a chantry priest for the soul of a dead patron.

MORTUARY. Customary payment of a dead parishioner's second-best animal or equivalent goods made to the parish rector in compensation for unpaid tithes. Compare HERIOT.

NAVE. The main body of a church where the laity stood; sometimes called "the people's church." By custom the laity were obliged to see to its up-keep. Compare CHANCEL.

NONES. See CANONICAL HOURS.

NOTARY. A public official with the power to write and certify the validity of legal instruments.

OCTAVE. The eighth day after a FEAST counting the feast, or the eight-day period itself. Compare VIGIL.

OFFERTORY. The section of the MASS preceding the CANON where gifts of bread and wine are offered for consecration.

OFFICE, DIVINE. See CANONICAL HOURS.

OFFICIAL (or COMMISSARY GENERAL). The chief legal officer of the bishop who administered the affairs of the diocese's court, called a consistory. Compare VICAR GENERAL. (By the fifteenth century, the offices of the OFFICIAL and the VICAR GENERAL were often merged.)

ORATORY. A private CHAPEL.

ORDINAL. A service book containing the sequence for the services of every day of the year.

ORDINARY (or JUDGE ORDINARY). The bishop of a diocese in his capacity as chief legal arbiter of the areas in his diocese under his jurisdiction. ARCHDEACONS also exercised some of the powers of the ordinary within their jurisdiction.

ORDINARY OF THE MASS. The fixed parts of the MASS that do not vary according to season, viz., *Kyrie, Gloria, Creed, Sanctus,* and *Agnus dei.* Compare PROPER.

ORDINATION. The sacrament by which a man becomes a priest through a bishop's laying on of hands and anointing. Ordination conveyed the power to administer all the sacraments except for Ordination and CONFIRMATION, which were reserved to bishops.

PARDONER (QUESTOR). A minor church officer, cleric or layman, who sold inexpensive parchment indulgences, sometimes under papal license. The proceeds of the sale supposedly went to religious houses, but the practice invited abuse, as Chaucer witnessed.

PARISH. A geographical and jurisdictional division within a diocese. The spiritual center of the parish was the parish church, to which all parishioners owed allegiance and revenues. They were obliged to receive the sacraments in their parish church as well as to be buried there, unless otherwise dispensed by their curate. The head of the parish was the RECTOR or, in his absence, the VICAR.

PARISH CLERK. The man or men who assisted the priest at mass and accompanied him during his visits to the sick. The parish clerks were also charged with the maintenance and the safekeeping of the church's books and utensils. Since clerks were often somewhat educated, they also could draw up last wills and other public documents. Compare AQUABAJULUS (whose duties were similar, though more limited), SEXTON, and CHURCHWARDEN.

PARISH PRIEST. Generally any secular priest attached to a parish, but especially the unbeneficed stipendiary clergy who assisted rectors and vicars. Compare CURATE and CHAPLAIN.

PARSON. See RECTOR.

PATRON. The person or corporation who possessed the right to make appointments to a benefice.

PAX-BOARD (or PAX-BRED). A small round or oblong plate of painted wood or metal. The KISS OF PEACE was passed from priest to people on this plate.

PECULIAR. Any area within a diocese outside the JURISDICTION of the bishop.

PENANCE (or CONFESSION). The SACRAMENT which granted absolution from sin to Christians who were contrite, orally confessed their sins to a priest, and performed some act of penance in recompense for their offense. By decree of the Fourth Lateran Council (1215), all Christians above the age of discretion (usually fourteen years old) were obliged to confess at least annually at Easter. Before the sixteenth century there were no confessional boxes; penitents knelt before the priest who sat in the nave, sometimes on a special "shriving pew."

PENITENTIARY. A local priest especially appointed by a bishop for a term to hear the confessions of the parish clergy within a deanery or archdeanery. As the bishop's deputy, he also could hear lay people's confessions and enjoin penance on them unless their crimes were those that could only be absolved by a bishop or the pope.

PENTECOST (or WHITSUNDAY). The seventh Sunday after Easter.

PETER'S PENCE (or ROME-SCOT). A hearth tax paid in England to the pope and fixed at £200 annually for the country. It was abolished in England in 1534.

PLACEBO. Latin, "I will please [the Lord]" [Ps. 114:9]. The first word of the VESPERS antiphon in the Office of the Dead.

PLURALISM. The practice of holding more than one benefice with cure of souls with or without dispensation.

PORTER (or DOOR-KEEPER). The lowest rank of the four MINOR ORDERS.

PORTION. See MOIETY.

PREBEND. A cathedral benefice was subdivided into many separate endowments called prebends, each of which supported one man called a prebendary. See CATHEDRAL and CANON (2).

PRELATE. An archbishop, bishop, abbot, or other church dignitary possessing JURISDICTION.

PRESENTATION. The act by which a patron nominates a candidate to a bishop to fill a vacant benefice in the patron's ADVOWSON.

PRIEST. The highest rank of the three MAJOR or HOLY ORDERS. In the middle ages a candidate for ordination to the priesthood had to be at least twenty-three years old, of good moral character and life, somewhat educated, free from notorious crimes, and hold a TITLE. See ORDINATION.

PRIME. See CANONICAL HOURS.

PRIMER (PRYMER, or BOOK OF HOURS). A basic prayer book for the laity. In either Latin or English, it contained prayers extracted from the BREVIARY and the MANUAL: for example, the CANONICAL HOURS of the Blessed Virgin, the seven Penitential Psalms (Pss. 6, 31, 37, 50, 101, 129, 142), the fifteen gradual psalms (Pss. 119–133), the PLACEBO and DIRIGE, the LITANY, and other prayers. It was often used as an elementary reader.

PRIOR. (1) The man second in rank after an ABBOT. (2) The head of a religious house that did not appoint an abbot (e.g., the mendicant orders).

PROCESSIONAL. A service book containing music and responses that accompanied processions held before mass on Sundays, feast days, and ROGATION DAYS.

PROCTOR. (1) A person who legally represents another; e.g., an attorney. (2) A tithe farmer. See FARMING A CHURCH.

PROCURATION. A small customary fee paid to a bishop or archdeacon during his visitation in lieu of providing him food and lodging.

PROPER. Those prayers and readings of the MASS that vary from day to day. Compare ORDINARY OF THE MASS.

PROVINCE. A collection of dioceses governed by an ARCHBISHOP.

PROVISION, PAPAL. The right of the pope to appoint a rector to a vacant benefice, regardless of its patron. The practice was outlawed in England by the Statutes of Provisors (1351, 1390), which were intermittently enforced. The Statutes of Praemunire (1353, 1365, 1393) forbade appeals to Rome over cases of patronage.

PSALTER. A book containing the 150 psalms said during the course of the week's DIVINE OFFICE.

PURIFICATION. See CHURCHING.

PYX. A small, locked, metal box in which the HOST was kept. Usually it was suspended by a cord over the altar. The host usually rested inside another square or round box inside the pyx. It was this inner box that was carried by the priest when visiting the sick.

QUADRAGESIMAL. A payment by the parish clergy for the CHRISM blessed by the bishop on Holy Thursday.

READER. See LECTOR.

RECTOR (or PARSON). The individual cleric or ecclesiastical corporation which claimed the right to the GREATER TITHES of a parish. Where the rector was an individual, he generally bore the responsibility of the CURE OF SOULS.

REGISTER. The record book of the daily administrative activities of a bishop.

REGULAR CLERGY. Clerics who belonged to a religious order and lived by a communal rule. Compare SECULAR CLERGY.

RELICS. The physical remains (primary relics) or personal effects (secondary relics) of a saint, believed to possess spiritual potency. Every ALTAR was required to contain the relic of some saint.

RELIQUARY. A container, often ornamented, for relics.

REQUIEM. The mass offered for the repose of the souls of the dead.

RESERVATION (of a benefice). The practice by which the pope held for himself the right to appoint a candidate to a vacant benefice. See PROVISION, PAPAL.

ROCHET. See VESTMENTS.

ROGATION DAYS (OR GANG DAYS OR CROSS DAYS). The Monday, Tuesday, and Wednesday before Ascension Thursday, and the Sunday prior to Ascension Thursday. During these days clergy and parishioners in solemn procession chanted litanies and supplications (rogations) for the coming harvest. Typically these were also the days that parishioners perambulated the boundaries of their parish. Sometimes a few young boys would be whipped at the boundaries so that their later recollection of the occasion would convey the memory of the parish's limits to the next generation.

ROOD-SCREEN. The wooden partition, surmounted by a large crucifix—the rood—that separated the chancel from the nave of the church. The rood-loft was the gallery across the top of the screen.

RURAL DEAN. The eyes and ears of the bishop at the local level. He was a parish rector or vicar appointed by the bishop to preside over the parishes in his area, passing on mandates from the bishop or archdeacon, issuing episcopal excommunications and citations to the CONSISTORY COURT, and insuring that clergy were resident in their benefices.

SACRAMENT. One of the seven ritual actions which bestows divine grace and special favor on its recipients according to Roman Catholic belief. The seven sacraments are BAPTISM, CONFIRMATION, PENANCE, the EUCHARIST, MATRIMONY, HOLY ORDERS, and EXTREME UNCTION (or the LAST ANOINTING).

SACRAMENTAL. Blessed objects and pious practices—e.g., holy water, blessed palms, lenten ashes, the sign of the cross, the rosary, grace before meals—that convey spiritual merit but are less efficacious than SACRAMENTS.

SACRAMENTARY. A book containing all the spoken rituals of the mass except for the gospels and epistles. Virtually the same book as, and ultimately replaced by, the MISSAL.

SANCTUARY. The physical area encompassed by the church and churchyard which granted anyone taking refuge within its boundaries immunity from seizure by secular law officers.

SECULAR CLERGY. Clerics who do not live according to a religious rule. Compare REGULAR CLERGY.

SEE. A bishop's DIOCESE.

SEQUESTRATION. The confiscation of the goods and revenues of a benefice until its incumbent complied with some injunction or mandate. Often applied to the benefice of a non-resident curate.

SEXT. (1) See CANONICAL HOURS. (2) The *Liber Sextus,* a collection of CANON LAW issued by Pope Boniface VIII in 1298.

SEXTON. Usually the PARISH CLERK'S assistant, charged with custodial duties such as keeping the church clean, ringing the church bells, or digging graves in the churchyard.

SIMONY. The crime of buying or selling ecclesiastical benefices or offices.

SINECURE. An ecclesiastical benefice without the CURE OF SOULS.

SONG (or READING) SCHOOL. An elementary school where boys about seven to twelve years old were taught basic reading.

SPIRITUALITIES. The property of a church—e.g., the church building, its sacred vessels and books, tithes and other offerings—theoretically immune from secular control.

STIPENDIARY PRIEST. An unbeneficed priest hired by a rector or vicar for an annual salary.

STOLE. See VESTMENTS.

SUBDEACON. The lowest rank of the three MAJOR or HOLY ORDERS. A subdeacon had to be at least eighteen years old.

SUBSIDY. Money, usually calculated as a tenth or fifteenth of annual revenues, collected from the clergy in aid of the king, pope, or bishop.

SUFFRAGAN BISHOP. Any bishop in relation to his archbishop, but more particularly, coadjutor bishops appointed by the pope to help a bishop administer his diocese. Coadjutor bishops, often friars, held all the spiritual powers of a bishop; but their sees were usually in the ancient lands now inaccessible since they were under Muslim control, and were thus described as dioceses *in partibus infidelium*. In England, suffragans often held Irish sees, equally inaccessible.

SUMMONER (or APPARITOR). Made notorious by Chaucer, the minor church officer charged with delivering citations summoning people to an ecclesiastical court.

SUSPENSION. Canonical CENSURE that temporarily relieved a cleric of his duties until he received absolution for some sin or crime, or that prevented a lay person from entering a church.

SYNOD. A council of clergy called to consider matters of church governance. It ranged in size from a small synod of the priests within a particular archdeaconry, to a gathering of all diocesan clergy, to a provincial assembly of clergy, secular and regular.

SYNODALS. A small customary fee collected by a bishop or archdeacon from those who attended their SYNODS.

TAPER. A tall, thin candle used in processions or for devotional purposes.

TEMPORALITIES. The material property of the clergy subject to secular jurisdiction. Compare SPIRITUALITIES.

TERCE (or TIERCE). See CANONICAL HOURS.

TITHES. The tenth part of the produce of nature—animal or agricultural—and the profits from labor, which parishioners owed annually to the rector of their parish. The GREATER or GARB TITHE was collected on all grain. The LESSER TITHE was collected on every other kind of goods, natural or man-made. Compare GLEBE and ALTARAGE.

TITLE. A benefice or some other means of material support without which a candidate could not be ordained.

TONSURE. The circular spot shaved bald on a cleric's head signifying his renunciation of the world and his enrollment in the clerical orders. The first tonsure could be received as early as age seven and signified the intent to enter clerical orders even before the reception of any orders.

TRANSLATION. (1) The transfer of a bishop from one diocese to another. (2) The transfer of a saint's relics from one church to another.

TRENTAL. A cycle of thirty masses said for a special intention, usually for the souls of the dead.

TUNIC. See VESTMENTS.

USE. The local liturgical adaptation of the Roman mass and rituals. Two uses predominated in medieval England: the use of Sarum (or Salisbury) also adopted by several other dioceses, and the use of York.

VACANCY. A benefice in which there is no incumbent.

VESPERS. See CANONICAL HOURS.

VESTMENTS. The clothing worn by priests and servers both at mass and while administering the sacraments. A full set of priest's mass vestments included an alb, amice, chasuble, girdle, maniple, and stole. A deacon wore the same but replaced the chasuble with the dalmatic. A subdeacon wore a tunic instead of the chasuble and stole.

ALB: A sleeved white gown reaching to the ankles.

AMICE: A white cloth hood usually worn around the shoulders.

CHASUBLE: The main vestment: a colored, sleeveless mantle covering the front and back and reaching from the neck to mid-calf.

COPE: A long cape worn over the shoulders in ceremonial processions.

DALMATIC: A wide-sleeved tunic reaching to the knees, worn by a deacon instead of the chasuble and by a bishop under his chasuble.

GIRDLE: A cord or sash belt worn around the waist of the alb.

MANIPLE: A narrow strip of colored cloth worn draped over the left arm.

ROCHET: Like a surplice, but sleeveless. It was often worn instead of a surplice, whose long sleeves could be a hindrance at baptisms, burials, etc.

STOLE: A colored sash worn by the deacon over the left shoulder crossing under the right arm, and by the priest over the neck crossing at the breast.

SURPLICE: A long, white, full-sleeved garment worn by priests, deacons, and subdeacons underneath the alb. Acolytes and choristers sometimes wore it in place of the alb.

TUNIC: Often identical with the dalmatic, though it usually had narrower sleeves. It was worn by subdeacons in place of the chasuble and by a bishop under his chasuble.

VICAR (or PERPETUAL VICAR). The priest entrusted with the CURE OF SOULS when a church had been appropriated to a religious house that was corporately its rector and held its major tithes. The Fourth Lateran Council (1215) guaranteed vicars a minimum wage. A vicar was under oath to reside perpetually in his parish.

VICAR GENERAL. An officer delegated by the bishop to handle routine diocesan business. Vicars general carried out most of the day-to-day administrative affairs of the bishop. Compare OFFICIAL.

VIGIL. The day before a FEAST.

VISITATION. The official on-site inspection by a bishop, his deputy, or—rare by the fourteenth century—an archdeacon, of a parish or other church within their jurisdiction. The inspection examined the moral life of the members of the parish and their priests as well as the physical condition of the church buildings. See DETECTIONS and COMPERTA.

Selected Bibliography
∾

Ault, Warren O. "The Village Church and the Village Community in Medieval England." *Speculum* 45 (1970): 197–215.

Barlow, Frank. *The English Church, 1000–1066: A History of the Later Anglo-Saxon Church.* 2nd ed. London: Longman, 1979.

Blair, John, and Richard Sharpe, eds. *Pastoral Care Before the Parish.* Leicester and New York: Leicester University Press, 1992.

Bowker, Margaret. *The Secular Clergy in the Diocese of Lincoln, 1495–1520.* Cambridge: Cambridge University Press, 1968.

Boyle, Leonard E. *Pastoral Care, Clerical Education and Canon Law, 1200–1400.* London: Variorum Reprints, 1981.

Cheney, C. R. *From Becket to Langton, English Church Government 1170–1213.* Manchester: Manchester University Press, 1956.

———. *English Synodalia of the Thirteenth Century.* Oxford: Oxford University Press, 1941. Rev. ed., 1968.

Cook, G. H. *The English Medieval Parish Church.* 3rd ed. London: Phoenix House, 1961.

Coulton, G. G. *Ten Medieval Studies.* Cambridge: Cambridge University Press, 1906. Reprint, Boston: Beacon Press, 1959.

Culbertson, Philip L., and Arthur Bradford Shippee, eds. *The Pastor: Readings from the Patristic Period.* Minneapolis: Fortress Press, 1990.

Cutts, Edward L. *Parish Priests and Their People in the Middle Ages in England.* London: SPCK, 1898. Reprint, New York: AMS Press, 1970.

Dickinson, J. C. *The Later Middle Ages: An Ecclesiastical History of England.* London: Adam and Charles Black, 1979.

Dohar, William J. *The Black Death and Pastoral Leadership: The Diocese of Hereford in the Fourteenth Century.* Philadelphia: University of Pennsylvania Press, 1995.

Drew, Charles. *Early Parochial Organisation in England: The Origins of the Office of Churchwarden.* St. Anthony's Hall Publications 7. London: St. Anthony's Press, 1954.

Duffy, Eamon. *The Stripping of the Altars: Traditional Religion in England, 1400–1580.* New Haven: Yale University Press, 1992.

Gasquet, F. A. *Parish Life in Mediaeval England.* London: Methuen, 1906.

Godfrey, John. *The English Parish Church, 600–1300.* London: SPCK, 1969.

Goering, Joseph. "The Changing Face of the Village Parish: the Thirteenth Century." In *Pathways to Medieval Peasants,* ed. J. Ambrose Raftis. Toronto: Pontifical Institute of Mediaeval Studies, 1981.

——. *William de Montibus (c. 1140–1213), The Schools and the Literature of Pastoral Care.* Toronto: Pontifical Institute of Mediaeval Studies, 1992.

Haines, Roy M. *Ecclesia Anglicana: Studies in the English Church of the Later Middle Ages.* Toronto: University of Toronto Press, 1989.

Hartridge, R. A. R. *A History of Vicarages in the Middle Ages.* Cambridge: Cambridge University Press, 1930. Reprint, New York: Barnes and Noble, 1968.

Heath, Peter. *Church and Realm, 1272–1461.* London: Fontana, 1988.

——. *The English Parish Clergy on the Eve of the Reformation.* London: Routledge and Kegan Paul; Toronto: University of Toronto Press, 1969.

Hughes, Jonathan. *Pastors and Visionaries: Religion and Secular Life in Late Medieval Yorkshire.* Woodbridge, Suffolk: Boydell, 1988.

Lawrence, C. H., ed. *The English Church and the Papacy in the Middle Ages.* London: Burns and Oates, 1965.

Lynch, Joseph. *The Medieval Church: A Brief History.* New York: Longman, 1992.

Manning, Bernard L. *The People's Faith in the Time of Wyclif.* Cambridge: Cambridge University Press, 1919.

Moorman, John R. H. *Church Life in England in the Thirteenth Century.* Cambridge: Cambridge University Press, 1955.

Owst, G. R. *Preaching in Medieval England.* Cambridge: Cambridge University Press, 1926.

Pantin, W. A. *The English Church in the Fourteenth Century.* Cambridge: Cambridge University Press, 1955.

——. "Medieval Priests' Houses in South-west England." *Medieval Archaeology* 1 (1957): 118–46.

Richardson, H. G. "The Parish Clergy of the Thirteenth and Fourteenth Centuries." *Transactions of the Royal Historical Society,* 3rd ser., 6 (1912): 89–127.

Rodes, Robert E., Jr. *Ecclesiastical Administration in Medieval England: The Anglo-Saxons to the Reformation.* Notre Dame, Ind.: University of Notre Dame Press, 1977.

Storey, R. L. *Diocesan Administration in the Fifteenth Century.* St. Anthony's Hall Publications 16. London: St. Anthony's Press, 1959.

Swanson, R. N. *Catholic England: Faith, Religion, and Observance before the Reformation.* Manchester: Manchester University Press, 1993.

————. *Church and Society in Late Medieval England*. Oxford: Blackwell, 1989.

Tanner, Norman P. *The Church in Late Medieval Norwich, 1370–1532*. Toronto: Pontifical Institute of Mediaeval Studies, 1984.

Thompson, A. Hamilton. *The English Clergy and Their Organization in the Later Middle Ages*. Oxford: Clarendon, 1947.

Vauchez, André. *The Laity in the Middle Ages: Religious Belief and Devotional Practices*. Edited by Daniel Bornstein. Translated by Margery J. Schneider. Notre Dame, Ind.: University of Notre Dame Press, 1993.

Acknowledgment of Sources in Copyright
᧜

No. 43. "An infamous pluralist, Bogo de Clare." Reprinted from G. G. Coulton, *Life in the Middle Ages* (1910, reprint 1967). Used by permission of the Cambridge University Press.

No. 46. "The life and character of a bishop." Reprinted from *Decrees of the Ecumenical Councils,* edited by Norman P. Tanner. Used by permission of the Georgetown University Press.

No. 47. "Episcopal authority in matters pertaining to the *cura animarum.*" Reprinted from *Decrees of the Ecumenical Councils,* edited by Norman P. Tanner. Used by permission of the Georgetown University Press.

No. 48. "The bishop's authority over benefices and their disposition." Reprinted from *Decrees of the Ecumenical Councils,* edited by Norman P. Tanner. Used by permission of the Georgetown University Press.

No. 49. "The duties of suffragan bishops." Reprinted from *English Historical Documents,* vol. 4, 1327–1485, ed. A. R. Myers (New York: Oxford University Press, 1969). Used by permission of Routledge, Ltd.

No. 53. "To a negligent archdeacon." Reprinted from *English Historical Documents,* vol. 3, 1189–1327, ed. Harry Rothwell (New York: Oxford University Press, 1975). Used by permission of Routledge, Ltd.

No. 57. "Appropriation of a parish to a monastic house." Reprinted from *The Bishop's Register,* ed. Clifford J. Offer (London: SPCK; New York: Macmillan, 1929).

No. 61. "The settlement of a dispute between two chantry chaplains." Reprinted from *English Historical Documents,* vol. 4, 1327–1485, ed. A. R. Myers (New York: Oxford University Press, 1969). Used by permission of Routledge, Ltd.

No. 64. "Papal regulations on the rights of the secular clergy and the friars." Reprinted from *Decrees of the Ecumenical Councils,* edited by Norman P. Tanner. Used by permission of the Georgetown University Press.

No. 66. "Carmelite friars licensed to preach." Reprinted from *The Bishop's Register,* ed. Clifford J. Offer (London: SPCK; New York: Macmillan, 1929).

No. 68. "Dominican friars deprive a parish priest of his burial dues." Reprinted from *English Historical Documents,* vol. 4, 1327–1485, ed. A. R. Myers (New York: Oxford University Press, 1969). Used by permission of Routledge, Ltd.

No. 77. "Annual confession: *Omnis utriusque sexus.*" Reprinted from *Decrees of the Ecumenical Councils,* edited by Norman P. Tanner. Used by permission of the Georgetown University Press.

No. 91. "A parish's budget: the accounts of the parish clergy of Hornsea." Reprinted from *English Historical Documents,* vol. 4, 1327–1485, ed. A. R. Myers (New York: Oxford University Press, 1969). Used by permission of Routledge, Ltd.

No. 92. "Daily expenses of a small clerical household." Reprinted from *English Historical Documents,* vol. 4, 1327–1485, ed. A. R. Myers (New York: Oxford University Press, 1969). Used by permission of Routledge, Ltd.

No. 94. "A country parson's goods." Reprinted from *English Historical Documents,* vol. 4, 1327–1485, ed. A. R. Myers (New York: Oxford University Press, 1969). Used by permission of Routledge, Ltd.

No. 99. "Exorbitant charges of chaplains." Reprinted from *The Bishop's Register*, ed. Clifford J. Offer (London: SPCK; New York: Macmillan, 1929).

No. 100. "Archbishop Simon Sudbury raises chaplains' wages." Reprinted from *English Historical Documents*, vol. 4, 1327–1485, ed. A. R. Myers (New York: Oxford University Press, 1969). Used by permission of Routledge, Ltd.

No. 102. "Royal protection for the clergy: the writ *Circumspecte agatis*." Reprinted from *English Historical Documents*, vol. 3, 1189–1327, ed. Harry Rothwell (New York: Oxford University Press, 1975). Used by permission of Routledge, Ltd.

No. 108. "A citation to unchaste clerks." Reprinted from *The Bishop's Register*, ed. Clifford J. Offer (London: SPCK; New York: Macmillan, 1929).

About the Editors
∾

John Shinners is Associate Professor and Chair of the Humanistic Studies Program at Saint Mary's College, Notre Dame, Indiana, and author of *Medieval Popular Religion, 1000–5000: A Reader* (1997).

William J. Dohar, C.S.C., is Associate Professor of the Department of History, University of Notre Dame, and author of *The Black Death and Pastoral Care: The Diocese of Hereford in the Fourteenth Century* (1995).